Laura Alter

THE FINAL
MONTHS

THE FINAL MONTHS

A Study of the Lives of 134 Persons Who Committed Suicide

ELI ROBINS, M.D.
Wallace Renard Professor of Psychiatry
Washington University School of Medicine
St. Louis, Missouri

New York   Oxford
OXFORD UNIVERSITY PRESS
1981

Copyright © 1981 by Oxford University Press, Inc.

Library of Congress Cataloging in Publication Data

Robins, Eli.
  The final months.

  Bibliography: p.
  Includes index.
  1. Suicide—Case studies.   I. Title. [DNLM:
1. Suicide.   2. Suicide—Psychology.   HV 6545 R632f]
RC569.R6   616.85'844509   81-1536
ISBN 0-19-502911-9   AACR2

Printing (last digit): 9 8 7 6 5 4 3 2 1

Printed in the United States of America

To Mandel E. Cohen

Acknowledgments

This book is the result of the intelligence, skill, and work of a number of people.

A large measure of the credit goes to the surviving families and friends of the suicide subjects. The cooperation and generosity of these surviving relatives and friends so soon after the deaths was gracious and exceedingly helpful.

The psychiatric interviews of the survivors were done by the following physicians: Drs. George E. Murphy, Robert W. Wilkinson, Jr., Seymour Gassner, Jack Kayes, and myself.

The evaluation of interviews for questions of reliability and diagnostic agreement was done by Dr. Murphy and myself.

Editorial work, initial writing of most of the vignettes, and the idea of the use of "score cards" were all those of Shannon Ravenel, who edited the manuscript from fetus to newborn.

The early typing, the careful marshalling, mothering, and annealing of the disparate aspects of the entire book is owed to Mary E. Lavazzi.

Thanks are due to Mary E. Cordes ("Betty") for a superb final typing of the manuscript—skillful and perceptive.

And finally, I am grateful to Jeffrey House of the Oxford University Press for his early encouragement and his later devil-take-the-hindmost attitude.

St. Louis, Mo.　　　　　　　　　　　　　　　　　　　　　　　　　　　　E.R.
June 1981

This study was supported in part by grants from the Alan Blumenthal Foundation for Mental Health, West Monroe, Louisiana, and by training grants from the National Institute of Mental Health.

Contents

Introduction   xi

1 First Considerations of the Investigators   3
2 Diagnostic Criteria Used in St. Louis to Determine Four Major Groups   7
3 Design of Interview Schedule to Determine the Prevalence of Symptoms Compared in the Four Major Diagnostic Groups   17
4 Affective Disorder—Description of the Sample Comprising the Largest of the Four Major Diagnostic Groups   47
5 Alcoholism—Description of the Sample Comprising the Second Largest of the Four Major Diagnostic Groups   221
6 The Miscellaneous Group—Description of the Clinical Group Comprising the Smallest Number in the Total Sample   321
7 The Psychiatrically Undiagnosed Group—Description of the 20 Subjects So Categorized   361
8 How Predictable Are Predictors of Suicide?   407
9 Before Suicide   423

Epilogue   431

Index   433

Introduction

This book describes a study of 134 suicides committed during a one-year period in the City of St. Louis and in St. Louis County (combined population in 1956–57 of about 1,500,000). The study, undertaken in the Department of Psychiatry, Washington University School of Medicine, was the first of three comprehensive studies (reported in English) of 100 or more unselected suicides. The second of these three studies was carried out in the Seattle area by Dorpat and Ripley and completed in 1958. The third study, by Barraclough, was completed some fifteen years later in England. Intermittent articles describing isolated aspects of suicide, such as communication of intent and diagnostic breakdown, have been published at intervals closely following each of these three similar studies. This is, however, the first comprehensive presentation of the full range of results from any one of them.

This is also the only presentation of a study of 100 or more unselected suicides in which each of the individual cases of suicide is described in a vignette so that readers may evaluate for themselves the clinical development of illnesses and the validity of diagnoses. Case vignettes include all relevant negative and positive symptoms as well as events ostensibly related to the suicides. For quick reference in comparing the diagnostic and nondiagnostic symptoms, each case presentation includes a symptom "score card."

There are a number of ways of investigating suicides. Of the nonclinical studies, the best known is Durkheim's sociological study.[1] His major work, *Suicide,* published in the late nineteenth century, was the first to gather sociological data systematically so that inferences as to the causes of suicide might be attempted from his findings. Durkheim studied suicide phenomena in different countries and in different provinces within those countries and related his findings to social structures and degrees of religious, domestic, and political integration of different peoples. His results had an apparent social basis which he believed was evidenced by the relative constancy of the rates for defined areas and defined social circumstances over a period of years. This constancy implied to him that social factors were dominant, and individual factors less so. To argue the latter point, he cited alcoholic insanity as an example of a specific cause of suicide and as an illness he considered largely nonsociological. As Dahlgren pointed out, "Durkheim treats the problem of suicide mainly from a sociological point of view: his book is of comparatively little importance from the psychiatric(al) point of view."[2] Since Durkheim's book, the sociological approach to the study of suicide has been more prevalent than the strictly psychological one (such as Shneidman and Farberow's).[3] More prevalent than either of these is the clinical approach. However, very few clinical studies deal with large numbers of subjects (e.g., more than fifty). A study of suicide from an "ecological" view (e.g., Sainsbury, 1955),[4] that is, one that mixes social, psychological, and some clinical aspects in examining the differences in suicide rates related to neighborhoods, social groups, and socioeconomic status, is becoming more common. The emphasis is termed ecological because it stresses equally neighborhood distribution, occupation, income, and illness as influences on suicide.

Although this book describes only completed suicides, the relationship of attempted suicide to completed suicide should be at least briefly mentioned here. There are two ways of looking at rates of completed suicide. The first, emphasizing completion, is to assess the proportion of a given number of unselected completed suicides, with histories of suicide attempts, to those without such histories. The other, emphasizing attempts, is to assess the rate of subsequent completed suicides among subjects who had attempted suicide. In the 1930s, von Andics[5] drew attention to the possibility that attempted suicide and completed suicide represented different phenomena. Following her lead, Dahlgren pointed out in 1945[2] as did Stengel and Cook later (in 1958)[6] that not only are attempted suicide and completed suicide different events, they occur in overlapping but different populations. Ettlinger's 1964 review[7] of eleven studies of attempted suicide indicated that, annually, from 1% to 2% of the persons attempting suicide will eventually complete suicide. These studies, even though they had follow-up periods as short as eight months and as long as twenty years, and had numbers of patients involved ranging from 19 to 1112, uncovered a strikingly narrow incidence of subsequent completed suicide. This finding suggests that in western culture the 1% to 2% annual incidence is a firm and consistent rate. Certainly, it is one that indicates the need for studies which keep separate as independent variables attempted suicide on the one hand and completed suicide on the other.

The decision, in St. Louis, to use our sample for a clinical study as opposed to any of the other kinds of studies described above, was based on the belief that the clinical study is inherently more comprehensive than studies limited, for example, to sociology or psychology or anthropology. The clinical approach involves looking at individual cases from many angles—medical history through doctor and hospital records, family studies through psychiatric interviews designed to collect symptom information from primary informants, social service and police record searches to determine school and job performance, and employer interviews to determine socioeconomic status and behavior away from home. In other words, the clinical investigation brings to the "ecological" study of suicide, medical and psychiatric training that is necessarily missing from the purely sociological or psychological approaches.

The point of bringing all that the clinical approach incorporates to bear on the study of over 100 cases of suicide is to reach the most accurate possible psychiatric classification of the sample. The word *possible* is, of course, the fly in the ointment, for a strictly clinical approach will not enable psychiatrists to progress beyond a certain level of accuracy in diagnosis. Until such a time when we are able, in the laboratory, to refine the techniques of psychopharmacological, neurochemical, and electrophysiological investigations of psychiatric disease, dependence upon clinical techniques of diagnosis is necessary. And even when the laboratory comes into its own, improved clinical techniques will insure that the direction of laboratory investigation is on target.

Therefore, this book, which describes in detail a painstakingly conceived and executed clinical study of 134 completed suicides, is written with a purpose that goes beyond the simply instructive—that similar large-scale studies will follow and build upon the techniques presented here. The need for more studies along these lines—with new emphases on aspects that have proven, over the years, to be of value in reaching the goal of improved diagnostic accuracy—is obvious.

As pointed out earlier, there have been only three studies published in English in which 100 or more completed suicides were studied clinically by interviewing primary informants and additional ancillary informants. The results of these three studies have been presented in more or less comparable forms (see tables). As a consequence, further similar studies are supplied with a firm basis from which to proceed. From the three studies have come results related to clinical diagnosis, previous psychiatric and medical illnesses, counts and listings of symptoms among the various diagnostic groups, and the bearing on suicide of antecedent circumstances. In one aspect—clinical diagnostic breakdown—all three studies reflect a dominant pattern despite the fact that the three groups of investigators were influenced by different kinds of psychiatric training and by different psychiatric philosophies.

B. Barraclough et al. (West Sussex County, Great Britain, 1966–68, 100 suicides)[8]
Depressive illness	70%
Alcoholism	15%
Schizophrenia	3%
Phobic-anxiety state	3%
Barbiturate dependence	1%
Acute schizo-affective disorder	1%
Not mentally ill	7%

(Depressive illness + Alcoholism = 85%)

T.L. Dorpat and H.S. Ripley (Seattle, Washington, 1957–58, 108 suicides)[9]
Depressive illness	28%
Alcoholism	26%
Schizophrenia	11%
Personality and sociopathic disorders	9%
Organic brain syndrome	4%
Miscellaneous	3%
Unspecified psychiatric illness	15%
No psychological information	5%

(Depressive illness + Alcoholism = 54%)

E. Robins et al. (St. Louis, Missouri, 1956–57, 134 suicides)[10]
Affective disorder, depressed phase	47%
Alcoholism	25%
Organic brain syndrome	4%
Schizophrenia	2%
Drug dependence	1%
Undiagnosed psychiatric illness	15%
Terminal medical illness	4%
Well	2%

(Affective disorder, depressed phase + Alcoholism = 72%)

Thus in three studies, completed over a ten-year period, we see that in combination, affective disorder, depressed phase, (or, as it is called by the other groups, depressive illness) and alcoholism were found to be the diagnoses predominantly associated with completed suicide with a mean of 70% of the 342 suicides studied. At the same time, schizophrenia, which has had the reputation of close association with suicide, was found to exist in a mean of only 5% of the overall samples.

As will be shown in the chapters that follow, there are numerous other aspects involved in completed suicide—such as the influence of hospitalization, previously attempted suicide, and preexisting medical disease—that can, through further study, add precision to diagnostic techniques and to a firmer basis for the next steps in the study of suicide—e.g., psychopharmacology, neurochemistry, and electrophysiology. These laboratory studies will, in turn, result in fewer mistakes in determining the degree of suicide risk in individual patients.

REFERENCES

1. Durkheim, E. *Suicide*. Edit. and trans. George Simpson. Glenco, Ill.: Free Press, 1951.
2. Dahlgren, K.G. *On Suicide and Attempted Suicide*. Lund, Sweden: A.-B. PH. Lindstedts Univ.-Bokhandel, 1945.
3. Shneidman, E.S. and Farberow, N.L. (eds.) *Clues to Suicide*. New York: The Blakiston Division, McGraw-Hill, 1957.
4. Sainsbury, P. *Suicide in London*. Maudsley Monograph #1. London: Chapman and Hall, 1955.
5. von Andics, M. *Über Sinn und Sinnlosigkeit des lebens*. Vienna: Gerold and Company, 1938.
6. Stengel, E. and Cook, N.G. *Attempted Suicide*. Maudsley Monograph #4. London: Chapman and Hall, 1958.
7. Ettlinger, R.W. Suicides in a group of patients who had previously attempted suicide. *Acta. Psychiat. Scand.* 40:363–378, 1964.
8. Barraclough, B., Bunch, J., Nelson, B. and Sainsbury, P. A hundred cases of suicide: Clinical aspects. *Brit. J. Psychiat.* 125:355–373, 1974.
9. Dorpat, T.L. and Ripley, H.S. A study of suicide in the Seattle area. *Comp. Psychiat.* 1(6):349–359, 1960.
10. Robins, E., Murphy, G.E., Wilkinson, R.H., Jr., Gassner, S. and Kayes, J. Some clinical considerations in the prevention of suicide based on a study of 134 successful suicides. *Amer. J. Public Health* 49(7):888–899, 1959.

THE FINAL
MONTHS

1

First Considerations of the Investigators

This study of 134 completed suicides—all those so adjudicated by the coroners of the City of St. Louis and St.Louis County in the one-year period between May 15, 1956, and May 15, 1957—had as its original purpose an attempt to answer the following questions:

1. What proportion of persons who commit suicide are clinically ill prior to death?
2. What is the nature and frequency of the illnesss from which these people suffer?
3. Are there psychiatric illnesses which, while common in the population, are rarely or never associated with a completed suicide?
4. What are some of the factors other than diagnosis that may be helpful in assessing the probability of suicide, or indicative of the possibility of suicide (predictors of suicide)?
5. In urban western society, to what degree is suicide a clinical problem as measured by the proortion of suicides who have been seen by physicians or psychiatrists or who have been hospitalized during or shortly before the last episode of illness?
6. What proportion of subjects are not psychiatrically ill at the time of their suicides?
7. Does the presence of medical or surgical illness seem to play a role in suicide?

Before the study officially began, a preliminary interview was designed to cover systematically the questions outlined above as well as many other aspects of the subject. In designing this preliminary interview, which we tested with five primary informants related to five suicides (none of whom were included in the final group of 134 St. Louis suicides), our aim was to develop a prototype of the interview form since one like it had never been composed for use with informants related to such a large group of consecutive suicides. It became evident in the testing of the preliminary interview that the questions finally included could not omit references to illnesses that were thought to have very little relationship to suicide. We believed it was as important to have specific information about those illnesses in which suicide was rare, or did not occur at all, as it was to gather information about those illnesses in which suicide had been thought to be relatively frequent. To cover these to aspects, i.e., the frequently and rarely suicide-associated illnesses, it was necessary to revise the interview in order to question informants specifically about individual symptoms of affective disorder, of alcoholism, and of schizophrenia. In the same effort, we revised the interview to include specific questions that would insure information concerning the illnesses rarely or never associated with suicide. These questions included a number of additional references to symptoms of anxiety neurosis, hysteria, and phobic neurosis.

Based on what we learned, a final interview form (see pp. 25–46) was designed for interviewing relatives or close friends within a few weeks or months following each suicide. This primary interview form was a systematic one in that over 95% of the responses were scored as "yes "no" or with a number. Any positive response was pursued with further questions insuring a minimum of undescribed positive answers. Completion of the interview required an average of over two hours. It covered past and present medical and psychiatric history, personal and social history, family history, and details of the completed suicide and of the events that led up to it.

The interview was carefully structured to insure that we could conclude whether or not a given psychiatric illness was present shortly before or at the time of suicide. The illnesses asked about were affective disorder, alcoholism, antisocial personality, anxiety neurosis, drug-dependence, homosexualty, hysteria, mental retardation, obsessive-compulsive neurosis, organic brain syndrome, phobic neurosis, and schizophrenia. Certain illnesses were not alluded to directly in the questioning, but as may be seen from the material in the individual case vignettes, any less expected illnesses such as fetishism, transsexualism, etc., would have come to the surface during the interview.

The interviews were conducted by six physicians.* A total of 305 primary and ancillary interviews were obtained concerning 119 subjects. There were 15 subjects for whom primary interviews were not obtained because of re-

---

*E. Robins, G.E. Murphy, J. Kayes, S. Gassner, W.H. Wilkinson, Jr., and P. O'Neal.

fusal by families or because an informant lived at a great enough distance to make a telephone interview necessary, which disqualified the interviewee as a primary informant. Ancillary interviews were conducted with other relatives, job associates, friends, clergymen, landladies, bartenders, nurses, attorneys, policemen, funeral home directors, and physicians. The completed interviews were independently evaluated for diagnosis by E.R. and G.E.M. and most disputed diagnoses were settled by mutual agreement utilizing the criteria developed for this study (see below). When there were unresolved disagreements with regard to diagnoses, or when neither E.R. nor G.E.M. could make a definite diagnosis, the suicide in question was categorized "psychiatrically undiagnosed."

Of the fifteen suicides for whom primary interviews were not obtained, thirteen were incomplete due to refusal. Most refusals were by family members (most often offspring) who believed that by not permitting the surviving spouse to be interviewed, or by not granting an interview themselves, they were protecting "family peace-of-mind" and privacy. The remaining two suicides for whom primary interviews were not obtained were transients who had no family members or close friends living within 500 miles of St. Louis.

While the primary interview provided the main source of information, record searches were done for each of the 134 suicides in the St. Louis Police Department records, the St. Louis Social Service Exchange, and in hospital records when it was known that the person in question had been a hospital patient.

Probably the most helpful ancillary informants were the physicians whom subjects had seen during the last months of their lives. The doctors' records which were made available to us both directly and by telephone contained detailed information concerning diagnostic symptoms, but unfortunately this valuable source of material was limited by the fact that 27% of the subjects had not consulted physicians during the last year of their lives.

2

Diagnostic Criteria Used in St. Louis To Determine Four Major Groups

In this sample of 134 completed suicides, the following psychiatric diagnoses were made: affective disorder, alcoholism, organic brain syndrome, schizophrenia, and drug dependence. There was also a group of subjects who were thought by the investigators to be psychiatrically ill, but for whom (for reasons described below) definite diagnoses were not made. Finally, there were two groups of subjects without apparent psychiatric disease—one group was made up of subjects who were terminally medically ill; the other included subjects who apparently were clinically well.

Diagnoses often thought to be associated with completed suicide that did not appear in this sample are uncomplicated obsessive compulsive neurosis, uncomplicated hysteria, and homosexuality. That there were no diagnoses of homosexuality among the 134 cases of completed suicide is probably evidence of the relative rarity of homosexuality rather than of a rarity of completed suicide among homosexuals.[1] On the other hand, the absence in the sample of cases of uncomplicated neurosis (a diagnosis that is not rare in the general population) *does* indicate the general rarity of completed suicide among subjects so diagnosed.[2-5] The sample subject who received a diagnosis of neurosis (hysteria) was one whose secondary diagnosis was drug dependence supporting the accepted observation that drug dependence is an illness associated wth completed suicide.[6] While hysteria is associated with a relatively high prevalence of attempted suicide,[7] completed suicide virtually never occurs in uncomplicated hysteria.

The diagnosis of affective disorder, depressed phase (the term "manic depressive disease" was used for affective disorder in an earlier publication),[8] was made when a subject met the criteria in four of six categories—two of which encompass individual symptoms and four of which describe the course of the illness. The six categories are as follows: 1. subject had been clinically well exclusive of attacks of affective disorder; 2. subject had had a previous episode of affective disorder; 3. discrete duration of last episode of affective disorder prior to suicide (two general durations—six months or less and twelve months or less—proved to be the most frequently reported: only 13 percent of the cases had had final episodes lasting longer than one year; the maximum duration was four years and that occurred in only one case); 4. complaints of "medical symptoms" such as insomnia, weight loss, and fatigue; 5. complaints of "psychological symptoms" such as sadness, loss of interest, and agitation; 6. disturbances in social behavior and decreases in social and recreational activity. A seventh category which included age of onset and family history of affective disorder was considered in each subject diagnosed as having had affective disorder. Although it was helpful in making the diagnoses clear, we did not require it as a criterion category.

These criteria are based on our clinical experience and on well documented clinical studies.[9] The diagnosis of affective disorder as used in this study includes the diagnoses of involutional melancholia and psychotic depressive reaction. The use of the term to include these entities has been justified by both clinical[10] and genetic[11] studies. And it is our clinical impression that so-called depressive neurosis is, in many instances, indistinguishable from affective disorder, depressed phase, without delusions or hallucinations or grossly apparent retardation. We believe this to be true in regard both to symptoms and clinical course.[12]

Chronic alcoholism was diagnosed in accordance with Keller's definition: "Alcoholism is a chronic behavioral disorder manifested by repeated drinking of alcoholic beverages in excess of the dietary and social uses of the community and to an extent that interferes with the drinker's health or his social or economic functioning."[13] This definition is in essential agreement with that of the World Health Organization.[14] There were nine items in the interview that were useful in eliciting a history of family, job, social, and medical difficulties related to alcoholism. In addition to these items, age of onset, defined as the age at which the person first got into difficulty because of drinking, and a family history of alcoholism were also considered in making a diagnosis.

Four of the following nine criteria were required for a diagnosis of alcoholism: 1. the informant thought the subject drank too much; 2. the subject drank daily; 3. the subject went on benders lasting at least 48 hours during which he neglected his usual responsibilities; 4. the subject's family objected to his drinking; 5. the subject had been arrested in relation to drinking; 6. the subject suffered from medical or psychiatric complications of drinking; 7. the subject had thought he drank too much; 8. the subject had job difficulties related to drinking; 9. the subject was involved in automobile accidents related to drinking.

While we are aware that there is ongoing discussion concerning alcoholism as a symptom of different diseases versus alcoholism as a disease entity, for the purposes of this study, it is considered as a single psychiatric disease.

The diagnostic features of organic brain syndrome (referred to in the early paper[8] as "chronic" brain syndrome) are memory difficulty, disorientation in time, inability to find one's way in familiar surroundings, inability to be trusted out alone, deterioration of reading skills, and difficulties with simple arithmetic. Three of these symptoms were required for a diagnosis of organic brain syndrome.

For a diagnosis of schizophrenia, at least seven of the following symptoms—in addition to the first (delusions and hallucinations)—had to have been present: conspicuous delusions or hallucinations; reduction in attachments and interests and impoverishment of human relationships; regressive behavior associated with inappropriate affect; conspicuous motor behavior exhibiting either marked generalized inhibition or excessive activity and excitation; expansive delusional system of omnipotence or genius; ideas of reference; silly behavior and mannerisms, unpredictable behavior; dissociative phenomena; autistic thinking; chronic apparent mental deterioration; rages and fights; hypochondriacal complaints; belief that "people" are spying on one or are "after" one; poor job history; excessive religious preoccupation; muteness.

Diagnosis of drug dependence was made when there were at least three of the following symptoms: addiction to drugs as manifested by increased tolerance and withdrawal symptoms when the drugs were unavailable; nightly drugs for sleeping; daily drug abuse; self-concern about taking too many drugs; family concern about too many drugs; inability to stop taking drugs.

Subjects were considered psychiatrically well if they had only two (or fewer) symptoms ordinarily part of a psychiatric illness. These two (or less) could not include delusions or hallucinations, formal thought disorder, dementia, delirium, or drug dependence.

Medical and surgical illnesses of the 134 subjects were diagnosed by the usual medical criteria. Some subjects had neither medical nor surgical illnesses. Others had one or more.

Each of the psychiatrically undiagnosed subjects was thought to have had a psychiatric illness. The symptoms and courses were, however, insufficiently clear—owing either to the informants' refusal, or to their inability to describe fully the subjects' final weeks—to permit a definite psychiatric diagnosis. In the initial report,[8] there were 25 such undiagnosed subjects. Over the ensuing 20 years, further information about five of these 25 sub-

TABLE 2.1 Clinical Findings in 134 Suicides

Diagnosis	Total	White Men	Black Men	White Women	Black Women	Total (%)
Affective disorder, depressed phase	63	43	2	18	0	47
Alcoholism	33	26	2	4	1	25
Organic brain syndrome	5	4	0	1	0	4
Schizophrenia	3	3	0	0	0	2
Drug dependence	2	1	0	1	0	1
Total psychiatrically diagnosed	106	77	4	24	1	79
Undiagnosed psychiatrically	20	15	1	4	0	15
Total psychiatrically ill, diagnosed and undiagnosed	126	92	5	28	1	94
Terminally medically ill	5	3	0	2	0	4
Neither psychiatrically nor medically ill	3	3	0	0	0	2

jects made it possible to make definite diagnoses, leaving 20 subjects still psychiatrically undiagnosed. The changes in diagnoses were: in three subjects, from undiagnosed psychiatric illness to affective disorder; and, in two subjects, from undiagnosed psychiatric illness to alcoholism.

The final diagnoses made for each of the 134 suicides were categorized by the investigators into four diagnostic groups: 1. subjects with major affective disorder, depressed phase; 2. subjects with alcoholism; 3. subjects with one of a group of miscellaneous psychiatric diseases (organic brain syndrome, schizophrenia, or drug dependence), subjects with terminal illnesses (carcinoma or lymphosarcoma) but without psychiatric illness and subjects considered well both medically and psychiatrically; and 4. psychiatrically "undiagnosed" subjects.

Three of the 134 subjects were considered to have been well, both psychiatrically and medically, at the time of their suicides. The remaining 131 subjects (98%) were diagnosed as clinically ill at the time of suicide. These 131 subjects included 5 who were medically terminally ill, but were without psychiatric illness. Thus 126 subjects—94% of the sample—were diagnosed as having been psychiatrically ill at the time of suicide. (See Table 2.1.)

The largest single diagnostic group was that comprising 63 subjects with major affective disorder. The next largest group was that comprising the 33 subjects with alcoholism. Third largest was the group of 20 subjects who were believed to be primarily psychiatrically ill, but not diagnosably so. The remaining subjects who received definite psychiatric diagnoses were five with organic brain syndrome, three with schizophrenia, and two with drug dependence. The two subjects with drug dependence were a white man and a white woman. The woman's first (chronological) diagnosis was hysteria, with drug dependence as a subsequent diagnosis.

Systematic description of psychiatric disease had been an ongoing interest of my group at Washington University who undertook the study of suicide. The diagnostic criteria finally drawn up for use in the study were in part based on DSM-I[15], but in larger part were based on our own clinical experience with psychiatric patients manifesting a wide range of symptoms of psychiatric diseases. Careful descriptions of the various courses of these diseases played a major role in our diagnoses and this aspect was emphasized in devising the criteria.

Fifteen years after the completion of the suicide study, the principal investigator, along with five other psychiatrists, published a paper entitled "Diagnostic Criteria for Use in Psychiatric Research."[16] This paper introduced what is familiarly known as the Feighner criteria. It presented specific diagnostic criteria for those adult psychiatric illnesses that have been sufficiently validated by precise clinical description, follow-up, and family studies to warrant their use in research as well as clinical practice.[17] Since the publication of this paper, the Feighner criteria have proven to be useful and accurate. Blashfield, at the University of Florida, Gainesville, has observed from *The Index Medicus* that between the 1972 publication and 1978, "there have been 611 citations to this article. This is an average of 87.3 citations per year. In contrast, the average article published in the *Archives of General Psychiatry* (which published the Feighner paper) receives only 2.1 citations per year" (personal communication, R. K. Blashfield).

In order to determine the validity of the original diagnoses arrived at by use of the 1956–57 criteria developed specifically for the suicide study, we applied the Feighner criteria to each of the 134 cases. We did this by means of a double-blind technique in which the cases were rediagnosed in chronological, numerical order and without reference to or knowledge of the original diagnoses.

By the original criteria, 63 of the 134 completed suicides had been diagnosed as having major affective disorder, depressed phase. By the Feighner criteria, 54 cases of affective disorder (three of which were "probable") were diagnosed. Each of these 54 was in the originally diagnosed group of 63. Of that original group, the Feighner criteria were not met by nine subjects. These nine were psychiatrically undiagnosed by the Feighner criteria; they did not meet the criteria for a *different* psychiatric disease. Of the 63 subjects originally diagnosed as having affective disorder, 45 were men and 18 were women. Of the 54 Feighner criteria diagnoses of affective disorder, 39 were in men (or "matched" the original diagnoses as explained above). The three "probable" diagnoses were all in men. There were 15 women whose diagnoses by the Feighner criteria matched the original 18 diagnoses.

TABLE 2.2 Validation of 1956–57 diagnoses through application of the Feighner criteria

	Total		"Matching" Diagnoses		"Probables" (Feighner)		No Match		Match Rate
	M	W	M	W	M	W	M	W	
Affective disorder	45	18	39	15	3*	0	6	3	86%
Alcoholism	28	5	24	3	6*	1*	4	2	82%
Miscellaneous									94%
organic brain syndrome	4	1	3	1	—	—	1	0	
schizophrenia	3	0	3	—	—	—	0	0	
drug dependence	1	1	1	1	—	—	0	0	
terminally medically ill	3	2	3†	2†	—	—	—	—	
neither psychiatrically nor medically ill	3	0	3†	0†	—	—	—	—	
Psychiatrically undiagnosed	16	4	16	4	—	—	0	0	100%
Total	103	31	92	26	9	1	11	5	88%

*Of the 45 men originally diagnosed as having affective disorder, 39 met the Feighner criteria for affective disorder. Of these, 6 fulfilled criteria for a "probable" diagnosis and were counted as "matches." Similarly, among the alcoholic subjects, 7 fulfilled the Feighner criteria for "probable" diagnoses and were counted as "matches."

†The Feighner criteria were not applicable to medical disease only or to no illness, either medical or psychiatric; however, they were applied to the 8 originally so diagnosed subjects (5 terminally medically ill, 3 neither psychiatrically nor medically ill) and, in failing to turn up any psychiatric diagnoses, matched the results of the original criteria.

Those 9 psychiatrically undiagnosed by the Feighner criteria included 6 men and 3 women. (See Table 2.2)

By the original criteria, 33 of the subjects were diagnosed as having alcoholism. By the Feighner criteria, 27 diagnoses matched (7 of these were "probable"). Again, those 6 who did not receive matching diagnoses did not meet the Feighner criteria for another psychiatric disease and fell into the Feighner criteria's psychiatrically undiagnosed category. There were 24 men of the original 28 whose Feighner diagnoses matched and 3 women of the original 5 whose Feighner diagnoses matched.

There were 20 subjects who were thought to be psychiatrically ill, but whose symptoms and courses were insufficiently clear to be diagnosable by either the original criteria or by the Feighner criteria. Of these 20, 16 were men and 4 were women. There were 8 men and 3 women in whom affective disorder symptoms predominated but did not meet either set of criteria. Failure to meet the criteria was most often because a subject had a few symptoms suggestive of affective disorder, but not enough of them for a definite or even "probable" diagnosis by either set of criteria. The same kinds of findings were true of three psychiatrically undiagnosed men in whom symptoms of alcoholism predominated; two men who had symptoms suggesting drug dependence; one man whose symptoms suggested schizophrenia; and two men and one woman whose symptoms suggested organic brain syndrome. In none of these was it clear whether failure to meet either set of criteria might have been due to insufficient information from the informants (although this did appear to be the case in 13 of the 20 subjects). One subject in the undiagnosed group was thought to be nearer being predominantly well, but this man was one of the 13 about whom we had insufficient information.

The miscellaneous group included 18 subjects—14 men and 4 women—with diagnoses by the original criteria of organic brain syndrome (in four men and one woman), schizophrenia (in three men), and drug dependence (in one man and one woman). The Feighner criteria matched each of these diagnoses with the exception of one man with organic brain syndrome who did not exhibit enough symptoms to meet the Feighner criteria. The remaining eight were five terminally ill subjects (three men and two women) who did not have a psychiatric illness and three men who were considered well.

In the entire group of 134 subjects, the diagnoses made by the Feighner criteria matched those made by the original criteria in 118 subjects—a matching rate of 88%.

The racial breakdown of the total sample of 134 subjects was 128 whites and 6 blacks. Among blacks, there were 5 men and 1 woman. There were 98 white men and 30 white women. In the subjects with major affective disorder, the ratio of men to women was 45 to 18, or 2.5:1; in the alcoholic group, the ratio was 28 men to 5 women (5.6:1); in the undiagnosed group, 16 men to 4 women (4:1). Combining the remaining diagnostic groups, with so few subjects in each—those with organic brain syndrome, schizophrenia, drug dependence, and those who were terminally ill or clinically well—into one group to which we shall refer hereafter as the miscellaneous group, the ratio of men to women was 14 to 4, or about 3.5:1.

The overwhelming preponderance of men—103 men to 31 women (more than 3:1)—in this particular sample is, presumably, a reflection of suicide as a disproportionately male phenomenon, at least in western society.[18,19] The national ratio of men to women who committed suicide in 1958 was 3.5:1.[20] In 1973, it was 2.7:1. In that year, the ratio of white men to white women increased from about 3:1 (ages 15–64) to 6:1 (ages 65–84) and increased further at above age 84 to around 11:1. This change in the ratio of men to women did not occur in blacks until age 84 when it decreased from 3:1 to 1.5:1.[21] It seems likely that this phenomenon exists regardless of diagnosis. However, given the small numbers of subjects in each of the five diagnostic groups making up our miscellaneous category, it would be presumptuous to draw firm conclusions about the individual diagnostic groups involving so few subjects.

There were only six (approximately 4%) blacks in our sample and the infrequency of suicide among blacks is a commonly described finding.[21] In our study, the ratio is 21.3:1, whites to blacks. In 1958, the national ratio of white suicides to black suicides was 27.1:1.[20] In 1973, the ratio was 16.9:1.[21]

The most common diagnosable illness associated with suicide in our study was major affective disorder, depressed phase. The second most common diagnosable illness associated with suicide was alcoholism. These two diagnoses accounted for 72% of the sample. If the assumption is made that the distribution of these diagnoses is similar in the 20 undiagnosed cases, then the two diagnoses would account for 82% of the 134 completed suicides.

Affective disorder has been shown, in a number of studies,[8,22] to have the highest rate of suicide, and alcoholism, in several other studies[23] is cited as the second most common diagnosis associated with completed suicide.

The prevalence of affective disorder and alcoholism in a representative sample (5,395 subjects) of a general population shown in Helagson's Iceland study[24] was 103 cases of affective disorder and 163 cases of true alcoholism as compared with 42 cases of schizophrenia. Unfortunately, there has not been a study of epidemiology of affective disorder, alcoholism, and schizophrenia in the United States. However, Helgason's methods are such that his findings are probably as comparable to eventual U.S. findings as such necessarily different national characteristics would permit.

REFERENCES

1. Saghir, M. and Robins, E. *Male and Female Homosexuality,* Baltimore: Williams & Wilkins, 1973.
2. Wheeler, E.O., et al. Neurocirculatory asthenia (anxiety neurosis, effort syndrome, neurasthenia). *JAMA* 142:878–888, 1950.
3. Marks, I.M. *Fears and Phobias,* New York: Academic Press, 1969.
4. Robins, E., Purtell, J.J. and Cohen, M.E. "Hysteria" in men. *N. Engl. J. Med.* 246:677–685, 1952.
5. Goodwin D.W., Guze, S.B. and Robins, E. Follow-up studies in obsessional neurosis. *Arch. Gen. Psychiat.* 20:182–187, 1969.
6. Barraclough, B.M. Poisoning cases: Suicide or accident. *Brit. J. Psychiat.* 124:526–530, 1974.
7. Schmidt, E.H., O'Neal, P. and Robins, E. Evaluation of suicide attempts as guide to therapy. *JAMA* 155:549–557, 1954.
8. Robins, E. et al. Some clinical considerations in the prevention of suicide based on a study of 134 successful suicides. *Amer. J. Public Health* 49(7):888–899, 1959.
9. Campbell, J.D. Mild manic-depressive psychosis, depressive type: Psychiatric and clinical significance. *J. Nerv. & Ment. Dis.* 112:206–236, 1950.

10. Lundquist, G. Prognosis and course in manic-depressive psychoses. A follow-up study of 319 first admissions. *Acta psychiat. et neurol. Scand.* (Suppl. 35):1–96, 1945.
11. Stenstedt, A. A study in manic-depressive psychosis. Clinical, social and genetic investigations. *Acta psychiat. et neurol. Scand.* (suppl. 79):1–111, 1952.
12. Ascher, E. A criticism of the concept of neurotic depression. *Amer. J. Psychiat.* 108:901–911, 1952.
13. Keller, M. Alcoholism: Nature and extent of the problem. *Ann. Amer. Acad. Polit. Social Sc.* 315:1–11, 1958.
14. World Health Organization. Expert Committee on Mental Health, Alcoholism Subcommittee (Second Report). *Tech. Rep. Ser.* 48:16, 1952.
15. *Diagnostic and Statistical Manual of Mental Disorders* (DSM I), Washington, D.C.: The American Psychiatric Association, 1952.
16. Feighner, J.P. et al. Diagnostic criteria for use in psychiatric research. *Arch. Gen. Psychiat.* 26:57–63, 1972.
17. Robins, E. and Guze, S.B. Establishment of diagnostic validity in psychiatric illness: Its application to schizophrenia. *Amer. J. Psychiat.* 126:7, 107–111, 1970.
18. McMahon, B., Johnson, S. and Pugh, T.F. Relation of suicide rates to social conditions. *Pub. Health Rep.* 78:285–93, 1963.
19. Dublin, L.I. *Suicide.* New York: Ronald Press, 1963.
20. *Vital Statistics of the United States, 1958.* Vol. II—Mortality (U.S.). Public Health Service, Washington, D.C., 1960.
21. *Vital Statistics of the United States, 1973.* Vol. II—Mortality (part A). U.S. Public Health Service, Rockville, Md., 1977.
22. Guze, S.B. and Robins, E. Suicide and primary affective disorders. *Brit. J. Psychiat.* 117:437–38, 1970.
23. World Health Organization. *Prevention of Suicide.* Public Health Papers 35:6, 1968.
24. Helgason, T. Epidemiology of mental disorders in Iceland. *Acta Psychiat. Scand.* 40(suppl. 73):1–258, 1964.

3

Design of Interview Schedule To Determine the Prevalence of Symptoms Compared in the Four Major Diagnostic Groups

The interviews for this study were designed to elicit, from primary and secondary informants, information that would indicate which illnesses were associated with completed suicide. The order of questions was determined in two ways. The first was based on an a priori idea, generally held, that affective disorder was the illness most commonly associated with completed suicide. The second was based on the realization that, prior to this study, there had been no published reports directly concerned with which illnesses might or might not be associated with a large number of consecutive completed suicides, nor had there been any studies assessing the frequency of association of other diagnosable psychiatric illnesses with large numbers of consecutive suicides.

The interview questions were drawn up in an order which initially emphasized symptoms thought to be common and important in affective disorder. Because affective disorder is characteristically an episodic illness—that is, episodic in contrast to most other functional psychiatric illnesses—a series of questions was devised to concentrate on the temporal development of illness during a subject's final year. The range of information covered was not, however, limited just to the final year. Whenever informants indicated the presence of chronic psychiatric illness, subsequent probe questions led to descriptions of the chronicity of recurrence in terms of length and progression from initial onset (sometimes as far back as 25 years) up through the last year of life.

In order to determine the presence or absence of a psychiatric disease in each of the subjects and to diagnose the disease as accurately as possible, the interviewers' questionnaire was designed to lead the interviewees through a step-by-step description of the subjects' last months. Questions concerning general behavior followed the questions about onset and duration; these in turn were followed by further questions with emphasis on more specific symptomatic behavior. The last were grouped in order to elicit information about specific symptoms considered to be commonly associated with various psychiatric illnesses. The questions were not posed in yes-or-no fashion, but rather in a way set up to lead the informant to more and more specific memories of the subjects' behavior and statements in an effort to pinpoint the correct diagnosis in each case (see interview, pp. 25–45). When an ultimate answer was obtained, however, it was scored by yes, no, or a number.

Once the interviews were completed and the questionnaire forms filled in, the individual symptoms were coded, counted, and computerized to enable us to ascertain the frequency of individual symptoms in the entire sample. To calculate the frequency of each symptom, the number of subjects on whom there was or was not the specific information was taken into account. Thus, for example, a prevalence of 28% for dizziness actually represents 30 subjects out of 108 about whom we had positive or negative information on dizziness.

To understand the variation in symptom frequency among different diagnostic groups, it is helpful to begin by looking at the symptom which, in the entire sample, had the highest prevalence. (See Table 3.1). Weight loss was reported to have been experienced by 60% of the suicidal subjects. (The percentage actually represents 67 of 112 subjects about whom we had positive or negative information about weight loss.) Broken down by diagnostic groups, weight loss was a symptom of 77% of subjects diagnosed as having had affective disorder, depressed phase; 29% of subjects with alcoholism; 83% of the subjects in the miscellaneous group; and 15% of the psychiatrically undiagnosed subjects.

The miscellaneous group had the highest proportion of subjects with weight loss. These were scattered among the psychiatrically ill subgroups (i.e., those with organic brain syndrome, schizophrenia, and drug dependence). Weight loss was not a symptom of any of the three subjects who were not clinically ill (psychiatrically or medically) included in the miscellaneous group. The fourth subject who did not lose weight was one with a psychiatric illness (organic brain syndrome). Of the five terminally medically ill subjects, four had lost weight; the fifty subject's family refused information. The much lower prevalence of the symptoms in the psychiatrically undiagnosed group is largely due to the relative lack of primary informants (only 40% of the undiagnosed subjects were reported on by primary informants) for the subjects included in the diagnostic category. The low prevalence among those subjects with alcoholism is somewhat surpris-

TABLE 3.1 Symptoms occurring in suicide subjects, in order of frequency (percentages)

	Total Sample	Affective Disorder	Alcoholism	Misc.	Undiagnosed
1. Weight loss	60	77	29	15	83
2. Nervousness	59	63	70	31	47
3. Insomnia	58	80	38	25	43
4. Weekly to daily drinking of alcohol	53	38	100	33	25
5. Loss of interest	52	73	33	0	57
6. Fatigue	50	60	41	8	62
7. Anorexia	49	71	38	0	29
8. Sadness	46	76	26	6	29
9. Joylessness	45	66	30	8	36
10. Tension ("high strung")	41	39	49	29	43
11. Easily hurt feelings	41	42	48	15	43
12. Suicidal ideas	40	38	48	14	50
13. Belief would never get well	39	48	27	23	50
14. Headaches	38	37	41	33	38
15. Crying easily	37	42	43	21	30
16. Weakness	36	48	24	13	38
17. Dyspnea	35	38	32	7	62
18. Less talkative	35	54	19	14	20
19. Informant's belief he/she drank too much	35	20	83	7	15
20. Inertia	34	51	26	0	21
21. Family objection to subject's drinking	32	18	66	14	36
22. Drifting from job to job 10 years prior to suicide	31	39	28	18	15
23. Drinking at time of suicide	30	15	82	23	0
24. Drugs for sleeping	30	33	32	8	33
25. Sexual indifference	29	41	25	0	20
26. Dizzy spells	28	35	24	13	23
27. Outbursts of rage	28	19	53	7	36
28. Ennui	28	43	20	0	17
29. Belief serious problem with part of body	28	33	24	21	21
30. Pain in extremities	26	32	19	0	46
31. Indecisiveness	26	40	11	14	14
32. Chest pain	25	24	24	0	57
33. Back pain	25	22	23	8	58
34. Complete silence at times	25	30	23	29	7
35. Without work for periods of more than 6 months	25	26	29	30	14
36. Benders	25	9	67	7	15
37. Abdominal pain	24	25	28	7	29
38. Not as clean as usual	23	20	19	54	7
39. Change in ordinary life style	23	28	26	21	0
40. Palpitations	23	26	20	0	31

	Total Sample	Affective Disorder	Alcoholism	Misc.	Undiagnosed
41. Vomiting	22	19	32	0	38
42. Constipation	22	23	9	0	31
43. Feelings of worthlessness/of being no good	22	20	33	14	14
44. Feelings of being a burden	21	26	16	7	29
45. Pain in joints	19	21	19	15	17
46. Statements of black future	19	20	17	14	21
47. Trouble with police	19	7	45	14	14
48. Nausea	19	15	21	0	38
49. Being fired from at least one job	19	12	28	25	17
50. Belief losing mind	18	22	18	0	20
51. Statement of feeling sad	18	17	27	0	21
52. Praying more than usual	17	19	11	17	25
53. Feeling that he/she drank too much	17	9	48	7	8
54. "Neurotic"	16	13	26	0	25
55. Chronic sickliness	16	11	17	14	31
56. Belief bad for his/her family	16	13	23	0	29
57. Worry about being "poverty stricken"	16	17	17	0	21
58. Change in way of dressing	16	23	16	0	7
59. More thought than usual about religion	16	18	10	15	23
60. Drugs for sleeping every night	16	25	10	0	8
61. Self-blame for own illness	15	13	21	0	21
62. Statements of being "no good"	15	13	23	7	14
63. Arrests for traffic violations	15	11	25	15	8
64. Sleeping drugs during daytime	15	20	10	8	15
65. Anxiety attacks	14	16	15	7	14
66. Poor memory	14	12	13	13	31
67. Trouble thinking	14	18	13	0	20
68. "Strange" behavior	14	12	16	7	29
69. Not caring for children	14	13	33	0	0
70. Job trouble due to drinking	14	7	45	0	0
71. Fears	13	9	21	0	21
72. Spending binges	13	4	32	7	14
73. Thoughts out of the ordinary	12	12	10	0	29
74. Repeated fainting spells	12	13	10	7	15
75. A lot of talk about sex	12	6	23	0	21
76. Quitting job due to difficulties with boss/fellow workers	12	10	17	13	8
77. Driving trouble associated with drinking	12	5	30	0	8
78. Arrests for drinking	12	6	34	0	0
79. Arrests for peace disturbance	12	7	23	7	8
80. Unnecessary self-blame for "things not being right"	11	8	14	8	21
81. Wearing dirty clothes	11	13	10	7	7

82. Deliberately injuring someone	11	4	27	0	14
83. Difficulty with simple arithmetic	11	8	13	8	21
84. Blurred vision	11	19	3	0	8
85. Guilt feelings	11	9	17	0	7
86. Loudness, noisiness	10	2	29	7	0
87. Reading and understanding less well	9	8	3	14	20
88. Walking off job for no known reason	9	10	13	0	7
89. Threatening someone	9	4	20	7	7
90. Paralysis	8	9	10	0	8
91. Seeming to feel like hurting someone	8	2	23	0	7
92. Neglecting children at least once	8	0	25	10	7
93. Feeling that he/she taking too many drugs	8	8	7	0	15
94. Loss of voice	7	9	0	0	23
95. "Stroke"	7	11	0	6	8
96. Belief had committed some sin	7	8	4	0	21
97. Informant's feeling he/she took too many drugs	7	6	7	8	15
98. Belief he/she lost all or most of money	7	0	14	8	14
99. Belief being spied upon	7	4	6	0	29
100. Belief pursued, tormented, etc.	7	6	6	0	20

ing since a common belief has been that suicidal alcoholics exhibit rapid weight loss prior to their suicides.

Analysis of this single symptom is undertaken here to show the problems, as well as the value, or dealing with symptom prevalence in four disparate diagnostic groups. It should be kept in mind that there are, in this study, two diagnostic groups—affective disorder ($N = 63$) and alcoholism ($N = 33$)—whose large numbers heavily influence the rate of symptom prevalence in the total sample. On the other hand, the mix of diagnoses in the miscellaneous group ($N = 18$) and the scarcity of information characteristic of the undiagnosed group ($N = 20$) results in rates which are less reliable and which might artifactually—if only slightly—increase, decrease, or not change at all the rates in the total sample of 134 subjects.

The other issue that is important to discuss here is the diversity of symptoms were recorded. In listing the symptoms in order of prevalence, I limited my observations to the first 100 (Table 3.1). As a consequence, the lowest prevalence rate in the 100 symptoms was 7%. Of the 58 additional symptoms not included in the master list of 100, 52 were symptoms with a prevalence of less than 7% (e.g., fits, amnesia, obsessions, compulsions, feelings of unreality, complaint of unusual tastes, belief being influenced by hypnosis, radio, or TV, overactivity, school suspension, inability to stop taking drugs at will). The remaining six symptoms omitted from the list of 100 most prevalent symptoms were sex specific.

The term diversity applies to these clinical symptoms in more than one way. The simplest is the great range of problems that the 158 symptoms represent; for example, problems from inertia to deliberately injuring someone physically. Another way of considering the concept of diversity is the observation of differences among diagnostic groups in prevalence rates of a single symptom. A striking example is the symptom "sadness," which was experienced by 46% of the total group, a percentage which would not, on the face of it, indicate the great difference in the prevalence among subjects with affective disorder and those with alcoholism. While 70% of those with affective disorder were reported to have "sadness," only 26% of those with alcoholism had the symptom. The rate in the undiagnosed group was 0%. It was 29% in the miscellaneous group.

On the other side of the coin, there are some symptoms whose prevalences among the four diagnostic groups are nearly identical. For instance, headache occurred in 38% of the total group and was almost identically represented in the four individual diagnostic groups: affective disorder—37%; alcoholism—41%; miscellaneous—38%; undiagnosed—33%. It is probable that headache is one of the most common symptoms humans suffer. Thus, due to the general prevalence of the complaint, its invariant level of prevalence in this sample—an asymptote—is not surprising.

Unexpected findings and surprising results were by-products of this study. The study and its questionnaire were for the most part designed along the usual lines of psychiatric investigation. However, because the matter under investigation was completed suicide, information concerning symptoms and course was necessarily second-hand. This kind of information may explain, at least to some extent, why certain findings in symptom prevalence were not what we might have expected. Good examples of this phenomenon are the prevalences shown for the symptom "loss of interest"—73% in affective disorder; 33% in alcoholism; 57% in miscellaneous; and 0% in undiagnosed. This is a symptom which ordinarily cannot be directly observed by informants and thus the figures given above, especially 0% in undiagnosed, probably, in the case of this symptom, say more about second-hand information than about the symptom prevalences important to diagnosis.

As noted, the most common symptom in the total sample was weight loss, which occurred in 60%. It was especially common in affective disorder (77%) and in the miscellaneous group (83%) and was much less common in alcoholism (29%) and in the undiagnosed group (15%). It was a surprise that this particular symptom was the most common and was about equally prevalent in affective disorder and the miscellaneous group, occurring in more than 75% in each. Symptoms diagnostic of affective disorder do include weight loss, but there are several other symptoms (such as sleep problems, poor concentration, feeling "low") having a higher prevalence given the distribution of diagnoses.[1]

There were three symptoms which surprised us by occurring at about the same levels in each of the four diagnostic groups. These symptoms were the aforementioned headache (which had a prevalence of about 40% in all four groups), remaining completely silent at times (a general prevalence of about 25%), and statements of a black future (a general prevalence of about 20%). Headache is a common symptom in depressed subjects and one which I expected to have a higher prevalence than the 37% it showed in the affective disorder group. I also expected a higher prevalence of headache in affective disorder than in the alcoholic group, where the prevalence was 41%. Similarly, silence, and expectation of black future are symptoms more common in affective disorder, depressed phase, than in other psychiatric illnesses. It surprised us, therefore, that their prevalences among the depressed subjects in our sample were as low as they were shown to be and that, at the same time, their prevalences in the other groups were so close to those found in the depressed group. Again, these unexpected figures may be the result of the impossibility of our directly interviewing the suicide subjects.

There were several symptoms usually considered most common in alcoholics, but which did not prove so in our study—shifting from job to job in the ten years immediately prior to suicide occurred in 28% of the alcoholics as opposed to 39% of the affective disorder group; not keeping one's self as clean as usual had a prevalence of only 19% in the alcoholic group as compared with a rate of 54% in the undiagnosed group; and nausea occurred in only 21% of the alcoholic subjects (second-hand information sources would once again seem likely to have had particular bearing on this figure) and in 38% of the miscellaneous group.

There were two other symptoms—statement of feeling sad, and belief that the family would be better off without the subject—which were, surprisingly, higher in the alcoholic group than in the affective disorder group where a higher prevalence would have been the expected finding (27% versus 17% and 23% versus 13%, respectively). These are particularly unexpected results when they are compared with the prevalence rates of two matching kinds of symptoms. Sadness itself was found in 70% of the affective disorder group and the feeling of being a burden was found in 26% of that group.

I have used the terms "surprising" and "unexpected" a good many times in this chapter. Indeed, a number of the symptom prevalence figures were not those I had anticipated. Even so, I am struck with the way in which the overall results of our study of a large number of consecutive suicides were closely related to the commonly held idea mentioned in the first paragraph of this chapter—that affective disorder is the illness most commonly associated with completed suicide.

This finding of more or less expected diagnostic breakdown is not vitiated by the secondary manner in which the occurrence of symptoms was elicited, presumably because the informants were observant and perceptive enough to avoid grossly misleading the interviewers.

All these findings on the prevalence of symptoms were of course derived from secondary information, and this resulted in some unexpected observations. Since suicide is an event in which affected families might benefit from and act on foreknowledge of symptoms, information gained in this secondhand manner is not a liability but an asset. It is useful to know which symptoms "show" to an extent that is noticeable to untrained informants. It is equally interesting to realize that certain symptoms commonly associated with specific psychiatric illnesses and suicide are interior symptoms not so likely to be noticed by close family and friends.

INTERVIEW FORM

Original interview form for informants of 134 completed suicides. (All identifying information was coded and kept in a locked file. This information was given to investigators with the informants' understanding of the above confidentiality safeguard.)

Psychiatric Diagnosis

　　　_____ 1. Affective disorder, depressed phase
　　　_____ 2. Affective disorder, manic phase
　　　_____ 3. Schizophrenia
　　　_____ 4. Organic brain syndrome
　　　_____ 5. Delirium
　　　_____ 6. Mental retardation
　　　_____ 7. Alcoholism
　　　_____ 8. Drug dependence
　　　_____ 9. Homosexuality
　　　_____ 10. Anxiety neurosis
　　　_____ 11. Phobic neurosis
　　　_____ 12. Hysteria
　　　_____ 13. Obsessive-compulsive neurosis
　　　_____ 14. Depressive neurosis
　　　_____ 15. Antisocial personality
　　　_____ 16. Undiagnosed psychiatric illness
　　　_____ 17. Psychiatric illness
　　　_____ 18. Terminal medical illness without psychiatric illness
　　　_____ 19. No current illness

Degree of confidence

　　　_____ Very
　　　_____ Moderate
　　　_____ Slight

Patient No. _____

Name _____
Maiden Name _____
Address _____
Phone _____
Other Name _____
Examiner _____ Birthplace _____
Date of exam _____ Population of birthplace _____
Time of exam _____ Religion _____
Date of act _____ Color _____
Date of inquest _____ Sibling rank
Coroner's No. _____ City _____   Total no. sibs _____
                    County _____   Sibs dead before pt. born _____
Age _____   Sibs dead before pt. 5 _____
Birth date _____   Sibs dead after pt. 5 _____
Sex _____
Marital status _____

Parents' Names	Parents' Address and Phone

Father's birthplace _____	Mother's birthplace _____
Father's occupation _____	Mother's occupation _____

Children's Names (2 or 3)	Children's Address

Spouse's Name _____
Spouse's Address
  and Phone _____

Whom was patient living with? (Description of household)

Name	Age	Sex	Relation to patient

Address and Telephone (if different than that above given for patient)

Informants

Name	Relation	Address	Est. age	Sex	Frequency of visits	Length of acquaintance	Phone
					per wk. / per mo.	(years)	

Relatives (3)

Name	Relation	Address

Current or Most Recent Occupation

_____ Kind of job and date held (be specific. If patient was unemployed, get this info for main source of support).

Name of Company
Address _____
Phone _____

Current or Most Recent *Physician* (M.D.) and any *Psychiatrist* (P) or Other *Counselor* (C) or *Chiropractor* (CH) or *Osteopath* (O)

Name	Ident.	Dates seen	Address	Phone

The Act

Tell me about what happened. (probe)

Why do you think he did this? (probe)

What have other persons said about why he did this?

Had he done anything else to try to solve this problem? (probe)

_____Did you have an idea something was the matter with him?
What was it? (probe)

_____Did anyone else, including a doctor, think anything was wrong with him?
What was it?

_____ When did this present trouble begin? (months)
_____ Was he like his usual self just before this time?
Was this trouble entirely new for him or was it a worsening of the way he generally was?
_____ Entirely new
_____ Recurrence after being well
_____ Worsening
_____ Can't tell
_____ Informant denies any trouble
During the time of this trouble (illness) did the patient:
_____ seem the same as at the beginning of the disease or after the illness was established
_____ seem better than at the beginning of the disease or after the illness was established
_____ seem to get worse steadily
_____ seem to get worse rather suddenly
_____ seem to get worse then better
_____ seem to get better then worse
_____ Did he believe he was ill?
_____ What did he think the illness was?

Did he talk to anyone about (dates):
_____ wanting to die
_____ being better off dead
_____ you (or his family) being better off if he were dead
_____ committing suicide
_____ any similar ideas

How did he do it? (not necessary to repeat if examiner is sure of details—applies for all questions down to Prior Events)

_____ Hanging   _____ Leaping
_____ Shooting   _____ Burning
_____ Poison   _____ Cutting
_____ Gas   _____ Auto wreck
_____ Drowning   _____ Other (specify)

_____ Was anyone in the room with him when he did it?
_____ Was anyone in the house with him? (or in yard or in garage)
_____ Was he entirely isolated when he did it?
_____ Time suicide committed
_____ Time of death
_____ Did he leave a note?
_____ What did the note say? (get copy)

_____ Where was he found?
_____ Who found him?
_____ Could anything be done for him when he was found?
_____ Taken to a hospital? (for Rx, not DOA)

Prior Events

	How many times?	When?

Did he mention ideas of committing suicide or killing himself ?
  to informant
  to family
  to relatives
  to friends
  to doctor
  to anyone		

Did he mention being depressed or did he look depressed or disgusted?
  to informant
  to family
  to relatives
  to friends
  to doctor
  to anyone		

Did he act more irritable and angry than usual?
  to informant
  to family
  to relatives
  to friends
  to doctor
  to anyone		

Was he under a doctor's care? (Dates are not exclusive. Fill in number of times saw M.D. or other practitioner in the given periods)
_____ Presently
_____ 1–3 months ago
_____ 3–6 months ago
_____ 6–12 months ago
_____ Over 12 months ago
_____ If he had a psychiatric illness, was he under a doctor's care for this illness? (or other practitioner)
_____ Was he under a doctor's care for some other illness? (or other practitioner)
_____ Was he seen by a psychiatrist or by someone else to help his nerves?

	In the year preceding patient's death, did any of these occur?	Related to suicide?
a. school trouble b. job trouble (fired, quit, lower income, promoted, demoted, higher income, couldn't take care of family or household) c. death of spouse, parent, child, relative, friend d. friction with spouse or lover e. divorce, separation, desertion f. friction with parent, sibling, child g. financial difficulties (in debt? in serious debt?) h. alcohol i. alcohol just before attempt j. pregnancy k. moved home l. moved city of residence m. feeling of disgrace n. sickness of relative or friend o. living alone or in an institution p. medical disease		

_____ Was one or more of these the most important reason(s) for his suicide? (fill in the appropriate letter[s].)

In the time just preceding his death would you say or did someone else say he was:
_____ depressed
_____ disgusted with self
_____ disgusted with the world

The Final Months

_____ feeling worthless
_____ blaming himself unduly for his own or family's troubles
_____ angry
_____ spiteful
_____ frustrated in a love relationship
_____ feeling he was a burden
_____ feeling neglected

_____ Was this an attempt to force attention to himself or his illness?

What do you think the effect of this will be on (household and relatives):

Person	Relation	See M.D.	Emotionally		Financially	On his living plans
			Acute	Long Term		

_____ Previous suicide attempts of patient (fill in number)

When	How	Why

Suicides in family (method, date, illness like patient's) (If this had happened, would you have known?)

	Successful	Attempt
_____ Father		
_____ Mother		
_____ Brother		
_____ Sister		
_____ Grandparent		
_____ Uncle		
_____ Aunt		
_____ Child		
_____ Spouse		
_____ Friend or other close person		

Operations (including lobotomy and tonsillectomy), Hospital Stays, Injuries

Date	Time in hospital	Why	Operation

Nonsurgical Hospitals (not including normal OB)

Date	Time in Hospital	Why

Mental Hospitals (sanitarium, state hospital, mental hospital, rest home)

Date	Time in hospital	Hospital name	Why

_____ If in mental hospital, was he like himself (completely well) between that time and the present?
If not, in what way was he not well?

_____ Number surgical hospitalizations (summary)
_____ Number general hospitals (summary)
_____ Number mental hospitals (summary)
_____ Number total hospitals (summary)
_____ Number injuries (doctor, missed work, coma, bad scars)

Present or Previous Serious Diseases

	Inclusive date	Diseases
Non-psychiatric (dates)		
Present disease (dates)		
Present physical disability		
Nervous breakdown		
Describe—Was there ever a time when he talked too much, was loud, overactive, couldn't take time to eat or sleep properly, bragged about himself, was too happy, irritable, would fight, couldn't do his job?)		
Manic attack		
Depressed attack		

If he had a nervous breakdown, was he completely well afterwards? _____
If not, in what way was he not himself?

Family Disease

	Relation	Inclusive date	Disease
Nervous breakdown			
Alcohol			
Mental hospital			
Nervous			
Like patient's			

(Let us review present illness which led to suicide. Review with relative if not clear in your mind or his. These are not necessarily direct questions to the informant, but are a means for the interviewer to score these data.)

_____ Was there a previous episode of this illness from which the patient fully and completely recovered?

_____ Date of present illness (the date it first began if this is an illness in which there has never been a full remission, *or,* if this is an episode of an illness in which there have been one or more complete remissions, the date of the *first* attack of illness.)

_____ Date of present episode (if there have been previous episodes from which the patient has fully recovered).

_____ Was there a recent (definite) worsening in the patient's symptoms? (This means an *exacerbation* of a previously established illness and not the *onset* of such an illness.)

_____ When did this worsening occur?

_____ Was there a recent (definite) improvement in the patient's symptoms?

_____ When did this improvement occur?

Symptoms

	Date began	Before present episode?	Part of present episode?
Dyspnea			
Palpitation			
Chest pain			
Dizziness			
Headache			
Anxiety attacks (apprehension, impending death, palpitation, shortness of breath, weakness, trembling)			
Fatigue			
Blindness			
Paralysis			
Loss of voice			
Fits			
Fainting spells			
Amnesia			
Stroke			
Visual blurring			
Weakness			
Weight loss			
Nausea			
Vomiting			
Abdominal pain			
Menstrual pain			
Menstrual irregularity			
Menstrual hemorrhage			
Sexual indifference			
Frigidity			
Impotence			

36 The Final Months

Pregnancy trouble			
Back pain			
Joint pain			
Extremity pain			
Nervous			
High-strung			
Cried easily			
Feelings hurt easily			
Moody			
Sensitive			
Always sickly (majority of life)			
"Neurotic"			
Outbursts of rage			
Crowd trouble			
Did he read or talk about suicides or accidental deaths or other violent deaths?			
Did he try to avoid hearing about or seeing violence in any form—either in the papers, movies, or TV?			
Fears (heights, streets, dark public conveyances, leaving home)			
Obsessions (injure someone)			
Compulsions (handwashing, locks, gas)			
Preoccupation (with any subject)			

In the past few days, weeks, or months, did any of these occur or had he ever had them before this?

_____ Weight loss   _____ Indecision
_____ Anorexia   _____ Loss of interest
_____ Insomnia   _____ Joylessness
_____ Fatigue   _____ Sadness
_____ Constipation   _____ Ennui
_____ Inertia

Reduction in affectionate relationships with:
_____ spouse
_____ children
_____ grandchildren
_____ other
_____ Reduction in sex drive
Diminished social relationships:
_____ see friends less
_____ less movies
_____ less TV
_____ less cards
_____ less sports
_____ less reading
_____ Job disability (housework, family care)
_____ Generally less active
_____ Looked depressed
Delusions (summary)
_____ sin
_____ guilt
_____ worthlessness
_____ somatic
_____ poverty
_____ Did he have any ideas you considered unusual for him or that you considered mistaken even though he wouldn't admit his mistake?
_____ Did he believe he had committed some sin?
_____ Did he believe he was worthless or no good?
_____ Did he believe his brain or intestines had rotted away or didn't function?
_____ Did he believe there was a serious difficulty with any other part of his body?
_____ Did he believe he was bad for his family and they would be better off without him?
_____ Did he feel he had made some mistake and that the police or tax people were after him?
_____ Did he believe he had lost most or all of his money?
_____ Did he worry about being poverty stricken?
_____ Did he believe he had lost his memory?
_____ Did he fear he was losing his mind?
_____ Did he blame himself for many things he felt were not right?
_____ Did he believe he would never get well?
_____ Did he blame himself for his own illness or believe that it was caused by his own mistakes or sins?
_____ Did he have hallucinations or complain of voices calling him bad names or saying he was no good?
_____ Did he say he was sad?
_____ Did he say he had a black future (without hope, nothing good will ever happen again, etc.)?

- _____ Did he say he was guilty?
- _____ Did he say he was no good?
- _____ Did he express any suicidal ideas?
- _____ Did he say he was "in the way" or a burden?
- _____ Was there ever a time in his life when he had feelings like these before?
- _____ Has he ever had a nervous breakdown that was in any way similar to this?
- _____ Did he complain of things seeming changed in some way?
- _____ Did he complain of things being unreal to him?
- _____ Did he complain of any unusual or different tastes?
- _____ Did he complain of any unusual smells?
- _____ Did he change the way he dressed?
- _____ Did he dress in dirty clothes?
- _____ Did he dress in unusual ways?
- _____ Did he keep himself as clean as he used to?
- _____ Did he talk about sex a lot?
- _____ Did he show sexual feelings toward persons he had not felt sexual toward before?
- _____ Did he say that anyone had been making sexual advances toward him, either real or imagined?
- _____ Did he seem to have any trouble thinking?
- _____ Did he talk less?
- _____ Were there times when he was almost completely silent even though other people tried to talk to him?
- _____ Did he have any thoughts out of the ordinary?
- _____ Had he thought much about religion lately?
- _____ Had he been reading the Bible a lot?
- _____ Had he been praying a lot?
- _____ Had he said that he had been communicating directly with God?
- _____ Was he loud and noisy?
- _____ Did he spend large sums of money?
- _____ Did he believe someone was spying on him?
- _____ Did he believe someone was robbing him?
- _____ Did he believe somebody was deliberately annoying him, trying to scare him, or was after him?
- _____ Did he believe he was being influenced by hypnosis, electrical waves, radio, or TV?
- _____ Did he believe that the house was wired?
- _____ Did he seem to believe that he was a special person or that he was someone else?
- _____ Did he believe someone was trying to harm him?
- _____ Did he believe someone was trying to kill him?
- _____ Had he talked about or acted as though he felt like hurting someone?
- _____ Had he hurt someone?
- _____ Had he talked about or acted as though he felt like killing someone?
- _____ Had he thrown something at a person?
- _____ Had he threatened someone?
- _____ Had he been afraid of hurting someone?

_____ Did he change his ordinary way of life?
_____ Did he behave strangely in any way?
_____ Did he believe someone had been reading his mind?
_____ Did he believe someone had been telling him what to do?
_____ Did he talk about having some special power?
_____ Did he say he had heard voices (when no one was around)?
_____ Did he say he had seen things that other people don't see?
_____ Was he very overactive and hard to slow down at times? (pathologically so)
_____ Were there times he was agitated and tense, when he would pace the floor, cry uncontrollably, not keep still?
_____ Had his memory gotten poor?
Yes No Did he know the date?
Yes No Could he find his way around by himself?
Yes No Did you trust him out of the house without a companion?
Yes No Could he read and understand things as well as ever?
Yes No Did he have any difficulties with simple arithmetic, such as having trouble making change?
_____ Any other symptoms?
I know that most people find it hard to talk about their sex life, but since this may be very important, I would like to know if you knew anything about his sex life that may have disturbed him or led to his suicide.

School History

_____ Grade reached

_____ Truancy

_____ Fighting

_____ Expulsion

_____ Suspension

Homes

_____ Length of time in St. Louis or St. Louis County. (years)
_____ Number of cities lived in. (list cities)

_____ Total number of homes lived in.
Brought up as child:
_____ on farm
_____ rural (less than 10,000)
_____ small city (10,000–100,000)
_____ large city (more than 100,000)
Most of life spent:
_____ on farm
_____ rural (less than 10,000)
_____ small city (10,000–100,000)
_____ large city (more than 100,000)
_____ Time in U.S., if foreign born.

Work History—Past 10 Years
(For most recent jobs and for jobs in past 2 years be sure to get exact income)

Income levels*:		
Week	Month	Year
$ 0–40	$ 0–150	$0 −2000
40–60	150–250	2000–3000
60–100	250–400	3000–5000
100–150	400–600	5000–7500
150+	600+	7500+

Date	Job	Where	Income	Why left

*Income levels refer to 1956–1957.

_____ Any income from pensions? (How long and how much)
_____ Any income from compensation—VA, job, due to injury or illness? (how long and how much)
_____ Most money ever made?
Ever much better off financially? (this must be done very carefully)
_____   as child
_____   as adult
_____ In general, did he do okay on his jobs?
_____ Did he used to (before 10 years ago) drift from job to job?
_____ Was he ever fired? How many times?
_____ Did he ever walk off a job for no good reason? How many times?
_____ Did he ever quit a job because of difficulties with boss or fellow employees? How many times?
_____ Did she ever have to stop taking care of children and house? How many times?
_____ Did he ever neglect his children?
_____ Total number of jobs
_____ Total length of working life
_____ Was he ever not working for a long period of time (more than 6 months) for any reason—illness, didn't want to work, couldn't find a job? How many times? How long each time?

Date	Reason

Marital History

Current marital status
_____ married   _____ widow
_____ divorced   _____ never married
_____ separated   _____ common law
_____ legal separation _____ bigamy
_____ deserted

Difficulties in present marriage if married and living with spouse?

Marriage no.	Inclusive date	How ended	Reason for incompatibility

Children, Stepchildren, Fosterchildren

Rank	Sex	Marriage no.	Date of birth	Date of death	Date permanently left home	Why left home

Parental Home

	Age of patient	Mother	Father
Divorced			
Separated (how long)			
Died			
Jailed (how long)			
Physical illness (how long)			
Mental illness (how long)			
Alcoholism			

_____ Was patient brought up in a foster home? (dates)
_____ Was patient brought up in an institution such as an orphan's home? (dates)
_____ Was patient brought up by relatives or friends? (dates)

Alcohol

_____ Did his family ever object to his drinking?
_____ Did he ever get into trouble at work because of drinking?
_____ Did he ever have trouble with auto driving (speeding, accident, etc.) because of drinking?
_____ Was he ever arrested, even for a few hours, because of drinking and/or peace disturbance?
_____ Did he ever go on benders?
_____ Did he think he drank too much?
_____ Did you think he drank too much for his own good?
_____ Were there times in his life, especially the past few weeks or months, that he drank too much?
_____ How frequently did he drink? (times/month)
_____ How much did he drink each day or each week? (amt./time period)
_____ Drinking at time of attempt?
Evaluation of alcoholic status
_____ chronic alcoholic

_____ heavy drinker
_____ mild drinker (normal social drinking)
_____ teetotaler

Arrests

_____ Did he ever have trouble with the police?
_____ Was he ever in reform school?

Was he ever arrested for	Date	Sentence	Time served	Where
Traffic violation Drinking Disturbing the peace Fighting Robbery Burglary Forgery Other				

Drugs

_____ Did he take drugs for sleeping?
_____ Every night?
_____ During the day?
_____ Was he ever addicted to dope?
_____ Did he ever want to stop taking drugs and couldn't?
_____ Did he think he took too many drugs?
_____ Did you think he took too many drugs?
            Evaluation of drug status
_____   addict
_____   took too many
_____   took occasionally
_____   none

Military

_____ Dates in service
_____ Overseas or combat decorations
_____ Kind of discharge
_____ Ever court martialed in service?

Religion and Social Life

_____ Did he belong to a church? (which denomination)
_____ How often did he go? (per month)
How devout was he?
_____ more than his friends or family
_____ less than his friends or family
_____ same as his friends or family
_____ Did he belong to any clubs or other organizations?
_____ Was he an officer or otherwise active in church groups or clubs?
Did he ever go to church?
_____ as child
_____ as adult
How often would he see his friends socially?
_____ 1 time per 2 weeks or more often
_____ 1 time per 2 to 4 weeks
_____ 1 time per 1 to 4 months
_____ 3 times per year or less
_____ How many people did he regularly see socially?
_____ Would his friends come to his house?
_____ Would he go to their houses?
_____ Both
_____ How many really close friends did he have?
Was a good part of his social life in
_____ his home
_____ friends' homes
_____ relatives' homes
_____ church
_____ bar or tavern
_____ with fellow employees after work

Home

_____ No. of rooms (identify and list every room, including bathrooms)
_____ Own own home (age of home)
_____ Rent home or apartment (amount of rent)
_____ Roomer
_____ Institution
_____ Live with relatives or friends
Summary
_____ living alone in house
_____ living alone in apartment
_____ living alone in room
_____ living with friends
_____ living with relatives
_____ living with family
_____ living in an institution

Condition of home
_____ good
_____ fair
_____ poor
_____ Census tract of residential neighborhood

From what you say there was no reason for suicide and yet there must be a reason? (probe)

Reliability of informant
_____ high
_____ OK
_____ questionable

Other Informants

No.	Name	Address and phone	Relation to patient	How close		How long
				per wk.	per mo.	(years)

Information:

Present illness, including previous episodes of same illness, if any, in prose:

REFERENCE

1. Cassidy, W.L., et al. Clinical observations in manic depressive disease: A quantitative study of one hundred manic-depressive patients and fifty medically sick controls. *JAMA* 164:1535–1546, 1957.

4

Affective Disorder— Description of the Sample Comprising the Largest of the Four Major Diagnostic Groups

Forty-seven percent (63 of 134) of the suicides were diagnosed as having had affective disorder, depressed phase, and represented the largest single diagnostic group in the sample.

In February 1959, an early report on one aspect of this study was published.[1] Later the same year, a second report was published.[2] In both of these publications, the psychiatric illness which I am here calling affective disorder, depressed phase, was called manic-depressive depression. It is uncertain when the word *affective* began to be widely used in association with manic-depressive illness. In the 1942 edition of *The Standard Nomenclature of Disease and Standard Nomenclature of Operations* (3rd edition, American Medical Association, Chicago) the phrase *affective reactions* was introduced. (It is not found in either of the earlier editions of the book, 1933 and 1935, even though at least three scientific papers—by Kantor in 1923,[3] by Ziegler in 1929,[4] and by Barker in 1930[5]—used the term in direct relation to manic-depressive illness.) Even so, the specific disorders listed under *affective reactions* in the 1942 Nomenclature were *manic depressive reaction* and *psychotic depressive reaction*. DSM-I,[6] published in 1952, apparently used those terms as models. By 1968, when DSM-II[7] was published, *major affective disorders* was used as a generic heading for *manic-depressive illness,* for *involutional melancholia,* and for *unspecified major affective disorder. Depressive neurosis* was not, however, listed under *major affective disorders.*

Clearly, it has been difficult for the psychiatric community to settle firmly on a good, descriptive term for the disease now fairly commonly known as affective disorder. One reason for the difficulty is the disagreement about whether psychiatrists are dealing with one disease or more than one. Another reason for the difficulty is that if they are dealing with only one, the implication must be that its various symptoms are examples of heterogeneous manifestations of a single underlying illness.

In the 1959 paper, we reported "Those [suicides] with manic-depressive disease were solely in the depressed phase at the time of their deaths. No person committed suicide while in the manic phase."[2] On reviewing the case histories for this book, I found that, indeed, as far as could be determined, none of the 63 subjects with affective disorder had ever had a manic episode. Careful descriptions of mania and depression, in which the two conditions are considered separately, are recent, even though Kraepelin introduced the concept more than 70 years ago.[8] In a study of several hundred cases of affective disorder, Stenstedt described depression and mania separately and found a ratio of 5 : 1, depression to mania.[9] Perris found a ratio of 6 : 1.[10] Manic episodes are generally known to lead to hospitalization in a higher proportion of cases than are depressive episodes, mania being the more disruptive of the two conditions. Unhospitalized depressive episodes are less often recorded and therefore it is likely that the true ratio is nearer to 10 or 15 to 1 than 5 or 6 to 1. For example, in the 899 cases of manic depressive illness reported by Kraepelin,[8] the ratio of depression to mania in hospitalized patients was 3 : 1, but as Kraepelin observed, if the number of patients with the combined form of the illness is included in the total and the number of attacks are counted and included as well, manic episodes become proportionately even more infrequent showing a ratio of depressive episodes to manic episodes of 6 : 1. Even so, it is unexpected, not to say unusual, to find not a single previous episode of mania in 63 unselected cases of affective disorder. That suicide was a common result should not negate the possibility of earlier manic episodes.

Table 4.1 shows that, regardless of disagreements about nomenclature, it is possible to comprehensively describe affective disorder, depressed phase, through its numerous symptomatic manifestations and their prevalences—in this sample, as high as 80% (insomnia) and as low as 2% (seeming to feel like hurting someone). There are 97 symptoms listed in the table—all those mentioned by informants as having been present in the suicidal subjects' behavior (those diagnosed as having affective disorder, depressed phase), conversation, physical condition, and mood. Before considering those 97 symptoms from a viewpoint specifically designed for this study of suicide, I should outline a more comprehensive way by which to evaluate and interpret subjects' symptoms and other manifestations of psychiatric disease in general. This approach is to regard them from five different aspects:[11] as the symptoms themselves, as chief complaints, as mental status findings, as natural history findings, and as family history findings. This kind of classification is not mutually exclusive and, depending on which viewpoint is

TABLE 4.1 Frequency of symptoms in affective disorder group (percentage)

Rank	Symptom	Total	Men	Women	Significance*
1.	Insomnia	80	76	92	NS
2.	Weight loss	77	75	81	NS
3.	Loss of interest	73	66	93	<.01
4.	Anorexia	71	67	85	NS
5.	Sadness	70	70	71	NS
6.	Joylessness	66	58	86	<.05
7.	Nervousness	63	69	47	NS
8.	Fatigue	60	59	64	NS
9.	Less talkative	54	55	50	NS
10.	Inertia	51	41	83	<.002
11.	Belief would never get well	48	46	55	NS
12.	Weakness	48	54	31	NS
13.	Ennui	43	41	58	NS
14.	Easily hurt feelings	42	42	43	NS
15.	Crying easily	42	45	31	NS
16.	Sexual indifference	41	50	13	<.005
17.	Indecision	40	34	64	<.05
18.	Drifting from job to job for more than ten years prior to suicide	39	39	38	NS
19.	Tension (high-strung)	39	35	50	NS
20.	Suicidal ideas	38	41	31	NS
21.	Weekly to daily drinking of alcohol	38	26	69	<.05
22.	Dyspnea	38	18	46	NS
23.	Headaches	37	38	33	NS
24.	Dizziness	35	36	33	NS
25.	Drugs for sleeping	33	23	67	<.01
26.	Belief serious problem with a part of his/her body	33	34	31	NS
27.	Constipation	33	24	100	<.0005
28.	Not caring for children	33	0	42	<.0005
29.	Pain in extremities	32	35	23	NS
30.	Complete silence at times	30	28	38	NS
31.	Change in usual life-style	28	23	46	NS
32.	Palpitations	26	22	44	NS
33.	Feeling of being a burden	26	15	100	<.0005
34.	Not working for more than 6 months	26	25	33	NS
35.	Drugs for sleeping every night	25	18	50	<.02
36.	Abdominal pain	25	23	31	NS
37.	Chest pain	24	24	23	NS
38.	Not as clean as usual	23	23	23	NS
39.	Change in way of dress	23	23	25	NS
40.	Belief losing his/her mind	22	20	38	NS
41.	Back pain	22	24	15	NS
42.	Pain in joints	21	19	30	NS
43.	Informant's belief he/she drank too much	20	27	0	<.005
44.	Feelings of worthlessness/being no good	20	16	40	NS
45.	Statement of black future	20	13	56	<.01
46.	Sleeping drugs during daytime	20	10	55	<.01

Rank	Symptom	Total	Men	Women	Significance*
47.	Outbursts of rage	19	20	14	NS
48.	Vomiting	19	20	18	NS
49.	Praying more than usual	19	17	43	<.05
50.	Blurred vision	19	23	8	NS
51.	Trouble in thinking	18	18	17	NS
52.	Family's objection to subject's drinking	18	24	0	<.0005
53.	More thoughts about religion than usual	18	13	33	NS
54.	Worry about being "poverty stricken"	17	15	23	NS
55.	Statement of feeling sad	17	17	17	NS
56.	Anxiety attacks	16	15	17	NS
57.	Nausea	15	15	16	NS
58.	Drinking at time of suicide	15	20	0	<.01
59.	"Neurotic"	13	12	17	NS
60.	Belief he/she bad for family	13	13	15	NS
61.	Self-blame for own illness	13	16	7	NS
62.	Statement of being no good	13	2	21	NS
63.	Repeated fainting spells	13	13	15	NS
64.	Wearing dirty clothes	13	18	0	<.01
65.	Poor memory	12	13	8	NS
66.	"Strange" behavior	12	10	15	NS
67.	Thoughts out of the ordinary	12	10	15	NS
68.	Chronic sickliness	11	13	7	NS
69.	Arrests for traffic violations	11	15	0	<.005
70.	"Strokes"	11	15	0	<.005
71.	Quitting job because of difficulties with boss or fellow workers	10	12	0	<.01
72.	Walking off job for no known reason	10	12	0	<.01
73.	Benders	9	12	0	<.01
74.	Feeling he/she drank too much	9	13	0	<.01
75.	Fears	9	10	7	NS
76.	Guilt feelings	9	8	14	NS
77.	Paralysis	9	13	0	<.01
78.	Loss of voice	9	10	8	NS
79.	Unnecessary self-blame for things not "being right"	8	8	8	NS
80.	Difficulty with simple arithmetic	8	8	7	NS
81.	Reading and understanding less well	8	11	0	<.05
82.	Feeling he/she took too many drugs	8	8	8	NS
83.	Belief he/she had committed some sin	8	5	14	NS
84.	Trouble with police	7	18	0	<.005
85.	Job trouble due to drinking	7	10	0	<.025
86.	Arrests for peace disturbance	7	7	7	NS
87.	Lot of talk about sex	6	8	0	NS
88.	Informant's belief subject took too many drugs	6	3	15	NS
89.	Belief being pursued, tormented, etc.	6	5	8	NS
90.	Arrests for drinking	6	8	0	NS
91.	Driving trouble associated with drinking	5	7	0	NS

92.	Deliberately injuring someone	4	5	0	NS
93.	Spending binges	4	5	0	NS
94.	Belief he/she being spied upon	4	3	8	NS
95.	Threatening someone	4	6	0	NS
96.	Loudness and noisiness	2	3	0	NS
97.	Seeming to feel like hurting someone	2	3	0	NS

*$P \leq 0.05$. The significance is whether the difference between the frequency of a symptom in men and in women reaches $P \leq 0.05$.

under consideration, an individual symptom might be observed in any one (or more) of the categories. On the other hand, some of these five ways of considering the symptoms necessarily omit certain of them as discussed below.

As chief complaints, the symptoms may be "psychological" in manifestation or "medical." "Psychological" chief complaints might include dysphoria (depression, sadness, joylessness, etc.), insomnia, fears, and difficulty in thinking and concentrating. Chief complaints are those symptoms which bother individual subjects most, regardless of the frequency of occurrence in a sample. Any one of these might occur in less than half a given sample, but would be, nevertheless, diagnostically helpful when present in an individual case. "Medical" chief complaints might include headache, abdominal pain, palpitation, fatigue, generalized trembling of the body. Again, the presence of any of these kinds of symptoms as a chief complaint is diagnostically informative.

In considering the symptoms simply as symptoms, it is helpful to subdivide the long list into subgroups as I will show a bit later in this chapter.

Considered as mental status findings, the symptoms include, for example, decreased speech and motor activity, immobile facies, untidiness, and depressive delusions (e.g. sin, guilt, nihilism).

Examples of natural history findings include previous episode of affective disorder, episodic attacks of affective disorder with intermittent periods of being well, psychiatric health except for affective disorder, and age of onset over 40 (there were 47 of 63 subjects, or 75%, with affective disorder whose age of onset was over 40).

Considered as family history findings, the list of symptoms must be seen as it would apply in diagnosing a subject's family members who either had or had not suffered from affective disorder, depressed phase, who had or had not suffered from another psychiatric disease, or who had or had not committed suicide.

One of these five methods of considering manifestations does present itself as the most obviously direct approach to assessment of affective disorder, depressed phase. As I have noted earlier, it is not difficult to accurately describe affective disorder, depressed phase, by its most prevalent symptoms. The high prevalences of certain symptoms have been shown in other studies. To discuss these widely diverse symptoms and their varying prevalences substantively, I have devised a classification system which groups the individual symptoms into 14 descriptive categories:

1. *Sleep problems*—insomnia, use of drugs for sleeping
2. *Appetite problems*—weight loss, anorexia
3. *Motivation difficulties*—loss of interest, ennui, sexual indifference, indifference toward own children
4. *Dysphoria*—sadness, joylessness, nervousness, no expectation of recovery, easily hurt feelings, crying easily, indecisiveness, "high-strung" (quotation marks indicate informants' choice of words), belief in serious problem with some part of body, statements of black future, outbursts of rage, worry about being poverty stricken, belief would never get well, statements of feeling sad, having fears, and seeming to feel like hurting someone
5. *Consequences of depression*—history of having drifted from job to job more than 10 years prior to suicide, ever having been unemployed for more than six months, quitting job because of difficulty with boss or fellow employees, walking off job for no known reason, strange behavior, change in usual way of life, change in usual way of dressing, wearing dirty clothes, not keeping self as clean as usual, "neurotic," thoughts out of the ordinary, praying more than usual, more thoughts about religion than usual
6. *Bodily symptoms*—fatigue, weakness, dyspnea, headaches, dizziness, constipation, pain in extremities, palpitation, abdominal pain, chest pain, back pain, pain in joints, vomiting, blurred vision, nausea, anxiety attacks, repeated fainting spells, having always been sickly, "stroke," paralysis, loss of voice
7. *Retardation*—talking less, inertia, complete silence at times, trouble thinking, difficulty with simple arithmetic, reading and understanding less well than usual, poor memory
8. *Self-blame*—feeling of being a burden, feelings of worthlessness or of being "no good," self-blame for own illness, statements of being "no good," feelings of guilt, unnecessary self-blame for things not being "right," belief bad for family and family would be better off without him
9. *Depressive delusions*—belief losing mind, belief had committed some sin
10. *Suicidal ideas*
11. *Manic-type symptoms*—much talk about sex, injuring someone deliberately, spending binges, loudness and noisiness
12. *Paranoid feelings*—belief being spied upon, thoughts about someone being "after" him, trying to annoy him, etc.

13. *Use of alcohol*—drinking alcohol weekly to daily, informant's belief subject drank too much, family objection to subject's drinking, subject's belief he drank too much, going on benders, job trouble owing to drink, arrests for peace disturbance, arrests owing to drinking, automobile accidents associated with drinking, trouble with police, arrests for traffic violations
14. *Illicit drug use or drug abuse*—informant's belief subject took too many drugs, illicit or licit, taking sleeping medicine during the day, nightly use of sleeping medicine, subject's belief he took too many drugs, illicit or licit

I have grouped the individual symptoms this way to show directly what constitutes the classifying variables that specifically diagnose affective disorder, depressed phase. For example, "dysphoria" has a meaning that, in affective disorder, encompasses at least 15 different symptoms (those listed above under "dysphoria" were the ones present in this particular sample). Seeing these symptoms together, the reader will more readily understand the elements of the kind of dysphoria that is characteristic of affective disorder.

I have also numbered the groups in such a way as to indicate—as far as is feasible—the prevalence of the groups of symptoms. For example, the most prevalent individual symptom in this sample was insomnia (80%) and one third of the subjects in this study diagnosed as having affective disorder took drugs for sleeping; thus, *sleep problems* is first on our list of 14 groups. I have done this so that the reader will have at least a sense of the relative importance of different kinds of symptoms in the diagnosis of affective disorder, depressed phase.

The point of this, then, is that the reader not be confronted with 97 symptoms to consider singly, but is able to see how they were interpreted by the psychiatrists involved in the study when making their diagnoses. An example of how complication is minimized is the *use of alcohol* group, in which one is able to see how the problem of alcoholism manifested itself among some subjects with affective disorder and how one may compare the individual symptom prevalences with the same symptoms as they are shown among alcoholic subjects (Table 3.1).

I have discussed above the symptoms descriptive of affective disorder. One further point should be made simply as a matter of interest. There is one symptom that occurs among depressed subjects with a prevalence surprisingly similar to its prevalence in the general population. I am referring to lifelong "nervousness," which I wish to differentiate from the kind of nervousness that occurs only during depressive episodes. Of the 45 men, there were 3 who were said to have suffered lifelong "nervousness"; of the 18 women, there were 2. Thus, 8% of the subjects diagnosed as having had affective disorder, depressed phase, had always been "nervous" (7% of the men; 11% of the women). Their "nervousness" was variously described among the three men: in man A as "nervousness," in man B "nervousness," moodiness, and easily hurt feelings, and in man C as uncontrolled and immoderate gambling along with a denial of "nervousness." Among the women, there were two who were considered "nervous": woman A had no somatic symptoms, but was described as timid, "nervous," and afraid of accidents; woman B was described as "being nervous."

As noted, these were lifelong qualities unrelated to episodes of affective disorder. The overall occurrence of 8% is reasonably near the prevalence of "nervousness" described by Helgason,[12] by Fremming,[13] and by Cohen,[14] and substantially lower than that described by Leighton[15] and by Srole.[16] This suicide study was not, of course, designed to investigate lifelong nervousness, but as an aside, it is interesting to note the similarity of the overall figure to the prevalence in the general population, which would seem to indicate that the presence of affective disorder neither prevents nor leads to the occurence of lifelong "nervousness."

The depressed phase of affective disorder is an illness that causes a plethora of symptoms and makes life miserable for those afflicted. The misery colors most personal and interpersonal aspects of life. Even when an attack of affective disorder is mild, it is still noticeably disabling and debilitating. The mildly depressed person suffers from feelings of poor self-image, inadequacy, and "the blues," in addition to the tendency to cry easily and to feel anxious. The person is often concerned about having some serious medical illness and about dying. These thoughts are frequent, repetitive, and difficult to avoid for any significant period of time. Despite these miseries, some people with mild depression are able to keep up with their daily responsibilities—if at an impaired level—and it is often not possible to determine the extent of depression in these cases.

In people who are more depressed, there is a crescendo effect during which the patients feel more and more worthless and less and less hopeful that the disease will ever recede. Along with this may come the problems of increased slowness and sluggishness of speech and movement, difficulty in responding to conversation even to the point of muteness, agitation manifested by nervous stalking, pulling of hair, hand-wringing, and restless brushing and rubbing of clothes. Another frequent complaint is that of inability to think, to concentrate, to feel emotion, and that the "head is empty." Delusions such as incurability, general self-blame, illness as a punishment for sin, and of abject poverty also occur. In our study, the informants did not report even a single occurrence of hallucination among the sample of 63 subjects with depression. Even so, the symptom is encountered in about one tenth of depressed subjects who are hospitalized for psychiatric reasons. An example is a criticizing voice accusing a patient of being the cause of his own problems.

The patient with an affective disorder is also virtually always afflicted with bodily symptoms. The lack of uninterrupted sleep, the presence of nausea, the loss of appetite, the resultant loss of weight, unrelieved pains, and trouble breathing combine to make life extremely unpleasant. There is also a deep sense of joylessness which involves a loss of interest in those aspects of life which are commonly associated with happiness—work, home, grandchildren, holidays, sex, reading, movies, company, etc.

Life becomes, for the depressed person, a painful existence without promise or expectation of relief. In the light of the description of such an existence, the reader may better understand the allure of suicide.

The following individual case histories, or vignettes, are presented in groups defined by sex and age. They are identified by case numbers and, in every case, the subject's family history of suicide and/or psychiatric disease and the subject's police record are noted. A "score card" showing the subject's symptoms against the original criteria and against the Feighner criteria is adjacent to each vignette in order to provide the reader with an additional quick reference to diagnostic information.

These vignettes and their "score cards" are presented at the end of this and the succeeding three chapters and describe the occurrence or absence of symptoms in each subject in such a way as to enable the reader to decide for himself whether he agrees or disagrees with the diagnoses reached. In eight of the case histories of affective disorder (006, 014, 043, 059, 061, 092, 126, and 131), the reader will be confronted with the same dilemma that faced the investigators; that is, which diagnosis to assign a subject who met the criteria for both affective disorder and alcoholism.

REFERENCES

1. Robins, E., Gassner, S., Kayes, J., Wilkinson, R.H., Jr. and Murphy, G.E. The communication of suicidal intent: A study of 134 consecutive cases of successful (completed) suicide. *Amer. J. Psychiat.* 115(8):724–733, 1959.
2. Robins, E., Murphy, G.E., Wilkinson, R.H., Jr., Gassner, S. and Kayes, J. Some clinical considerations in the prevention of suicide based on a study of 134 successful suicides. *Amer. J. Public Health* 49(7):888–899, 1959.
3. Kantor, J.R. The psychology of feeling or affective reactions. *Amer. J. Psychology* 34:433–463, 1923.
4. Ziegler, L.H. Clinical phenomena associated with depressions, anxieties and other affective or mood disorder. *Amer. J. Psychiat.* 8:849–879, 1929.
5. Barker, L.F. The Relations of Psychology to Medicine and the Recognition and Treatment of Commoner Affective Disorders: Porter Lectures, Series 1, University Extension Division. University of Kansas, Lawrence, Kansas: 26–63, 1930.
6. *Diagnostic and Statistical Manual, Mental Disorders* (DSM I), Washington, D.C.: The American Psychiatric Association, 1952.
7. *Diagnostic and Statistical Manual of Mental Disorders* (DSM II). Washington, D.C.: The American Psychiatric Association, 1968.

8. Kraepelin, E., *Manic-Depressive Insanity and Paranoia*. Trans. R.M. Barclay from 8th German Edition of the "Text Book of Psychiatry," vols. iii and v, and edit. by G.M. Robertson. Edinburgh: E. and S. Livingstone, 1921.
9. Stenstedt, A. A study in manic depressive psychosis. Clinical, social and genetic investigations. *Acta psychiat. et neurol Scand.* (suppl. 79):1–111, 1952.
10. Perris, C. (ed.). A study of bipolar (manic-depressive) and unipolar recurrent depressive psychoses. *Acta psychiat. Scand.* 42 (suppl. 194):1–184, 1966.
11. Robins, E. Recognition and management of the seriously suicidal patient. *Medical Science* 8:78–94, 1960.
12. Helgason, T. Epidemiology of mental disorders in Iceland. *Acta psychiat. Scand.* 40 (suppl. 173) 1964.
13. Fremming, K.H. *The Expectation of Mental Infirmity in a Sample of the Danish Population.* London: The Eugenics Society and Cassell and Co. Ltd., 1951.
14. Kannel, W.B., Dawber, T.R. and Cohen, M.E. The electrocardiogram in neurocirculatory asthenia (anxiety neurosis or neurasthenia): A study of 203 neurocirculatory asthenia patients and 757 healthy controls in the Framingham study. *Ann. Internal Med.* 49:1351–1360, 1959.
15. Leighton, D.C., Harding, J.S., Maclin, D.B., Macmillan, A.M. and Leighton, A.H. *The Character of Danger.* New York: Basic Books, 1963.
16. Srole, L., Langes, T.S., Michael, S.T., Opler, M.K. and Rennie, T.A.C. *Mental Health in the Metropolis:* The Midtown Manhattan Study, Vol. 1. New York: McGraw-Hill, 1962.

AFFECTIVE DISORDER, SUBGROUP 1

Men aged 48 and under* (N = 11)

004 Informants: Wife, employer, police records

This 33-year-old white machinist changed to the night shift one month before his death. At about the same time he began to complain of being depressed, of being disgusted with the world, of fatigue, of visual blurring, and of pains in his legs. He also became increasingly nervous; he was especially provoked by his children making noise. He became somewhat withdrawn socially and less talkative at home. His wife felt that these symptoms were mild to moderate in intensity and did not believe they represented a drastic change. The symptoms were, however, unusual for him since he was not a nervous or complaining person ordinarily.

About one week before his death he became more irritable. On the day of his suicide the children wanted to go swimming. He refused them permission, but his wife contradicted him and allowed them to go swimming. After the children were gone he wanted to go boating with his wife but she did not want to go, saying that they would wait for the children. He said, "Now we know who's boss." He then went into the basement and hanged himself.

His employer stated that he was an excellent worker and that he had worked efficiently to the end, never appearing morose or withdrawn on the job. His suicide was a surprise to everyone at the plant.

The informants could give no information on life stress that may have contributed to his suicide.

Family history: Two brothers suffered from chronic alcoholism.
Arrest record: At ages 18 and 20 he was arrested for speeding. At age 23 he was arrested for car theft. No subsequent arrests.

---

*In the two largest diagnostic groups, affective disorder and alcoholism, there were (except in regard to women with alcoholism) sufficient numbers to calculate a standard deviation for age. Thus the middle age-categories represent the mean ages ± SD, and account for two-thirds of each sex-diagnostic group. About one-sixth of these groups were therefore older than the upper age limit of the mid-age category and one-sixth were younger than the lower limit.

Case No. 004 M X F ___ Age 33

ST. LOUIS SUICIDE STUDY CRITERIA FOR MAJOR AFFECTIVE DISORDER

Diagnosis required four of the six following categories, A–F. Category G was helpful in diagnosis, but not necessary.

A. Clinically well, exclusive of attacks of major affective disorder X

B. Previous episode(s) of major affective disorder ___

C. Discreteness (and duration) of final attack:
   6 months or less X
   12 months or less ___

D. "Medical" symptoms:
   insomnia ___
   anorexia ___
   weight loss ___
   low energy, weakness fatigue X
   constipation ___

E. Psychological symptoms:
   "blue" feeling, depression, sadness X
   diminished motor activity ___
   loss of interest ___
   diminished sexual interest and activity ___
   undertalkativeness X
   low expectancy of recovery; expectation of "black" future ___
   feeling of being a burden ___
   indecisiveness ___
   feelings of worthlessness or guilt X
   agitation ___
   personal untidiness ___
   difficulty in thinking and concentration ___
   delusions ___

F. Disturbances in social behavior: decreased social and recreational activity X

G. Miscellaneous items:
   age of onset 40 and over ___
   family history of affective disorder X

FEIGHNER CRITERIA FOR MAJOR AFFECTIVE DISORDER

Diagnosis required all three of the following categories.

A. Dysphoric mood (depressed, sad, blue, despondent, hopeless, "down in dumps," irritable, fearful, worried, discouraged) X

B. At least 5 of following for definite; at least 4 of following for probable:
   poor appetite or weight loss: 2 lb/wk, 10 lb/yr ___
   sleep difficulties ___
   loss of energy (fatigue, tiredness) X
   agitation or retardation ___
   loss of interest in usual activities or decreased sex drive ___
   complaints or actual diminished ability to think/concentrate ___
   feelings of guilt, self-reproach ___
   recurrent thoughts of death and/or suicide ___

C. A psychiatric illness lasting <u>at least one month</u> with no pre-existing psychiatric condition (schizophrenia, anxiety neurosis, phobic neurosis, obsessive-compulsive neurosis, hysteria, alcoholism, drug dependence, antisocial personality, homosexuality, transsexualism, mental retardation, anorexia nervosa, organic brain syndrome) or life-threatening or incapacitating illness X

054 Informants: Wife, hospital records

This 41-year-old white man had been married twice. The first marriage ended nine years prior to his suicide when the wife left the subject for another man. Within a year after his divorce, he moved to St. Louis from Ohio and, about three years later, married his second wife.

He and his second wife had been married for five years when he died. The subject was employed as an inspector and sprayer for an exterminating company, and although he was regularly employed, there never seemed to be enough money to support the family. His wife felt he drank too much (one to ten beers nightly) and described him as a "heavy drinker." She reported that he had suffered from headaches all his life and that he had always been a sensitive man with easily hurt feelings.

About three years before his death, the subject saw a doctor because of chest pain, palpitation, and shortness of breath. The doctor x-rayed his chest and discovered a collapsed lung. On learning this news, the subject went home and wept. According to hospital records investigated after his death, the subject had visited a hospital clinic six years prior to his suicide because he had broken his glasses. Doctors at the clinic diagnosed alternating exotropia. He was operated on and was followed by his doctors for one year, during which time his vision was normal.

One year before his death, he began to experience intermittent spells of depression which his wife described as characterized by gloominess, loss of appetite, loss of initiative, dissatisfaction with his job, fatigue, vomiting, looking and seeming depressed and disgusted. These "spells" came and went, with no intervening manic episodes. During them he mentioned suicide several times, asking his wife where she had hidden the shotgun, and saying he wished a car would run over him. Six months before his death, he was mugged on his way home from a neighborhood bar, knocked unconscious, and robbed.

Two months prior to his suicide, all his symptoms worsened. He believed he was physically very ill and that he would never get well. He complained of fatigue which kept him from going to work. He slept heavily all day and not at all at night. He complained of numbness in his legs, he seemed to have trouble thinking clearly, he spoke less, and stopped going to the bar to drink with his buddies. During this time, he spoke of his relatives in Ohio being "against him" (he was never more specific than this) and of the possibility of going back to the church. He was a member of the Salvation Army, as was his wife, and although she attended regularly, he had not attended in three years. During the last two months of his life he lost interest in sex and, in the last two weeks, lost his taste for alcohol and stopped drinking altogether.

On the day of the suicide, he was, according to his wife, in much better spirits than usual and had been talking happily with her family which was gathered at their corner grocery store. At about 1:00 PM, he went up to their apartment to change his clothes. A half hour later he shot himself with the shotgun he had apparently found sometime before and bought shells for. His wife discovered him, still alive, shortly after 1:30. He was taken to a hospital where he died that evening. He left a note asking his wife to pay all the outstanding bills they owed and saying he hoped his family was happy.

Family history: Because she had known him only five years and had never met his family, the wife knew very little about his background. However, she did not believe that anyone in his immediate family had a psychiatric illness.
Arrest record: None.

Case No. *054* M _X_ F __ Age _41_

ST. LOUIS SUICIDE STUDY CRITERIA FOR MAJOR AFFECTIVE DISORDER

Diagnosis required four of the six following categories, A–F. Category G was helpful in diagnosis, but not necessary.

- A. Clinically well, exclusive of attacks of major affective disorder _X_
- B. Previous episode(s) of major affective disorder _X_
- C. Discreteness (and duration) of final attack:
  - 6 months or less __
  - 12 months or less _X_
- D. "Medical" symptoms:
  - insomnia _X_
  - anorexia _X_
  - weight loss __
  - low energy, weakness fatigue _X_
  - constipation __
- E. Psychological symptoms:
  - "blue" feeling, depression, sadness _X_
  - diminished motor activity __
  - loss of interest __
  - diminished sexual interest and activity _X_
  - undertalkativeness __
  - low expectancy of recovery; expectation of "black" future _X_
  - feeling of being a burden __
  - indecisiveness __
  - feelings of worthlessness or guilt __
  - agitation __
  - personal untidiness __
  - difficulty in thinking and concentration _X_
  - delusions _X_
- F. Disturbances in social behavior: decreased social and recreational activity _X_
- G. Miscellaneous items:
  - age of onset 40 and over __
  - family history of affective disorder __

FEIGHNER CRITERIA FOR MAJOR AFFECTIVE DISORDER

Diagnosis required all three of the following categories.

A. Dysphoric mood (depressed, sad, blue, despondent, hopeless, "down in dumps," irritable, fearful, worried, discouraged) _X_

B. At least 5 of following for definite; at least 4 of following for probable:
 poor appetite or weight loss: 2 lb/wk, 10 lb/yr _X_
 sleep difficulties _X_
 loss of energy (fatigue, tiredness) _X_
 agitation or retardation _X_
 loss of interest in usual activities or decreased sex drive _X_
 complaints or actual diminished ability to think/concentrate _X_
 feelings of guilt, self-reproach __
 recurrent thoughts of death and/or suicide __

C. A psychiatric illness lasting <u>at least one month</u> with no pre-existing psychiatric condition (schizophrenia, anxiety neurosis, phobic neurosis, obsessive-compulsive neurosis, hysteria, alcoholism, drug dependence, antisocial personality, homosexuality, transsexualism, mental retardation, anorexia nervosa, organic brain syndrome) or life-threatening or incapacitating illness _X_

---

059 Informants: Wife, brother, sister-in-law, physicians, hospital records

This 45-year-old white man was educated through the 12th grade and married for the first time at age 29 just before leaving to serve overseas for two years during World War II. He received an honorable discharge, returned home to rural Missouri, and divorced his first wife. He moved to St. Louis and, at age 32 or 33, married his second wife with whom he was living at the time of his death. He was employed by a machine company as a lather and made a fairly good and steady income. His wife said he had not had more than ten jobs in his life and that he had been fired only once.

A longtime, heavy drinker, the subject was also a chronic asthmatic and had suffered from asthma-associated symptoms—dyspnea, palpitation, chest pain—all his life.

In describing him, his wife emphasized that he had had a wide circle of close friends and that as a couple they had had an active social life. She said her husband had always been a sensitive, rather moody person given to occasional outbursts of rage and that he cried easily and had feelings which were easily hurt. She and the subject's mother felt that he drank too much for his own good. She said that he had been arrested at least once for drunken driving and that, although he had gone on occasional benders, his drinking had never interfered with his work.

A year before his death, a favorite brother who had been "like a Santa Clause to the family" died. The subject's family physician felt this loss had precipitated the onset of a depressive episode and that the subject continued to be depressed throughout the last year of his life. His wife disagreed. She felt he had been his usual self until he was involved in an automobile accident six weeks before he died. He was drunk at the time of the accident and was charged with causing it. He suffered a concussion, head lacerations, and multiple rib fractures and the experience clearly frightened him. After a two-day hospitalization, he told his wife and his family doctor that he was quitting drinking and indeed he had no alcohol until the evening of his suicide, when he drank one beer.

After the accident he began to worry constantly about whether he would be allowed to drive again (he had cancelled his insurance shortly before the accident) as driving was necessary to his work. He worried also about how he would pay for the damages and injuries to the other car and its occupants. He complained of headaches and worried about the injury to his head. He suffered from increasing anorexia, weight loss, insomnia, fatigue, inertia, indecision, loss of interest, weakness, and anxiety attacks. He lost all interest in sex and was generally less interested in his wife. He rejoined the Baptist Church in which he had been raised as a child and began attending services regularly. At home he prayed often and read the Bible, neither of which he had done before. His old interests diminished—he stopped watching TV, reading the paper, playing cards, and going to the movies. He began to see less and less of his friends.

During this time, he visited two physicians. His family doctor, who believed that his depression had been well established before the accident, wanted to help him quit drinking and offered hypnosis. The subject seemed interested, but maintained that he could "take care of it himself." The other doctor saw the subject several times in the last four months of his life in connection with his asthma and reported only that the subject had never "really opened up to him."

His wife stated that his depressive symptoms grew steadily worse toward the end. She said that he looked depressed, that he spoke often of feeling worthless, and that he blamed himself for his troubles and for what he considered to be his black future. He did not make any comments about wanting to die or about suicide.

On the last evening of his life, a payday, he and his wife went grocery shopping with some friends. In the friends' car, he mentioned his worry about whether he would ever be allowed to drive again. The friends came back to his house after shopping and stayed until after midnight. After they had left, the subject drank one can of beer, his first in six weeks, after which he and his wife prepared for bed. While she was in the bathroom, he found his gun and shot himself. He was taken to a hospital where he died the next day. He left a note which said only, "Dear E." His wife was puzzled by this, for while one of her names is Elizabeth, it was not the name he called her by.

Family history: No family history of psychiatric illness.
Arrest record: Charged with drunken driving resulting in accident and injury six weeks prior to suicide.

Case No. 059 M X F__ Age 45

ST. LOUIS SUICIDE STUDY CRITERIA FOR MAJOR AFFECTIVE DISORDER

Diagnosis required four of the six following categories, A–F. Category G was helpful in diagnosis, but not necessary.

A. Clinically well, exclusive of attacks of major affective disorder ___

B. Previous episode(s) of major affective disorder ___

C. Discreteness (and duration) of final attack:
   6 months or less __X__
   12 months or less ___

D. "Medical" symptoms:
   insomnia __X__
   anorexia __X__
   weight loss __X__
   low energy, weakness fatigue __X__
   constipation ___

E. Psychological symptoms:
   "blue" feeling, depression, sadness __X__
   diminished motor activity __X__
   loss of interest __X__
   diminished sexual interest and activity __X__
   undertalkativeness ___
   low expectancy of recovery; expectation of "black" future __X__
   feeling of being a burden ___
   indecisiveness __X__
   feelings of worthlessness or guilt __X__
   agitation ___
   personal untidiness ___
   difficulty in thinking and concentration ___
   delusions ___

F. Disturbances in social behavior: decreased social and recreational activity __X__

G. Miscellaneous items:
   age of onset 40 and over __X__
   family history of affective disorder ___

FEIGHNER CRITERIA FOR MAJOR AFFECTIVE DISORDER

Diagnosis required all three of the following categories.

A. Dysphoric mood (depressed, sad, blue, despondent, hopeless, "down in dumps," irritable, fearful, worried, discouraged) __X__

B. At least 5 of following for definite; at least 4 of following for probable:
   poor appetite or weight loss: 2 lb/wk, 10 lb/yr __X__
   sleep difficulties __X__
   loss of energy (fatigue, tiredness) __X__
   agitation or retardation ____
   loss of interest in usual activities or decreased sex drive __X__
   complaints or actual diminished ability to think/concentrate ____
   feelings of guilt, self-reproach __X__
   recurrent thoughts of death and/or suicide ____

C. A psychiatric illness lasting <u>at least one month</u> with no pre-existing psychiatric condition (schizophrenia, anxiety neurosis, phobic neurosis, obsessive-compulsive neurosis, hysteria, alcoholism, drug dependence, antisocial personality, homosexuality, transsexualism, mental retardation, anorexia nervosa, organic brain syndrome) or life-threatening or incapacitating illness __X__

---

072 Informants: Wife, doctor, social service records

This 31-year-old white man had been, according to his wife, sexually inadequate throughout their ten-year marriage. Six months before his death, he had been hospitalized for three weeks for an appendectomy. While he was in the hospital, his wife told him she wanted a divorce, which she believed precipitated his depression.

He had completed sixth grade and, until drafted during World War II, moved from job to job. He served in the Army overseas and was given an honorable discharge. Shortly afterward, he married. He and his wife had three children. He was steadily employed at one job at a florist shop throughout his marriage and was, when he died, making the most money he had ever earned. He had no religious affiliation.

His wife described him as always having been "high-strung" and moody. She said he had never had many friends and had no real interests in anything except himself. She said he had never been "much in bed" nor ever really able to satisfy her, but that he had, at one time, undergone special medical treatments which had temporarily improved his sexual performance. As soon as he quit these treatments, however, he was "no good" again.

She said her husband's depression began six months prior to his suicide and described his symptoms as insomnia, weight loss (he lost 20–30 pounds in the last months of his life), feelings of being neglected, feelings of self-blame, of worthlessness, joylessness, sadness, and disgust. She said he had had outbursts of rage, that once he had tried to choke her, and another time had broken up some furniture. She also said that he had often paced the floor, crying and wringing his hands, and that he talked a great deal about sex.

His doctor, who had seen him several times in the last six months, said he had complained of back pain and asked to be checked for kidney disease (which he did not have). One month before his death, he had seemed to the doctor nervous and worried, but "not particularly depressed." The tranquilizers he had been given had not helped his insomnia, so the doctor prescribed others. He reported that he had noted no change in his patient's weight and that the patient had never mentioned his sex life.

Although his wife had filed for divorce at the time of his appendectomy and he had moved in with his mother when he was released from the hospital, he returned to his wife a month later. For the last five months of his life, he slept at home (though not "as man and wife"), but took his meals out. One month prior to his suicide, he began to talk about wanting to die, about being better off dead, and about his family being better off if he were dead. He threatened many times to commit suicide, but his wife thought he was just trying to get attention and sympathy. Her father, on the other hand, felt concerned that he might kill his wife and family as well as himself. On the night before his suicide, he brought home some poison which he said he intended to use to kill himself. The next evening he tried to "attack" his wife sexually. When she pushed him away, he drank the poison and ran from the house. The police found him an hour or so later and took him to a hospital where he died after about an hour.

Family history: There was no family history of psychiatric illness.
Arrest record: None.

Case No. 072 M X F __ Age 31

ST. LOUIS SUICIDE STUDY CRITERIA FOR MAJOR AFFECTIVE DISORDER

Diagnosis required four of the six following categories, A-F. Category G was helpful in diagnosis, but not necessary.

A. Clinically well, exclusive of attacks of major affective disorder X

B. Previous episode(s) of major affective disorder __

C. Discreteness (and duration) of final attack:
    6 months or less X
    12 months or less __

D. "Medical" symptoms:
    insomnia X
    anorexia __
    weight loss X
    low energy, weakness X
    fatigue __
    constipation __

E. Psychological symptoms:
    "blue" feeling, depression, sadness X
    diminished motor activity __
    loss of interest __
    diminished sexual interest and activity __
    undertalkativeness __
    low expectancy of recovery; expectation of "black" future __
    feeling of being a burden X
    indecisiveness __
    feelings of worthlessness or guilt X
    agitation X
    personal untidiness __
    difficulty in thinking and concentration __
    delusions __

F. Disturbances in social behavior: decreased social and recreational activity __

G. Miscellaneous items:
    age of onset 40 and over __
    family history of affective disorder __

FEIGHNER CRITERIA FOR MAJOR AFFECTIVE DISORDER

Diagnosis required all three of the following categories.

A. Dysphoric mood (depressed, sad, blue, despondent, hopeless, "down in dumps," irritable, fearful, worried, discouraged) X

B. At least 5 of following for definite; at least 4 of following for probable:
    poor appetite or weight loss: 2 lb/wk, 10 lb/yr X
    sleep difficulties X
    loss of energy (fatigue, tiredness) __
    agitation or retardation X
    loss of interest in usual activities or decreased sex drive __
    complaints or actual diminished ability to think/concentrate __
    feelings of guilt, self-reproach X
    recurrent thoughts of death and/or suicide X

C. A psychiatric illness lasting <u>at least one month</u> with no pre-existing psychiatric condition (schizophrenia, anxiety neurosis, phobic neurosis, obsessive-compulsive neurosis, hysteria, alcoholism, drug dependence, antisocial personality, homosexuality, transsexualism, mental retardation, anorexia nervosa, organic brain syndrome) or life-threatening or incapacitating illness X

080 Informant: Wife

This 29-year-old white man was described by his wife as having been a "happy-go-lucky" person who usually refused to worry about money matters. He was, she said, "always smiling." The only characteristic that did not fit her general description of him was what she believed to be hypochondria. All his life he had identified with other people's illnesses. As examples, she told of her husband's having had to go to a doctor because he had developed severe throat pain when his father-in-law had strep throat and of his having dizziness accompanied by pain in his left arm, symptoms that matched the father-in-law's angina symptoms. Ironically, he appeared to have been a fairly healthy man and had never been hospitalized for any reason. His father, who was ill with stomach cancer during most of his son's adolescence, died when the subject was 20. Apparently something of a problem as a child, he was expelled from his grammar school and ended his education after 8th grade. He spent two years in the Navy during World War II and received an honorable discharge. He married his wife when he was 22 and they had two children.

At the time of his death, the subject had been working for eight years as a press man at a printing company. There was a rumor that the company was considering closing down one of its presses and the subject was concerned about the possibility of losing his job. His wife said that he began to talk about this worry two weeks prior to his suicide. Two other incidents occurred at this time to add to his worries. He began to bleed from his rectum and, though he did not consult a doctor, his wife is certain that he believed he might have cancer like his father's. When his mother, from whom he had borrowed $300, called to ask him if he could repay her, he began to fret about his bills and to worry more about losing his job. His wife said that though it was unusual for him to worry about money, he had had similar worries one year earlier which also had been precipitated by unpaid bills. She said that the previous episode, during which he had manifested many depressive symptoms, lasted about a week and then subsided when things "straightened themselves out." He had said once during that week that she wouldn't have to pay the bills if he died. She also remembered that, for the last year, he had been more self-conscious about his short stature (he was five feet six inches tall) and had said several times that standing next to tall men made him feel like killing himself.

For the last two weeks of his life, the subject suffered from insomnia, anorexia, weight loss (ten pounds), fatigue, weakness, and sexual indifference. At work, he asked a friend if "100 Anacin would kill a person," but he did not mention any suicidal ideas to his wife or family. He had never had close friends nor much of a social life outside his family. His wife said he was generally less active. He watched much less TV, spoke less, and at times seemed not to have heard when she talked to him. She said he looked depressed and disgusted throughout those last two weeks.

One week before his death he complained of abdominal pain and, on the day of his suicide, he was said to have felt very ill at work. That night, when he came home, he attached a hose to his car exhaust and closed himself in the car with the motor running. His wife discovered his body sometime later in the evening. He left no note.

Family history: An aunt and an uncle had killed themselves (in separate incidents) some years in the past. One sister was said to have been currently "depressed" due to marital troubles. Her symptoms were described as being similar to her brother's.

Arrest record: None.

Case No. *080* M _X_ F __ Age *29*

ST. LOUIS SUICIDE STUDY CRITERIA FOR MAJOR AFFECTIVE DISORDER

Diagnosis required four of the six following categories, A–F. Category G was helpful in diagnosis, but not necessary.

- A. Clinically well, exclusive of attacks of major affective disorder __X__
- B. Previous episode(s) of major affective disorder ___
- C. Discreteness (and duration) of final attack:
  - 6 months or less __X__
  - 12 months or less ___
- D. "Medical" symptoms:
  - insomnia __X__
  - anorexia __X__
  - weight loss __X__
  - low energy, weakness __X__
  - fatigue __X__
  - constipation ___
- E. Psychological symptoms:
  - "blue" feeling, depression, sadness __X__
  - diminished motor activity __X__
  - loss of interest ___
  - diminished sexual interest and activity __X__
  - undertalkativeness ___
  - low expectancy of recovery; expectation of "black" future ___
  - feeling of being a burden ___
  - indecisiveness ___
  - feelings of worthlessness or guilt __X__
  - agitation ___
  - personal untidiness ___
  - difficulty in thinking and concentration ___
  - delusions ___
- F. Disturbances in social behavior: decreased social and recreational activity ___
- G. Miscellaneous items:
  - age of onset 40 and over ___
  - family history of affective disorder __X__

Affective Disorder—The Largest Group

FEIGHNER CRITERIA FOR MAJOR AFFECTIVE DISORDER

Diagnosis required all three of the following categories.

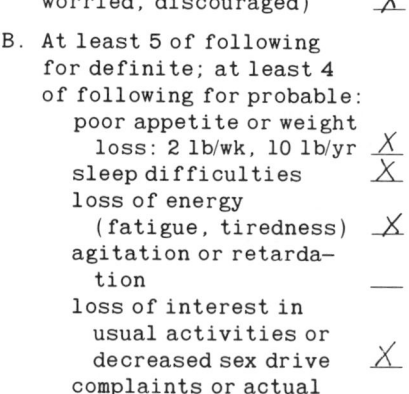

A. Dysphoric mood (depressed, sad, blue, despondent, hopeless, "down in dumps," irritable, fearful, worried, discouraged) __X__

B. At least 5 of following for definite; at least 4 of following for probable:
   - poor appetite or weight loss: 2 lb/wk, 10 lb/yr __X__
   - sleep difficulties __X__
   - loss of energy (fatigue, tiredness) __X__
   - agitation or retardation __—__
   - loss of interest in usual activities or decreased sex drive __X__
   - complaints or actual diminished ability to think/concentrate __—__
   - feelings of guilt, self-reproach __X__
   - recurrent thoughts of death and/or suicide __X__

C. A psychiatric illness lasting <u>at least one month</u> with no pre-existing psychiatric condition (schizophrenia, anxiety neurosis, phobic neurosis, obsessive-compulsive neurosis, hysteria, alcoholism, drug dependence, antisocial personality, homosexuality, transsexualism, mental retardation, anorexia nervosa, organic brain syndrome) or life-threatening or incapacitating illness __X__

082 Informants: Wife, employer

This 39-year-old white man was, according to his wife, a well-adjusted man who had, at the time of his suicide, "some slight financial difficulties, but nothing bigger than he had had many times before."

Although he married at 19, he finished four years of college and was, at the time of his death, employed as an accountant. He had converted to Catholicism, his wife's religion, when his three children were growing up and going to Sunday School.

His wife denied any trouble or any reasons for his suicide. She said he had shown no symptoms of depression, that he had never drunk to excess, that he was in good physical health, and that their family life was happy.

However, she did report that for a period of six weeks about two years prior to his suicide he had suffered from what seemed to be a "nervous breakdown." This was, she thought, precipitated by his brief unemployment at the time. She said he had paced, cried, been unable to sleep, and had lost weight. He had not seen either a physician or a psychiatrist and, after that six-week episode, had been entirely himself again. She repeatedly denied that any of those previous symptoms had recurred in the weeks or days just before his suicide.

His employer reported that the subject had been a congenial, conscientious, and interested worker though he at times seemed to feel inadequate in his work. The employer had noticed that about six weeks before his death he had withdrawn into himself. He stopped eating lunch with the other employees and when questioned said that he was having problems with his family. He did not specify, but repeated that he was worried about his home life. He was never heard to make any suicidal comments and there was no record of any unusual absenteeism.

On the first working day after the New Year, he got up, dressed, and ate breakfast as usual. He said his routine goodbyes and told his wife he'd see her at 5 PM. He then went down into his basement and shot himself. He left no note.

Family history: There was no family history of psychiatric illness.
Arrest record: None.

Case No. 084 M X F __ Age 39

ST. LOUIS SUICIDE STUDY CRITERIA FOR MAJOR AFFECTIVE DISORDER

Diagnosis required four of the six following categories, A–F. Category G was helpful in diagnosis, but not necessary.

A. Clinically well, exclusive of attacks of major affective disorder   X

B. Previous episode(s) of major affective disorder   X

C. Discreteness (and duration) of final attack:
   6 months or less   X
   12 months or less   __

D. "Medical" symptoms:
   insomnia   __
   anorexia   __
   weight loss   __
   low energy, weakness   __
   fatigue   __
   constipation   __

E. Psychological symptoms:
   "blue" feeling, depression, sadness   __
   diminished motor activity   __
   loss of interest   X
   diminished sexual interest and activity   __
   undertalkativeness   X
   low expectancy of recovery; expectation of "black" future   __
   feeling of being a burden   __
   indecisiveness   __
   feelings of worthlessness or guilt   __
   agitation   __
   personal untidiness   __
   difficulty in thinking and concentration   __
   delusions   __

F. Disturbances in social behavior: decreased social and recreational activity   X

G. Miscellaneous items:
   age of onset 40 and over   __
   family history of affective disorder   __

FEIGHNER CRITERIA FOR MAJOR AFFECTIVE DISORDER

Diagnosis required all three of the following categories.

A. Dysphoric mood (depressed, sad, blue, despondent, hopeless, "down in dumps," irritable, fearful, worried, discouraged) _X_

B. At least 5 of following for definite; at least 4 of following for probable:
- poor appetite or weight loss: 2 lb/wk, 10 lb/yr ___
- sleep difficulties ___
- loss of energy (fatigue, tiredness) ___
- agitation or retardation ___
- loss of interest in usual activities or decreased sex drive _X_
- complaints or actual diminished ability to think/concentrate ___
- feelings of guilt, self-reproach ___
- recurrent thoughts of death and/or suicide ___

C. A psychiatric illness lasting <u>at least one month</u> with no pre-existing psychiatric condition (schizophrenia, anxiety neurosis, phobic neurosis, obsessive-compulsive neurosis, hysteria, alcoholism, drug dependence, antisocial personality, homosexuality, transsexualism, mental retardation, anorexia nervosa, organic brain syndrome) or life-threatening or incapacitating illness _X_

---

086 *Informants: Mother, brother-in-law, sister, employer*

This 42-year-old white man completed 11 grades of school and served for four years overseas during World War II. He saw combat, was decorated, and given an honorable discharge. His mother described him as always having been nervous and high-strung, somewhat like his father (who had been "nervous" all his life) and had once been hospitalized for a "nervous breakdown."

The subject had been married three times. His first wife divorced him for another man after five years of marriage. The second wife divorced him for incompatibility three years prior to his suicide, and after she left him he had an episode of depression lasting about a month during which he suffered anorexia, weight loss, and insomnia. At that time he made no suicidal threats and was not known to have cried. Two years before his death, he married his third wife and was as happy as he had ever been, according to informants. He loved the last wife and was, at her request, in the process of converting to Catholicism. A year after their marriage, they moved into a new house of which he was extremely proud. The family reported that the third wife was beginning to display the characteristics of "a wanter," constantly demanding more and more. The subject, who had a history of job shifts, gaining a bit in salary with each move, changed jobs twice the last year of his life. He held his last job, as a baker, for about ten months and his salary was the highest of his career.

Relations between the subject and his wife deteriorated to the point of constant fighting. Though they were both heavy drinkers—the subject averaged five to six beers nightly—neither was described as alcoholic. The wife assaulted her husband in their fights and was once supposed to have split his ear. In their last fight, the subject picked up a knife and pointed it at his wife who immediately "quieted down." When the subject returned from work the next day, he found she had packed up and left, having first arranged to have the gas and electricity turned off. Distraught, he called her at her parents' home and begged her to return, but she refused.

For the next week, the subject stayed in the empty, cold house, not bathing, shaving, or eating much. He did not go to work and never bothered to have the utilities restarted. His brother-in-law discovered the situation at the end of the week and took him home with him. For the last three weeks of his life, he seemed slightly better. He went to work every day, though his employer reported that he broke down and cried on returning and that he was obviously depressed the rest of his time at the bakery. He ate better, dressed better, and was, for one week, it seemed to his mother, a little less depressed. However, at some point during those weeks, he wrote a note which was found later. It said, "I want to be buried next to dad." There was no other mention of suicidal intent, either at home or at work. His insomnia, anorexia, sadness, ennui, and general lack of interest persisted and he made frequent statements about feeling sad and about his "black future." He telephoned his wife a few times during those weeks and cried after each call. He spoke less and less and was known to have been praying a great deal.

There was a brief time about one week before his suicide when he seemed suddenly much better and, for a day or two, he ate well, gaining back 2 pounds of the 20 he had lost in the last month. The improvement did not last and three days before his death he grew much worse. He complained of bad headaches and of being unable to think. The weekend before his death he refused to go out with the family and was lethargic and depressed when they returned. On the following Monday, he left for work at the usual time, but did not show up at the bakery. His whereabouts for most of the day were unaccounted for, but in the late afternoon, he turned up at his wife's parents' home. There he shot and wounded his wife and both her parents. While the wife's wounds were not severe, her parents were seriously injured. He then went to a railroad track near a neighborhood he had lived in before marrying his third wife and put his head down on the track just in

Affective Disorder—The Largest Group

time to be killed by the oncoming train. His mother remembered that he had told her of his wife's taunts that one day she'd "send him back" to the shabby neighborhood that he chose as the scene of his suicide.

Family history: As mentioned, the subject's father had been hospitalized once for a "nervous breakdown" and characterized as "nervous" all his life. The subject's sister was also described as "nervous."
Arrest record: None.

Case No. *086* M X F __ Age *42*

ST. LOUIS SUICIDE STUDY CRITERIA FOR MAJOR AFFECTIVE DISORDER

Diagnosis required four of the six following categories, A–F. Category G was helpful in diagnosis, but not necessary.

- A. Clinically well, exclusive of attacks of major affective disorder __X__
- B. Previous episode(s) of major affective disorder __X__
- C. Discreteness (and duration) of final attack:
   - 6 months or less __X__
   - 12 months or less ___
- D. "Medical" symptoms:
   - insomnia __X__
   - anorexia __X__
   - weight loss __X__
   - low energy, weakness ___
   - fatigue ___
   - constipation ___
- E. Psychological symptoms:
   - "blue" feeling, depression, sadness __X__
   - diminished motor activity ___
   - loss of interest __X__
   - diminished sexual interest and activity ___
   - undertalkativeness __X__
   - low expectancy of recovery; expectation of "black" future __X__
   - feeling of being a burden ___
   - indecisiveness ___
   - feelings of worthlessness or guilt ___
   - agitation ___
   - personal untidiness __X__
   - difficulty in thinking and concentration __X__
   - delusions ___
- F. Disturbances in social behavior: decreased social and recreational activity ___
- G. Miscellaneous items:
   - age of onset 40 and over ___
   - family history of affective disorder __X__

FEIGHNER CRITERIA FOR MAJOR AFFECTIVE DISORDER

Diagnosis required all three of the following categories.

A. Dysphoric mood (depressed, sad, blue, despondent, hopeless, "down in dumps," irritable, fearful, worried, discouraged) __X__

B. At least 5 of following for definite; at least 4 of following for probable:
   poor appetite or weight loss: 2 lb/wk, 10 lb/yr __X__
   sleep difficulties __X__
   loss of energy (fatigue, tiredness) __X__
   agitation or retardation ____
   loss of interest in usual activities or decreased sex drive __X__
   complaints or actual diminished ability to think/concentrate __X__
   feelings of guilt, self-reproach ____
   recurrent thoughts of death and/or suicide ____

C. A psychiatric illness lasting <u>at least one month</u> with no pre-existing psychiatric condition (schizophrenia, anxiety neurosis, phobic neurosis, obsessive-compulsive neurosis, hysteria, alcoholism, drug dependence, antisocial personality, homosexuality, transsexualism, mental retardation, anorexia nervosa, organic brain syndrome) or life-threatening or incapacitating illness __X__

---

114 Informants: Sister-in-law, psychiatrist

This 29-year-old white man, a college graduate, married at age 23 and was married for five years during which time he worked for several years as an engineer. He and his wife had no children and, for one year of their marriage, she worked to support the subject while he tried unsuccessfully to write a novel. He was divorced by his wife seven months prior to his suicide.

After his divorce, he was said to have become irritable on his job and either was fired or quit under pressure. He moved to Columbia, Missouri, in order to go to the University of Missouri for a master's degree in English literature. Shortly after starting his courses in the fall, he began to suffer from a growing fear of his own inadequacy and from worry about his judgment, his past worth, and his competence. Worse at the end of the fall semester, he moved back to St. Louis to live with his older brother and family and to continue his studies at the St. Louis branch of the university. During the three months he was at his brother's house, he became noticeably more depressed and anxious. He worried about "sponging off his brother" and about being in the family's way. He no longer had a social life outside the family, which he told his sister-in-law was at a doctor's recommendation and with which he agreed. He let his brother make all his decisions for him and he accompanied the family to church several times though his sister-in-law believed he had not been a church goer for many years previous to his stay with them.

Six weeks before his suicide, at his brother's instigation, he began to see a psychiatrist on a weekly basis. He complained to her of inertia, helplessness, feelings of incompetence, guilt, and worthlessness. He believed he was failing in graduate school (though his grades had been excellent) and had a "nearly paralyzing anxiety" about his future. He also complained of alternating between having no appetite and overeating, and of difficulty staying asleep. He told her that he had experienced a similar episode about two years earlier which he said had lasted nearly a year. The psychiatrist's records described the subject as becoming "increasingly withdrawn and unkempt" over the period of their sessions and she noted that she suspected him of having suicidal inclinations though he denied them. She urged him, directly and through his brother, to agree to hospitalization. He refused and his brother did not want to "push." During their last appointment, she told him that she could not be responsible for him unless he agreed to go into the hospital. When he again refused, she discharged him. That night, he drove off in his car to a lonely country road and shot himself. He left no note.

Family history: The subject's mother was described as having been "nuts" since the subject was 10 years old. When he was 12 or 13, he discovered her in the midst of a suicide attempt, after which she was hospitalized for several years. She was, at the time of his death, living in a nursing home. His sister was said to have been "temperamentally like her brother."

Arrest record: None.

Case No. 114 M X F __ Age 29

ST. LOUIS SUICIDE STUDY CRITERIA FOR MAJOR AFFECTIVE DISORDER

Diagnosis required four of the six following categories, A-F. Category G was helpful in diagnosis, but not necessary.

- A. Clinically well, exclusive of attacks of major affective disorder X
- B. Previous episode(s) of major affective disorder X
- C. Discreteness (and duration) of final attack:
  - 6 months or less __
  - 12 months or less X
- D. "Medical" symptoms:
  - insomnia X
  - anorexia X
  - weight loss X
  - low energy, weakness X
  - fatigue __
  - constipation __
- E. Psychological symptoms:
  - "blue" feeling, depression, sadness X
  - diminished motor activity __
  - loss of interest __
  - diminished sexual interest and activity __
  - undertalkativeness __
  - low expectancy of recovery; expectation of "black" future __
  - feeling of being a burden X
  - indecisiveness __
  - feelings of worthlessness or guilt X
  - agitation __
  - personal untidiness X
  - difficulty in thinking and concentration __
  - delusions X
- F. Disturbances in social behavior: decreased social and recreational activity X
- G. Miscellaneous items:
  - age of onset 40 and over __
  - family history of affective disorder X

FEIGHNER CRITERIA FOR MAJOR AFFECTIVE DISORDER

Diagnosis required all three of the following categories.

- A. Dysphoric mood (depressed, sad, blue, despondent, hopeless, "down in dumps," irritable, fearful, worried, discouraged) X
- B. At least 5 of following for definite; at least 4 of following for probable:
  - poor appetite or weight loss: 2 lb/wk, 10 lb/yr X
  - sleep difficulties X
  - loss of energy (fatigue, tiredness) X
  - agitation or retardation __
  - loss of interest in usual activities or decreased sex drive __
  - complaints or actual diminished ability to think/concentrate __
  - feelings of guilt, self-reproach X
  - recurrent thoughts of death and/or suicide __
- C. A psychiatric illness lasting **at least one month** with no pre-existing psychiatric condition (schizophrenia, anxiety neurosis, phobic neurosis, obsessive-compulsive neurosis, hysteria, alcoholism, drug dependence, antisocial personality, homosexuality, transsexualism, mental retardation, anorexia nervosa, organic brain syndrome) or life-threatening or incapacitating illness X

118 Informants: Wife, employer

This 47-year-old white man had moved to St. Louis County from a small Missouri town three years before his suicide because his wife had been offered a good job as a school teacher. He had many relatives in the small town he had left and had graduated from its high school and worked for many years as an electrician for a strip mining company there. He had been married for 25 years and had one son.

His wife described him as having been a nervous, high-strung, hot-tempered man who was "always on the go." Once in St. Louis, however, he had been generally less active. He had seemed fatigued and somewhat indecisive. They had fewer friends due to the move and those they did make they saw only rarely. A Baptist, he was a teetotaler all his life, never took drugs, and avoided doctors.

For the first two and a half years in St. Louis, the subject worked as a bus driver and school custodian. Five months before his death, he changed to a job "with a better future"—tube tester for a local aircraft manufacturer. Although the pay was good, he did not like the job because he said people at the plant "weren't as friendly as at the mine." According to plant personnel records, sometime not long before his death he had fainted at work. In the infirmary, he explained this as a result of having a cold, working too many hours, and "nerves" from overwork. He told the doctor there he had been hospitalized seven years earlier for five days because of "nerves" from overwork, pain around the heart, shortness of breath, and tightness in his chest. His work record showed an above average level of dependability and cooperation, and no absences.

Though his wife at first denied any change in her husband's behavior in the months and weeks just prior to his suicide, she did remember that he had, in the last several weeks, lost about six pounds. One night three weeks before his death, he had paced the floor, crying uncontrollably and rubbing his arms. She said that during the last two weeks of his life, he had seemed happier and that he had bought extra groceries, which she saw as a sign of good spirits. However, she also remembered that he had, in those two weeks, mentioned a friend from back home who, in attempting to commit suicide by hanging, "hadn't done the job right" and had been discovered and cut down before he died.

On the morning of his suicide, the subject got up earlier than his wife to make his 7 AM shift and left the house. When his wife got up, she found a note from his which said, "Don't look in the shed. Call the police." A neighbor called the police who discovered his dead body hanging in the shed behind the house. Later, his wife realized that he had left all his papers out where she would find them. She said she had no idea why he had killed himself.

Family history: There was no family history of psychiatric illness.
Arrest record: None.

Case No. *118* M _X_ F ___ Age *47*

ST. LOUIS SUICIDE STUDY CRITERIA FOR MAJOR AFFECTIVE DISORDER

Diagnosis required four of the six following categories, A–F. Category G was helpful in diagnosis, but not necessary.

- A. Clinically well, exclusive of attacks of major affective disorder _X_
- B. Previous episode(s) of major affective disorder _X_
- C. Discreteness (and duration) of final attack:
    - 6 months or less _X_
    - 12 months or less ___
- D. "Medical" symptoms:
    - insomnia ___
    - anorexia ___
    - weight loss _X_
    - low energy, weakness fatigue _X_
    - constipation ___
- E. Psychological symptoms:
    - "blue" feeling, depression, sadness _X_
    - diminished motor activity _X_
    - loss of interest ___
    - diminished sexual interest and activity ___
    - undertalkativeness ___
    - low expectancy of recovery; expectation of "black" future ___
    - feeling of being a burden ___
    - indecisiveness _X_
    - feelings of worthlessness or guilt ___
    - agitation _X_
    - personal untidiness ___
    - difficulty in thinking and concentration ___
    - delusions ___
- F. Disturbances in social behavior: decreased social and recreational activity _X_
- G. Miscellaneous items:
    - age of onset 40 and over _X_
    - family history of affective disorder ___

Affective Disorder—The Largest Group

FEIGHNER CRITERIA FOR MAJOR AFFECTIVE DISORDER

Diagnosis required all three of the following categories.

A. Dysphoric mood (depressed, sad, blue, despondent, hopeless, "down in dumps," irritable, fearful, worried, discouraged) _X_

B. At least 5 of following for definite; at least 4 of following for probable:
   poor appetite or weight loss: 2 lb/wk, 10 lb/yr _X_
   sleep difficulties ___
   loss of energy (fatigue, tiredness) _X_
   agitation or retardation _X_
   loss of interest in usual activities or decreased sex drive ___
   complaints or actual diminished ability to think/concentrate ___
   feelings of guilt, self-reproach ___
   recurrent thoughts of death and/or suicide _X_

C. A psychiatric illness lasting <u>at least one month</u> with no pre-existing psychiatric condition (schizophrenia, anxiety neurosis, phobic neurosis, obsessive-compulsive neurosis, hysteria, alcoholism, drug dependence, antisocial personality, homosexuality, transsexualism, mental retardation, anorexia nervosa, organic brain syndrome) or life-threatening or incapacitating illness _X_

122 Informants: Lawyer and friend, physician

This 45-year-old white, married man was described by his friends and his doctor as a "typical manic-depressive"—the life of the party one day, down in the dumps the next. Because his wife left town immediately after his death and we were thus unable to interview her, his lawyer (who was also a good friend) agreed to act as the primary informant. He had most recently seen the subject six weeks before his death and thus his answers were not always as full or as detailed as they might have been had he seen the subject more recently and more often.

The subject was the son of Russian immigrants. His father was a junk buyer and peddler who was able to help his son not only through college, but through law school as well. Although he graduated from law school, he did not choose a legal career but rather one in sales at which he was very successful. During World War II, he served two years overseas in the Navy as a junior officer and received an honorable discharge. He was married for 17 years and had three daughters. His wife was said to have "worshipped" him.

The subject had spent most of his life in Wisconsin where he had met and married his wife. About 14 years before his death, he experienced the first of his severe depressions, walked off the job he had there, and moved his family to St. Louis. Within four years, he and a partner had established their own business in St. Louis as manufacturer's representatives and the subject moved quickly into a high income bracket. A compulsive worker, he was tense about business and a worrier. There were, however, no reasons for any undue business worries on his part at the time of his suicide, according to his lawyer, but the subject had expressed concern about not being in the "top group" economically. His lawyer felt he did not meet his own standards economically or socially.

A moderate social drinker, he and his wife had "dozens" of friends and an active social life. However, the subject was known to have had only one close, "confidential" friend.

The lawyer believed that he was about three months into one of his cyclical depressions at the time of his death. He had been irritable with his family and friends, joyless, generally less active, short-tempered, and depressed-looking for about that length of time. A brother-in-law in Wisconsin was very ill during this period, which the lawyer believed had an effect on him. Six weeks before his suicide, he saw his doctor, also a friend, and complained of being "nervous" and of having insomnia. The doctor advised him to get psychiatric help as he had advised him to do two years earlier during another episode. As before the advice went unheeded.

The subject had yet another friend, a druggist, who the lawyer believed kept him over-supplied with the barbiturates he took nightly for sleeping.

On the morning of his suicide, the subject had made plans for an upcoming business trip. Also on the day of his death he copied out a passage from a book he had apparently been reading called *How to Live 365 Days a Year*. The passage was: "I'm going to keep my attitude calm and cheerful—right now." He was found in his closed garage inside his car with the engine running. His lawyer commented that "if the sun had been shining that day, he wouldn't have done it. It was an impulse he acted on."

Family history: The subject's lawyer had no information about psychiatric illness in the family.
Arrest record: None.

Case No. 122 M _X_ F ___ Age 45

ST. LOUIS SUICIDE STUDY CRITERIA FOR MAJOR AFFECTIVE DISORDER

Diagnosis required four of the six following categories, A-F. Category G was helpful in diagnosis, but not necessary.

- A. Clinically well, exclusive of attacks of major affective disorder _X_
- B. Previous episode(s) of major affective disorder _X_
- C. Discreteness (and duration) of final attack:
  - 6 months or less _X_
  - 12 months or less ___
- D. "Medical" symptoms:
  - insomnia _X_
  - anorexia ___
  - weight loss ___
  - low energy, weakness ___
  - fatigue ___
  - constipation ___
- E. Psychological symptoms:
  - "blue" feeling, depression, sadness _X_
  - diminished motor activity ___
  - loss of interest _X_
  - diminished sexual interest and activity _X_
  - undertalkativeness ___
  - low expectancy of recovery; expectation of "black" future ___
  - feeling of being a burden ___
  - indecisiveness ___
  - feelings of worthlessness or guilt ___
  - agitation ___
  - personal untidiness ___
  - difficulty in thinking and concentration ___
  - delusions ___
- F. Disturbances in social behavior: decreased social and recreational activity _X_
- G. Miscellaneous items:
  - age of onset 40 and over ___
  - family history of affective disorder ___

FEIGHNER CRITERIA FOR MAJOR AFFECTIVE DISORDER

Diagnosis required all three of the following categories.

- A. Dysphoric mood (depressed, sad, blue, despondent, hopeless, "down in dumps," irritable, fearful, worried, discouraged) _X_
- B. At least 5 of following for definite; at least 4 of following for probable:
  - poor appetite or weight loss: 2 lb/wk, 10 lb/yr ___
  - sleep difficulties _X_
  - loss of energy (fatigue, tiredness) _X_
  - agitation or retardation ___
  - loss of interest in usual activities or decreased sex drive _X_
  - complaints or actual diminished ability to think/concentrate ___
  - feelings of guilt, self-reproach _X_
  - recurrent thoughts of death and/or suicide ___
- C. A psychiatric illness lasting at least one month with no pre-existing psychiatric condition (schizophrenia, anxiety neurosis, phobic neurosis, obsessive-compulsive neurosis, hysteria, alcoholism, drug dependence, antisocial personality, homosexuality, transsexualism, mental retardation, anorexia nervosa, organic brain syndrome) or life-threatening or incapacitating illness _X_

126 Informants: Parents

This 36-year-old white man killed himself five months after being divorced. He finished grade school, joined the Marines at an early age, and remained in the service for six years. He saw overseas combat, was decorated, and given an honorable discharge at the end of World War II.

At age 25, he returned to St. Louis, married, and found work at a brewery. He and his wife had three sons. The subject was a daily drinker and was thought by his family to drink too much for his own good. He had three or four close friends whom he saw regularly at a favorite tavern. A devout Roman Catholic, he never missed a Sunday mass and was considered by his family to be more "religious" than themselves.

Seven or eight months before his suicide, his wife left him and their children to move to Chicago to be near a married man. The subject, along with his wife's mother and brother, went to Chicago and brought her back, but after only a short time at home she returned to Chicago. The subject moved into a rooming house and his three boys went to live with his parents. Around Christmas time, six months before his death, he began to show his depression. He cried on Christmas day because of his wife's absence, he made statements that he "couldn't live without her," and he began to go on fairly regular benders. His mother noticed that he looked depressed much of the time and that he seemed to eat very little the last six months of his life (during which time he lost a total of about 20 pounds). Just before Christmas, he was involved in a minor automobile accident and suffered a cut on his head. He complained of headaches for two weeks following the accident.

Five months before his suicide, the subject and his wife were legally divorced, but he still wanted her back and made all kinds of excuses to see her. By that time, she had left Chicago and taken up with a second man, a Coast Guardsman who was due to be transferred a month or two later. Apparently, she hinted to the subject that when the Coast Guardsman left she would come back to him.

His depression increased noticeably during the last months, to the point that he was always sad, always joyless. One week before his death, he had a quarrel with his mother and went on a prolonged bender. He did not show up at work the last week of his life and spent most of his time in taverns. There seemed to be one further factor involved at that point—the possibility that a woman he had been seeing was pregnant and that it was his child. At any rate, he stayed drunk most of the week. The day before his suicide, he borrowed his brother-in-law's rifle "to go hunting" and the brother-in-law later recalled that he had looked depressed. He spent the next day in a tavern where he told friends, "You'll see my death notice in the paper." Late that evening, he drove to his parents' home, parked his car in back of their house, propped the rifle he had borrowed between his knees, and shot himself in the head. No one heard the shot that evening, but a neighbor noticed someone "sleeping" in the car next morning and alerted his parents. When the subject's mother went out to wake him, she discovered his dead body. No suicide note was found.

Family history: There was no family history of psychiatric illness.
Arrest record: None.

Case No. *126* M _X_ F ___ Age *36*

ST. LOUIS SUICIDE STUDY CRITERIA FOR MAJOR AFFECTIVE DISORDER

Diagnosis required four of the six following categories, A–F. Category G was helpful in diagnosis, but not necessary.

A. Clinically well, exclusive of attacks of major affective disorder _X_

B. Previous episode(s) of major affective disorder ___

C. Discreteness (and duration) of final attack:
    6 months or less _X_
    12 months or less ___

D. "Medical" symptoms:
    insomnia ___
    anorexia _X_
    weight loss _X_
    low energy, weakness _X_
    fatigue _X_
    constipation ___

E. Psychological symptoms:
    "blue" feeling, depression, sadness _X_
    diminished motor activity _X_
    loss of interest _X_
    diminished sexual interest and activity ___
    undertalkativeness ___
    low expectancy of recovery; expectation of "black" future ___
    feeling of being a burden ___
    indecisiveness ___
    feelings of worthlessness or guilt ___
    agitation ___
    personal untidiness ___
    difficulty in thinking and concentration ___
    delusions ___

F. Disturbances in social behavior: decreased social and recreational activity ___

G. Miscellaneous items:
    age of onset 40 and over ___
    family history of affective disorder ___

FEIGHNER CRITERIA FOR MAJOR AFFECTIVE DISORDER

Diagnosis required all three of the following categories.

A. Dysphoric mood (depressed, sad, blue, despondent, hopeless, "down in dumps," irritable, fearful, worried, discouraged) __X__

B. At least 5 of following for definite; at least 4 of following for probable:
   - poor appetite or weight loss: 2 lb/wk, 10 lb/yr __X__
   - sleep difficulties ____
   - loss of energy (fatigue, tiredness) __X__
   - agitation or retardation ____
   - loss of interest in usual activities or decreased sex drive __X__
   - complaints or actual diminished ability to think/concentrate ____
   - feelings of guilt, self-reproach ____
   - recurrent thoughts of death and/or suicide __X__

C. A psychiatric illness lasting <u>at least one month</u> with no pre-existing psychiatric condition (schizophrenia, anxiety neurosis, phobic neurosis, obsessive-compulsive neurosis, hysteria, alcoholism, drug dependence, antisocial personality, homosexuality, transsexualism, mental retardation, anorexia nervosa, organic brain syndrome) or life-threatening or incapacitating illness __X__

AFFECTIVE DISORDER, SUBGROUP 2

Men aged 49–67 (N = 25)

001   Informants: Wife, two psychiatrists, hospital records

This 55-year-old white semi-skilled laborer suffered from "nervous trouble" that began in his youth. It was not possible to characterize his early chronic nervousness further. At age 30 he had a " nervous breakdown" which, according to the psychiatrist who was caring for him in his last illness, was a "typical depression" with marked incapacitation, but for which he was not hospitalized. During his thirties he remained active and was not incapacitated despite his chronic nervousness even though he had rather frequent job changes without apparent reason. At age 40 he had a second attack of depression and was fired because of inefficiency. This attack lasted some months until he returned to his usual state, which lasted until age 50 when he again became depressed. This third depression continued for almost four years. Toward the end of that time, he complained of sadness, lack of pep, no interest in anything, extreme tension, marked insomnia, and inability to work. One year prior to his death he received electroshock therapy with remarkable improvement. For a period of three months he felt well, was able to work, and remarried. Then, eight or nine months prior to his death he again became ill. He went to a psychiatrist complaining of constipation and despondency, in addition to the previously described symptoms. He was not able to work and went to a farm, but soon returned without feeling any better. He became despondent and began to fear he was losing his mind. He then went to another psychiatrist. He became very indecisive, delusionally preoccupied with having done something wrong, complained of having no feelings and of not being able to taste or smell, and finally became almost mute. Six months prior to his death, he was hospitalized for three months and received electroshock and insulin shock therapy with a partial remission for a short while. However, he remained despondent and tired. Three weeks prior to his death his condition worsened. He stated he was so much weaker that he could not work. He stopped eating and lost 25 pounds (according to his wife) in the last three weeks of his life. He became almost completely unable to sleep, stopped talking except in monosyllables, cried frequently, and said he ought to go to the State Hospital, that he was a burden to his family, that the "game was over," and that he wished the Lord would take him if he had to suffer as he had been. He lost his interest in his family, his job, the world about him, and his friends. He became fearful of reading the paper and of watching movies and television because he might see or read about violence or people dying.

On the day of his suicide he reiterated his feelings of being a burden and his fears of becoming an invalid, and complained of his inability to dress himself. His wife left the room where he was lying in bed. Within a few minutes he shot himself. When his wife ran into the room, he was still conscious and told her he had done this because he did not want to be a burden. He was taken to a hospital where he died a few hours later.

In addition to his chronic nervousness and frequent job changes, he had married four times, in each instance to a woman older than himself. The psychiatrist, who had seen him only when he was ill, judged that he was an overly dependent person.

None of the informants was able to recall any current life stress that may have contributed to his suicide.

Family history: No family history of psychiatric illness.
Arrest records: None.

Case No. *001* M *X* F __ Age *55*

ST. LOUIS SUICIDE STUDY CRITERIA FOR MAJOR AFFECTIVE DISORDER

Diagnosis required four of the six following categories, A-F. Category G was helpful in diagnosis, but not necessary.

A. Clinically well, exclusive of attacks of major affective disorder __X__	diminished sexual interest and activity undertalkativeness	__X__
B. Previous episode(s) of major affective disorder __X__	low expectancy of recovery; expectation of "black" future	__X__
C. Discreteness (and duration) of final attack:	feeling of being a burden	__X__
6 months or less __X__	indecisiveness	__X__
12 months or less ___	feelings of worthlessness or guilt	___
	agitation	__X__
D. "Medical" symptoms:	personal untidiness	___
insomnia __X__	difficulty in thinking and concentration	___
anorexia __X__	delusions	__X__
weight loss __X__		
low energy, weakness __X__	F. Disturbances in social behavior: decreased social and recreational activity	
fatigue __X__		
constipation __X__		__X__
E. Psychological symptoms:		
"blue" feeling, depression, sadness __X__	G. Miscellaneous items: age of onset 40 and over	___
diminished motor activity __X__	family history of affective disorder	___
loss of interest __X__		

FEIGHNER CRITERIA FOR MAJOR AFFECTIVE DISORDER

Diagnosis required all three of the following categories.

A. Dysphoric mood (depressed, sad, blue, despondent, hopeless, "down in dumps," irritable, fearful, worried, discouraged) X

B. At least 5 of following for definite; at least 4 of following for probable:
   poor appetite or weight loss: 2 lb/wk, 10 lb/yr X
   sleep difficulties X
   loss of energy (fatigue, tiredness) X
   agitation or retardation X
   loss of interest in usual activities or decreased sex drive X
   complaints or actual diminished ability to think/concentrate ___
   feelings of guilt, self-reproach X
   recurrent thoughts of death and/or suicide X

C. A psychiatric illness lasting <u>at least one month</u> with no pre-existing psychiatric condition (schizophrenia, anxiety neurosis, phobic neurosis, obsessive-compulsive neurosis, hysteria, alcoholism, drug dependence, antisocial personality, homosexuality, transsexualism, mental retardation, anorexia nervosa, organic brain syndrome) or life-threatening or incapacitating illness X

006 Informants: Wife, two physicians

This 63-year-old black railroad carpenter had suffered from arthritis for some years. About two years prior to his death his arthritis worsened somewhat although he was still able to work. One year before his death, his symptoms changed. He developed headaches, pains throughout his body and extremities, epigastric discomfort, dizzy spells, visual blurring, chronic fatigue, feelings of weakness, anorexia, insomnia (requiring sedation), constipation, and complete absence of sex drive. Associated with these symptoms were marked despondency, loss of interest, diminished social activities, self-blame for his illness, a belief that he would never get well, self-disgust, nervousness, diminished motor activity, undertalkativeness with occasional periods during which he would not talk at all, concern that he was losing his memory, and many ideas of suicide and death. These latter ideas included preoccupation with suicidal and accidental deaths as reported in the newspapers, and statements that he wanted to die and was going to commit suicide. He told his wife of his great concern that she might die first, leaving no one to take care of him, and that he might have a stroke. He constantly reminded his wife that she was not to spend too much money for his burial.

He saw physicians for these complaints on two occasions, six months and three months before his death. Aside from moderate hypertension and osteoarthritis, there was no positive evidence of other medical disease. Just before seeing the first physician he had remained in bed for three weeks. At that time his job aggravated him greatly, but he changed to a more congenial job without any lessening of his symptoms. Other than the possible aggravation of his work, the informants knew of no other life stresses.

His wife said that he had been an excessive drinker for many years. This excessive drinking was demonstrated by the information that his wife objected to his drinking, that he believed he drank too much, that he got into trouble at work because of drinking, and that he had been arrested at least twice for drinking and peace disturbance. It was of interest that during his last illness his drinking diminished.

On the morning of his suicide he told his wife not to buy a new summer hat or new clothes for him because he would not need them. A few minutes later he hung up his hat and coat, took off his glasses, went down to the basement and hanged himself. His meticulous preparations had led his wife to believe that he was only going to tidy up the yard or basement.

Family history: Alcoholic brother.
Arrest record: At least two arrests for peace disturbance and drunken behavior.

Case No. _006_ M _X_ F __ Age _63_

ST. LOUIS SUICIDE STUDY CRITERIA FOR MAJOR AFFECTIVE DISORDER

Diagnosis required four of the six following categories, A–F. Category G was helpful in diagnosis, but not necessary.

- A. Clinically well, exclusive of attacks of major affective disorder ___
- B. Previous episode(s) of major affective disorder ___
- C. Discreteness (and duration) of final attack:
  - 6 months or less ___
  - 12 months or less _X_
- D. "Medical" symptoms:
  - insomnia _X_
  - anorexia _X_
  - weight loss ___
  - low energy, weakness _X_
  - fatigue _X_
  - constipation _X_
- E. Psychological symptoms:
  - "blue" feeling, depression, sadness _X_
  - diminished motor activity _X_
  - loss of interest _X_
  - diminished sexual interest and activity _X_
  - undertalkativeness _X_
  - low expectancy of recovery; expectation of "black" future _X_
  - feeling of being a burden ___
  - indecisiveness ___
  - feelings of worthlessness or guilt _X_
  - agitation ___
  - personal untidiness ___
  - difficulty in thinking and concentration _X_
  - delusions ___
- F. Disturbances in social behavior: decreased social and recreational activity _X_
- G. Miscellaneous items:
  - age of onset 40 and over _X_
  - family history of affective disorder ___

FEIGHNER CRITERIA FOR MAJOR AFFECTIVE DISORDER

Diagnosis required all three of the following categories.

- A. Dysphoric mood (depressed, sad, blue, despondent, hopeless, "down in dumps," irritable, fearful, worried, discouraged) _X_
- B. At least 5 of following for definite; at least 4 of following for probable:
  - poor appetite or weight loss: 2 lb/wk, 10 lb/yr _X_
  - sleep difficulties _X_
  - loss of energy (fatigue, tiredness) _X_
  - agitation or retardation _X_
  - loss of interest in usual activities or decreased sex drive _X_
  - complaints or actual diminished ability to think/concentrate _X_
  - feelings of guilt, self-reproach _X_
  - recurrent thoughts of death and/or suicide _X_
- C. A psychiatric illness lasting <u>at least one month</u> with no pre-existing psychiatric condition (schizophrenia, anxiety neurosis, phobic neurosis, obsessive-compulsive neurosis, hysteria, alcoholism, drug dependence, antisocial personality, homosexuality, transsexualism, mental retardation, anorexia nervosa, organic brain syndrome) or life-threatening or incapacitating illness _X_

008 Informants: Wife, physician, hospital records

This 64-year-old white fireman was raised in an orphan's home from age eight, following his father's death. He joined the fire department at an early age and was still a member of the department at the time of his death. Prior to his last episode of illness, he had had at least four "nervous breakdowns"—25, 15, 10 and 5 years before his death. These breakdowns were characterized by despondency, crying, suicidal ideas, weakness, insomnia, and inability to work. Each of these episodes lasted for some months. Between episodes he was not depressed, did not have any of the above symptoms, and worked well and steadily. His wife felt that he had always been a "nervous" person, but said that he did not complain of any symptoms nor did he go to doctors except for the episodic breakdowns.

For the last few years he suffered from mild prostatism, but was otherwise well and able to work until approximately 9 to 12 months prior to his death. At that time he developed episodes of right upper quadrant pain, vomiting, and jaundice. Three months before his death he had a cholecystectomy which relieved the symptoms just enumerated. These latter symptoms never again bothered him. At about the time of the operation he again became depressed. He convalesced from the operation for a month, becoming increasingly depressed, and then returned to work. His first day at work he decided to go home because he "just couldn't do his job." He complained to his wife that she and the doctor were withholding the truth from him. He believed (wrongly) that the operation had revealed some incurable disease, and it was not possible to reassure him concerning this belief.

At that time he returned to the hospital because of his prostatism, but no surgical treatment was given because the condition was considered to be mild. He became very agitated while at home, restlessly pacing from room to room. At other times he would sit almost motionless for prolonged periods. His speech diminished greatly and there were times when he could not answer questions nor participate in a conversation. He began to lose weight, to cry easily, and to say that he was a burden on his family and that he would never get well. He developed insomnia and became nervous and increasingly despondent. His appetite failed. Children began to annoy him. He stopped watching television and reading the newspaper except for reports about suicides, which he read avidly. He complained of feelings of worthlessness. He prayed and read the Bible with much greater frequency than was usual for him. He talked about wanting to die, committing suicide, being better off dead, and his family being better off if he were dead. He expressed these latter ideas to his wife, his family, his friends, his job associates, his physician, and his minister. At the same time that he spoke of suicide, he was also very fearful that he might not only "hurt" himself but also that he might "hurt his wife." On one occasion he threatened to drink Drano.

Just a few days before going into a hospital, about six weeks before his suicide, he began to complain of pain in his scrotum. On the day of his admission to the hospital he made a suicide attempt with carbon monoxide. He remained in the hospital for 17 days. During this time he remained depressed and spoke of suicide. His scrotal pain was diagnosed as acute epididymitis, and he was discovered also to have syphilitic aortitis. He was transferred to a mental hospital, but was discharged in a few days, three weeks prior to his suicide.

During the next three weeks he remained depressed. The same symptoms continued, except that he no longer spoke of committing suicide. His wife was concerned, however, that he might commit suicide and hid the car keys from him. On the day of his death he took her to serve as an election official at a voting booth. When he did not return at noon to pick her up she became alarmed. He was found dead in his garage with the doors closed and the car motor running.

The only current stress that his wife knew about was the cholecystectomy and the acute epididymitis.

Family history: There was no family history of psychiatric illness.
Arrest record: None.

Case No. 008 M X F___ Age 64

ST. LOUIS SUICIDE STUDY CRITERIA FOR MAJOR AFFECTIVE DISORDER

Diagnosis required four of the six following categories, A-F. Category G was helpful in diagnosis, but not necessary.

- A. Clinically well, exclusive of attacks of major affective disorder ___
- B. Previous episode(s) of major affective disorder _X_
- C. Discreteness (and duration) of final attack:
  - 6 months or less _X_
  - 12 months or less ___
- D. "Medical" symptoms:
  - insomnia _X_
  - anorexia ___
  - weight loss _X_
  - low energy, weakness _X_
  - fatigue ___
  - constipation ___
- E. Psychological symptoms:
  - "blue" feeling, depression, sadness _X_
  - diminished motor activity _X_
  - loss of interest _X_
  - diminished sexual interest and activity ___
  - undertalkativeness _X_
  - low expectancy of recovery; expectation of "black" future _X_
  - feeling of being a burden _X_
  - indecisiveness ___
  - feelings of worthlessness or guilt _X_
  - agitation _X_
  - personal untidiness ___
  - difficulty in thinking and concentration ___
  - delusions _X_
- F. Disturbances in social behavior: decreased social and recreational activity ___
- G. Miscellaneous items:
  - age of onset 40 and over _X_
  - family history of affective disorder ___

FEIGHNER CRITERIA FOR MAJOR AFFECTIVE DISORDER

Diagnosis required all three of the following categories.

- A. Dysphoric mood (depressed, sad, blue, despondent, hopeless, "down in dumps," irritable, fearful, worried, discouraged) _X_
- B. At least 5 of following for definite; at least 4 of following for probable:
  - poor appetite or weight loss: 2 lb/wk, 10 lb/yr _X_
  - sleep difficulties _X_
  - loss of energy (fatigue, tiredness) _X_
  - agitation or retardation _X_
  - loss of interest in usual activities or decreased sex drive _X_
  - complaints or actual diminished ability to think/concentrate ___
  - feelings of guilt, self-reproach _X_
  - recurrent thoughts of death and/or suicide _X_
- C. A psychiatric illness lasting at least one month with no pre-existing psychiatric condition (schizophrenia, anxiety neurosis, phobic neurosis, obsessive-compulsive neurosis, hysteria, alcoholism, drug dependence, antisocial personality, homosexuality, transsexualism, mental retardation, anorexia nervosa, organic brain syndrome) or life-threatening or incapacitating illness _X_

014 Informants: Daughter-in-law; hospital and social service records

This 67-year-old white widowed retired part-time plumber had been a confirmed alcoholic for the 18 years that the informant had known him. So far as she knew, he had drunk excessively all his adult life, but there was a verified history of only 18 years. He drank daily and there were times when he would go on "benders." His drinking had led to his being fired from numerous jobs, being arrested on five occasions, and being in recurrent troubles with his wife, when she was alive, and with his family. He and his wife were said to have had many arguments and fights during which, according to the informant, he would lose his temper and assault his wife. About 12 years prior to his death, he suffered a "stroke" which briefly gave him some difficulty using one hand. At that time, his physician suggested he curtail his drinking. He had, by that time, a constant tremor which the informant believed was related to his drinking. About seven years before his death, his wife died from an intra-abdominal carcinoma. After her death he complained of feelings of loneliness and depression. However, these feelings did not reach any great intensity and did not appreciably change his patterns of living and drinking. About four to five years before his death he began to worry about his doors being locked for fear of being robbed. He frequently complained, after bouts of drinking, that something was missing and that he had been robbed. He did not complain to the police, however, and the informant believes that on many of these occasions he had not been robbed, although other times she believed he had been. About two years before his death he saw a physician because of chest pains, which were diagnosed as angina pectoris. At that time he also complained of a "knot" in his stomach and developed a fear of stomach cancer which remained with him until his death. He also began to fear being alone, especially when drinking. As a result, he spent a large proportion of the remaining two years of his life with his son and daughter-in-law, although he still maintained an independent room apart from his relatives.

About 18 months before his death, he began having an affair with a married woman some years his junior. He and his son had violent disagreements about this relationship, but it was not broken off until later. He also felt the neighbors were critical of his relationship with the woman. Six months prior to his suicide, he became markedly depressed. He began to complain of severe non-radiating left anterior chest pain, smothering feelings, palpitation, severe insomnia with much waking during the night, dizziness, headaches, sadness, loss of interest, diminished social relationships, and a feeling he would never get better. Though he had previously taken a great deal of pride in his appearance, he became slovenly and dirty in dress and appearance. He began to speak less and to become more irritable. Two months later, four months before his death, he and the married woman finally broke up. The informant did not know what led to the breakup or who had taken the initiative. Three months prior to his death he called the woman and told her she would not have to hear from him again. He then cut his wrist with a butcher knife. He was admitted to a general hospital where it was found that he had cut himself deeply enough to sever two tendons. It was also found that he had an old anteroseptal infarct. He told the physicians in the hospital that he was depressed over his chest pains and wanted to "leave this world." He also described the symptoms noted above. A psychiatric consultation was requested. The psychiatrist noted depression, feelings of being a burden, and some psychomotor retardation. Admission to a psychiatric hospital was advised, but was refused by the patient and his family.

Shortly after his general hospital discharge, he gave his daughter-in-law a sealed envelope containing his insurance papers and policies. He became preoccupied with these policies, asking the informant about them daily—and sometimes more often—until his death. Three weeks before his suicide, he bought a gun without giving a reason for doing so. His depression decreased and his excessive drinking continued. Two days prior to his suicide, he told his neighbors that they would "find a dead man on the street." The neighbors did not realize he was talking about himself, but believed he was talking about a 90-year-old man who lived in the neighborhood. The subject moved out of his son's home and into his own room. The night before his death he told his companions in a tavern that he was going to commit suicide. They did not believe him. The next day, apparently while drunk, he killed himself by shooting himself in the head.

The informant believed that the suicide attempt and the suicide itself were related to feelings of spite, frustration, and neglect. At the same time she believed that he was severely depressed to a degree and in a way that she had never seen.

Family history: There was no family history of psychiatric illness.
Arrest record: Five arrests beginning at age 46 for destruction of property and trespassing, fugitive from sheriff, peace disturbance, and driving while intoxicated.

Case No. 014 M _X_ F ___ Age _67_

ST. LOUIS SUICIDE STUDY CRITERIA FOR MAJOR AFFECTIVE DISORDER

Diagnosis required four of the six following categories, A-F. Category G was helpful in diagnosis, but not necessary.

- A. Clinically well, exclusive of attacks of major affective disorder ___
- B. Previous episode(s) of major affective disorder ___
- C. Discreteness (and duration) of final attack:
  - 6 months or less _X_
  - 12 months or less ___
- D. "Medical" symptoms:
  - insomnia _X_
  - anorexia ___
  - weight loss ___
  - low energy, weakness ___
  - fatigue ___
  - constipation ___
- E. Psychological symptoms:
  - "blue" feeling, depression, sadness _X_
  - diminished motor activity _X_
  - loss of interest _X_
  - diminished sexual interest and activity ___
  - undertalkativeness _X_
  - low expectancy of recovery; expectation of "black" future _X_
  - feeling of being a burden _X_
  - indecisiveness ___
  - feelings of worthlessness or guilt ___
  - agitation ___
  - personal untidiness _X_
  - difficulty in thinking and concentration _X_
  - delusions _X_
- F. Disturbances in social behavior: decreased social and recreational activity _X_
- G. Miscellaneous items:
  - age of onset 40 and over ___
  - family history of affective disorder ___

FEIGHNER CRITERIA FOR MAJOR AFFECTIVE DISORDER

Diagnosis required all three of the following categories.

- A. Dysphoric mood (depressed, sad, blue, despondent, hopeless, "down in dumps," irritable, fearful, worried, discouraged) _X_
- B. At least 5 of following for definite; at least 4 of following for probable:
  - poor appetite or weight loss: 2 lb/wk, 10 lb/yr ___
  - sleep difficulties _X_
  - loss of energy (fatigue, tiredness) ___
  - agitation or retardation _X_
  - loss of interest in usual activities or decreased sex drive _X_
  - complaints or actual diminished ability to think/concentrate _X_
  - feelings of guilt, self-reproach _X_
  - recurrent thoughts of death and/or suicide _X_
- C. A psychiatric illness lasting <u>at least one month</u> with no pre-existing psychiatric condition (schizophrenia, anxiety neurosis, phobic neurosis, obsessive-compulsive neurosis, hysteria, alcoholism, drug dependence, antisocial personality, homosexuality, transsexualism, mental retardation, anorexia nervosa, organic brain syndrome) or life-threatening or incapacitating illness ___

023 Informants: *Wife, psychiatrist, internist; employment and hospital records*

This 67-year-old white semi-retired design engineer had held a responsible and well-paying job with the same industrial firm for 44 years. He had married at age 29 and had two children. His wife was described as dull, unimaginative, and a chronic complainer, and his sister as a very dominating person. He was said to have been besieged and beset at home, at least in his later years. However, he never had psychiatric symptoms and was not psychiatrically ill until age 55 when he developed a typical psychotic depressive episode for which he was hospitalized and received electroshock therapy. He recovered completely and went back to work. Four years later he developed another depressive episode for which he received outpatient electroshock therapy. He again recovered completely and returned to work. About two years prior to his death he wanted to retire and did so. At the insistence of the company, he modified his retirement so that he worked part time on a number of inventions. His employers considered him an unusually ingenious and creative designer and wanted his services, even if only part time. At the time of his first episode of psychiatric disease, he had just designed a large and industrially important machine which saved the company $1.5 million annually over a period of seven years. As part of his illness, however, he worried about his competence and about whether the machine would do the job.

Four months prior to his suicide, after having been well for over three years, he again became ill. One of the first changes noted was that he stopped working, saying that he could no longer compete with younger workers. He became irritable and despondent. He developed extreme nervousness, and dyspnea and chest pain related to his nervousness. He complained of fatigue, dizziness, visual blurring and anorexia. He tired easily. Severe insomnia developed. At that time, he went to his internist, but refused to go to a psychiatrist because he feared having to receive shock therapy again. His condition worsened. He ruminated about being a burden on his family, about the family spending all their money on him, and about his wife having no money for her future. He lost weight and developed bouts of diarrhea. He lost interest in everything, showing a diminution in affectionate relationships with his family and in his usual social and recreational activities. He complained that he would never get well, bathed and shaved only infrequently, and dressed in dirty clothes. He paced the floor in an agitated fashion. Worried about impotence and loss of libido, he received injections from his physician, had intercourse a few times, and then stopped for fear intercourse would damage his nerves. He repeatedly talked about wanting to die, and said that he and his family would be better off if he were dead, that he was going to commit suicide, and that he was going to get off the face of the earth. About two weeks prior to his death, all of his symptoms increased in intensity and remained so until his suicide. A day before his death he saw a notice in the paper of the suicide of a prominent person and said, "He must have been depressed just as I am." On the morning of his suicide he waked early, went to the basement, and hanged himself.

Family history: There was no family history of psychiatric illness.
Arrest record: None.

Case No. *023* M _X_ F ___ Age *67*

ST. LOUIS SUICIDE STUDY CRITERIA FOR MAJOR AFFECTIVE DISORDER

Diagnosis required four of the six following categories, A–F. Category G was helpful in diagnosis, but not necessary.

A. Clinically well, exclusive of attacks of major affective disorder _X_

B. Previous episode(s) of major affective disorder _X_

C. Discreteness (and duration) of final attack:
   6 months or less _X_
   12 months or less ___

D. "Medical" symptoms:
   insomnia _X_
   anorexia _X_
   weight loss _X_
   low energy, weakness _X_
   fatigue _X_
   constipation ___

E. Psychological symptoms:
   "blue" feeling, depression, sadness _X_
   diminished motor activity ___
   loss of interest _X_
   diminished sexual interest and activity _X_
   undertalkativeness ___
   low expectancy of recovery; expectation of "black" future _X_
   feeling of being a burden _X_
   indecisiveness ___
   feelings of worthlessness or guilt _X_
   agitation _X_
   personal untidiness _X_
   difficulty in thinking and concentration ___
   delusions _X_

F. Disturbances in social behavior: decreased social and recreational activity _X_

G. Miscellaneous items:
   age of onset 40 and over _X_
   family history of affective disorder ___

FEIGHNER CRITERIA FOR MAJOR AFFECTIVE DISORDER

Diagnosis required all three of the following categories.

A. Dysphoric mood (depressed, sad, blue, despondent, hopeless, "down in dumps," irritable, fearful, worried, discouraged) __X__

B. At least 5 of following for definite; at least 4 of following for probable:
- poor appetite or weight loss: 2 lb/wk, 10 lb/yr __X__
- sleep difficulties __X__
- loss of energy (fatigue, tiredness) __X__
- agitation or retardation __X__
- loss of interest in usual activities or decreased sex drive __X__
- complaints or actual diminished ability to think/concentrate __—__
- feelings of guilt, self-reproach __X__
- recurrent thoughts of death and/or suicide __X__

C. A psychiatric illness lasting <u>at least one month</u> with no pre-existing psychiatric condition (schizophrenia, anxiety neurosis, phobic neurosis, obsessive-compulsive neurosis, hysteria, alcoholism, drug dependence, antisocial personality, homosexuality, transsexualism, mental retardation, anorexia nervosa, organic brain syndrome) or life-threatening or incapacitating illness __X__

025 Informants: Sister, brother, sister-in-law, wife

When he died at age 62, this white married man had spent 40 years at his profession as a barber. He was brought to Missouri from Germany by his parents when he was a small child and spent the rest of his life in St. Louis. He was raised a Catholic, but even as a child, rejected organized religion and, as an adult, often argued with his sister about the existence of God. She also remembers his asking "What is life worth living for?" for three or four years before he died, but not in a particularly morose way.

He had married at age 23. He and his wife had no children, which he is said to have regretted. He was described by his sister as being a sensitive man who cried easily and whose feelings were easily hurt, but at the same time a happy and outgoing person. He ran his own barber shop where he enjoyed seeing and talking with his regular customers. He enjoyed a daily beer or two, but never drank to excess. Always a heavy man, he had an average weight of about 240 pounds. When he was 27, he developed a double hernia, but, "afraid of doctors," he refused ever to have it treated. At about age 57, he developed what his sister described as "sciatic rheumatism," which caused intermittent leg pain. Again, he refused to see a doctor about this.

When he was 40, his parents were divorced. This came as a great blow to him, as did their deaths some years later. Seven months before his own death, his wife fractured her hip and was hospitalized for over two months. About that time, his business slowed due to a rise in the price of haircuts. He had rent to pay on both his house and his shop plus the hospital costs. For about a year and a half before this he had seemed slightly depressed. His wife had been home from the hospital only a few weeks when she had to return to be operated on for appendicitis. Three weeks following that operation, again at home, she developed pneumonia and once more returned to the hospital. During this period, her husband became increasingly withdrawn and despondent, often commenting on his worthlessness and the uselessness of life. He stopped going out, watching TV, reading, watching sports, and seeing movies, explaining that, without his wife with him, he didn't feel like it. He showed joylessness and sadness, and after her third hospitalization, he told his sister "I have always had good sailing and this has thrown me in a turnstile and I can't get out. Death is the only place I'll find peace." He began to lose weight, about 60 pounds in six months. His customers reported that he would often turn them away, saying, "Go home; I don't feel like cutting hair today." He also began to pray a lot, which was unusual for him.

Two months before his death, while his wife was still in the hospital recovering from pneumonia, her doctors discovered she had cancer and removed part of her large intestine. His sister-in-law said he was told of this development and that he understood it; his sister, on the other hand, did *not* believe he "knew." In any case, he became extremely withdrawn, answering people in monosyllables, staring into space, sitting silently apart from his wife at the hospital and gazing out her window. He complained of terrible pain in both his legs, of fatigue, of bad headaches, and abdominal pain from his hernia. He made frequent remarks about his "black future," his fear of death, and of what would become of him when his wife died ("If she dies, I'm going to be a bum."). He slept and ate poorly. He gave away his motor boat and his guns and said to his sister, who was aware of his lifelong fear of drowning, "Don't be surprised if you find that I walked into the water." In the last six weeks of his life, he began to have trouble reading and understanding certain words that he had always known the meaning of and his sister said that she had had to do his telephoning for him during that time. He complained of things around him changing and asked, "Is it me or conditions around me that have changed?"

Ten days before his death, his wife came home from the hospital. The day before he died, he gave her an anniversary card, the first card he had given her in their 39-year marriage. On the morning of his suicide he had breakfast with his wife and surprised her by talking about things he hadn't mentioned in years. She said he seemed much calmer and that, leaving the house after breakfast, he called out cheerfully, "I'll see you at lunch."

Sometime in the morning he parked his car under a bridge and walked off a landing into the river. His body later washed up on the bank and was found by the police.

On learning of his suicide, his wife is reported to have cried, "We agreed to do it together. Why have you left me alone?" A note he left for her stated, "I am tired and I fear the future. You have my insurance. Goodbye."

Family history: A brother was under a doctor's care for "nerves" and is said to have had a psychiatric illness like the subject's.
Arrest record: None.

Case No. *025* M *X* F __ Age *62*

ST. LOUIS SUICIDE STUDY CRITERIA FOR MAJOR AFFECTIVE DISORDER

Diagnosis required four of the six following categories, A–F. Category G was helpful in diagnosis, but not necessary.

A. Clinically well, exclusive of attacks of major affective disorder *X*

B. Previous episode(s) of major affective disorder __

C. Discreteness (and duration) of final attack:
   6 months or less *X*
   12 months or less __

D. "Medical" symptoms:
   insomnia *X*
   anorexia *X*
   weight loss *X*
   low energy, weakness fatigue *X*
   constipation __

E. Psychological symptoms:
   "blue" feeling, depression, sadness *X*
   diminished motor activity __
   loss of interest *X*
   diminished sexual interest and activity __
   undertalkativeness *X*
   low expectancy of recovery; expectation of "black" future *X*
   feeling of being a burden __
   indecisiveness __
   feelings of worthlessness or guilt *X*
   agitation __
   personal untidiness __
   difficulty in thinking and concentration *X*
   delusions __

F. Disturbances in social behavior: decreased social and recreational activity *X*

G. Miscellaneous items:
   age of onset 40 and over *X*
   family history of affective disorder *X*

Affective Disorder—The Largest Group 101

FEIGHNER CRITERIA FOR MAJOR AFFECTIVE DISORDER

Diagnosis required all three of the following categories.

A. Dysphoric mood (depressed, sad, blue, despondent, hopeless, "down in dumps," irritable, fearful, worried, discouraged) _X_

B. At least 5 of following for definite; at least 4 of following for probable:
 poor appetite or weight loss: 2 lb/wk, 10 lb/yr _X_
 sleep difficulties _X_
 loss of energy (fatigue, tiredness) _X_
 agitation or retardation ___
 loss of interest in usual activities or decreased sex drive _X_
 complaints or actual diminished ability to think/concentrate _X_
 feelings of guilt, self-reproach ___
 recurrent thoughts of death and/or suicide _X_

C. A psychiatric illness lasting <u>at least one month</u> with no pre-existing psychiatric condition (schizophrenia, anxiety neurosis, phobic neurosis, obsessive-compulsive neurosis, hysteria, alcoholism, drug dependence, antisocial personality, homosexuality, transsexualism, mental retardation, anorexia nervosa, organic brain syndrome) or life-threatening or incapacitating illness _X_

027 Informants: Wife, job supervisor, physician; hospital and social service records

This 58-year-old white World War I veteran was described by his wife as having been nervous and inadequate all his life, as "not a strong man" (a sexual reference) and "a mama's boy." He had been chronically tired, hypochondriacal, suspicious, and moody for as long as anyone could remember.

He served overseas in the Army (1918–19), saw combat, and was given an honorable discharge. At age 24, he married a woman six years his senior. They had no children of their own, but when the subject was 28 applied to take in a foster child. They were turned down because of their constant bickering. A few years later they adopted a baby daughter. The family was, at that time, on relief and receiving regular grocery orders. The subject worked only sporadically from the time of his Army discharge until 12 years before his suicide when he got work as a U.S. Postal Service trucking clerk. His wife complained that in the first months at the Post Office he drank heavily after work "with the boys." At age 41 he and his wife applied again to board a child and their application was again disapproved because both of them were judged by the agency to be "neurotic" and only "moderately competent."

He was hospitalized three times for "nervousness" (at age 39 for three months, at age 41 for six weeks, and at age 54 for nine weeks). At age 43 he developed an aortic aneurysm and at 53, hypertensive cardiovascular disease was diagnosed. At about that time, he also developed a noticeable tremor of his left hand which persisted until he died. For the last seven years of his life, he complained of steadily increasing fatigue.

About four or five years prior to his suicide, he inherited almost $100,000 from a sister. He became suspicious and fearful that someone would take his money. His wife said he had plans to divorce her when he got the money. Instead, a year before his death, he had all his assets put in his wife's name without informing her. His suspiciousness led to cutting out nearly all social contact and he became more and more irritable. He had no sexual relations with his wife for the last four years of his life. During that time, his daughter and her children were living in his house and he displayed an uncharacteristic and undue fondness for his daughter. One year before his death, all his symptoms grew worse. His daughter remarried at that time and when she became pregnant about ten months before he died, he showed extreme jealousy. His long time pattern of qaurreling with his wife intensified and he frequently accused her of neglecting his needs in favor of their daughter's. At the Post Office, he was shifted to more isolated tasks as his conflicts with the other employees increased. He slept poorly, often sitting up in a chair all night to relieve his dyspnea. Three months before he died, he developed habits of blank staring, of long chewing at meals, of crying, sometimes uncontrollably, over TV programs, of lapsing into long silences, and of pacing. He began to threaten suicide. He spoke many times of "doing the Dutch Act" and once pantomimed shooting himself in the head.

Six weeks prior to his death, when his hypertensive cardiovascular disease was becoming incapacitating, he saw his doctor who advised him to cut out all alcohol (until that time, he drank only moderately, two or three beers a day) and put him on a low salt diet. He began to take sleeping pills at night and during the day. Three weeks later, he was sent home sick from work. His doctor refused to give him permission to return, telling the wife that he was "a mighty sick man." Thereafter, he worried constantly about being "laid off," even though he had accumulated nearly 1,000 hours of sick leave. He suffered from insomnia, dizzy spells, anorexia, nausea, vomiting, and intermittent blurred vision. He often commented that he would be better off dead and twice he was discovered with the gas on. Two weeks before his suicide, the doctor agreed, at his wife's suggestion, to hospitalize him. A few days before his death, he went to a picnic and ate an inordinate amount, explaining that he knew he would "never come back from the hospital." The hospital was contacted and on a Friday he received a card scheduling admission for the following Monday.

The next morning, he was up early. He sat in the yard for a while, ate a good breakfast, put on carefully chosen, clean clothes, and went to a tavern where he spent $30 to treat everyone there to a round of drinks. Back at home before lunch, he clung to his wife in an odd manner, holding onto her dress and following her step for step. After lunch, his wife, daughter, and grandchildren went shopping. When they returned they found his body in the garage. He had slashed his left wrist with a razor blade and bled to death.

Family history: The subject's mother was a "nervous" woman and a chronic alcoholic.
Arrest record: None.

Case No. *027* M _X_ F __ Age *58*

ST. LOUIS SUICIDE STUDY CRITERIA FOR MAJOR AFFECTIVE DISORDER

Diagnosis required four of the six following categories, A-F. Category G was helpful in diagnosis, but not necessary.

A. Clinically well, exclusive of attacks of major affective disorder   ___

B. Previous episode(s) of major affective disorder   _X_

C. Discreteness (and duration) of final attack:
   6 months or less   ___
   12 months or less   ___

D. "Medical" symptoms:
   insomnia   _X_
   anorexia   _X_
   weight loss   ___
   low energy, weakness fatigue   _X_
   constipation   ___

E. Psychological symptoms:
   "blue" feeling, depression, sadness   ___
   diminished motor activity   _X_
   loss of interest   ___
   diminished sexual interest and activity   _X_
   undertalkativeness   _X_
   low expectancy of recovery; expectation of "black" future   _X_
   feeling of being a burden   _X_
   indecisiveness   ___
   feelings of worthlessness or guilt   ___
   agitation   _X_
   personal untidiness   ___
   difficulty in thinking and concentration   ___
   delusions   ___

F. Disturbances in social behavior: decreased social and recreational activity   _X_

G. Miscellaneous items:
   age of onset 40 and over   ___
   family history of affective disorder   _X_

FEIGHNER CRITERIA FOR MAJOR AFFECTIVE DISORDER

Diagnosis required all three of the following categories.

A. Dysphoric mood (depressed, sad, blue, despondent, hopeless, "down in dumps," irritable, fearful, worried, discouraged) __X__

B. At least 5 of following for definite; at least 4 of following for probable:
   poor appetite or weight loss: 2 lb/wk, 10 lb/yr __X__
   sleep difficulties __X__
   loss of energy (fatigue, tiredness) _____
   agitation or retardation __X__
   loss of interest in usual activities or decreased sex drive __X__
   complaints or actual diminished ability to think/concentrate _____
   feelings of guilt, self-reproach _____
   recurrent thoughts of death and/or suicide __X__

C. A psychiatric illness lasting <u>at least one month</u> with no pre-existing psychiatric condition (schizophrenia, anxiety neurosis, phobic neurosis, obsessive-compulsive neurosis, hysteria, alcoholism, drug dependence, antisocial personality, homosexuality, transsexualism, mental retardation, anorexia nervosa, organic brain syndrome) or life-threatening or incapacitating illness _____

037 Informants: Wife, physician

This 53-year-old white carpenter, the son of a Kentucky farmer, had lived all his adult life in St. Louis. His wife of 31 years described him as a sensitive person with easily hurt feelings, but from many other statements about him, he appears to have been extremely steady and reliable. They had no children, but enjoyed a pleasant social life. Though raised as a Baptist, he was a moderate social drinker and attended church only rarely.

Three years before his death, he suffered a heart attack and was hospitalized for two weeks. A year later, he suffered a second attack and six months after that, a third. Due to his heart disease, he was pensioned by the railroad for two years. His doctor prescribed digitalis for congestive heart failure. Some months before his death, he was able to return to the same job he had held previously and was, according to his wife, happy and functioning well. She denied any depressive symptoms, but his doctor felt that he had been depressed since his first heart attack and reported that he spoke little and that his appetite, weight, and strength decreased in the last year.

Two weeks prior to his suicide, when his half-brother from Indiana left after a visit, he cried hard trying to tell him goodbye. This was the first time his wife had ever seen him cry. In the days that followed, he had spells of extreme nervousness and frequent crying. Three days before his suicide, he went to work as usual, but was brought home at noon by his foreman who said he had begun to shake and sob at work. While the foreman was telling his wife about this, the subject stood by a tree crying uncontrollably. He had been suffering from a severe headache for two days and had had an episode of vomiting a few days before that. The next day, his doctor put him in the hospital for his nerves. As he entered the hospital, he said to his wife, "This is the end. I'll never get out of here alive. I'm ready to go." He was put in a private room and a staff member was assigned to watch him and record what he said. He appeared to be confused and hallucinating, complaining that "nobody believed him." When his wife returned to visit him the next day, she found him weak, but rid of the headache and seemingly happier. Very early the next morning, he managed to hang himself with a belt tied around his neck and to the foot of his bed. His body was found seated on the floor at the end of the bed. He left an unsigned note which said, "Please do not blame my wife for this, she knows nothing about . . . nor does anyone else."

Family history: There was no family history of psychiatric illness.
Arrest record: None.

Case No. 037 M __ F X__ Age 53

ST. LOUIS SUICIDE STUDY CRITERIA FOR MAJOR AFFECTIVE DISORDER

Diagnosis required four of the six following categories, A-F. Category G was helpful in diagnosis, but not necessary.

- A. Clinically well, exclusive of attacks of major affective disorder ___
- B. Previous episode(s) of major affective disorder ___
- C. Discreteness (and duration) of final attack:
  - 6 months or less ___
  - 12 months or less X
- D. "Medical" symptoms:
  - insomnia ___
  - anorexia X
  - weight loss X
  - low energy, weakness fatigue X
  - constipation ___
- E. Psychological symptoms:
  - "blue" feeling, depression, sadness X
  - diminished motor activity ___
  - loss of interest ___
  - diminished sexual interest and activity ___
  - undertalkativeness X
  - low expectancy of recovery; expectation of "black" future X
  - feeling of being a burden ___
  - indecisiveness ___
  - feelings of worthlessness or guilt ___
  - agitation X
  - personal untidiness ___
  - difficulty in thinking and concentration X
  - delusions ___
- F. Disturbances in social behavior: decreased social and recreational activity ___
- G. Miscellaneous items:
  - age of onset 40 and over X
  - family history of affective disorder ___

FEIGHNER CRITERIA FOR MAJOR AFFECTIVE DISORDER

Diagnosis required all three of the following categories.

- A. Dysphoric mood (depressed, sad, blue, despondent, hopeless, "down in dumps," irritable, fearful, worried, discouraged) X
- B. At least 5 of following for definite; at least 4 of following for probable:
  - poor appetite or weight loss: 2 lb/wk, 10 lb/yr X
  - sleep difficulties ___
  - loss of energy (fatigue, tiredness) X
  - agitation or retardation X
  - loss of interest in usual activities or decreased sex drive ___
  - complaints or actual diminished ability to think/concentrate X
  - feelings of guilt, self-reproach ___
  - recurrent thoughts of death and/or suicide ___
- C. A psychiatric illness lasting <u>at least one month</u> with no pre-existing psychiatric condition (schizophrenia, anxiety neurosis, phobic neurosis, obsessive-compulsive neurosis, hysteria, alcoholism, drug dependence, antisocial personality, homosexuality, transsexualism, mental retardation, anorexia nervosa, organic brain syndrome) or life-threatening or incapacitating illness X

043 Informants: Wife, physician

This 53-year-old white man was, at the time of his death, married to his third wife, a woman 12 years his junior. His first two marriages, both of undetermined duration, ended in divorce. He had two sons, one by each of the earlier marriages. The first son was, at the time of the subject's death, in a state penitentiary having been convicted a second time for the same unspecified crime. The subject had not communicated with that son since the conviction, and his second son was dead.

His third wife, to whom he had been married for 16 years, described him as a temperamental man who had been moody, sensitive, hot-tempered, "neurotic," and "high-strung" all his life. At 18, he had spent one year in the Navy, but was discharged because of some unspecified "trouble." According to his wife, this discharge prevented him from ever being able to get defense work. For many years, he had had brief periods of depression, occurring in the spring, when he would quit work for a week or so and lie around the house, after which he would gradually feel better and return to his job.

In the 20 years his wife had known him, he had had seven jobs, the last one as a packer for a moving company for eight years. He was known as a good worker though perfectionistic and hot-tempered. He "quit" his last job three or four times due to temper, but was always recalled by his employer.

A heavy drinker all of his adult life, his drinking patterns were quite set. He was rarely known to start drinking at home. Rather, he began in the morning with a few drinks at work and continued after work at the tavern. Though he might share a beer or two with his wife while watching TV, he was never drunk at home on the weekends. For the last five years of his life, he drank heavily nearly every workday and was drunk at least four times a week. He worried about his drinking, believing that he would never be able to stop and that his neighbors criticized him for it. He had been arrested once or twice for drunken driving and on several occasions the police impounded his car and sent him home in a cab.

Five or six years before he died, he had a six-month episode in which the symptoms were chest pain, dyspnea, dizziness, morning nausea, abdominal pain, palpitation, leg cramps, fatigue, and sadness. He quit working for the duration of these symptoms and spent much of his time in bed. The symptoms gradually diminished without his ever seeing a physician. At the end of six months, he returned to work. At about the time of onset of the chest pains, etc., his mother died of a long-term illness and his son was sentenced to prison, but it was not clear whether or not he felt his symptoms were in reaction to either of these events. In any case, from that time on, his drinking increased, he had less time for and interest in his wife, and he continued to feel "bad" physically. He explained his heavier drinking by saying he felt "so bad" he couldn't work without drinking. Even so, he visited a doctor only once in those years and then for "cold and cough." With his wife he shared no interests, his only topic of conversation was his work, and he talked a great deal about how much better he was at packing than his fellow workers.

Three years prior to his death, he and his wife bought a new house in order to get away from their old neighborhood's tavern crowd and, for a time, things were better. He stopped drinking, came directly home after work, and showed interest in improving his new house and yard. This lasted only briefly and he soon lapsed back into his old habits.

About a year before he died, he began to lose interest in all aspects of his life except work and drinking with his buddies. He saw a favorite brother much less often and his sexual activity diminished greatly. Though never impotent, he told his wife he was "no good anymore" and that she needed a younger man. He was moodier and more irritable with her and once, when drunk, he displayed angry jealousy and threatened to beat her if ever he caught her "having a good time." He seemed upset by any kind of violence shown on TV or described in the papers. He complained occasionally of feeling as if he were in a "trance" and of not being able to think straight. When feeling especially poorly, he complained of an odd taste in his mouth. He seemed generally tired, weaker, and less sure of himself and of his performance at work. Once or twice, when drunk, he said he'd be better off dead.

Six months later, all of the above symptoms had grown noticeably worse. In additon, he was again beginning to experience chest pain, dyspnea, dizziness, anorexia, and weight loss. He lost ten pounds in the last six months of his life. His lack of interest became even more pronounced and he was extremely nervous and tense about his job. His take-home pay decreased about this time, probably because he was working shorter hours. He was pale, had trouble sleeping, and had several severe nosebleeds. He was sad and depressed in appearance and his wife reported that he began to shave, bathe, and change his clothes less and less often. One week before he died, he was not able to sleep at all and said, "If this doesn't stop, I'll have to do something about it." His wife suggested seeing a doctor on the weekend.

On the day of his suicide, a Saturday, he came home about 5 PM. He had been drinking at work and went right out again to a tavern where he drank a good deal more. An hour or so later, he returned from the tavern, staggering, with a case of beer for the weekend. He said to his wife, who was watching television, "I brought you six cold ones," and then, "See, I can get just as drunk here as in the old neighborhood." She heard him in the basement moving things around. A few minutes later, she heard a shot, went to the basement and discovered that he had shot himself in the head with a shotgun and was dead. When asked why he might have committed suicide, she answered, "Nobody can understand why he did it."

Family history: Two brothers were alcoholics, one for more than 16 years. The other was described as having had "nervous" troubles. One son was in the penitentiary twice.
Arrest record: None obtained.

Case No. *043* M _X_ F __ Age _53_

ST. LOUIS SUICIDE STUDY CRITERIA FOR MAJOR AFFECTIVE DISORDER

Diagnosis required four of the six following categories, A-F. Category G was helpful in diagnosis, but not necessary.

- A. Clinically well, exclusive of attacks of major affective disorder ___
- B. Previous episode(s) of major affective disorder _X_
- C. Discreteness (and duration) of final attack:
  - 6 months or less ___
  - 12 months or less _X_
- D. "Medical" symptoms:
  - insomnia _X_
  - anorexia _X_
  - weight loss _X_
  - low energy, weakness _X_
  - fatigue _X_
  - constipation ___
- E. Psychological symptoms:
  - "blue" feeling, depression, sadness _X_
  - diminished motor activity ___
  - loss of interest _X_
  - diminished sexual interest and activity _X_
  - undertalkativeness ___
  - low expectancy of recovery; expectation of "black" future ___
  - feeling of being a burden ___
  - indecisiveness ___
  - feelings of worthlessness or guilt _X_
  - agitation ___
  - personal untidiness _X_
  - difficulty in thinking and concentration _X_
  - delusions ___
- F. Disturbances in social behavior: decreased social and recreational activity _X_
- G. Miscellaneous items:
  - age of onset 40 and over ___
  - family history of affective disorder _X_

FEIGHNER CRITERIA FOR MAJOR AFFECTIVE DISORDER

Diagnosis required all three of the following categories.

A. Dysphoric mood (depressed, sad, blue, despondent, hopeless, "down in dumps," irritable, fearful, worried, discouraged) __X__

B. At least 5 of following for definite; at least 4 of following for probable:
- poor appetite or weight loss: 2 lb/wk, 10 lb/yr __X__
- sleep difficulties ____
- loss of energy (fatigue, tiredness) __X__
- agitation or retardation ____
- loss of interest in usual activities or decreased sex drive __X__
- complaints or actual diminished ability to think/concentrate __X__
- feelings of guilt, self-reproach __X__
- recurrent thoughts of death and/or suicide __X__

C. A psychiatric illness lasting <u>at least one month</u> with no pre-existing psychiatric condition (schizophrenia, anxiety neurosis, phobic neurosis, obsessive-compulsive neurosis, hysteria, alcoholism, drug dependence, antisocial personality, homosexuality, transsexualism, mental retardation, anorexia nervosa, organic brain syndrome) or life-threatening or incapacitating illness ____

044 Informants: Wife, physician

This 64-year-old white laborer had, until a bad fall three and a half months before his death, worked a full eight-hour day digging ditches and laying pipe for a plumbing company. He grew up on his father's farm, stopped school after the 5th grade, and worked full time from the age of 14. He had been happily married to a woman his own age for 45 years and they had raised three children. He and his wife had lived in St. Louis County for 33 years in a home he had built himself. Raised a Lutheran, he attended church infrequently. According to his wife, he had many friends, five or six of whom were close ones he saw at least once a week. He was only a moderate social drinker. Sometime after his fall, his doctor had told him of some changes in his lungs, whereupon he began to worry about possible lung trouble. He experienced some chest pains while in the hospital after the fall, but they disappeared once he was back at home.

In the accident, he had fractured one hip and several ribs and was, as a result, hospitalized for about six weeks. On his return home, he used crutches for a few weeks, but was soon able to walk on his own and wanted to go back to work. One month before his suicide, he went to see his boss about returning to his old job at the plumbing company. The boss refused to take him back and he returned home in tears, a state that was most unusual for him. Although his wife said that he had been slightly more "nervous" after the accident, until the denial of his job, his spirits had been as good as ever. After the boss's rejection, he cried easily and showed anger at the mere thought of his boss. In his wife's opinion, he was obviously depressed and irritable (especially with his grandchildren whom he had always enjoyed), but she denied any inertia, delusions, loss of appetite, any weight loss, or suicidal remarks. Even so, she admitted having hidden a gun away some weeks before his death.

A week or two before his suicide, his boss reconsidered and agreed to take him back, but only on a full-time basis and without any special considerations of his age or injuries. This did not serve to diminish his depression for he worried a great deal about whether he would be able, after three and a half months off, to resume a full day of ditch digging. He suffered from insomnia and was given sleeping pills by his doctor.

On the morning he was to start back to work, he got up early, dressed, and ate breakfast. His wife reported that his eyes looked "funny"—bloodshot and glassy—though she knew he had had at least five hours of sleep the night before. At 7:30 AM, he went out to his garage where he shot himself in the head with a shotgun and died instantly. He left a note which indicated that he had not wanted to be a burden on his family.

Family history: There was no family history of psychiatric illness.
Arrest record: None.

Case No. 044 M X F___ Age 64

ST. LOUIS SUICIDE STUDY CRITERIA FOR MAJOR AFFECTIVE DISORDER

Diagnosis required four of the six following categories, A-F. Category G was helpful in diagnosis, but not necessary.

- A. Clinically well, exclusive of attacks of major affective disorder **X**
- B. Previous episode(s) of major affective disorder ___
- C. Discreteness (and duration) of final attack:
  - 6 months or less **X**
  - 12 months or less ___
- D. "Medical" symptoms:
  - insomnia **X**
  - anorexia ___
  - weight loss ___
  - low energy, weakness ___
  - fatigue ___
  - constipation ___
- E. Psychological symptoms:
  - "blue" feeling, depression, sadness **X**
  - diminished motor activity ___
  - loss of interest ___
  - diminished sexual interest and activity ___
  - undertalkativeness ___
  - low expectancy of recovery; expectation of "black" future ___
  - feeling of being a burden **X**
  - indecisiveness ___
  - feelings of worthlessness or guilt ___
  - agitation ___
  - personal untidiness ___
  - difficulty in thinking and concentration ___
  - delusions ___
- F. Disturbances in social behavior: decreased social and recreational activity ___
- G. Miscellaneous items:
  - age of onset 40 and over **X**
  - family history of affective disorder ___

FEIGHNER CRITERIA FOR MAJOR AFFECTIVE DISORDER

Diagnosis required all three of the following categories.

- A. Dysphoric mood (depressed, sad, blue, despondent, hopeless, "down in dumps," irritable, fearful, worried, discouraged) **X**
- B. At least 5 of following for definite; at least 4 of following for probable:
  - poor appetite or weight loss: 2 lb/wk, 10 lb/yr ___
  - sleep difficulties **X**
  - loss of energy (fatigue, tiredness) ___
  - agitation or retardation ___
  - loss of interest in usual activities or decreased sex drive ___
  - complaints or actual diminished ability to think/concentrate ___
  - feelings of guilt, self-reproach ___
  - recurrent thoughts of death and/or suicide ___
- C. A psychiatric illness lasting <u>at least one month</u> with no pre-existing psychiatric condition (schizophrenia, anxiety neurosis, phobic neurosis, obsessive-compulsive neurosis, hysteria, alcoholism, drug dependence, antisocial personality, homosexuality, transsexualism, mental retardation, anorexia nervosa, organic brain syndrome) or life-threatening or incapacitating illness **X**

048 Informants: Physician, psychiatrist (no primary informant)

Because no one who had known this 66-year-old white man well would agree to be interviewed, very little is known about the events that led to his suicide.

It is know that he was married, that he had at least one married son, and that he had been pensioned from the Post Office. He saw a doctor after having suffered very severe depression for two or three months. He told the doctor he had "funny" ideas, but would not tell what they were. He was sleeping poorly. He had no known delusions. The doctor referred him to a psychiatrist whom he saw a day or two before his death. The psychiatrist noted no organic symptoms, no previous history of depression, and no delusions. He reported that the patient had been suffering "agitated depression" for a few weeks, that he had lost weight and had also lost all interest in things he once enjoyed. He saw the patient only once. A day or two later, he was informed that the patient had hanged himself.

Family history: None obtained
Arrest record: None

Case No. 048 M X F__ Age 66

ST. LOUIS SUICIDE STUDY CRITERIA FOR MAJOR AFFECTIVE DISORDER

Diagnosis required four of the six following categories, A-F. Category G was helpful in diagnosis, but not necessary.

- A. Clinically well, exclusive of attacks of major affective disorder ___
- B. Previous episode(s) of major affective disorder ___
- C. Discreteness (and duration) of final attack:
  - 6 months or less _X_
  - 12 months or less ___
- D. "Medical" symptoms:
  - insomnia _X_
  - anorexia ___
  - weight loss _X_
  - low energy, weakness fatigue ___
  - constipation ___
- E. Psychological symptoms:
  - "blue" feeling, depression, sadness _X_
  - diminished motor activity ___
  - loss of interest _X_
  - diminished sexual interest and activity ___
  - undertalkativeness ___
  - low expectancy of recovery; expectation of "black" future ___
  - feeling of being a burden ___
  - indecisiveness ___
  - feelings of worthlessness or guilt ___
  - agitation _X_
  - personal untidiness ___
  - difficulty in thinking and concentration ___
  - delusions ___
- F. Disturbances in social behavior: decreased social and recreational activity _X_
- G. Miscellaneous items:
  - age of onset 40 and over ___
  - family history of affective disorder ___

FEIGHNER CRITERIA FOR MAJOR AFFECTIVE DISORDER

Diagnosis required all three of the following categories.

- A. Dysphoric mood (depressed, sad, blue, despondent, hopeless, "down in dumps," irritable, fearful, worried, discouraged) _X_
- B. At least 5 of following for definite; at least 4 of following for probable:
  - poor appetite or weight loss: 2 lb/wk, 10 lb/yr _X_
  - sleep difficulties _X_
  - loss of energy (fatigue, tiredness) ___
  - agitation or retardation _X_
  - loss of interest in usual activities or decreased sex drive _X_
  - complaints or actual diminished ability to think/concentrate ___
  - feelings of guilt, self-reproach ___
  - recurrent thoughts of death and/or suicide ___
- C. A psychiatric illness lasting <u>at least one month</u> with no pre-existing psychiatric condition (schizophrenia, anxiety neurosis, phobic neurosis, obsessive-compulsive neurosis, hysteria, alcoholism, drug dependence, antisocial personality, homosexuality, transsexualism, mental retardation, anorexia nervosa, organic brain syndrome) or life-threatening or incapacitating illness _X_

049 Informants: Son, wife, physician, hospital records

This 65-year-old white man was born in Vienna, Austria. His father died when he six and he and his mother immigrated to the U.S. when he was 11. Although he had completed 6th grade in Austria and was a good student, he did not attend school in the U.S. He married at age 18 and he and his wife had been living in St. Louis for 45 years when he died. They had two children—a married son, and a daughter who was living at home.

The subject was described by his son as having been very slow-moving all of his life. In his youth, he had trained to be a furniture finisher and had been a union cabinet finisher for at least ten years before he died. The quality of his work was good, but, because of his slowness, he had trouble holding regular jobs. He was always the first to be laid off and, consequently, in his 50 years of work, he had had about 20 or 25 different jobs.

Until three years before his death, he had been a fairly happy person with an adequate income (in spite of his sporadic career) and a moderately active social life. He liked to read, to play cards, to watch TV, and he enjoyed keeping his house in good repair. He tended always to have been "sickly" (even so, there were no records of any serious illnesses or hospitalizations) and "tired," but these symptoms seemed to his family just part of his slow-moving ways. Raised a Catholic, he had not been a member of any church for many years. He drank only very moderately.

Three years prior to his suicide, he was sent out of town on a job which involved the finishing of a new bank. Instead of taking the agreed upon one week to complete the job, he took three weeks, which caused the bank's opening to be delayed. He never called the contractor to explain his slowness and, when he returned to St. Louis, he was fired (as opposed to being laid off) for the first time in his life. This upset him greatly and seemed to his family to bring on a complete personality change. He gave up his daily beer. No longer cheerful and jolly at family gatherings, he became just the opposite—sad, joyless, uninterested. From that time on, he worked very little, even around his own house, and spent much of his time sitting or lying down by himself. He spoke less, read, watched TV, and played cards less, and gradually stopped seeing his friends. His appetite was poor, his fatigue grew worse, he was generally irritable, moody, and sensitive. His feelings were easily hurt and, when it was necessary for his wife to enter a hospital briefly, he cried to himself and trembled. According to his son, he did not have trouble sleeping. Rather, he seemed to sleep too much. He lost interest in his personal appearance and sometimes went for days without shaving or bathing. He looked depressed and disgusted and he began to suffer anxiety attacks with apprehension, shortness of breath, palpitation, and trembling. However, if he was worried about anything in particular, he never spoke of it to his family. He seemed to be withdrawing from them into himself.

One year before his suicide, all of his symptoms had become noticeably worse. About that time, he walked off a job—something he had never done—saying flatly that he could not work any more. Finally, at his family's insistence, he went to a physician who referred him to an outpatient clinic at a psychiatric hospital. There, over a period of two months, he received five electroshock treatments. For a short while, he seemed better, but then relapsed. He was eating almost nothing (in the last six months of his life he lost a total of 20 pounds) and his family took him back to the clinic. He received seven additional shock treatments over the next two months. Again he improved and four months before his death he was, according to the hospital records, making plans to work again and had "increased outside interests." He was discharged as an outpatient, but the improvement did not last long. He never managed to get back to work and all his old symptoms returned. His depression deepened and, two weeks before he died, he again visited the clinic and was told that he would have to have more shock treatments. He feared these and did not want to return to the clinic again. He began to spend most of his time lying on a mattress in his attic. His son recalled that, toward the end, he had a strange sort of "little cry." Though he was much quieter with his family, he talked to himself often and he slept a great deal. According to both his son and his wife, he had no delusions of worthlessness or guilt and he made no remarks about "being better off dead" or of "being a burden."

On the weekend of his suicide, his wife and daughter had gone away to the country to visit relatives. This was something they did every three or four weeks and, once before, he had refused to let them back into the house. When they returned from this two-day visit on Monday, they found he had hanged himself from a banister in the attic.

Family history: There was no family history of psychiatric illness.
Arrest record: None.

Case No. 049 M X F___ Age 65

ST. LOUIS SUICIDE STUDY CRITERIA FOR MAJOR AFFECTIVE DISORDER

Diagnosis required four of the six following categories, A-F. Category G was helpful in diagnosis, but not necessary.

- A. Clinically well, exclusive of attacks of major affective disorder __X__
- B. Previous episode(s) of major affective disorder __X__
- C. Discreteness (and duration) of final attack:
    - 6 months or less ____
    - 12 months or less __X__
- D. "Medical" symptoms:
    - insomnia ____
    - anorexia __X__
    - weight loss __X__
    - low energy, weakness fatigue __X__
    - constipation ____
- E. Psychological symptoms:
    - "blue" feeling, depression, sadness __X__
    - diminished motor activity __X__
    - loss of interest __X__
    - diminished sexual interest and activity ____
    - undertalkativeness __X__
    - low expectancy of recovery; expectation of "black" future ____
    - feeling of being a burden ____
    - indecisiveness ____
    - feelings of worthlessness or guilt ____
    - agitation ____
    - personal untidiness ____
    - difficulty in thinking and concentration ____
    - delusions ____
- F. Disturbances in social behavior: decreased social and recreational activity __X__
- G. Miscellaneous items:
    - age of onset 40 and over __X__
    - family history of affective disorder ____

FEIGHNER CRITERIA FOR MAJOR AFFECTIVE DISORDER

Diagnosis required all three of the following categories.

- A. Dysphoric mood (depressed, sad, blue, despondent, hopeless, "down in dumps," irritable, fearful, worried, discouraged) __X__
- B. At least 5 of following for definite; at least 4 of following for probable:
    - poor appetite or weight loss: 2 lb/wk, 10 lb/yr __X__
    - sleep difficulties __X__
    - loss of energy (fatigue, tiredness) __X__
    - agitation or retardation __X__
    - loss of interest in usual activities or decreased sex drive __X__
    - complaints or actual diminished ability to think/concentrate ____
    - feelings of guilt, self-reproach ____
    - recurrent thoughts of death and/or suicide ____
- C. A psychiatric illness lasting at least one month with no pre-existing psychiatric condition (schizophrenia, anxiety neurosis, phobic neurosis, obsessive-compulsive neurosis, hysteria, alcoholism, drug dependence, antisocial personality, homosexuality, transsexualism, mental retardation, anorexia nervosa, organic brain syndrome) or life-threatening or incapacitating illness __X__

050 Informants: Wife, physician, clinic records

This 63-year-old white married man was raised on a farm and was illiterate at the time of his death. Married for 35 years, he and his wife owned their own home. Unemployed for 11 years when he died, he had held many jobs as a laborer over the course of his life, but had often gone without work for several years at a time. He had enlisted in the Army in 1918 and was discharged 72 days later. His wife said the records listed the reason for discharge simply as "disability," and did not know what the nature of the disability was. She worked full time until nine months before her husband's death when she took time off to spend with him.

She described her husband as always having been a sensitive, "high-strung" person. About four years before his suicide, he had become ill with Parkinson's Disease and arteriosclerosis. Up until that time, he had drunk to what she considered to be excess—about five or six beers a day—but after the onset of his illness, gave up drinking almost entirely. Thereafter an occasional single beer always "made him reel."

The wife reported that the subject's feelings of hopelessness and worthlessness were a result of the clinic doctors having told him that he had a brain disease and that he would, in her words, "die a horrible death." From that point on, she said, he was preoccupied with his disease, afraid of losing his mind, afraid of being a burden, afraid he would never get well.

Over the last four years prior to his suicide, the subject suffered three or four anxiety attacks with accompanying shortness of breath, palpitation, weakness, trembling, and apprehension. His wife remembered that it was also during this time that he began to exhibit very easily hurt feelings, to cry easily, and to be much more nervous than he had been before. About two and a half or three years before he died, at about the same time he quit drinking, he stopped going to the tavern to play cards with his friends. He became increasingly dependent on his wife and let his social life dwindle away. He lost his voice whenever he was especially nervous. He developed anorexia, nausea, and vomiting, was unable to keep solids down in the mornings, and lost 18 pounds in the last three years of his life. He lost interest in his appearance and was careless about his clothes. The tremors and stiffness in his extremities worsened. He spoke often of being a burden and of the possibility of suicide. He frequently said to his wife, "I can't live like this," and on waking would wonder aloud if he could "make it through one more day." Even though he would say to his wife now and again, "I don't think I'm really losing my mind, do you?" he felt the neighbors were watching him for signs of insanity.

Two months before he killed himself, his physical condition deteriorated noticeably. His tremors were more pronounced, his vomiting was worse, and he had developed a roar in his left ear. Although his wife denied that he had any loss of memory, she did say that he tended to get confused in a room where two or three people were talking at once. She also denied that he had trouble sleeping, but she reported that, in the last weeks of his life, he was sad, joyless, had lost almost all interest in things other than his health, that he constantly paced the floor crying (always careful to pull the shades so the neighbors wouldn't see him). She said that he began to think more about religion (raised a Baptist, his adult church attendance had been scanty) and that the week before he died he went to a faith healer. He also refused that last week to leave the house without her.

On the day of his death, his wife went to a nearby store, leaving him alone in the house. When she returned, she found him dead in the kitchen. He had propped a rifle on the sink board and shot himself through the mouth.

Family history: One brother spent a brief period in a mental hospital (in 1910) for "nervous breakdown." There was no other family history of psychiatric illness.

Arrest record: None.

Case No. 050 M X F___ Age 63

ST. LOUIS SUICIDE STUDY CRITERIA FOR MAJOR AFFECTIVE DISORDER

Diagnosis required four of the six following categories, A-F. Category G was helpful in diagnosis, but not necessary.

- A. Clinically well, exclusive of attacks of major affective disorder ___
- B. Previous episode(s) of major affective disorder ___
- C. Discreteness (and duration) of final attack:
  - 6 months or less X
  - 12 months or less ___
- D. "Medical" symptoms:
  - insomnia ___
  - anorexia X
  - weight loss X
  - low energy, weakness ___
  - fatigue ___
  - constipation ___
- E. Psychological symptoms:
  - "blue" feeling, depression, sadness X
  - diminished motor activity ___
  - loss of interest X
  - diminished sexual interest and activity ___
  - undertalkativeness ___
  - low expectancy of recovery; expectation of "black" future X
  - feeling of being a burden X
  - indecisiveness ___
  - feelings of worthlessness or guilt ___
  - agitation X
  - personal untidiness X
  - difficulty in thinking and concentration X
  - delusions X
- F. Disturbances in social behavior: decreased social and recreational activity X
- G. Miscellaneous items:
  - age of onset 40 and over X
  - family history of affective disorder X

FEIGHNER CRITERIA FOR MAJOR AFFECTIVE DISORDER

Diagnosis required all three of the following categories.

- A. Dysphoric mood (depressed, sad, blue, despondent, hopeless, "down in dumps," irritable, fearful, worried, discouraged) X
- B. At least 5 of following for definite; at least 4 of following for probable:
  - poor appetite or weight loss: 2 lb/wk, 10 lb/yr X
  - sleep difficulties ___
  - loss of energy (fatigue, tiredness) ___
  - agitation or retardation X
  - loss of interest in usual activities or decreased sex drive X
  - complaints or actual diminished ability to think/concentrate X
  - feelings of guilt, self-reproach ___
  - recurrent thoughts of death and/or suicide X
- C. A psychiatric illness lasting <u>at least one month</u> with no pre-existing psychiatric condition (schizophrenia, anxiety neurosis, phobic neurosis, obsessive-compulsive neurosis, hysteria, alcoholism, drug dependence, antisocial personality, homosexuality, transsexualism, mental retardation, anorexia nervosa, organic brain syndrome) or life-threatening or incapacitating illness X

051   Informant: Wife

This 61-year-old white man had been a highly successful lawyer and, until a few months before his death, a senior partner in his law firm. His mother was a devout, orthodox Jew who doted on her son, but was rigid in her insistence that he work to get the best possible marks at school, that he practice his music long hours, that he in general "get ahead." According to the informant, he married the first girl he ever took out and did so after an intervening automobile accident which had left her terribly scarred. He and the first wife had one daughter and had been married for over 30 years when he divorced her to marry his second wife, a much younger woman. He waited for the divorce for several years in consideration of his mother who had threatened to disown him should he divorce his first wife.

Long before his final troubles, the subject had suffered from obsessive gambling and, about five or six months before his suicide, his gambling losses mounted overwhelmingly. Deeply in debt to professional gamblers, he was totally preoccupied with efforts to get hold of money to repay them. He let his law business slide and, after it was discovered that he had been embezzling money from an aunt of his, his law firm asked for his resignation. Eventually he was forced to sell his house.

His wife reported that he developed depressive symptoms at the time of his financial crisis, 15 or 16 months prior to his suicide, but she was uncertain as to which came first. At any rate, he appeared for the first time in his life depressed, disgusted, and agitated. He suffered from insomnia and anorexia, and often threatened suicide in the presence of his wife and family. He lost some weight, though not a great deal, and he was continually gambling unsuccessfully to try to make up his losses.

One week before his suicide, his wife left him and moved in with her sister. This was a blow to him. Although he had sold his house—for cash, most of which disappeared within six weeks—he was, the last week before his death, still living in it alone. On the morning of his suicide, he went to an expensive hotel and ordered an elaborate breakfast. Afterwards, he telephoned his wife to describe it, which she felt was most unlike him. Sometime later he asphyxiated himself with the exhaust fumes in a car he had apparently rented specially for that purpose.

Family history: The subject's only child experienced a single episode called "nervous breakdown" at the age of 25 (approximately). She recovered and had no recurrences. There was no other record of family psychiatric illness.

Arrest record: None.

Case No. 051 M__ X F__ Age 61

ST. LOUIS SUICIDE STUDY CRITERIA FOR MAJOR AFFECTIVE DISORDER

Diagnosis required four of the six following categories, A-F. Category G was helpful in diagnosis, but not necessary.

- A. Clinically well, exclusive of attacks of major affective disorder __X__
- B. Previous episode(s) of major affective disorder ____
- C. Discreteness (and duration) of final attack:
  - 6 months or less ____
  - 12 months or less __X__
- D. "Medical" symptoms:
  - insomnia __X__
  - anorexia __X__
  - weight loss __X__
  - low energy, weakness ____
  - fatigue ____
  - constipation ____
- E. Psychological symptoms:
  - "blue" feeling, depression, sadness __X__
  - diminished motor activity ____
  - loss of interest ____
  - diminished sexual interest and activity ____
  - undertalkativeness ____
  - low expectancy of recovery; expectation of "black" future ____
  - feeling of being a burden ____
  - indecisiveness ____
  - feelings of worthlessness or guilt __X__
  - agitation __X__
  - personal untidiness ____
  - difficulty in thinking and concentration ____
  - delusions ____
- F. Disturbances in social behavior: decreased social and recreational activity __X__
- G. Miscellaneous items:
  - age of onset 40 and over __X__
  - family history of affective disorder __X__

FEIGHNER CRITERIA FOR MAJOR AFFECTIVE DISORDER

Diagnosis required all three of the following categories.

- A. Dysphoric mood (depressed, sad, blue, despondent, hopeless, "down in dumps," irritable, fearful, worried, discouraged) __X__
- B. At least 5 of following for definite; at least 4 of following for probable:
  - poor appetite or weight loss: 2 lb/wk, 10 lb/yr __X__
  - sleep difficulties __X__
  - loss of energy (fatigue, tiredness) ____
  - agitation or retardation __X__
  - loss of interest in usual activities or decreased sex drive ____
  - complaints or actual diminished ability to think/concentrate ____
  - feelings of guilt, self-reproach __X__
  - recurrent thoughts of death and/or suicide __X__
- C. A psychiatric illness lasting <u>at least one month</u> with no pre-existing psychiatric condition (schizophrenia, anxiety neurosis, phobic neurosis, obsessive-compulsive neurosis, hysteria, alcoholism, drug dependence, antisocial personality, homosexuality, transsexualism, mental retardation, anorexia nervosa, organic brain syndrome) or life-threatening or incapacitating illness __X__

056 Informant: Neighbor

This 56-year-old white man, a German immigrant who had lived in the United States for 30 years and in St. Louis for 26, was living alone at the time of his death. His common-law wife of more than 20 years had suffered a stroke four months earlier and had been placed in a St. Louis nursing home by her relatives.

According to a neighbor who knew the couple well and had seen them daily for a number of years, they had been living together very happily until the woman's stroke. Both of them had worked and shared expenses. The small house which they had owned jointly had been put in the subject's name several years earlier when the woman had been ill and temporarily out of work. The neighbor felt that the subject had been a fairly steady, stable person. He had been employed for ten years as a restaurant's pot washer and she said he drank only once a week, on his day off. On that one day, however, it had been his custom to spend all of it drinking a case of beer. Even so, she never knew this day-long drinking jag to cause him any trouble and the only arrest she had heard of was that, according to another neighbor, he had been imprisoned at Ft. Leavenworth during the Second World War because of a fight he started when someone called him a Nazi. The informant was not certain of the truth of this story nor of another neighborhood rumor that he had a legal wife alive either in Germany or somewhere else in the States. To her personal knowledge, he had no relatives in the United States and only one close friend, an elderly German lady living in St. Louis. Raised a Catholic, he was not known to have attended church.

The neighbor believed that his wife's stroke brought on the subject's sudden and severe depression. From the time the wife was taken away, he seemed totally lost and despondent and would ask his neighbors the same question over and over: "What am I going to do?" He claimed to be unable to cook or to start his furnace. He lost interest in life, was sad and joyless, and spoke frequently of his worry about how to get money and whether he would be responsible for his wife's medical bills. He looked depressed and disgusted, and complained of anorexia, insomnia, and fatigue. He cried whenever he saw his wife. He became increasingly nervous and, two months before he died, complained of dizziness associated with the nervousness.

Soon after his wife's stroke, he spoke of wanting to die. Though he also mentioned reading of other people's suicides and accidental deaths, he did not begin to speak of killing himself until about a month before his death. Then he talked of killing both himself and his wife. He became more and more preoccupied with this subject and that of guns. He also began to indicate that he believed that his wife, by falling ill, had betrayed him. He told his neighbor that she "ruined our lives when she had the stroke."

Two weeks before his suicide, the subject mailed a note to his wife's brother-in-law asking him to inform the police or his lawyer that he was going to kill himself and that he wanted his house sold and the money used for the care of his wife. After the note was received, he was not seen for several days. When he reappeared, the police were notified. They called at his house briefly, saying when they left that he was "all right."

He was seen about this time by a county social worker who arranged to have his wife transferred from the private nursing home chosen by her relatives to the state hospital. This did not seem to ease his fears and worries and he continued to appear dazed, weak, and unable to think. He spoke more and more often about suicide; so often, in fact, that one week before his death he was fired from his job because of his constant talk of it. This upset him badly and his state of mind deteriorated noticeably. He told his neighbor that he was suffering from dyspnea, abdominal pains, and sleeplessness.

On a Monday evening, his old friend, the German lady, telephoned to check on him. She reported that he had sounded drunk on the phone. On Wednesday, the neighbor went into his house to let his dog out and found his dead body on his bed. A twenty-two rifle was propped between his knees and there were two bullet wounds in his body. He had left the following note: "I fell down the cellar steps today, I might as well blow my top."

Family history: The informant had no information concerning the subject's family background or family psychiatric illness.
Arrest record: None obtained.

Case No. 056 M X F__ Age 56

ST. LOUIS SUICIDE STUDY CRITERIA FOR MAJOR AFFECTIVE DISORDER

Diagnosis required four of the six following categories, A-F. Category G was helpful in diagnosis, but not necessary.

- A. Clinically well, exclusive of attacks of major affective disorder X
- B. Previous episode(s) of major affective disorder __
- C. Discreteness (and duration) of final attack:
  - 6 months or less X
  - 12 months or less __
- D. "Medical" symptoms:
  - insomnia X
  - anorexia X
  - weight loss __
  - low energy, weakness X
  - fatigue X
  - constipation __
- E. Psychological symptoms:
  - "blue" feeling, depression, sadness X
  - diminished motor activity __
  - loss of interest X
  - diminished sexual interest and activity __
  - undertalkativeness __
  - low expectancy of recovery; expectation of "black" future __
  - feeling of being a burden __
  - indecisiveness __
  - feelings of worthlessness or guilt __
  - agitation X
  - personal untidiness __
  - difficulty in thinking and concentration X
  - delusions X
- F. Disturbances in social behavior: decreased social and recreational activity __
- G. Miscellaneous items:
  - age of onset 40 and over X
  - family history of affective disorder __

FEIGHNER CRITERIA FOR MAJOR AFFECTIVE DISORDER

Diagnosis required all three of the following categories.

- A. Dysphoric mood (depressed, sad, blue, despondent, hopeless, "down in dumps," irritable, fearful, worried, discouraged) X
- B. At least 5 of following for definite; at least 4 of following for probable:
  - poor appetite or weight loss: 2 lb/wk, 10 lb/yr X
  - sleep difficulties X
  - loss of energy (fatigue, tiredness) X
  - agitation or retardation X
  - loss of interest in usual activities or decreased sex drive X
  - complaints or actual diminished ability to think/concentrate X
  - feelings of guilt, self-reproach __
  - recurrent thoughts of death and/or suicide X
- C. A psychiatric illness lasting at least one month with no pre-existing psychiatric condition (schizophrenia, anxiety neurosis, phobic neurosis, obsessive-compulsive neurosis, hysteria, alcoholism, drug dependence, antisocial personality, homosexuality, transsexualism, mental retardation, anorexia nervosa, organic brain syndrome) or life-threatening or incapacitating illness X

057 Informants: Son, physician

This 63-year-old white carpenter had completed 7th grade and had worked for his own living since he was 13 years old. He married at 22 and he and his wife spent the 41 years of their married life in St. Louis. They had two children, a married son who also lived in St. Louis, and a married daughter who lived with her husband in the subject's six-room house. For the last ten years of his life, he had been successfully self-employed.

Five years before his death, he suffered a coronary thrombosis which was followed by progressive congestive heart disease and associated symptoms of edema, fatigue, dyspnea, palpitation, and weakness. He took life much easier after his heart attack, but continued to work steadily and to make a good income. However, his heart failure was gradually incapacitating and, a year prior to his death, he was hospitalized in an osteopathic hospital for two weeks because of dyspnea and shortness of breath. After he was released from the hospital, he gave up working and began to see his doctor, an osteopathic physician, at regular two-week intervals. The doctor supposedly told him his heart "had worn out five years before."

Ten months before his suicide, his closest sister died. Four months later he was again hospitalized for his heart condition. Once home from the hospital, he became depressed and anxious and for the last six months of his life, he complained to his doctor of a diminished sex drive and of irrational fears that his house would "cave in" or be "bombed." Twice he cried at the doctor's office as he discussed an automobile accident he had had about that time, which he felt represented a "blow by society." The doctor prescribed tranquilizers, but they aggravated his depression. With his family he displayed the symptoms of his depression—moodiness, loss of interest, insomnia, indecision, sadness, ennui. Accustomed to attending a Baptist church every Sunday, he began to attend only occasionally. He stopped going with his son to a fishing and hunting camp on the Mississippi River. He watched TV less, played cards less, and was generally less active. Despite his lack of interest in going to church services, he read the Bible a great deal during these six months. He often spoke of his fears of becoming a burden on his wife and children and of his worries about not earning any money. Though the family tried to reassure him—he owned his house, had a regular pension, and his wife worked—his despondency continued. The family urged him to see a psychiatrist, but he refused. Gradually, he stopped seeing his close friends with whom he had enjoyed a pleasantly active social life. As his son put it, "He finally just gave up." His insomnia worsened toward the end "because he was worrying," but he did not experience anorexia, constipation, or sudden weight loss (over the last five years he had gradually lost 25 pounds due to his heart condition). Other than the insomnia, no other symptoms seemed to worsen noticeably just prior to his suicide.

He was found, by his son-in-law, early one fall afternoon. He had hanged himself in his garage having left a note for his son-in-law instructing him to look in the garage and then inform his wife.

Family history: Father had been an alcoholic and had committed suicide.
Arrest record: None.

Case No. *057* M X F__ Age *63*

ST. LOUIS SUICIDE STUDY CRITERIA FOR MAJOR AFFECTIVE DISORDER

Diagnosis required four of the six following categories, A–F. Category G was helpful in diagnosis, but not necessary.

- A. Clinically well, exclusive of attacks of major affective disorder ___
- B. Previous episode(s) of major affective disorder ___
- C. Discreteness (and duration) of final attack:
  - 6 months or less X
  - 12 months or less ___
- D. "Medical" symptoms:
  - insomnia X
  - anorexia ___
  - weight loss ___
  - low energy, weakness X
  - fatigue ___
  - constipation ___
- E. Psychological symptoms:
  - "blue" feeling, depression, sadness X
  - diminished motor activity X
  - loss of interest X
  - diminished sexual interest and activity X
  - undertalkativeness ___
  - low expectancy of recovery; expectation of "black" future ___
  - feeling of being a burden X
  - indecisiveness X
  - feelings of worthlessness or guilt ___
  - agitation X
  - personal untidiness ___
  - difficulty in thinking and concentration ___
  - delusions X
- F. Disturbances in social behavior: decreased social and recreational activity X
- G. Miscellaneous items:
  - age of onset 40 and over X
  - family history of affective disorder X

FEIGHNER CRITERIA FOR MAJOR AFFECTIVE DISORDER

Diagnosis required all three of the following categories.

A. Dysphoric mood (depressed, sad, blue, despondent, hopeless, "down in dumps," irritable, fearful, worried, discouraged) __X__

B. At least 5 of following for definite; at least 4 of following for probable:
  poor appetite or weight loss: 2 lb/wk, 10 lb/yr ___
  sleep difficulties __X__
  loss of energy (fatigue, tiredness) __X__
  agitation or retardation __X__
  loss of interest in usual activities or decreased sex drive __X__
  complaints or actual diminished ability to think/concentrate ___

 feelings of guilt, self-reproach ___
 recurrent thoughts of death and/or suicide ___

C. A psychiatric illness lasting <u>at least one month</u> with no pre-existing psychiatric condition (schizophrenia, anxiety neurosis, phobic neurosis, obsessive-compulsive neurosis, hysteria, alcoholism, drug dependence, antisocial personality, homosexuality, transsexualism, mental retardation, anorexia nervosa, organic brain syndrome) or life-threatening or incapacitating illness ___

064 Informant: *Wife*

This 60-year-old white man was born in St. Louis and was an only child. The subject married at age 29 and he and his wife lived in his parents' home until a month before his suicide.

A high school graduate, the subject attended business college, and after serving two years in the Army during World War I, was employed as a trust officer in a St. Louis bank. He lost the job during the depression, and was, according to his wife, "too old" (he was 47) to find work once the depression had ended. Five years after his marriage, his mother, who disliked her son's wife, went to bed—for no obvious physical reasons—and remained there until her death five years before her son's. At about the time his mother took to her bed, the subject suffered a "nervous breakdown" after an appendectomy. This apparent depression, which occurred 31 years prior to his suicide, lasted a few months, but did not require hospitalization. The symptoms did not recur until four or five months before his death.

For the last 15 years of his life, the subject stayed at home to care for his parents while his wife worked to support the family.

After the mother's death, the father, though physically ill, remained mentally alert and the "head of the house," keeping the house keys, turning off the lights at night, and so forth. About a year and a half before his suicide, the subject, who felt he could no longer properly care for his father, put him in a nursing home. The old man never forgave his son and cursed him every time he visited. The subject would return from these visits saying he wasn't sure he could stand seeing his father again.

Four or five months prior to his suicide, he began to lose his appetite. Although he did not appear depressed to his wife, her sister felt that he was depressed. About six weeks before he died, he and his wife bought a new, smaller house. He refused to buy new furniture or clothing, saying they would wait "until the move." This was unlike him and worried his wife. Once they had moved, he was unable to sleep well and began to lose weight rapidly. He stopped watching television, but otherwise continued his usual routine. He attended church about twice a month, as was his custom, and continued to visit regularly with one or two close relatives.

The evening before his suicide he was preparing for his weekly visit to his father the next day. He assembled the things he meant to take to his father, then sat down, and, holding his head in his hands, said to his wife, "I can't face father." They went to bed early without watching the TV programs they usually saw on Saturday evenings. Unable to sleep, he woke his wife several times during the night. When he got up his mood seemed "very good." His wife was in the basement when she heard a shot and the sound of breaking glass. She rushed upstairs where she found that her husband had shot himself to death.

Family history: There was no family history of psychiatric illness. An uncle of the subject's committed suicide many years prior to the subject's death.

Arrest record: None.

Case No. _064_ M _X_ F ___ Age _60_

ST. LOUIS SUICIDE STUDY CRITERIA FOR MAJOR AFFECTIVE DISORDER

Diagnosis required four of the six following categories, A–F. Category G was helpful in diagnosis, but not necessary.

- **A.** Clinically well, exclusive of attacks of major affective disorder ___
- **B.** Previous episode(s) of major affective disorder _X_
- **C.** Discreteness (and duration) of final attack:
  - 6 months or less _X_
  - 12 months or less ___
- **D.** "Medical" symptoms:
  - insomnia _X_
  - anorexia _X_
  - weight loss _X_
  - low energy, weakness ___
  - fatigue ___
  - constipation ___
- **E.** Psychological symptoms:
  - "blue" feeling, depression, sadness _X_
  - diminished motor activity ___
  - loss of interest _X_
  - diminished sexual interest and activity ___
  - undertalkativeness ___
  - low expectancy of recovery; expectation of "black" future ___
  - feeling of being a burden ___
  - indecisiveness ___
  - feelings of worthlessness or guilt ___
  - agitation _X_
  - personal untidiness ___
  - difficulty in thinking and concentration ___
  - delusions ___
- **F.** Disturbances in social behavior: decreased social and recreational activity _X_
- **G.** Miscellaneous items:
  - age of onset 40 and over _X_
  - family history of affective disorder _X_

FEIGHNER CRITERIA FOR MAJOR AFFECTIVE DISORDER

Diagnosis required all three of the following categories.

- **A.** Dysphoric mood (depressed, sad, blue, despondent, hopeless, "down in dumps," irritable, fearful, worried, discouraged) _X_
- **B.** At least 5 of following for definite; at least 4 of following for probable:
  - poor appetite or weight loss: 2 lb/wk, 10 lb/yr _X_
  - sleep difficulties _X_
  - loss of energy (fatigue, tiredness) ___
  - agitation or retardation ___
  - loss of interest in usual activities or decreased sex drive _X_
  - complaints or actual diminished ability to think/concentrate ___
  - feelings of guilt, self-reproach _X_
  - recurrent thoughts of death and/or suicide ___
- **C.** A psychiatric illness lasting <u>at least one month</u> with no pre-existing psychiatric condition (schizophrenia, anxiety neurosis, phobic neurosis, obsessive-compulsive neurosis, hysteria, alcoholism, drug dependence, antisocial personality, homosexuality, transsexualism, mental retardation, anorexia nervosa, organic brain syndrome) or life-threatening or incapacitating illness _X_

071 Informants: Brother, landlady, hospital records

This 63-year-old white worker in a shoe factory had never married and was living alone in a rooming house at the time of his death. The second of five children born to an immigrant couple, he had quit school in the fifth grade to help support his family. By the time of his suicide, he had worked in factories for 53 years. A younger brother described the subject as never having been close to any of his siblings, as having had easily hurt feelings, and as having been a "loner."

On Christmas, about one year before his suicide, the subject had spent the day with his brother and other members of the family. He was, at that time, said to have been his usual self—"not happy, not sad." Three months later his landlady telephoned the younger brother to say that she wished he would come to visit the subject as he had lost a lot of weight and she was worried about him. When the brother arrived at the rooming house, he found the subject lying in bed in dirty clothes and greatly in need of a bath. His rooms were cluttered and his weight had dropped 70 pounds to 130. The subject, who was angry at the intrusion, told his brother that he "had nothing to live for" and that he figured he would just stop eating altogether until he died. The brother took the subject home with him, made him bathe, and fed him a large meal which he ate hungrily. The brother then took responsibility for seeing to the subject's welfare and had him in for a meal and TV several times a week until his death nine months later.

In May the subject was taken by his brother to the outpatient clinic of a psychiatric hospital. This was done near the time of a suicide attempt on the subject's part, but the brother could not recall whether the first visit to the clinic was preceded or followed by the attempt. In any case, the hospital records note that the patient reported a gradual onset of malaise with loss of interest, insomnia, worry about the future, weight loss, and a feeling that "life was not worth living." The records also noted "no crying, no delusions." The patient admitted having thought of suicide two years before, when he had lost a job. He also told the doctors that his New Year's resolution had been to stop drinking beer and this had ended his custom of stopping every evening after work at a neighborhood tavern to drink beer with the other regular customers. Thus, for four months, he had cut himself off from his main source of outside contact.

The hospital records noted that, one and a half months later, the patient had had two electroshock treatments and was "better—eats and sleeps good." The records showed that two weeks later he had been found by his landlady in the basement of the rooming house with a rope, but that he had insisted he was there to do his laundry. He was due to come back to the clinic for further shock treatment, but had never returned.

For the last six months of his life, the subject seemed to his brother to be "fine again." He did, perhaps, speak a little less and complained of a shoulder pain, but otherwise, he appeared to his brother and sister-in-law to be more or less recovered. He regained 35 pounds, continued to work regularly, and also continued to visit them three or four times a week. Nine months after the brother had found the subject in his room, there was a severe cold snap and the subject did not go to his brother's house for several consecutive evenings, nor did he go out to his job for that week. At the end of that week, the brother was notified by the landlady that his body had been found in his rooms. He had hanged himself by looping a cord around a door hinge and then around his neck. He had then slipped off the chair he had been sitting on. He left no note.

Family history: One brother had "taken to drink" excessively for one year, at the end of which he had died of pneumonia. There was no further family history of psychiatric illness.
Arrest record: None.

Case No. *071* M _X_ F ___ Age *63*

ST. LOUIS SUICIDE STUDY CRITERIA FOR MAJOR AFFECTIVE DISORDER

Diagnosis required four of the six following categories, A–F. Category G was helpful in diagnosis, but not necessary.

A. Clinically well, exclusive of attacks of major affective disorder _X_

B. Previous episode(s) of major affective disorder ___

C. Discreteness (and duration) of final attack:
   6 months or less ___
   12 months or less _X_

D. "Medical" symptoms:
   insomnia _X_
   anorexia ___
   weight loss _X_
   low energy, weakness ___
   fatigue ___
   constipation ___

E. Psychological symptoms:
   "blue" feeling, depression, sadness _X_
   diminished motor activity _X_
   loss of interest _X_
   diminished sexual interest and activity ___
   undertalkativeness _X_
   low expectancy of recovery; expectation of "black" future _X_
   feeling of being a burden ___
   indecisiveness ___
   feelings of worthlessness or guilt ___
   agitation ___
   personal untidiness _X_
   difficulty in thinking and concentration ___
   delusions ___

F. Disturbances in social behavior: decreased social and recreational activity _X_

G. Miscellaneous items:
   age of onset 40 and over _X_
   family history of affective disorder ___

FEIGHNER CRITERIA FOR MAJOR AFFECTIVE DISORDER

Diagnosis required all three of the following categories.

A. Dysphoric mood (depressed, sad, blue, despondent, hopeless, "down in dumps," irritable, fearful, worried, discouraged) __X__

B. At least 5 of following for definite; at least 4 of following for probable:
 - poor appetite or weight loss: 2 lb/wk, 10 lb/yr __X__
 - sleep difficulties __X__
 - loss of energy (fatigue, tiredness) ____
 - agitation or retardation ____
 - loss of interest in usual activities or decreased sex drive __X__
 - complaints or actual diminished ability to think/concentrate ____
 - feelings of guilt, self-reproach ____
 - recurrent thoughts of death and/or suicide __X__

C. A psychiatric illness lasting <u>at least one month</u> with no pre-existing psychiatric condition (schizophrenia, anxiety neurosis, phobic neurosis, obsessive-compulsive neurosis, hysteria, alcoholism, drug dependence, antisocial personality, homosexuality, transsexualism, mental retardation, anorexia nervosa, organic brain syndrome) or life-threatening or incapacitating illness __X__

089 *Informants: Foster son, Catholic Charity records*

The family of this 62-year-old white man was reluctant to give an interview and though his foster son finally agreed, the interview was brief and did not provide many details.

The subject was the son of a farmer and, when his father retired, he took over the family farm and ran it for the next 40-odd years. He and his wife had one child, a daughter who died at age five. Twenty years later, they applied to a Catholic adoption agency for a foster child and their foster son went to live with them when he was 14 years old. According to the agency records, the subject and his wife were good, intelligent people and treated the foster child as if he were their natural son.

The subject is said to have always worked hard and been happy on the family farm. However, about two and a half years before his suicide, he sold it to a developer, moved to a house in suburban St. Louis, and went to work as a truck driver for the County Highway Department. From that time on, he was sad and depressed. His son said he lost interest in everything and that he told his family there was nothing for him to live for. He also stated that, without his farm to work, he was useless. He rarely smiled and complained that he could not sleep.

During the last two years of his life, he bought—and immediately sold—two other farms. He had shown great enthusiasm before the actual purchases, but once the final papers were signed, had insisted that he had made a mistake and made arrangements for resales. He was, just prior to his suicide, in the midst of this process for the third time and was to have signed the final purchase papers for a farm the day after his suicide.

His son reported that the subject had long suffered from a stomach ailment which required that he drink much milk and cream. This had caused him to gain 60 pounds, all of which he lost gradually over the last few years of his life.

Three weeks before he died, the subject was temporarily laid off by the Highway Department. He worried a great deal about money because of this, but his son believed that there had been a good bit of money in his savings. In the very last weeks, the subject had seemed slightly better to his son.

He committed suicide by shooting himself. No details of the act were given.

Family history: No information was given.
Arrest record: None.

Case No. 089 M X F __ Age 62

ST. LOUIS SUICIDE STUDY CRITERIA FOR MAJOR AFFECTIVE DISORDER

Diagnosis required four of the six following categories, A-F. Category G was helpful in diagnosis, but not necessary.

- A. Clinically well, exclusive of attacks of major affective disorder X
- B. Previous episode(s) of major affective disorder X
- C. Discreteness (and duration) of final attack:
  - 6 months or less ___
  - 12 months or less ___
- D. "Medical" symptoms:
  - insomnia X
  - anorexia ___
  - weight loss X
  - low energy, weakness fatigue ___
  - constipation ___
- E. Psychological symptoms:
  - "blue" feeling, depression, sadness X
  - diminished motor activity ___
  - loss of interest X
  - diminished sexual interest and activity ___
  - undertalkativeness ___
  - low expectancy of recovery; expectation of "black" future ___
  - feeling of being a burden X
  - indecisiveness X
  - feelings of worthlessness or guilt X
  - agitation ___
  - personal untidiness ___
  - difficulty in thinking and concentration ___
  - delusions ___
- F. Disturbances in social behavior: decreased social and recreational activity ___
- G. Miscellaneous items:
  - age of onset 40 and over X
  - family history of affective disorder ___

FEIGHNER CRITERIA FOR MAJOR AFFECTIVE DISORDER

Diagnosis required all three of the following categories.

- A. Dysphoric mood (depressed, sad, blue, despondent, hopeless, "down in dumps," irritable, fearful, worried, discouraged) X
- B. At least 5 of following for definite; at least 4 of following for probable:
  - poor appetite or weight loss: 2 lb/wk, 10 lb/yr X
  - sleep difficulties X
  - loss of energy (fatigue, tiredness) ___
  - agitation or retardation ___
  - loss of interest in usual activities or decreased sex drive X
  - complaints or actual diminished ability to think/concentrate ___
  - feelings of guilt, self-reproach X
  - recurrent thoughts of death and/or suicide ___
- C. A psychiatric illness lasting <u>at least one month</u> with no pre-existing psychiatric condition (schizophrenia, anxiety neurosis, phobic neurosis, obsessive-compulsive neurosis, hysteria, alcoholism, drug dependence, antisocial personality, homosexuality, transsexualism, mental retardation, anorexia nervosa, organic brain syndrome) or life-threatening or incapacitating illness X

092 Informants: Brother, physician, hospital records

This 65-year-old white man was raised a Catholic and remained devoutly religious all his life. He left school after the fifth grade and went to work at age 13. He married at about age 25 and was the father of two daughters.

Although the subject was a chronic alcoholic, he had, according to his brother, been a "happy" man who loved his wife very much and was good to her. He had worked for the same steel company for 46 years as foundry foreman. For the last three or four years, in preparation for his retirement, he had been head of security police at the foundry. His brother described his alcoholism as taking the form of not very heavy daily drinking ("one or two beers a night") interspersed with yearly benders which often caused him to be hospitalized for "straightening out." Seven or eight months prior to his suicide, he had gone on one of these binges because he felt he was being eased out of his job by a younger man. He was hospitalized for three weeks following that bender and, when released, seemed to his brother and wife unusually depressed. He was more nervous and complained of fatigue, weakness, insomnia, and anorexia. His weight dropped 30 pounds in the last six months of his life. He began to see his doctor regularly due to his worry about his health, which he felt he had ruined with alcohol. He was despondent, lethargic, and restless around the house and uninterested in keeping up his property. He looked depressed and lost interest in his appearance and cleanliness. In the last two months of his life, he lost his taste for liquor and beer and stopped drinking almost altogether.

According to his brother, about a month before his suicide, he seemed to feel a little better and, though his insomnia and anorexia continued, he stopped seeing his doctor.

The physician's report differed slightly from that of the subject's brother. He diagnosed the subject as an alcoholic of long standing with cirrhosis and depression. He had had to hospitalize him several times following his drinking bouts and felt he was definitely suicidal. After the last hospitalization during which he had received electroshock treatments, the doctor had recommended that he be institutionalized. The family refused. The doctor also reported that the subject had not retired from his job, but had been fired because of his drinking.

Old hospital records indicated repeated hospitalizations for alcoholism over the last 20 years of the subject's life. According to one report, he had experienced a similar depressive episode ten years earlier, which had also been precipitated by fears of being replaced in his job. At that time he admitted his daily, non-bender quota of whiskey to be "three or four shots."

The subject missed mass the Sunday before his suicide, a lapse extremely unusual for him. The next morning, he got up at his usual time, put trousers

Affective Disorder—The Largest Group

and a shirt on over his pajamas and went down to the basement of his house to stoke the furnace. Awhile later, when he had not come up again, his wife went to the basement and discovered that he had hanged himself from a ceiling pipe. He left no note.

Family history: A sister had committed suicide 20 years previously during a "nervous breakdown." The subject's father had been a chronic alcoholic.
Arrest record: None.

Case No. *098* M X F __ Age *65*

ST. LOUIS SUICIDE STUDY CRITERIA FOR MAJOR AFFECTIVE DISORDER

Diagnosis required four of the six following categories, A-F. Category G was helpful in diagnosis, but not necessary.

- A. Clinically well, exclusive of attacks of major affective disorder ___
- B. Previous episode(s) of major affective disorder X
- C. Discreteness (and duration) of final attack:
    - 6 months or less ___
    - 12 months or less X
- D. "Medical" symptoms:
    - insomnia X
    - anorexia X
    - weight loss X
    - low energy, weakness X
    - fatigue X
    - constipation ___
- E. Psychological symptoms:
    - "blue" feeling, depression, sadness X
    - diminished motor activity X
    - loss of interest X
    - diminished sexual interest and activity ___
    - undertalkativeness ___
    - low expectancy of recovery; expectation of "black" future ___
    - feeling of being a burden ___
    - indecisiveness ___
    - feelings of worthlessness or guilt ___
    - agitation X
    - personal untidiness X
    - difficulty in thinking and concentration ___
    - delusions ___
- F. Disturbances in social behavior: decreased social and recreational activity ___
- G. Miscellaneous items:
    - age of onset 40 and over X
    - family history of affective disorder X

FEIGHNER CRITERIA FOR MAJOR AFFECTIVE DISORDER

Diagnosis required all three of the following categories.

A. Dysphoric mood (depressed, sad, blue, despondent, hopeless, "down in dumps," irritable, fearful, worried, discouraged) _X_

B. At least 5 of following for definite; at least 4 of following for probable:
   poor appetite or weight loss: 2 lb/wk, 10 lb/yr _X_
   sleep difficulties _X_
   loss of energy (fatigue, tiredness) _X_
   agitation or retardation _X_
   loss of interest in usual activities or decreased sex drive _X_
   complaints or actual diminished ability to think/concentrate ___
   feelings of guilt, self-reproach ___
   recurrent thoughts of death and/or suicide ___

C. A psychiatric illness lasting <u>at least one month</u> with no pre-existing psychiatric condition (schizophrenia, anxiety neurosis, phobic neurosis, obsessive-compulsive neurosis, hysteria, alcoholism, drug dependence, antisocial personality, homosexuality, transsexualism, mental retardation, anorexia nervosa, organic brain syndrome) or life-threatening or incapacitating illness _X_

093 Informants: Friend and employee, attorney, police records (murder + suicide)

This 62-year-old white pharmacist and owner of his own drug store was a member of a prominent Latin American family. As a young man he had come to St. Louis to study medicine. He met a local girl and married her. For unknown reasons, he changed from medicine to pharmacy and received a degree cum laude. During their marriage his wife became increasingly and grotesquely fat. In addition, she developed an illness and though she was operated on she continued to become more and more of an invalid. They had not had sexual relations for years and she had not left the house for more than two years prior to his death. For the last 10 or 15 years, he had had a black mistress and his wife, aware of this relationship, made his life at home miserable.

Despite these many problems, he had remained an effective pharmacist and manager of his store. He was a hard worker, arriving at work at 8:30 AM and not leaving until 10 PM. He had little or no social life. Until 18 months prior to his suicide, he had never shown any signs of nervousness, or unusual behavior. At that time, he began to be nervous, tense, and irritable. About a year before his death he suggested to his wife that they both commit suicide. Except for the moderate nervousness and irritability noted above, the informant had, at that time, noted no disturbances in his behavior. Shortly afterward a competitor opened a drug store in the same block and business slackened greatly. In spite of this, he was not in financial difficulties and left an estate of $80,000.

During the last six months of his life he became increasingly nervous and irritable. At work he paced back and forth, waving his arms, and telling his employees all his troubles. He was disgusted with himself and with the state of the world, often saying, "The world has gone to hell." As his depression and sadness increased, he lost interest in his work. The informant knew of no other symptoms, such as weight loss, anorexia, or insomnia. His attorney, on the other hand, believed he did have insomnia and there was a note written to the attorney in which he mentioned that his "mind was going," without elaborating on the meaning of this statement.

On the day of his suicide, just as he was leaving the drug store, he turned and, with a flamboyant gesture, shouted to his employees, "Goodbye, everybody!" This behavior, as well as that described above, was distinctly unusual for him. He went home and that evening he killed his wife, by hitting her several times in the head with a hatchet as she lay in bed. He then committed suicide with poison. The informant was surprised that he had killed his wife, suggesting that perhaps he had not planned to kill her but had done it because he felt she could not take care of herself without him. The informant also stated that he believed his wife had an abdominal malignancy and might have killed her out of mercy.

Family history: There was no history of psychiatric illness in the subject's family.
Arrest record: One arrest for a moving traffic offense at age 43.

Case No. 093 M X F __ Age 62

ST. LOUIS SUICIDE STUDY CRITERIA FOR MAJOR AFFECTIVE DISORDER

Diagnosis required four of the six following categories, A-F. Category G was helpful in diagnosis, but not necessary.

- A. Clinically well, exclusive of attacks of major affective disorder **X**
- B. Previous episode(s) of major affective disorder **X**
- C. Discreteness (and duration) of final attack:
  - 6 months or less **X**
  - 12 months or less ___
- D. "Medical" symptoms:
  - insomnia **X**
  - anorexia ___
  - weight loss ___
  - low energy, weakness ___
  - fatigue ___
  - constipation ___
- E. Psychological symptoms:
  - "blue" feeling, depression, sadness ___
  - diminished motor activity ___
  - loss of interest **X**
  - diminished sexual interest and activity ___
  - undertalkativeness ___
  - low expectancy of recovery; expectation of "black" future ___
  - feeling of being a burden ___
  - indecisiveness ___
  - feelings of worthlessness or guilt **X**
  - agitation **X**
  - personal untidiness ___
  - difficulty in thinking and concentration **X**
  - delusions ___
- F. Disturbances in social behavior: decreased social and recreational activity ___
- G. Miscellaneous items:
  - age of onset 40 and over ___
  - family history of affective disorder **X**

FEIGHNER CRITERIA FOR MAJOR AFFECTIVE DISORDER

Diagnosis required all three of the following categories.

- A. Dysphoric mood (depressed, sad, blue, despondent, hopeless, "down in dumps," irritable, fearful, worried, discouraged) **X**
- B. At least 5 of following for definite; at least 4 of following for probable:
  - poor appetite or weight loss: 2 lb/wk, 10 lb/yr ___
  - sleep difficulties **X**
  - loss of energy (fatigue, tiredness) **X**
  - agitation or retardation **X**
  - loss of interest in usual activities or decreased sex drive **X**
  - complaints or actual diminished ability to think/concentrate **X**
  - feelings of guilt, self-reproach ___
  - recurrent thoughts of death and/or suicide **X**
- C. A psychiatric illness lasting <u>at least one month</u> with no pre-existing psychiatric condition (schizophrenia, anxiety neurosis, phobic neurosis, obsessive-compulsive neurosis, hysteria, alcoholism, drug dependence, antisocial personality, homosexuality, transsexualism, mental retardation, anorexia nervosa, organic brain syndrome) or life-threatening or incapacitating illness **X**

110 Informants: Wife, physician, hospital records

This 63-year-old black man had married a second wife 23 years his junior four years prior to his suicide. Because she had not known him for very long, the wife was unable to provide complete information about his background.

She did know that he had been educated to the 4th grade and had lived in St. Louis for more than 30 years. His first marriage, which lasted some 30 years and produced four children, was ended by his first wife's death. His occupation for the last 37 years of his life was hide stripper and butcher. He had worked for a national packing company for 32 years and for a smaller, local packing company for the last five years. He belonged to no social clubs, had few friends, and confined his social life mostly to visiting relatives. He drank only occasionally and moderately. He was living with his wife and her 11-year-old daughter at the time of his death.

A daughter by his first marriage is reported to have stated that her father had had "a nervous breakdown" 20 years previously and had attempted suicide at that time.

Two months before his death, he began to suffer from nervousness, weakness, insomnia, and irritability, symptoms his wife had never before known him to have. One month before his death, his irritability toward his wife had developed into anger and he beat her severely several times. He complained of chills and fever, of abdominal pain, of weakness, and of anorexia and insomnia. By that time, he felt too "poorly" to work and spent most of his days at home in bed. Believing he might be suffering from a "virus," he went to a hospital where he described the above symptoms as well as hoarseness, dizziness, a weight loss of 19 pounds, and a reduction in sex drive. He told the doctors he had experienced a similar episode 12 years earlier which had lasted six weeks. Hospital records noted, in addition to his other symptoms, "mild depression."

Because hospital x-rays indicated an unidentifiable abdominal mass, he was operated on for a stomach biopsy and, at the same time, his appendix was removed. The biopsy results were entirely negative. The subject was informed of this and released from the hospital as soon as he had recovered from the operation.

At home from the hospital for three days, his depression and irritability continued and he seemed unconvinced that he did not have stomach cancer. His insomnia persisted and the night before his suicide he again beat his wife cruelly. The next night, she went to bed before he did. She was awakened at 5 AM by a shot, got up, and discovered her husband's body in another room. No note was found.

Family history: The informant did not have information concerning psychiatric illness in the subject's family history.
Arrest record: None.

Case No. 110 M X F __ Age 63

ST. LOUIS SUICIDE STUDY CRITERIA FOR MAJOR AFFECTIVE DISORDER

Diagnosis required four of the six following categories, A-F. Category G was helpful in diagnosis, but not necessary.

- A. Clinically well, exclusive of attacks of major affective disorder X
- B. Previous episode(s) of major affective disorder X
- C. Discreteness (and duration) of final attack:
  - 6 months or less X
  - 12 months or less __
- D. "Medical" symptoms:
  - insomnia X
  - anorexia X
  - weight loss X
  - low energy, weakness X
  - fatigue __
  - constipation __
- E. Psychological symptoms:
  - "blue" feeling, depression, sadness X
  - diminished motor activity X
  - loss of interest __
  - diminished sexual interest and activity X
  - undertalkativeness __
  - low expectancy of recovery; expectation of "black" future X
  - feeling of being a burden __
  - indecisiveness __
  - feelings of worthlessness or guilt __
  - agitation X
  - personal untidiness __
  - difficulty in thinking and concentration __
  - delusions __
- F. Disturbances in social behavior: decreased social and recreational activity __
- G. Miscellaneous items:
  - age of onset 40 and over X
  - family history of affective disorder __

FEIGHNER CRITERIA FOR MAJOR AFFECTIVE DISORDER

Diagnosis required all three of the following categories.

- A. Dysphoric mood (depressed, sad, blue, despondent, hopeless, "down in dumps," irritable, fearful, worried, discouraged) X
- B. At least 5 of following for definite; at least 4 of following for probable:
  - poor appetite or weight loss: 2 lb/wk, 10 lb/yr X
  - sleep difficulties X
  - loss of energy (fatigue, tiredness) X
  - agitation or retardation __
  - loss of interest in usual activities or decreased sex drive X
  - complaints or actual diminished ability to think/concentrate __
  - feelings of guilt, self-reproach __
  - recurrent thoughts of death and/or suicide __
- C. A psychiatric illness lasting at least one month with no pre-existing psychiatric condition (schizophrenia, anxiety neurosis, phobic neurosis, obsessive-compulsive neurosis, hysteria, alcoholism, drug dependence, antisocial personality, homosexuality, transsexualism, mental retardation, anorexia nervosa, organic brain syndrome) or life-threatening or incapacitating illness X

127 Informants: Brother, physician

This 65-year-old white married man was scheduled to have eye surgery three days after his suicide. His brother believed he was afraid of the operation and that he was not confident that it would be successful.

Born and raised in St. Louis, he finished six years of school and had, at the time of his death, been working to support himself for well over 45 years. He had been married twice. The first marriage, which lasted an unspecified length of time, ended in divorce due to the wife's infidelity. The second marriage, still formally intact at his death, produced one child, a son.

Seven months before his death, the subject had had to give up his 20-year job as a stationery engraver because of his failing sight. This happened just before he was eligible to retire and receive social security benefits. Shortly thereafter, he moved from his and his wife's house in the suburbs to his brother's house in St. Louis, ostensibly to be closer to the eye specialist. However, his brother indicated that troubles with his wife made the move doubly practical for the subject. He was not a sociable man and rarely saw his three or four close friends. Even so, he did enjoy visiting his various relatives every Sunday with his brother.

By the time of his death, he had lost 90% of his vision and the eye specialist who was treating him had planned an operation to remove cataracts from each eye. According to his brother, the subject was skeptical of the doctor's assurances that he would be "OK" after the operation and he was afraid that, instead, he would be left totally blind. The subject also feared cancer, a disease from which his mother had died. The eye doctor, when contacted after the subject's suicide, reported that his patient seemed to him to be alert and intelligent and "not particularly depressed, although he was the type."

According to his brother, the subject had not seemed depressed or especially fearful until about four weeks before his suicide. At that time, he had begun to express his fear of the operation, his depression and disgust at his condition, and his fear of cancer. He said he was having trouble getting to sleep at night and that his thoughts kept him awake. He also complained of fatigue and weakness, but what struck his brother as most unusual was his refusal to make the Sunday visits to relatives which he had always enjoyed. His brother could not remember his ever having been nervous or depressed prior to this episode and felt certain that his depression was an entirely new condition.

On the day of his suicide, the subject's brother left for work. He called him, as was his custom, to check on his brother. When he got no answer, he called again later in the morning and still got no answer. When he arrived home at 3 PM, he found his brother dead in bed, having shot himself in the head. A neighbor later recalled having heard what sounded like a shot about 7 AM. There was no note.

Family history: There was no family history of psychiatric illness.
Arrest record: None.

Case No *127* M *X* F __ Age *65*

ST. LOUIS SUICIDE STUDY CRITERIA FOR MAJOR AFFECTIVE DISORDER

Diagnosis required four of the six following categories, A-F. Category G was helpful in diagnosis, but not necessary.

A. Clinically well, exclusive of attacks of major affective disorder _X_

B. Previous episode(s) of major affective disorder ___

C. Discreteness (and duration) of final attack:
    6 months or less _X_
    12 months or less ___

D. "Medical" symptoms:
    insomnia _X_
    anorexia ___
    weight loss ___
    low energy, weakness _X_
    fatigue _X_
    constipation ___

E. Psychological symptoms:
    "blue" feeling, depression, sadness _X_
    diminished motor activity ___
    loss of interest _X_
    diminished sexual interest and activity ___
    undertalkativeness ___
    low expectancy of recovery; expectation of "black" future _X_
    feeling of being a burden ___
    indecisiveness ___
    feelings of worthlessness or guilt ___
    agitation ___
    personal untidiness ___
    difficulty in thinking and concentration ___
    delusions _X_

F. Disturbances in social behavior: decreased social and recreational activity _X_

G. Miscellaneous items:
    age of onset 40 and over ___
    family history of affective disorder ___

FEIGHNER CRITERIA FOR MAJOR AFFECTIVE DISORDER

Diagnosis required all three of the following categories.

A. Dysphoric mood (depressed, sad, blue, despondent, hopeless, "down in dumps," irritable, fearful, worried, discouraged) _X_

B. At least 5 of following for definite; at least 4 of following for probable:
   poor appetite or weight loss: 2 lb/wk, 10 lb/yr ___
   sleep difficulties _X_
   loss of energy (fatigue, tiredness) _X_
   agitation or retardation ___
   loss of interest in usual activities or decreased sex drive _X_
   complaints or actual diminished ability to think/concentrate ___
   feelings of guilt, self-reproach ___
   recurrent thoughts of death and/or suicide _X_

C. A psychiatric illness lasting <u>at least one month</u> with no pre-existing psychiatric condition (schizophrenia, anxiety neurosis, phobic neurosis, obsessive-compulsive neurosis, hysteria, alcoholism, drug dependence, antisocial personality, homosexuality, transsexualism, mental retardation, anorexia nervosa, organic brain syndrome) or life-threatening or incapacitating illness _X_

131 Informants: Wife, psychiatrist

This 49-year-old white married man had suffered from convulsions for 20 years as the result of a lesion of one temporal lobe and was, according to his psychiatrist, organically impaired and "of limited ability to handle stress." He finished six grades of school. He was said to have been unpopular with other children, which his mother had always explained as being due to his severe psoriasis, but others felt that he had been distinctly "odd" even as a child. In adolescence, he and some other boys were caught trying to steal a car and he spent a short time in reform school. His mother had related that once in his youth he had told her, while shaving, that someday he would slit his throat from "ear to ear."

He married at the age of 21 and his wife described the early years of their marriage as turbulent. He was a drinker and a womanizer, always loud and boisterous when drunk, and had been jailed for drunk driving and disorderly conduct several times. At age 29, he suffered what his wife called "a nervous breakdown" during which his behavior became very peculiar. She said he had been constantly "on the go," that he had listened to the radio turned up full blast, drunk excessively, and laughed and cried alternately. He believed (incorrectly) that he had a lot of money to spend and one evening he brought another woman home to sleep in their bed. The night before he was committed to a state sanitarium, he slept with a butcher knife in his grasp. He spent six months at the sanitarium where his condition was diagnosed as syphillis of the central nervous system and was treated with heavy metals and malaria. During his hospitalization, he developed convulsions which were kept under partial control with dilantin and phenobarbital. His wife felt that his personality had changed after his releaase from the sanitarium, and that he was much quieter and easier to live with although he was "never happy again except when he was drunk." He continued to drink heavily (two cases of beer a week) and sometimes, when drunk, he made vague allusions to killing himself, such as "Don't be surprised if something should happen to me" and requests that his body be "given to medical science." A year after leaving the hospital, he opened an auto repair shop and did well with it until, according to his wife, he began to lose his mechanical skill three years later. At that point, he found work at a brewery. His convulsions continued and he also experienced "blank blackouts" which were always preceded by olfactory auras. Because of this, his wife limited their social life to home visits with very old friends as she worried about new acquaintances not understanding her husband's condition and unwittingly hurting his feelings. She described him as a man whose feelings had always been easily hurt, and as always have been "neurotic," sickly, sensitive, nervous, and "high-strung." She also reported that he had always cried easily.

After four years at the brewery, he lost his job and was unable to find another until nine years before his death when he got a job as caretaker at an estate. Three years before his death, he fell from a truck and fractured his spine. His wife felt that this may have precipitated a gradual decline in his state of mind. Both she and the subject's doctor believed that he had looked increasingly depressed during the last three years, that his feelings of guilt at not being a good provider and his worry about losing his mind "again" began to get the better of him. His wife said that he complained more and more of fatigue, weakness, of his work getting harder, and of back pain. She also reported that his sex drive was diminished during those years and that he drank far less than he had previously.

A year before his death, his mother, who had been living with them, had to be put in a nursing home due to her senility. The subject's sisters refused to help financially which caused friction and further money worries. Four months before his suicide, he became obviously worse. His convulsions increased in frequency. He suffered from "forgetfulness" (or so he feared), insomnia, anorexia, weight loss, and a loss of interest, especially in TV and reading. Having lost his caretaking job and been out of work for several months, he had, ten days before his death, been hired as caretaker at another estate and had just moved into the house provided there.

The day before he died, the subject and his wife visited his mother. After the visit, he seemed happier than usual and they went on to his brother-in-law's to play cards. However, on the way home, he said, "I used to remember the Lord's Prayer, but I've even forgotten that."

The next morning, when his wife woke about 7, he was not in bed. She found him unconscious on the living room sofa, his face cold and clammy, but his body warm. She thought he was having a convulsion, covered him with blankets, and went for help. He was taken by ambulance to a hospital where he died shortly after arriving. Later a note was found indicating that he had taken pills intended for his mother because he "needed them for his back and arm" (he had burned his arm recently and it was still painful). His psychiatrist, who had seen him most recently ten months before his death, felt that due to his inability to handle stress, family problems had accumulated to the point that he felt he couldn't cope and he had simply taken a quick way out from under the pressure.

Family history: All the members of his immediate family were described as "nervous" and his father had been a chronic alcoholic.

Arrest history: Arrest as juvenile offender (car theft). Several arrests as adult, for drunken driving, peace disturbance, drunk and disorderly conduct.

Case No. 131 M _X_ F __ Age 49

ST. LOUIS SUICIDE STUDY CRITERIA FOR MAJOR AFFECTIVE DISORDER

Diagnosis required four of the six following categories, A–F. Category G was helpful in diagnosis, but not necessary.

- A. Clinically well, exclusive of attacks of major affective disorder —
- B. Previous episode(s) of major affective disorder —
- C. Discreteness (and duration) of final attack:
  - 6 months or less X
  - 12 months or less —
- D. "Medical" symptoms:
  - insomnia X
  - anorexia X
  - weight loss X
  - low energy, weakness X
  - fatigue X
  - constipation —
- E. Psychological symptoms:
  - "blue" feeling, depression, sadness X
  - diminished motor activity —
  - loss of interest X
  - diminished sexual interest and activity X
  - undertalkativeness —
  - low expectancy of recovery; expectation of "black" future —
  - feeling of being a burden X
  - indecisiveness —
  - feelings of worthlessness or guilt X
  - agitation —
  - personal untidiness —
  - difficulty in thinking and concentration X
  - delusions X
- F. Disturbances in social behavior: decreased social and recreational activity X
- G. Miscellaneous items:
  - age of onset 40 and over X
  - family history of affective disorder X

FEIGHNER CRITERIA FOR MAJOR AFFECTIVE DISORDER

Diagnosis required all three of the following categories.

- A. Dysphoric mood (depressed, sad, blue, despondent, hopeless, "down in dumps," irritable, fearful, worried, discouraged) X
- B. At least 5 of following for definite; at least 4 of following for probable:
  - poor appetite or weight loss: 2 lb/wk, 10 lb/yr X
  - sleep difficulties X
  - loss of energy (fatigue, tiredness) X
  - agitation or retardation —
  - loss of interest in usual activities or decreased sex drive X
  - complaints or actual diminished ability to think/concentrate X
  - feelings of guilt, self-reproach X
  - recurrent thoughts of death and/or suicide X
- C. A psychiatric illness lasting at least one month with no pre-existing psychiatric condition (schizophrenia, anxiety neurosis, phobic neurosis, obsessive-compulsive neurosis, hysteria, alcoholism, drug dependence, antisocial personality, homosexuality, transsexualism, mental retardation, anorexia nervosa, organic brain syndrome) or life-threatening or incapacitating illness X

132 Informants: Wife, hospital records

This 66-year-old white married man had finished 8th grade, married at age 21, and worked for more than 40 years as a clerk with a railroad company. He and his wife had one child, a son who was killed in the Korean War.

The subject, described by his wife as "nervous," was not, in her opinion, a particularly sensitive or moody person. He was not sociable and rarely saw anyone other than his wife and her sister. His only membership in an organization was in the railroad workers' union. Although the subject's physical health was generally good, he had in the last several years of his life suffered from increasingly severe arthritis.

Seven years before his suicide, he experienced a first depressive episode which lasted about three weeks. Following his spontaneous recovery, he was completely well until about five months before his death. At that time, he was having a great deal of discomfort and pain from his arthritis which finally forced him to take laeave from work. His wife remembered that about a month before he took the sick leave, he had told her that his superiors at the office had begun to give him a great deal of extra work and that they put pressure on him to finish it quickly. At the railroad hospital, doctors treated the arthritis with "some new drug" (not cortisone) which helped the pain but seemed to precipitate a second depressive episode. He began to complain of insomnia, forgetfulness, nervousness about his work, fatigue, and a feeling of worthlessness. His wife said he put up a "good front" at work and with outsiders, but when alone with her, "he let his true feelings show." Apparently they were very sad feelings and he asked his regular physician for "shock treatment," but was told he didn't need it. He began to lose interest in everything around him, lost all interest in sex, and complained about his inability to concentrate. Six weeks before his death, he told his wife he was no good for anything anymore, that he knew he would never get well, and that he was going to kill himself. She responded by asking what would happen to her. Three weeks before his suicide, he woke her during the night to tell her he was "afraid," but she never asked him what it was he feared.

He was hospitalized by his doctor briefly a month before his suicide, both for treatment of his painful arthritis and because of his depression. For the last two weeks he cried uncontrollably and he often stated his fear that he was "losing his mind."

On the day of his suicide, a Sunday, his wife left him alone in the house while she went to church. When she returned she found that he had hanged himself. He left no note.

Family history: There was no family history of psychiatric illness.
Arrest record: None.

Case No. 132 M X F __ Age 66

ST. LOUIS SUICIDE STUDY CRITERIA FOR MAJOR AFFECTIVE DISORDER

Diagnosis required four of the six following categories, A–F. Category G was helpful in diagnosis, but not necessary.

- A. Clinically well, exclusive of attacks of major affective disorder ___
- B. Previous episode(s) of major affective disorder X
- C. Discreteness (and duration) of final attack:
  - 6 months or less X
  - 12 months or less ___
- D. "Medical" symptoms:
  - insomnia X
  - anorexia ___
  - weight loss ___
  - low energy, weakness fatigue X
  - constipation ___
- E. Psychological symptoms:
  - "blue" feeling, depression, sadness X
  - diminished motor activity X
  - loss of interest X
  - diminished sexual interest and activity X
  - undertalkativeness ___
  - low expectancy of recovery; expectation of "black" future X
  - feeling of being a burden X
  - indecisiveness ___
  - feelings of worthlessness or guilt X
  - agitation X
  - personal untidiness ___
  - difficulty in thinking and concentration X
  - delusions X
- F. Disturbances in social behavior: decreased social and recreational activity ___
- G. Miscellaneous items:
  - age of onset 40 and over X
  - family history of affective disorder ___

FEIGHNER CRITERIA FOR MAJOR AFFECTIVE DISORDER

Diagnosis required all three of the following categories.

- A. Dysphoric mood (depressed, sad, blue, despondent, hopeless, "down in dumps," irritable, fearful, worried, discouraged) X
- B. At least 5 of following for definite; at least 4 of following for probable:
  - poor appetite or weight loss: 2 lb/wk, 10 lb/yr ___
  - sleep difficulties X
  - loss of energy (fatigue, tiredness) X
  - agitation or retardation X
  - loss of interest in usual activities or decreased sex drive X
  - complaints or actual diminished ability to think/concentrate X
  - feelings of guilt, self-reproach X
  - recurrent thoughts of death and/or suicide X
- C. A psychiatric illness lasting <u>at least one month</u> with no pre-existing psychiatric condition (schizophrenia, anxiety neurosis, phobic neurosis, obsessive-compulsive neurosis, hysteria, alcoholism, drug dependence, antisocial personality, homosexuality, transsexualism, mental retardation, anorexia nervosa, organic brain syndrome) or life-threatening or incapacitating illness X

AFFECTIVE DISORDER, SUBGROUP 3
Men aged 68 and over (N = 9)

012 Informants: Son, physician, social service records

This 68-year-old white iron works layout man retired two years before his death. As far as the informants were aware, he remained his usual self until one year prior to his suicide, when he became "depressed" and developed a cancer phobia. He complained of his year-long depression and feared cancer when he saw his physician only three weeks before his death. His family, however, noted no change in his behavior or speech until approximately six months prior to his death when his wife developed a stasis ulcer on her leg. He seemed to become, according to his son, too concerned about his wife's illness. He still showed no notable behavioral change. Two months prior to his death he began to worry about the condition of his house. It was not clear to his family what the source of his worry was, but they realized that this was a very unusual worry for him. Six weeks prior to his death his wife went to the hospital for one week where her condition was found to be satisfactory. During this week, however, he became manifestly concerned about her, showed agitation by pacing and restlessness, refused to stay with his son, believed his wife had cancer, and repeatedly said, "Mom won't come home." Following his wife's return home nothing unusual—except the undefined worry about his house—was noted about his behavior, until three weeks prior to his death. He suddenly woke his wife one night and said, "Let's get out of here! The house is going to cave in." It took his wife some time to reassure and quiet him. Around this same time he said to his son, "I'm going to throw everything in your lap." He began to complain bitterly about an asymptomatic hernia that he had had for 20 years. He went to a physician with a complaint of abdominal pain. The doctor found no medical or surgical condition to account for the complaint. He saw his physician twice more, the last time one day before his suicide. These last two visits were for urinary retention. In each instance he was able, with urging, to void. Catheterization on one occasion showed a 50 ml residual.

For the last three weeks of his life there was a crescendo of symptoms, delusions, and psychological disturbances. He became depressed and nervous and developed the delusion that he was poverty-stricken. He also told his wife, "Don't stand in front of the house. The people next door won't like it and they'll yell at you." He began to speak of dying, saying to his wife, "You and I are going to die here [at home]," and to his son, "Mother and I are going to die here." He told his son, "I'm going to put everything in your hands." He also commented, "The medicines are going to kill me." He became less active, very much less talkative, and complained that he was too ill to work in his garden. He stopped seeing his friends, quit going fishing, quit playing cards, and lost interest in sports. He looked pale and would frequently stare at his wife without reason. He lost 15 pounds in weight and complained of anorexia, weakness, and fatigue. In the last two or three days he became very passive and indecisive. His sons recalled that while they were all repairing a cistern, he took directions from them, which was unusual for him.

On the day of his suicide he woke very early in the morning and was not able to go back to sleep. During that day he seemed little different from the way he had been the past three weeks. His sons had come over again to work on the cistern and went home in the early afternoon. He told his wife he was going to take a nap in the basement where there was a bed. He went down to the basement and his wife found him hanging an hour or two hours later. He had hanged himself with a rope obviously prepared for the purpose. He had braided a one-quarter inch washline into a rope more than one inch in diameter, made a noose, thrown it over a beam, and stepped off a chair with one foot, dying with his other foot still on the chair.

Family history: A cousin hanged himself 53 years previously.
Arrest record: None.

Case No. 013 M _X_ F ___ Age _68_

ST. LOUIS SUICIDE STUDY CRITERIA FOR MAJOR AFFECTIVE DISORDER

Diagnosis required four of the six following categories, A–F. Category G was helpful in diagnosis, but not necessary.

- A. Clinically well, exclusive of attacks of major affective disorder __X__
- B. Previous episode(s) of major affective disorder ___
- C. Discreteness (and duration) of final attack:
  - 6 months or less __X__
  - 12 months or less ___
- D. "Medical" symptoms:
  - insomnia __X__
  - anorexia __X__
  - weight loss __X__
  - low energy, weakness __X__
  - fatigue __X__
  - constipation ___
- E. Psychological symptoms:
  - "blue" feeling, depression, sadness __X__
  - diminished motor activity ___
  - loss of interest __X__
  - diminished sexual interest and activity ___
  - undertalkativeness __X__
  - low expectancy of recovery; expectation of "black" future ___
  - feeling of being a burden ___
  - indecisiveness __X__
  - feelings of worthlessness or guilt ___
  - agitation __X__
  - personal untidiness ___
  - difficulty in thinking and concentration ___
  - delusions __X__
- F. Disturbances in social behavior: decreased social and recreational activity __X__
- G. Miscellaneous items:
  - age of onset 40 and over __X__
  - family history of affective disorder __X__

FEIGHNER CRITERIA FOR MAJOR AFFECTIVE DISORDER

Diagnosis required all three of the following categories.

- A. Dysphoric mood (depressed, sad, blue, despondent, hopeless, "down in dumps," irritable, fearful, worried, discouraged) __X__
- B. At least 5 of following for definite; at least 4 of following for probable:
  - poor appetite or weight loss: 2 lb/wk, 10 lb/yr __X__
  - sleep difficulties __X__
  - loss of energy (fatigue, tiredness) __X__
  - agitation or retardation __X__
  - loss of interest in usual activities or decreased sex drive __X__
  - complaints or actual diminished ability to think/concentrate ___
  - feelings of guilt, self-reproach ___
  - recurrent thoughts of death and/or suicide __X__
- C. A psychiatric illness lasting <u>at least one month</u> with no pre-existing psychiatric condition (schizophrenia, anxiety neurosis, phobic neurosis, obsessive-compulsive neurosis, hysteria, alcoholism, drug dependence, antisocial personality, homosexuality, transsexualism, mental retardation, anorexia nervosa, organic brain syndrome) or life-threatening or incapacitating illness __X__

016 Informants: Wife, physician

This 74-year-old white steamfitter had worked at an industrial concern for a number of years (more than ten). He had married twice and had had two children by his first marriage. His first wife had died about 25 years before and he married his second wife five years later. His second wife described him as being an active person and a good husband. She felt that he was high-strung and said his feelings were easily hurt, but neither he nor she thought he was emotionally ill. He had not had symptoms of psychiatric disease and had never gone to a physician for nervousness.

About four months prior to his death his behavior changed. He became nervous and went to his general physician complaining of nervousness and depression. His doctor believed that the patient had undergone a definite change. There were no symptoms of senile brain disease or of a stroke. His doctor put him on sedation and injections without appreciable effect. He began to worry about his approaching retirement, saying that the pension due him would not be enough to support his wife and himself. When visiting his doctor he constantly appeared to want to get something "off his chest," but was unable to. During this four-month period his wife became worried about the possibility of suicide and tried to keep the car keys hidden from him. His physician believed, without any direct evidence, that his suicide had been carefully planned well ahead of time.

He complained of dizziness, a pain in his head, anorexia, severe insomnia, and constipation. The pain in his head was extremely aggravating to him and toward the end he said repetitively, "All I have is trouble. I can't stand the pain any longer." He became disgusted with himself and with his surroundings, and irritable. He began telling his wife, "I don't have long to live." During the last two months he became worse. He was agitated and frequently paced the floor. He was unable to work, lost interest in reading and TV, and saw his friends less. He suffered from marked feelings of inertia. During the last two weeks his condition worsened even more. He complained of feelings of weakness. It was apparent that he had lost a considerable amount of weight. Even during the last two weeks, however, he would have occasional "good" days when he seemed almost like himself. On the night before his suicide he told his wife that he felt better than he had any time in the previous four months. Early the next morning she went to his room—he had taken to sleeping in a separate bedroom—saw that he was sleeping, and went back to bed. On waking later in the morning she discovered that he had found the hidden car keys and had gone into the garage. He had closed the garage doors and started the motor and by the time his wife found him he was dead from carbon monoxide poisoning.

Family history: There was no family history of psychiatric illness.
Arrest record: None.

Case No. **016** M __ F **X** Age **74**

ST. LOUIS SUICIDE STUDY CRITERIA FOR MAJOR AFFECTIVE DISORDER

Diagnosis required four of the six following categories, A-F. Category G was helpful in diagnosis, but not necessary.

- A. Clinically well, exclusive of attacks of major affective disorder __X__
- B. Previous episode(s) of major affective disorder ____
- C. Discreteness (and duration) of final attack:
  - 6 months or less __X__
  - 12 months or less ____
- D. "Medical" symptoms:
  - insomnia __X__
  - anorexia __X__
  - weight loss __X__
  - low energy, weakness __X__
  - fatigue ____
  - constipation __X__
- E. Psychological symptoms:
  - "blue" feeling, depression, sadness ____
  - diminished motor activity ____
  - loss of interest __X__
  - diminished sexual interest and activity ____
  - undertalkativeness __X__
  - low expectancy of recovery; expectation of "black" future ____
  - feeling of being a burden ____
  - indecisiveness ____
  - feelings of worthlessness or guilt ____
  - agitation __X__
  - personal untidiness ____
  - difficulty in thinking and concentration ____
  - delusions __X__
- F. Disturbances in social behavior: decreased social and recreational activity __X__
- G. Miscellaneous items:
  - age of onset 40 and over __X__
  - family history of affective disorder ____

FEIGHNER CRITERIA FOR MAJOR AFFECTIVE DISORDER

Diagnosis required all three of the following categories.

- A. Dysphoric mood (depressed, sad, blue, despondent, hopeless, "down in dumps," irritable, fearful, worried, discouraged) __X__
- B. At least 5 of following for definite; at least 4 of following for probable:
  - poor appetite or weight loss: 2 lb/wk, 10 lb/yr __X__
  - sleep difficulties __X__
  - loss of energy (fatigue, tiredness) __X__
  - agitation or retardation __X__
  - loss of interest in usual activities or decreased sex drive __X__
  - complaints or actual diminished ability to think/concentrate ____
  - feelings of guilt, self-reproach ____
  - recurrent thoughts of death and/or suicide __X__
- C. A psychiatric illness lasting <u>at least one month</u> with no pre-existing psychiatric condition (schizophrenia, anxiety neurosis, phobic neurosis, obsessive-compulsive neurosis, hysteria, alcoholism, drug dependence, antisocial personality, homosexuality, transsexualism, mental retardation, anorexia nervosa, organic brain syndrome) or life-threatening or incapacitating illness __X__

019 Informants: Wife, internist, physician

This 79-year-old white retired assistant maintenance engineer had been married for 58 years. His wife described him as always having been a nervous person, but without clinical symptoms. He had never been to a doctor for nervousness and had been an active and steady worker (40 years for the same organization). His wife said that he liked to have his own way and that the family usually gave in. He became angry relatively infrequently, but when he did, he was very angry. In respect to his anger and liking to have his own way, he was said to have been very like his father. For some years he would on occasion, when angry, say "I feel like jumping off the free bridge." There was, however, no increase in suicidal communications in the months prior to his death. About 20 or more years prior to his suicide he developed appendicitis and an appendiceal abscess. Following this illness he had a residual mass in his abdomen and recurrent pain in the same region. Although the pain was never severe, it was bothersome. Seven years prior to his death he complained of chest pain and went to an internist who diagnosed him as having arteriosclerotic heart disease with angina pectoris and arteriosclerotic mitral insufficiency. He retired six years prior to his death. Over the next three years he received nitrites and occasional aminophyllin from the internist, but he never required diuretics or digitalis. For the last four years of his life his cardiac symptoms diminished and he did not see a doctor.

Three years prior to his suicide he began to complain of recurrent insomnia, specifically of early morning waking. His wife believed that this was an isolated symptom until a year later, when he developed total impotence. He complained bitterly about the latter difficulty. According to his wife he remained in his usual health except for these two symptoms until one year prior to his death. Then he began to "slow down" and to become depressed and irritable. Even though he was more irritable, his episodes of severe anger ceased. He complained of weakness and fatigue. About six months after the onset of these symptoms he went on a self-imposed diet and lost 60 pounds. Although it is not clear when he stopped dieting, he had become anorexic and continued to lose weight until death. About two months prior to his suicide he became much less talkative and less active. He lost interest in many of his activities. One month later he began to suffer from more severe abdominal pain and he developed diarrhea. Two weeks later, his physician found evidence of his old appendiceal abscess and found a carcinoma of the colon. One week prior to his death the doctor reported these findings to him and told him that he needed surgery. He refused, saying that he would not undergo a colostomy. After a few days, however, he did decide to undergo surgery and arrangements were made for him to enter the hospital. Two evenings before he was due to go into the hospital he, his wife, son, and daughter-in-law were sitting in the living room. He went to his bedroom, turned off the light, and closed the door. Since the latter action was so unusual, his wife hurried up the steps, turned on the light, and saw him in front of his dresser. He turned, held up a pair of underpants, and smiled. His wife assumed he was going to change his underwear and left. Three to four minutes later a shot was heard, but there was no sound of a fall. Rushing upstairs, his family found him on the floor dead, shot through the head. Since they had not heard a fall they assumed he lay down on the floor before shooting himself. His family and the doctor believed he committed suicide because he was afraid of the operation, because a neighbor of his had recently died a lingering death from gastrointestinal cancer, and/or because he wanted to spare his wife.

Family history: His son was an alcoholic. His daughter was said to be very "nervous." A maternal uncle had shot himself 60 years previously. *Arrest record:* None.

Case No. *019* M*M* F__ Age *79*

ST. LOUIS SUICIDE STUDY CRITERIA FOR MAJOR AFFECTIVE DISORDER

Diagnosis required four of the six following categories, A-F. Category G was helpful in diagnosis, but not necessary.

A. Clinically well, exclusive of attacks of major affective disorder X

B. Previous episode(s) of major affective disorder X

C. Discreteness (and duration) of final attack:
    6 months or less X
    12 months or less __

D. "Medical" symptoms:
    insomnia X
    anorexia X
    weight loss X
    low energy, weakness X
    fatigue X
    constipation __

E. Psychological symptoms:
    "blue" feeling, depression, sadness X
    diminished motor activity X
    loss of interest __

    diminished sexual interest and activity X
    undertalkativeness X
    low expectancy of recovery; expectation of "black" future __
    feeling of being a burden __
    indecisiveness __
    feelings of worthlessness or guilt __
    agitation __
    personal untidiness __
    difficulty in thinking and concentration __
    delusions __

F. Disturbances in social behavior: decreased social and recreational activity __

G. Miscellaneous items:
    age of onset 40 and over X
    family history of affective disorder X

FEIGHNER CRITERIA FOR MAJOR AFFECTIVE DISORDER

Diagnosis required all three of the following categories.

A. Dysphoric mood (depressed, sad, blue, despondent, hopeless, "down in dumps," irritable, fearful, worried, discouraged) _X_

B. At least 5 of following for definite; at least 4 of following for probable:
   poor appetite or weight loss: 2 lb/wk, 10 lb/yr _X_
   sleep difficulties _X_
   loss of energy (fatigue, tiredness) _X_
   agitation or retardation _X_
   loss of interest in usual activities or decreased sex drive _X_
   complaints or actual diminished ability to think/concentrate ___

   feelings of guilt, self-reproach ___
   recurrent thoughts of death and/or suicide ___

C. A psychiatric illness lasting <u>at least one month</u> with no pre-existing psychiatric condition (schizophrenia, anxiety neurosis, phobic neurosis, obsessive-compulsive neurosis, hysteria, alcoholism, drug dependence, antisocial personality, homosexuality, transsexualism, mental retardation, anorexia nervosa, organic brain syndrome) or life-threatening or incapacitating illness _X_

030 Informants: Daughter, physician

This white 80-year-old custodian had retired five years before his death. Following his retirement he spent most of his time around his house. He had chronic joint pains of low intensity which did not interfere with his activities. During that period, and perhaps before, he drank about three bottles of beer daily. His daughter thought that once in a while he drank too much for his own good, but there was no real evidence of alcoholism. About two years before death his thinking became noticeably slower, but he showed no confusion or disorientation. At that time he complained of mild dyspnea, but no cause could be found for this complaint. He also became increasingly fatigued. About a year prior to his death he began to complain of recurrent mild dizziness. He continued in this fashion until two or three months prior to his death when he began to lose interest in things about him. He quit going to church, stopped reading the newspaper, and saw his friends less. He was mildly depressed and talked less. About two weeks prior to his suicide he fell and broke his wrist. The physician who attended him noted the depression, but did not attempt to elicit any specific symptoms of depression. His physician did note that he was alert and not senile. At this time, or perhaps for a few weeks prior to this, he told his wife that he was tired of living and that he was going to commit suicide. For a long time prior to this, probably at least a few years, he would say when tired, "Oh well, I may be wearing a wooden overcoat." On the day of his suicide he went to his physician to have his broken wrist attended to and was told that the wrist was responding well. He then went home and told his wife he was going to the basement to nap. There he shot himself in the head. The only possible life stresses that his daughter knew were that his wife was ill and that he had broken his wrist. Although his wife was not bedridden at the time of his suicide, she was seriously ill and died a few months after his death.

Family history: There was no family history of psychiatric illness.
Arrest record: None.

Case No. *030* M *M* F __ Age *80*

ST. LOUIS SUICIDE STUDY CRITERIA FOR MAJOR AFFECTIVE DISORDER

Diagnosis required four of the six following categories, A-F. Category G was helpful in diagnosis, but not necessary.

- A. Clinically well, exclusive of attacks of major affective disorder *X*
- B. Previous episode(s) of major affective disorder __
- C. Discreteness (and duration) of final attack:
    - 6 months or less *X*
    - 12 months or less __
- D. "Medical" symptoms:
    - insomnia __
    - anorexia __
    - weight loss __
    - low energy, weakness *X*
    - fatigue *X*
    - constipation __
- E. Psychological symptoms:
    - "blue" feeling, depression, sadness *X*
    - diminished motor activity __
    - loss of interest *X*
    - diminished sexual interest and activity __
    - undertalkativeness *X*
    - low expectancy of recovery; expectation of "black" future __
    - feeling of being a burden __
    - indecisiveness __
    - feelings of worthlessness or guilt __
    - agitation __
    - personal untidiness __
    - difficulty in thinking and concentration *X*
    - delusions __
- F. Disturbances in social behavior: decreased social and recreational activity *X*
- G. Miscellaneous items:
    - age of onset 40 and over *X*
    - family history of affective disorder __

FEIGHNER CRITERIA FOR MAJOR AFFECTIVE DISORDER

Diagnosis required all three of the following categories.

A. Dysphoric mood (depressed, sad, blue, despondent, hopeless, "down in dumps," irritable, fearful, worried, discouraged) _X_

B. At least 5 of following for definite; at least 4 of following for probable:
   - poor appetite or weight loss: 2 lb/wk, 10 lb/yr ___
   - sleep difficulties ___
   - loss of energy (fatigue, tiredness) _X_
   - agitation or retardation ___
   - loss of interest in usual activities or decreased sex drive _X_
   - complaints or actual diminished ability to think/concentrate _X_
   - feelings of guilt, self-reproach ___
   - recurrent thoughts of death and/or suicide _X_

C. A psychiatric illness lasting <u>at least one month</u> with no pre-existing psychiatric condition (schizophrenia, anxiety neurosis, phobic neurosis, obsessive-compulsive neurosis, hysteria, alcoholism, drug dependence, antisocial personality, homosexuality, transsexualism, mental retardation, anorexia nervosa, organic brain syndrome) or life-threatening or incapacitating illness _X_

---

061 Informants: Wife, physicians; hospital and social service records

This 68-year-old white man immigrated to the United States from Russia when he was in his late 20's and had lived in St. Louis for more than 35 years at the time of his death. He was married and, though his widow agreed to discuss the events leading to his suicide, she could not during the actual interview seem to answer many of the questions satisfactorily.

According to her, her husband, whom she described as a moderate social drinker, had always worked in the garment industry and, though he changed jobs often (she thought he had had 10 to 15 different jobs in the last ten years of his life), this was, she said, "the custom" in his line of work. She said he had never been out of work and that he made a steady and adequate income throughout their marriage. He owned his own house in St. Louis which he and his wife shared with a daughter and her husband. He was devoutly religious and attended the Russian Orthodox Church regularly. His wife said he had a few close friends whom he saw about every two weeks or so.

Until three weeks before his suicide, when he awoke one morning with an earache, he was his usual self, she said. He went to his doctor about his ear but got no relief. He could not work because of the pain and because of a humming noise in the ear, which bothered him a great deal. For the last three weeks of his life, he lay around the house, pounding his pillow in frustration, demanding that "the damn thing" (the TV) be turned off, and complaining bitterly of sleeplessness and anorexia. Two weeks before he died, he said to his wife, "Mama, let's go to Russia." She was surprised, as she could not remember his ever having said anything similar. On the morning of his suicide, he sent his wife from their bedroom to the kitchen to fix his breakfast. As soon as she was out of the room, he shot himself in the head. He did not die immediately and was rushed to a hospital where he died several hours later. He left no note.

His wife's description of her husband's state of mind during his last year—"his usual self"—and her denial of any depressive symptoms prior to the onset of his earache in the last weeks of his life conflict with reports from two of the subject's physicians. A heart specialist, who had hospitalized the subject 16 months prior to his death because of chest pains, described his patient's behavior in the hospital as "bizarre" and noted depressive symptoms including insomnia and extreme quiet. He also noted that the referring family physician had described the patient as a chronic alcoholic. This last seems plausible in the light of the specialist's final diagnosis of liver abnormality and his prescription of a cirrhosis diet.

The subject was hospitalized again three months before his death, this time for tests for possible TB. The tests were negative, though x-rays showed some evidence of an old infection. The hospital and doctor's report of the patient's behavior include the phrases "progressively uncooperative," "irritable," "complaint of insomnia," "bordering on psychotic depression," "whole family hard to deal with."

According to the records of the Jewish Employment and Vocational Service, the subject applied for help in finding a job when he was seasonally laid off 13 months before his death. The agency social worker noted the following facts—that the subject was very religious and thus would not work on Saturdays; that he had been educated only through the 5th grade and that though he could read, he could not spell; that he had three children; that he was neat and well groomed; and, finally, that he was not a citizen of the U.S.

Family history: Nothing is known of the subject's family background.
Arrest record: None.

Case No. __061__ M __M__ F ___ Age __68__

ST. LOUIS SUICIDE STUDY CRITERIA FOR MAJOR AFFECTIVE DISORDER

Diagnosis required four of the six following categories, A–F. Category G was helpful in diagnosis, but not necessary.

- A. Clinically well, exclusive of attacks of major affective disorder __X__
- B. Previous episode(s) of major affective disorder ___
- C. Discreteness (and duration) of final attack:
  - 6 months or less ___
  - 12 months or less ___
- D. "Medical" symptoms:
  - insomnia __X__
  - anorexia __X__
  - weight loss ___
  - low energy, weakness ___
  - fatigue ___
  - constipation ___
- E. Psychological symptoms:
  - "blue" feeling, depression, sadness __X__
  - diminished motor activity ___
  - loss of interest ___
  - diminished sexual interest and activity ___
  - undertalkativeness __X__
  - low expectancy of recovery; expectation of "black" future ___
  - feeling of being a burden ___
  - indecisiveness ___
  - feelings of worthlessness or guilt ___
  - agitation __X__
  - personal untidiness ___
  - difficulty in thinking and concentration ___
  - delusions ___
- F. Disturbances in social behavior: decreased social and recreational activity __X__
- G. Miscellaneous items:
  - age of onset 40 and over __X__
  - family history of affective disorder ___

FEIGHNER CRITERIA FOR MAJOR AFFECTIVE DISORDER

Diagnosis required all three of the following categories.

- A. Dysphoric mood (depressed, sad, blue, despondent, hopeless, "down in dumps," irritable, fearful, worried, discouraged) __X__
- B. At least 5 of following for definite; at least 4 of following for probable:
  - poor appetite or weight loss: 2 lb/wk, 10 lb/yr __X__
  - sleep difficulties __X__
  - loss of energy (fatigue, tiredness) ___
  - agitation or retardation __X__
  - loss of interest in usual activities or decreased sex drive __X__
  - complaints or actual diminished ability to think/concentrate ___
  - feelings of guilt, self-reproach ___
  - recurrent thoughts of death and/or suicide ___
- C. A psychiatric illness lasting __at least one month__ with no pre-existing psychiatric condition (schizophrenia, anxiety neurosis, phobic neurosis, obsessive-compulsive neurosis, hysteria, alcoholism, drug dependence, antisocial personality, homosexuality, transsexualism, mental retardation, anorexia nervosa, organic brain syndrome) or life-threatening or incapacitating illness ___

062 Informants: Wife, brother; medical and hospital records

From all accounts, this 75-year-old white former teacher and elementary school principal was, throughout his life, a reasonable, considerate, responsible man. He was described also as a "sensitive man" whose feelings were easily hurt. His parents were both healthy, exceptionally long-lived people.

After teacher's college, he went on to graduate school, earning a Master's Degree in education. He taught in elementary schools in three small Illinois towns before moving to Chicago where he lived and worked in education for 30 years. He was principal of a Chicago elementary school for 12 years until his formal retirement at 65, ten years before his death. For three years after retirement, he taught part-time at a branch of the state university. Though never rich he made a consistently good living.

Married at 42, he and his wife had three daughters. Fully retired the last seven years of his life, he was active and well until about three months before he died. He owned a fair-sized house and 40 acres of land in rural Illinois where they lived in retirement on a small but adequate pension. Except for his wife's poor health their life seems to have been peaceful.

He was generally healthy. He suffered from chronic, typical migraine headaches until he was 62 when he was operated on for appendicitis, after which the headaches ceased. Three times—ten years, four years, and three months before his death—he lost strength in his left hand with an aftermath of tremor which gradually cleared completely the first time, partially the second, and remained the last time. A week or so before his death he saw a doctor for complaints concerning his eyesight which he believed had been failing for two months. He also admitted that, since that time, he had feared his mind was slipping, that he had been worrying a lot, had been easily distracted and inattentive. Other symptoms he mentioned were fatigue, a slight weight loss, a worsening of the tremor in his left hand, and intermittent insomnia. He had begun to be very tense and often found himself pacing the floor. He was referred to a psychiatrist who felt that the patient was suffering from severe guilt delusions and depression and admitted him to a psychiatric hospital. Two recent incidents that seemed to precipitate his state—the first, the changing, a month before his death, of his property title to one of "joint tenancy" in order to immediately provide for his wife in the event of his death; and the second, his inability to perform sexually. The deed change symbolized disgrace to him and, just prior to his hospitalization, he stated he had "committed a crime" and tried to telephone the police. Later, he told his brother that the police had been waiting for him all night on his porch. The impotence, which had been total for two months, symbolized old age to him and his wife reported he had been very upset by it. Other signs of depression remembered in retrospect by his wife and brothers were a decline in general activity and sociability in the last three months of his life. He had talked less, appeared "down," worried excessively, seemed less interested in his wife, his family, his clothes. He mentioned several times that his family would be better off if he were dead. They also remembered that his circulation and color had been poor. The obvious effects of the built delusions occurred only four days before he was hospitalized.

On admission to the hospital, he was clearly worried about how he would pay for the costs of his illness. He felt he could not be helped and spoke of his fear of having to go to a state hospital. Otherwise, he was quiet and withdrawn. Eight days later, during an occupational therapy session, he surreptitiously obtain an awl, took it to the men's rest room and, in one attempt, pushed it through his chest wall and into his heart. He died within ten minutes and was dead when found. Two weeks before his hospitalization, perhaps in reference to the deed change, he had been heard to mutter, "Maybe you're trying to kill us off."

Family history: One sibling was known to have had "nervous problems" but was never hospitalized. One brother was an alcoholic.
Arrest record: None.

Case No. 062 M X F __ Age 75

ST. LOUIS SUICIDE STUDY CRITERIA FOR MAJOR AFFECTIVE DISORDER

Diagnosis required four of the six following categories, A-F. Category G was helpful in diagnosis, but not necessary.

- A. Clinically well, exclusive of attacks of major affective disorder __X__
- B. Previous episode(s) of major affective disorder ____
- C. Discreteness (and duration) of final attack:
  - 6 months or less __X__
  - 12 months or less ____
- D. "Medical" symptoms:
  - insomnia __X__
  - anorexia ____
  - weight loss __X__
  - low energy, weakness fatigue __X__
  - constipation ____
- E. Psychological symptoms:
  - "blue" feeling, depression, sadness __X__
  - diminished motor activity __X__
  - loss of interest __X__
  - diminished sexual interest and activity __X__
  - undertalkativeness __X__
  - low expectancy of recovery; expectation of "black" future ____
  - feeling of being a burden __X__
  - indecisiveness ____
  - feelings of worthlessness or guilt ____
  - agitation __X__
  - personal untidiness __X__
  - difficulty in thinking and concentration __X__
  - delusions __X__
- F. Disturbances in social behavior: decreased social and recreational activity __X__
- G. Miscellaneous items:
  - age of onset 40 and over __X__
  - family history of affective disorder ____

FEIGHNER CRITERIA FOR MAJOR AFFECTIVE DISORDER

Diagnosis required all three of the following categories.

- A. Dysphoric mood (depressed, sad, blue, despondent, hopeless, "down in dumps," irritable, fearful, worried, discouraged) __X__
- B. At least 5 of following for definite; at least 4 of following for probable:
  - poor appetite or weight loss: 2 lb/wk, 10 lb/yr __X__
  - sleep difficulties __X__
  - loss of energy (fatigue, tiredness) __X__
  - agitation or retardation __X__
  - loss of interest in usual activities or decreased sex drive __X__
  - complaints or actual diminished ability to think/concentrate __X__
  - feelings of guilt, self-reproach __X__
  - recurrent thoughts of death and/or suicide ____
- C. A psychiatric illness lasting <u>at least one month</u> with no pre-existing psychiatric condition (schizophrenia, anxiety neurosis, phobic neurosis, obsessive-compulsive neurosis, hysteria, alcoholism, drug dependence, antisocial personality, homosexuality, transsexualism, mental retardation, anorexia nervosa, organic brain syndrome) or life-threatening or incapacitating illness __X__

075 Informants: Hospital records, physician (refusal)

Because none of his relatives would agree to an interview and because no one else who knew him well could be found, the details of this 86-year-old white man's life are not known.

It is known that, at the time of his death, he was living alone in a St. Louis hotel. He had never married and had retired from dentistry some 25 years earlier. The manager of the hotel said she had never seen friends visit him.

According to his doctor, about 18 months before his suicide, he returned to St. Louis from a trip to San Francisco. Because he had caught a heavy cold in California, he visited his doctor who put him in a general hospital a day later when the cold and cough had worsened. In the hospital, it was determined that he had had heart trouble for seven or eight years, that both his parents had died of cirrhosis, that he was accustomed to drinking three to five beers a day, and that he was at that time living with his nephew. The diagnoses made during the hospitalization were 1) chronic asthmatic bronchitis, 2) prostatic hypertrophy, 3) hypotensive vascular heart disease, and 4) generalized arteriosclerosis. After three weeks of treatment, he was released.

Six months before his suicide, he underwent prostatic surgery at another hospital. One month prior to his death, he saw his doctor because of a tender mass he had discovered under his right nipple. He said the mass seemed to become enlarged when he took the estrogen tablets prescribed following the prostate operation. His doctor admitted him again to the hospital and the tumor was surgically removed. He was discharged a week after the operation. Once back in his rooms at the hotel, he complained to his doctor that he was suffering from insomnia, anorexia, and depression. His doctor told him that, at his age, it sometimes took longer to snap back from surgery. After his suicide, the doctor said he felt that his remark had only served to make the patient feel worse. He was said to have told a friend he planned to commit suicide, but this could not be verified. In any case, he shot himself a little over one month after his release from the hospital. In a will he had made one month prior to his death, he left his estate to an orphan's home in Belleville, Missouri. His relatives were said to have tried to have the will broken. When an effort was made by interviewers to contact his nephew (for this study), they were told that the nephew did not wish to be interviewed.

Family history: No information about a family history of psychiatric illness was available.
Arrest record: None.

Case No. 075 M X F__ Age 86

ST. LOUIS SUICIDE STUDY CRITERIA FOR MAJOR AFFECTIVE DISORDER

Diagnosis required four of the six following categories, A–F. Category G was helpful in diagnosis, but not necessary.

- A. Clinically well, exclusive of attacks of major affective disorder ___
- B. Previous episode(s) of major affective disorder ___
- C. Discreteness (and duration) of final attack:
  - 6 months or less X
  - 12 months or less ___
- D. "Medical" symptoms:
  - insomnia X
  - anorexia X
  - weight loss ___
  - low energy, weakness fatigue ___
  - constipation ___
- E. Psychological symptoms:
  - "blue" feeling, depression, sadness X
  - diminished motor activity ___
  - loss of interest ___
  - diminished sexual interest and activity ___
  - undertalkativeness ___
  - low expectancy of recovery; expectation of "black" future ___
  - feeling of being a burden ___
  - indecisiveness ___
  - feelings of worthlessness or guilt ___
  - agitation ___
  - personal untidiness ___
  - difficulty in thinking and concentration ___
  - delusions ___
- F. Disturbances in social behavior: decreased social and recreational activity X
- G. Miscellaneous items:
  - age of onset 40 and over ___
  - family history of affective disorder ___

FEIGHNER CRITERIA FOR MAJOR AFFECTIVE DISORDER

Diagnosis required all three of the following categories.

- A. Dysphoric mood (depressed, sad, blue, despondent, hopeless, "down in dumps," irritable, fearful, worried, discouraged) X
- B. At least 5 of following for definite; at least 4 of following for probable:
  - poor appetite or weight loss: 2 lb/wk, 10 lb/yr X
  - sleep difficulties X
  - loss of energy (fatigue, tiredness) ___
  - agitation or retardation ___
  - loss of interest in usual activities or decreased sex drive ___
  - complaints or actual diminished ability to think/concentrate ___
  - feelings of guilt, self-reproach ___
  - recurrent thoughts of death and/or suicide X
- C. A psychiatric illness lasting at least one month with no pre-existing psychiatric condition (schizophrenia, anxiety neurosis, phobic neurosis, obsessive-compulsive neurosis, hysteria, alcoholism, drug dependence, antisocial personality, homosexuality, transsexualism, mental retardation, anorexia nervosa, organic brain syndrome) or life-threatening or incapacitating illness X

117 Informants: Daughter-in-law, hospital records

This 71-year-old white man had, because of financial problems, moved with his wife into his son's home three weeks before his suicide. His daughter-in-law, who had known him for 10 years and had seen him every day for the last three weeks of his life, volunteered to discuss the subject's suicide. Because his wife was too upset for consultation, there was uncertainty about many aspects of his early life.

His daughter-in-law knew that he had been born in St. Louis and had worked as a tailor. She did not know how long he and his wife had been married, but knew that they had adopted their one son at birth 31 years earlier. She knew nothing of the subject's parents, siblings, or other close relatives. She said that he and his wife had had almost no social life, that their only friends were their old neighbors, and that their outings had been restricted to visits to their son's home. A life-long teetotaler, he had also never taken drugs.

The subject's wife had mentioned that he had been losing weight and looking depressed for two or three months before the move and his depressed state was obvious to his daughter-in-law as soon as he was settled in her home. She said that he had lost 30 pounds by the time he died and that he had had no appetite the last three weeks of his life. He had spent his time "sitting around," not even watching TV wrestling of which he was fond. She noted that he had also been silent for long periods of time. He had complained of "feeling bad" and, the last week of his life, he had complained of his nose bothering him and of headaches. His wife told the daughter-in-law that he had spoken to her several times in the last two or three months of killing himself, and that he had talked of it at least twice since the move to their son's.

The informant knew that the subject had had heart trouble and ulcers for more than ten years and that he was on an ulcer diet. According to hospital records he had been hospitalized for two months because of a coronary thrombosis 15 years before his suicide. A month or two later, he spent two days in the hospital for similar symptoms, but signed himself out before a definite diagnosis had been made. There was no further record of heart trouble. Eleven years before his death, he was seen in the hospital clinic several times because of a duodenal ulcer. One week before his death, he appeared at the clinic complaining of feeling "tired all over," of having no pep, and of being constipated. He was scheduled to return in 10 days to see an ear, nose, and throat specialist for sinusitis.

On the day of his suicide, the subject got up in "good spirits" and drove his granddaughter to scool. He kissed her as she got out of the car as he usually did. He then drove back to his son's house, parked in front, entered the house, got his gun, returned to the car, and, lying on the back seat, shot himself. His daughter-in-law, sent out by his wife to see what was keeping him, discovered his body a few minutes later. He left no note.

Family history: The informant had no information concerning psychiatric illness in the family history.
Arrest record: None

Case No. *117* M X F __ Age *71*

ST. LOUIS SUICIDE STUDY CRITERIA FOR MAJOR AFFECTIVE DISORDER

Diagnosis required four of the six following categories, A-F. Category G was helpful in diagnosis, but not necessary.

A. Clinically well, exclusive of attacks of major affective disorder __

B. Previous episode(s) of major affective disorder __

C. Discreteness (and duration) of final attack:
   6 months or less X
   12 months or less __

D. "Medical" symptoms:
   insomnia __
   anorexia X
   weight loss X
   low energy, weakness X
   fatigue X
   constipation X

E. Psychological symptoms:
   "blue" feeling, depression, sadness X
   diminished motor activity X
   loss of interest X
   diminished sexual interest and activity __
   undertalkativeness X
   low expectancy of recovery; expectation of "black" future __
   feeling of being a burden __
   indecisiveness __
   feelings of worthlessness or guilt __
   agitation __
   personal untidiness __
   difficulty in thinking and concentration __
   delusions __

F. Disturbances in social behavior: decreased social and recreational activity X

G. Miscellaneous items:
   age of onset 40 and over __
   family history of affective disorder __

FEIGHNER CRITERIA FOR MAJOR AFFECTIVE DISORDER

Diagnosis required all three of the following categories.

A. Dysphoric mood (depressed, sad, blue, despondent, hopeless, "down in dumps," irritable, fearful, worried, discouraged) _X_

B. At least 5 of following for definite; at least 4 of following for probable:
   - poor appetite or weight loss: 2 lb/wk, 10 lb/yr _X_
   - sleep difficulties ___
   - loss of energy (fatigue, tiredness) _X_
   - agitation or retardation ___
   - loss of interest in usual activities or decreased sex drive _X_
   - complaints or actual diminished ability to think/concentrate ___
   - feelings of guilt, self-reproach ___
   - recurrent thoughts of death and/or suicide _X_

C. A psychiatric illness lasting <u>at least one month</u> with no pre-existing psychiatric condition (schizophrenia, anxiety neurosis, phobic neurosis, obsessive-compulsive neurosis, hysteria, alcoholism, drug dependence, antisocial personality, homosexuality, transsexualism, mental retardation, anorexia nervosa, organic brain syndrome) or life-threatening or incapacitating illness _X_

133 Informants: Son, physician

This 78-year-old white married man graduated from college and worked for 25 years in St. Louis as a civil engineer. He married at the age of 30 and he and his wife had two sons. At 54 he inherited money from his mother's family and retired. He had a large income from investments and was content not to work. He served as St. Louis Police Commissioner for four years in his late 50's. He and his wife spent every summer in Wisconsin and winters in an expensive hotel suite in St. Louis. He belonged to several St. Louis social clubs where he spent most of his winter days reading, playing bridge, and lunching with his many friends. He was a mild social drinker.

Both his son and his family doctor described him as a man overconcerned with his physical health. He had suffered for years from tinnitus which bothered him greatly and which he battled until his death. About 20 years before he died, his doctor jokingly suggested suicide as a means of stopping it and he himself referred to the possibility, also jokingly, several times over the years. Rather a demanding person, he expected—and got—attention and service, and his wife was said to have "babied him a little." He was a pacifist and did not allow his children or grandchildren to play with toy guns or watch violent programs on television. For the last ten years of his life, he suffered from insomnia and took sleeping pills nightly.

His son felt that he had begun to be even more preoccupied with his health about one year before his death. Starting then, the tinnitus and insomnia seemed to bother him more and he saw his doctor more often, looking for ways to relieve them. He relied more and more on his sleeping pills and, when two of his old friends died, their loss saddened him and he talked often about their deaths. Both his son and his wife noticed that he was increasingly irritable and that he looked depressed.

Six weeks before his suicide, he had a slight stroke which left him partially paralysed for less than a week. For several days after the paralysis disappeared, he complained of unsteadiness, dizziness when turning over in bed, and restlessness. However, once the effects of the stroke had waned, he seemed to "brighten up" and to feel generally better. A week before his death, another old friend died and this had a definitely depressing effect. He visited his doctor that week and laughed in an embarrassed way when the doctor tried to reassure him. When he left the office, he seemed happier.

He committed suicide by jumping from the roof of one of his social clubs at 9:30 one morning. He had left a note for his wife addressed to "the loveliest and best woman in the world" and mentioned not wanting to become a burden. A second note, indicating those who should be notified of his suicide, was found on his body. His son felt that he had not been long planning his suicide, that it had been an impulsive act.

Family history: A nephew had committed suicide at age 35. One of his sons was an alcoholic and a sister and one other son were described as "nervous."

Arrest record: None.

Case No. *133* M X F__ Age *78*

ST. LOUIS SUICIDE STUDY CRITERIA FOR MAJOR AFFECTIVE DISORDER

Diagnosis required four of the six following categories, A-F. Category G was helpful in diagnosis, but not necessary.

A. Clinically well, exclusive of attacks of major affective disorder X

B. Previous episode(s) of major affective disorder __

C. Discreteness (and duration) of final attack:
   6 months or less __
   12 months or less X

D. "Medical" symptoms:
   insomnia X
   anorexia __
   weight loss __
   low energy, weakness __
   fatigue __
   constipation __

E. Psychological symptoms:
   "blue" feeling, depression, sadness X
   diminished motor activity __
   loss of interest __
   diminished sexual interest and activity __
   undertalkativeness __
   low expectancy of recovery; expectation of "black" future __
   feeling of being a burden X
   indecisiveness __
   feelings of worthlessness or guilt __
   agitation __
   personal untidiness __
   difficulty in thinking and concentration __
   delusions __

F. Disturbances in social behavior: decreased social and recreational activity __

G. Miscellaneous items:
   age of onset 40 and over __
   family history of affective disorder X

FEIGHNER CRITERIA FOR MAJOR AFFECTIVE DISORDER

Diagnosis required all three of the following categories.

A. Dysphoric mood (depressed, sad, blue, despondent, hopeless, "down in dumps," irritable, fearful, worried, discouraged) X

B. At least 5 of following for definite; at least 4 of following for probable:
   poor appetite or weight loss: 2 lb/wk, 10 lb/yr __
   sleep difficulties X
   loss of energy (fatigue, tiredness) __
   agitation or retardation __
   loss of interest in usual activities or decreased sex drive __
   complaints or actual diminished ability to think/concentrate __
   feelings of guilt, self-reproach __
   recurrent thoughts of death and/or suicide X

C. A psychiatric illness lasting <u>at least one month</u> with no pre-existing psychiatric condition (schizophrenia, anxiety neurosis, phobic neurosis, obsessive-compulsive neurosis, hysteria, alcoholism, drug dependence, antisocial personality, homosexuality, transsexualism, mental retardation, anorexia nervosa, organic brain syndrome) or life-threatening or incapacitating illness X

AFFECTIVE DISORDER, SUBGROUP 4

Women aged 45 and under (N = 3)

112   Informants: Husband, elder daughter, physician

This 42-year-old white woman, married for 22 years and the mother of three children, was extremely close to both her immediate and extended families.

Her husband described his wife as "never smiling," always high-strung, a perfectionist, and a person whose feelings were easily hurt. A Methodist, she was a regular church goer. She had never drunk alcohol nor taken any drugs. She was devoted to her large family and took her husband and children to her parents' every Sunday for dinner. Outside the family, she had only one close friend whom she saw about once a week.

A year and a half before her death, she became unhappy, worried, and depressed when her son went off to college. She visited him every weekend and took him groceries. This episode ended when the son dropped out of college after three months and returned home.

The subject had suffered from what informants described as a "chronically infected bladder" for many years. She also had a long history of irregular menstrual periods and abdominal pain. For the last three years of her life she had been having "hot flashes" and she had an exaggerated fear of menopause. About six weeks before her death, she began to tell her husband that, when he and the children weren't around, she became "very depressed." She said she was fine when he was home and indeed, neither he nor her daughter had noticed any unusual joylessness, sadness, disgust, or fatigue. Two weeks before she died, she told her husband she never wanted to go to a mental hospital and made him promise that if things "got bad" he would lock her in a room upstairs. They had never discussed such things before. She continued her rather exacting housekeeping routine, kept up with her family obligations, and regularly visited her mother who was in the hospital for a cataract operation. She expressed worry about her mother several times and, about ten days before her suicide, she went to the family doctor on her own and complained to him of feeling "depressed" and fearing she was "losing her mind." He prescribed 25 mg of thorazine per day and she reported some relief of her symptoms. The doctor had no suspicions of her suicidal intentions. In the last six weeks of her life, she had lost between 10 and 15 pounds and suffered nightly insomnia. She reported neither of these symptoms to her doctor.

Her family said she was "especially sweet" the last week of her life. The night before she killed herself, she asked her daughter, while combing her hair, "What would you do with out me?" The next morning, she was sweeter and more attentive than ever and her husband said, "She kissed me better than she ever had before." Once the family had all left for work and school, she straightened the house, finished some ironing, went upstairs to her bedroom, and shot herself. She left no note.

Family history: Two uncles and one brother were chronic alcoholics. The subject's father was "nervous" all his life, often threatened to kill himself when his children crossed him, and "fainted" frequently. An uncle, who had been physically ill, committed suicide eight months before the subject's death.

Arrest record: None.

Case No. *112* M ___ F *X* Age *42*

ST. LOUIS SUICIDE STUDY CRITERIA FOR MAJOR AFFECTIVE DISORDER

Diagnosis required four of the six following categories, A–F. Category G was helpful in diagnosis, but not necessary.

- A. Clinically well, exclusive of attacks of major affective disorder ___
- B. Previous episode(s) of major affective disorder *X*
- C. Discreteness (and duration) of final attack:
    - 6 months or less *X*
    - 12 months or less ___
- D. "Medical" symptoms:
    - insomnia *X*
    - anorexia ___
    - weight loss *X*
    - low energy, weakness ___
    - fatigue ___
    - constipation ___
- E. Psychological symptoms:
    - "blue" feeling, depression, sadness *X*
    - diminished motor activity ___
    - loss of interest ___
    - diminished sexual interest and activity ___
    - undertalkativeness ___
    - low expectancy of recovery; expectation of "black" future *X*
    - feeling of being a burden ___
    - indecisiveness ___
    - feelings of worthlessness or guilt ___
    - agitation ___
    - personal untidiness ___
    - difficulty in thinking and concentration *X*
    - delusions ___
- F. Disturbances in social behavior: decreased social and recreational activity ___
- G. Miscellaneous items:
    - age of onset 40 and over *X*
    - family history of affective disorder *X*

FEIGHNER CRITERIA FOR MAJOR AFFECTIVE DISORDER

Diagnosis required all three of the following categories.

A. Dysphoric mood (depressed, sad, blue, despondent, hopeless, "down in dumps," irritable, fearful, worried, discouraged) X

B. At least 5 of following for definite; at least 4 of following for probable:
   - poor appetite or weight loss: 2 lb/wk, 10 lb/yr X
   - sleep difficulties X
   - loss of energy (fatigue, tiredness) —
   - agitation or retardation —
   - loss of interest in usual activities or decreased sex drive —
   - complaints or actual diminished ability to think/concentrate X
   - feelings of guilt, self-reproach —
   - recurrent thoughts of death and/or suicide X

C. A psychiatric illness lasting <u>at least one month</u> with no pre-existing psychiatric condition (schizophrenia, anxiety neurosis, phobic neurosis, obsessive-compulsive neurosis, hysteria, alcoholism, drug dependence, antisocial personality, homosexuality, transsexualism, mental retardation, anorexia nervosa, organic brain syndrome) or life-threatening or incapacitating illness X

002 Informants: Internist and friend, psychiatrist, social service records (refusal)

This 42-year-old white housewife was born into a wealthy family, went to private schools, and studied music. She was described as outgoing, warm, poised, a good hostess, and a good mother and wife. Her home life was described as congenial until the onset of her first troubles at age 37. At that time she developed abdominal pain about which she became panicky and overconcerned. No medical or surgical disease was found to explain this symptom. At that time she began to suffer episodes during which she was generally fearful and afraid to leave her home. She would not go out alone and wanted her husband with her. During these times she was depressed and had severe insomnia. Flitting from one thing to another, she was unable to sustain interest in any one thing. She also complained of fatigue and an inability to enjoy anything. She withdrew from her active social life, failed to take care of her child, and became very undertalkative. A marked antagonism to her husband gradually developed.

There were two or three such episodes with intervening periods when she was her usual self. The last episode (from which she never recovered) began 18 months prior to her death. In addition to the symptoms noted above she developed psychomotor retardation, severe anorexia, intractable insomnia, and feelings that people stared at her because she was inferior and no good. Her appearance became increasingly disheveled as she neglected her personal care. She repeatedly stated (to her husband) that she was going to commit suicide.

Her husband said that the day before her suicide the symptoms became even more severe. That night she took an overdose of sleeping medicine and was found dead in bed the next morning.

Since neither her relatives nor a close friend was interviewed there is no evidence available concerning possible life stresses as precipitating events for the suicide. Her psychiatrist did not offer information concerning any such stresses except for the antagonism toward her husband whenever she was ill.

Family history: There was no family history of psychiatric illness.
Arrest record: None.

Case No. *002* M___ F *X* Age *42*

ST. LOUIS SUICIDE STUDY CRITERIA FOR MAJOR AFFECTIVE DISORDER

Diagnosis required four of the six following categories, A-F. Category G was helpful in diagnosis, but not necessary.

A. Clinically well, exclusive of attacks of major affective disorder *X*

B. Previous episode(s) of major affective disorder *X*

C. Discreteness (and duration) of final attack:
   6 months or less ___
   12 months or less ___

D. "Medical" symptoms:
   insomnia *X*
   anorexia *X*
   weight loss ___
   low energy, weakness ___
   fatigue ___
   constipation ___

E. Psychological symptoms:
   "blue" feeling, depression, sadness ___
   diminished motor activity *X*
   loss of interest ___
   diminished sexual interest and activity ___
   undertalkativeness *X*
   low expectancy of recovery; expectation of "black" future ___
   feeling of being a burden ___
   indecisiveness ___
   feelings of worthlessness or guilt *X*
   agitation *X*
   personal untidiness *X*
   difficulty in thinking and concentration *X*
   delusions ___

F. Disturbances in social behavior: decreased social and recreational activity *X*

G. Miscellaneous items:
   age of onset 40 and over ___
   family history of affective disorder ___

Affective Disorder—The Largest Group

FEIGHNER CRITERIA FOR MAJOR AFFECTIVE DISORDER

Diagnosis required all three of the following categories.

A. Dysphoric mood (depressed, sad, blue, despondent, hopeless, "down in dumps," irritable, fearful, worried, discouraged) _X_

B. At least 5 of following for definite; at least 4 of following for probable:
  poor appetite or weight loss: 2 lb/wk, 10 lb/yr _X_
  sleep difficulties _X_
  loss of energy (fatigue, tiredness) _X_
  agitation or retardation _X_
  loss of interest in usual activities or decreased sex drive _X_
  complaints or actual diminished ability to think/concentrate _X_
  feelings of guilt, self-reproach _X_
  recurrent thoughts of death and/or suicide _X_

C. A psychiatric illness lasting <u>at least one month</u> with no pre-existing psychiatric condition (schizophrenia, anxiety neurosis, phobic neurosis, obsessive-compulsive neurosis, hysteria, alcoholism, drug dependence, antisocial personality, homosexuality, transsexualism, mental retardation, anorexia nervosa, organic brain syndrome) or life-threatening or incapacitating illness _X_

---

090 Informants: Husband, son, hospital records

This 40-year-old white married woman, had made at least two attempts to kill herself before her successful suicide. She completed 10 grades in school and at 16 she was briefly married to a boy her age. The marriage was annulled shortly before the birth of a son. A year or two later, she married again and spent about 13 years with the second husband. She was said to have been happy in that marriage. However, when her favorite brother returned from the service at the end of World War II, she quarreled with her husband, left him, and went off with her brother. The two of them went into the nightclub business together. After two years, she and the brother divided their profits and each invested in their own nightclub.

The subject's nightclub failed and, about that time, when she and her son were living alone in St. Louis, she attempted suicide with an overdose of sleeping pills. Her mother had recently died and she was said to have reacted strongly—not eating, crying uncontrollably, and pacing. Her son was very young at the time and was not, in retrospect, certain whether the suicide attempt coincided with that episode, but the dates make it seem likely. In any event, she was taken to a general hospital where her stomach was pumped. She had apparently written a note which the police took. That first attempt occurred seven years before her death.

The following year, she married her third husband, a man 10 years older than herself. According to him, their marriage was happy, especially the last two years. Even so, four years prior to her suicide, they separated for a period during which she was "depressed" and hospitalized for a few days in a Catholic psychiatric hospital. A second, less serious suicide attempt occurred at about that time, when following a miscarriage, she "nicked" her wrists.

According to the history she gave to a consulting psychiatrist during her final hospitalization five months before her death, she had discovered, three years earlier, that her husband was unfaithful. She told the psychiatrist that he had filed for divorce a year later, but that the judge had denied it on the grounds that his wife was "too sick." Like her husband, she claimed that the last two years of their marriage had been very happy.

Her husband described her as always having been a high-strung person whose feelings were easily hurt. He said she had suffered for years from migraine headaches, palpitation, and dyspnea, and for the last four years she had been "nervous."

A year and a half before her death, she had quit her job as a waitress due to increasing tiredness. One year before her death, she underwent surgery for bleeding ulcers. A partial gastrectomy was performed and she remained in the hospital for three weeks. Five months later, she was readmitted to the hospital for a condition diagnosed as "anxiety reaction." She had been suffering from weakness, dizziness, insomnia, nausea, vomiting, weight loss, abdominal pain, and depression. The nausea, vomiting, and weight loss had evidently continued since her operation, but the depression and weakness were new. She was kept in the hospital two weeks and released.

Back at home, she was too weak to do housework or to see her friends. Her insomnia continued. About five months before her death, her favorite brother died and, from that point on, she became steadily worse. She cried constantly, and a month later she was again admitted to the hospital complaining of "no pep" and continued weight loss (by then she was down to 80 pounds). She was seen by a psychiatrist to whom she admitted that a great part of her third marriage had been unhappy, that she was terribly upset by her brother's death and by the guilt she felt at "not having taken better care of him." She denied any depression even though she admitted keeping the flag that had covered her brother's coffin constantly in view and spending much of her time rereading his old letters. The psychiatrist felt that she was moderately depressed and, though she made no direct suicidal comments, that she was "possibly suicidal" and in need of psychiatric care on a closed ward.

She was, however, released at the end of a week and allowed to go home where she appeared to be more cheerful, to sleep better, and to look better for the next two months. She continued to lose weight and her husband said

FEIGHNER CRITERIA FOR MAJOR AFFECTIVE DISORDER

Diagnosis required all three of the following categories.

A. Dysphoric mood (depressed, sad, blue, despondent, hopeless, "down in dumps," irritable, fearful, worried, discouraged) _X_

B. At least 5 of following for definite; at least 4 of following for probable:
   - poor appetite or weight loss: 2 lb/wk, 10 lb/yr _X_
   - sleep difficulties _X_
   - loss of energy (fatigue, tiredness) _X_
   - agitation or retardation _X_
   - loss of interest in usual activities or decreased sex drive _X_
   - complaints or actual diminished ability to think/concentrate ___
   - feelings of guilt, self-reproach _X_
   - recurrent thoughts of death and/or suicide ___

C. A psychiatric illness lasting <u>at least one month</u> with no pre-existing psychiatric condition (schizophrenia, anxiety neurosis, phobic neurosis, obsessive-compulsive neurosis, hysteria, alcoholism, drug dependence, antisocial personality, homosexuality, transsexualism, mental retardation, anorexia nervosa, organic brain syndrome) or life-threatening or incapacitating illness _X_

105 *Informants: Daughter, physician, psychiatrist*

This 58-year-old white Catholic woman had been a widow for 23 years at the time of her suicide. She was the 4th of 13 siblings. She attended school for only the first three years and then worked on her father's farm. She moved to St. Louis when she was 18, was married at 19, had her only child, a daughter, when she was 23, and lost her husband at 35. She worked for the last 20 years of her life as a seamstress for a clothing manufacturer and was entirely self-supporting. At the time of her death, she was living alone in a separate apartment at the rear of her daughter's house.

She had been a healthy woman for most of her life. She was not a social person and saw her two or three friends no more than twice a month.

About six months before her death, she began to suffer from a burning sensation in her urinary tract. She went to her doctor who treated her symptoms medically for a few months without success. He could find no evidence of physical cause for her discomfort and when she admitted to him that she was also suffering from increasingly severe insomnia, anorexia, and anxiety about the possibility of cancer, he suspected a "phobic anxiety" and referred her to a psychiatrist. Although she could not understand how her mind could cause pain in her bladder, she reluctantly agreed to see the psychiatrist. Her last words to her doctor were that it might be "too late" by the time she had her appointment with the psychiatrist.

According to her daughter, her trouble was entirely new and she had never known her mother to have been depressed until the last six months of her life. In those months, however, the subject experienced loss of interest, feelings of uselessness, of being a burden, of never getting well, of self-disgust, palpitation, dysuria, "burning" in the chest, pains in the back of her head, anorexia, weight loss (more than 20 pounds in six months), constipation, inertia, indecision, joylessness, sadness, ennui, and in the last week of her life, increasing irritability toward her daughter and her family.

She kept her appointment with the psychiatrist on a Thursday. He reported that the patient described her nervousness, tension, lost interest, belief in a black future, a bad taste in her mouth, and an inability to eat or sleep. She denied any suicidal ideas, but was quoted by her daughter as having stated, "If I had any poison around here, I'd take it." The psychiatrist diagnosed acute depression with strong suicidal tendencies and recommended immediate hospitalization and electroshock therapy. Even though the subject had packed her suitcase in preparation for entering the hospital, the family conferred and decided to get one more opinion before hospitalizing her. The next morning, an appointment was made with another psychiatrist for the following week and the daughter reported that her mother seemed better. By evening, however, she was again extremely depressed. She refused to spend the night in her daughter's house and insisted on going alone to her own apartment. Sometime during the night, she cut her throat and died in the early hours of Saturday morning. She left the following note: "Dear God forgive me for what I'm about to do. I can't stand it any longer."

Family history: There was no family history of psychiatric illness.
Arrest record: None.

Case No. *105* M __ F _X_ Age *58*

ST. LOUIS SUICIDE STUDY CRITERIA FOR MAJOR AFFECTIVE DISORDER

Diagnosis required four of the six following categories, A-F. Category G was helpful in diagnosis, but not necessary.

- A. Clinically well, exclusive of attacks of major affective disorder _X_
- B. Previous episode(s) of major affective disorder ___
- C. Discreteness (and duration) of final attack:
  - 6 months or less _X_
  - 12 months or less ___
- D. "Medical" symptoms:
  - insomnia _X_
  - anorexia _X_
  - weight loss _X_
  - low energy, weakness fatigue _X_
  - constipation _X_
- E. Psychological symptoms:
  - "blue" feeling, depression, sadness _X_
  - diminished motor activity ___
  - loss of interest _X_
  - diminished sexual interest and activity ___
  - undertalkativeness ___
  - low expectancy of recovery; expectation of "black" future _X_
  - feeling of being a burden _X_
  - indecisiveness _X_
  - feelings of worthlessness or guilt _X_
  - agitation ___
  - personal untidiness ___
  - difficulty in thinking and concentration ___
  - delusions ___
- F. Disturbances in social behavior: decreased social and recreational activity ___
- G. Miscellaneous items:
  - age of onset 40 and over _X_
  - family history of affective disorder ___

FEIGHNER CRITERIA FOR MAJOR AFFECTIVE DISORDER

Diagnosis required all three of the following categories.

- A. Dysphoric mood (depressed, sad, blue, despondent, hopeless, "down in dumps," irritable, fearful, worried, discouraged) _X_
- B. At least 5 of following for definite; at least 4 of following for probable:
  - poor appetite or weight loss: 2 lb/wk, 10 lb/yr _X_
  - sleep difficulties _X_
  - loss of energy (fatigue, tiredness) _X_
  - agitation or retardation ___
  - loss of interest in usual activities or decreased sex drive _X_
  - complaints or actual diminished ability to think/concentrate ___
  - feelings of guilt, self-reproach _X_
  - recurrent thoughts of death and/or suicide ___
- C. A psychiatric illness lasting <u>at least one month</u> with no pre-existing psychiatric condition (schizophrenia, anxiety neurosis, phobic neurosis, obsessive-compulsive neurosis, hysteria, alcoholism, drug dependence, antisocial personality, homosexuality, transsexualism, mental retardation, anorexia nervosa, organic brain syndrome) or life-threatening or incapacitating illness _X_

125 Informants: Physician, hospital records (*no primary informant, refusal*)

Because no primary informant was available for an interview concerning the suicide of this 61-year-old white woman, investigators were dependent upon information given by her family doctor and on hospital records.

Her early background is unknown. She married in her late thirties and had no children, but her doctor described her as a "mother surrogate" to her younger siblings. He also said she had told him she had been nervous all of her life.

Five years before her suicide, her husband developed hemiplegia and was hospitalized. In an apparent reaction, the subject suffered depression and somatic delusions, and received electroshock treatments at a psychiatric hospital. Once her husband had come home again and she was able to take care of him herself, she was fine. She remained well throughout his long illness. However, when he finally died, 18 months before her suicide, she again suffered from acute, agitated depression and was hospitalized in order to receive more shock treatments. While she was in the hospital, her relatives sold her house and thus, on discharge from the hospital, she was faced with living alone in an apartment and the necessity of finding work.

A year before her death, she suffered the onset of another depressive episode, was hospitalized for several months, and received more shock treatments which resulted in temporary remissions. On release from the hospital, she was given tranquilizers and eight months before her death, she made a first suicide attempt by swallowing a "handful" of hyoscine tablets. She was taken to a general hospital by a brother, recovered from the poisoning in ten days, and was released to a nursing home. Although her doctor said that he thought she was "ashamed" of this attempt, a nurse's notes recorded her own comment that she wished she could "throw herself out the hospital window."

Six weeks before her suicide, she left the nursing home to move in with a couple whom the doctor had found and felt would provide her with pleasant surroundings and, more important, company. During her stay in their home she remarked at least once to her doctor that she had "made a mess" of her life, that she "saw no reason to go on," and that she wished he had let her die when she had first tried to kill herself. She asked her hosts several times about the pipes running along the ceiling in their basement and, when she did succeed in committing suicide, it was by hanging herself from one of those pipes. No suicide note was found.

Family history: There was no information concerning psychiatric illess in the subject's family history.
Arrest record: None.

Case No. 125 M __ F X Age 61

ST. LOUIS SUICIDE STUDY CRITERIA FOR MAJOR AFFECTIVE DISORDER

Diagnosis required four of the six following categories, A-F. Category G was helpful in diagnosis, but not necessary.

A. Clinically well, exclusive of attacks of major affective disorder X

B. Previous episode(s) of major affective disorder X

C. Discreteness (and duration) of final attack:
   6 months or less __
   12 months or less X

D. "Medical" symptoms:
   insomnia __
   anorexia __
   weight loss __
   low energy, weakness __
   fatigue __
   constipation __

E. Psychological symptoms:
   "blue" feeling, depression, sadness X
   diminished motor activity __
   loss of interest __
   diminished sexual interest and activity __
   undertalkativeness __
   low expectancy of recovery; expectation of "black" future X
   feeling of being a burden __
   indecisiveness __
   feelings of worthlessness or guilt X
   agitation X
   personal untidiness __
   difficulty in thinking and concentration __
   delusions X

F. Disturbances in social behavior: decreased social and recreational activity X

G. Miscellaneous items:
   age of onset 40 and over X
   family history of affective disorder X

FEIGHNER CRITERIA FOR MAJOR AFFECTIVE DISORDER

Diagnosis required all three of the following categories.

A. Dysphoric mood (depressed, sad, blue, despondent, hopeless, "down in dumps," irritable, fearful, worried, discouraged) X

B. At least 5 of following for definite; at least 4 of following for probable:
   poor appetite or weight loss: 2 lb/wk, 10 lb/yr __
   sleep difficulties __
   loss of energy (fatigue, tiredness) __
   agitation or retardation X
   loss of interest in usual activities or decreased sex drive __
   complaints or actual diminished ability to think/concentrate __
   feelings of guilt, self-reproach X
   recurrent thoughts of death and/or suicide X

C. A psychiatric illness lasting at least one month with no pre-existing psychiatric condition (schizophrenia, anxiety neurosis, phobic neurosis, obsessive-compulsive neurosis, hysteria, alcoholism, drug dependence, antisocial personality, homosexuality, transsexualism, mental retardation, anorexia nervosa, organic brain syndrome) or life-threatening or incapacitating illness X

134 Informants: Daughter, physician

This 62-year-old white married woman told her daughter a few weeks before she committed suicide that she felt she had too little to do. She had finished six grades in school, married at 29, and had two children.

Her life seemed to have revolved mostly around her family. She had no close friends except her sisters and brothers, and almost all of her social activity took place in the homes of relatives. She and her husband owned a pleasant house and seemed to be financially secure. She did not drink alcohol at all and had never taken drugs of any kind until six weeks before her death when her doctor prescribed sleeping pills and tranquilizers. Her daughter described her as a person whose feelings were easily hurt, but not as "nervous" or moody.

Four years before she died, her son was killed in the Army. She was appropriately upset by his death, but adjusted well to it in time. At the time of her own death, her younger sister was suffering from cancer, a disease that had killed both her father and her uncle and therefore worried her greatly.

About two months prior to her suicide, she began to appear depressed and seemed less interested in what went on around her. Her grandchildren got on her nerves as they never had before, and she claimed to feel worthless. She saw her doctor six weeks before her death and, as mentioned above, he prescribed sleeping pills and tranquilizers to treat her "reactive depression" which he felt was the result of hypertension and encephalopathy. His opinion was that she was not suicidal at that time and not acutely depressed. He reported that she had no previous history of depression.

The last three or four weeks of her life, she complained of fatigue, anorexia, insomnia, and weakness. Her family observed that she was bored and listless and had lost all her previous enthusiasm and interest in life. She could never seem to get around to her spring cleaning, a chore she usually plunged into with vigor. The only interest she did show was in reading the Bible and discussing religion, which represented a total reversal of her lifelong disinterest in religion.

The day before her suicide, she baby-sat for her daughter and told the daughter as she was leaving for home that she felt terribly weak. Her husband was away on a business trip and her daughter called at noon the next day to check on her mother, but got no answer. When the subject's husband arrived at home at 5 PM he was unable to find his wife, although her glasses were in the house, indicating she hadn't gone far. He called his daughter, and finally the police, who found her body in the garage where she had hanged herself. She left no note.

Family history: An uncle had committed suicide. There was no other family history of suicide or psychiatric illness.
Arrest record: None.

Case No 134 M___ F X Age 62

ST. LOUIS SUICIDE STUDY CRITERIA FOR MAJOR AFFECTIVE DISORDER

Diagnosis required four of the six following categories, A–F. Category G was helpful in diagnosis, but not necessary.

- A. Clinically well, exclusive of attacks of major affective disorder **X**
- B. Previous episode(s) of major affective disorder **X**
- C. Discreteness (and duration) of final attack:
  - 6 months or less **X**
  - 12 months or less ___
- D. "Medical" symptoms:
  - insomnia **X**
  - anorexia **X**
  - weight loss ___
  - low energy, weakness **X**
  - fatigue **X**
  - constipation ___
- E. Psychological symptoms:
  - "blue" feeling, depression, sadness **X**
  - diminished motor activity **X**
  - loss of interest **X**
  - diminished sexual interest and activity ___
  - undertalkativeness ___
  - low expectancy of recovery; expectation of "black" future ___
  - feeling of being a burden ___
  - indecisiveness ___
  - feelings of worthlessness or guilt **X**
  - agitation ___
  - personal untidiness ___
  - difficulty in thinking and concentration ___
  - delusions ___
- F. Disturbances in social behavior: decreased social and recreational activity **X**
- G. Miscellaneous items:
  - age of onset 40 and over **X**
  - family history of affective disorder **X**

FEIGHNER CRITERIA FOR MAJOR AFFECTIVE DISORDER

Diagnosis required all three of the following categories.

- A. Dysphoric mood (depressed, sad, blue, despondent, hopeless, "down in dumps," irritable, fearful, worried, discouraged) **X**
- B. At least 5 of following for definite; at least 4 of following for probable:
  - poor appetite or weight loss: 2 lb/wk, 10 lb/yr **X**
  - sleep difficulties **X**
  - loss of energy (fatigue, tiredness) **X**
  - agitation or retardation **X**
  - loss of interest in usual activities or decreased sex drive ___
  - complaints or actual diminished ability to think/concentrate ___
  - feelings of guilt, self-reproach **X**
  - recurrent thoughts of death and/or suicide ___
- C. A psychiatric illness lasting <u>at least one month</u> with no pre-existing psychiatric condition (schizophrenia, anxiety neurosis, phobic neurosis, obsessive-compulsive neurosis, hysteria, alcoholism, drug dependence, antisocial personality, homosexuality, transsexualism, mental retardation, anorexia nervosa, organic brain syndrome) or life-threatening or incapacitating illness **X**

AFFECTIVE DISORDER, SUBGROUP 6
Women aged 62 and over (N = 3)

079 Informants: Daughter, son-in-law, physicians, hospital records

This 60-year-old white Jewish woman escaped from Germany to the United States 16 years before her death. She was, at the time of the escape, 53 years old and twice widowed, her second husband having died three years earlier. Escaping with her was most of her immediate family—a son, a daughter, a son-in-law, and one grandchild. The family settled in St. Louis where the subject lived with her daughter and son-in-law.

The subject, who came from a well-to-do family, learned English quickly and through religious organizations made many friends in her new home. She led an active, pleasant life until six months before her death when it was discovered that she had cancer of the colon.

In a successful operation, the cancer was removed. Three months later, she returned to the hospital so that the colostomy could be surgically closed. She had been repelled by secretions from the colostomy, over which she had had practically no control. Following the second operation, she was noted in the hospital record as having been unusually upset and as having said, "I've lived my life and am too old for them to do anything more on me." She was discharged in a week, but only a few days later she developed a blockage. The surgical closure ruptured and an emergency cecostomy was performed. She was again distressed, but most striking was her revulsion at the secretions from the cecal colostomy. At home again, she avoided her friends for fear of embarrassment and was intermittently depressed by her condition. Although she had little pain, she repeatedly asked for pain killers or barbiturates, which she was not given. She mentioned on several occasions that she and her family would be better off if she were dead and was quoted as having said, "In cases like this, the only thing to do is take poison." She discussed ways and means of suicide, but never actually told anyone she meant to kill herself, though she had long considered suicide an appropriate way out of certain difficult situations. She had carried a lethal dose of sedative in her purse during her escape from Germany and had kept it with her for many years afterwards.

Her daughter and son-in-law described her as a person who had been "high-strung" all of her life. They said she tended toward excitability and that she had always reacted dramatically toward illness and hospitalization, even though she had herself been reasonably healthy most of her life except for headaches which had not increased in frequency or severity toward the end of her life. When she was 30 years old, she had suffered severe depression and loneliness for a year after her first husband's death, but had not been hospitalized. At age 40, she developed a blockage of the common bile duct and a cholecystectomy was performed. One year before her death, she had seen a doctor because of "fainting spells." No diagnosis was made and the spells gradually disappeared.

Her son-in-law, a physician, had noted no changes due to age except for a slight and progressive deafness the last three years and a coarse tremor, seemingly associated with tension. He did not feel that she had undergone any real behavior changes or that she had exhibited any symptoms of true, sustained depression.

One and a half months after the cecostomy (which had in the meantime been closed), the subject suffered another blockage and a second rupture, and entered the hospital for the fifth time in six months. This time, in early December, she issued an ultimatum to her doctor to the effect that if her problems had not been satisfactorily taken care of by Christmas, she would "see the end." She remained in the hospital through the month due to a series of complications. She became increasingly irritable with her doctor and the nurses. Three days before her suicide, another blockage developed and she suffered nausea and further discomfort.

On Christmas Day, shortly after seeing her doctor and son-in-law, both of whom had reassured her that they believed she would be all right and that she did not have a recurrence of cancer, she removed the screen from the window of her seventh-floor room and jumped to her death. A note she had written before her final hospitalization and kept with her was found on the ground near her body. In the note, she said she wanted her family to be happy and not to mourn her. She gave as her reason for suicide that she could not "go on anymore."

Family history: A niece had an undescribed mental illness for which she had received electroshock therapy every six months for ten years.

Arrest record: None.

Case No. 079 M___ F X Age 69

ST. LOUIS SUICIDE STUDY CRITERIA FOR MAJOR AFFECTIVE DISORDER

Diagnosis required four of the six following categories, A-F. Category G was helpful in diagnosis, but not necessary.

- A. Clinically well, exclusive of attacks of major affective disorder ___
- B. Previous episode(s) of major affective disorder X
- C. Discreteness (and duration) of final attack:
  - 6 months or less X
  - 12 months or less ___
- D. "Medical" symptoms:
  - insomnia ___
  - anorexia ___
  - weight loss ___
  - low energy, weakness fatigue ___
  - constipation ___
- E. Psychological symptoms:
  - "blue" feeling, depression, sadness ___
  - diminished motor activity ___
  - loss of interest ___
  - diminished sexual interest and activity ___
  - undertalkativeness ___
  - low expectancy of recovery; expectation of "black" future X
  - feeling of being a burden X
  - indecisiveness ___
  - feelings of worthlessness or guilt ___
  - agitation X
  - personal untidiness ___
  - difficulty in thinking and concentration ___
  - delusions ___
- F. Disturbances in social behavior: decreased social and recreational activity X
- G. Miscellaneous items:
  - age of onset 40 and over ___
  - family history of affective disorder X

FEIGHNER CRITERIA FOR MAJOR AFFECTIVE DISORDER

Diagnosis required all three of the following categories.

- A. Dysphoric mood (depressed, sad, blue, despondent, hopeless, "down in dumps," irritable, fearful, worried, discouraged) X
- B. At least 5 of following for definite; at least 4 of following for probable:
  - poor appetite or weight loss: 2 lb/wk, 10 lb/yr ___
  - sleep difficulties ___
  - loss of energy (fatigue, tiredness) ___
  - agitation or retardation X
  - loss of interest in usual activities or decreased sex drive ___
  - complaints or actual diminished ability to think/concentrate ___
  - feelings of guilt, self-reproach ___
  - recurrent thoughts of death and/or suicide X
- C. A psychiatric illness lasting **at least one month** with no pre-existing psychiatric condition (schizophrenia, anxiety neurosis, phobic neurosis, obsessive-compulsive neurosis, hysteria, alcoholism, drug dependence, antisocial personality, homosexuality, transsexualism, mental retardation, anorexia nervosa, organic brain syndrome) or life-threatening or incapacitating illness ___

026 Informants: Physician, friend (no primary informant, refusal)

This 70-year-old white woman had been widowed 22 months prior to her suicide. Because a willing informant with close knowledge of the woman and her background could not be found, her family history and the specific events leading to her suicide are unknown. It is known that the husband's fatal illness was cancer, that he suffered considerably the last two years of his life, and that his death left his widow lonely, depressed, and worried about her own health. She was said to have stated years before that if she ever had cancer she would kill herself and that she told a close friend the day before her death that she was going to commit suicide. She was financially well off and lived alone from the time of her husband's death until her own.

A year before she died, she had had one eye removed because of glaucoma, and, for two months before her death, she had suffered from a severe and painful case of shingles. Her doctor reported that the pain continued even after healing and that she feared some more serious disease. He had prescribed treatment for depression as she had been eating and sleeping poorly and losing weight even before the onset of the shingles.

She committed suicide by taking an overdose of Seconal, a drug she had kept in her house for five years and used occasionally for sleeping. She left a note, the contents of which are unknown.

Family history: There was no information about a family history of psychiatric illness.
Arrest record: None.

Case No. *026* M___ F *X* Age *70*

ST. LOUIS SUICIDE STUDY CRITERIA FOR MAJOR AFFECTIVE DISORDER

Diagnosis required four of the six following categories, A–F. Category G was helpful in diagnosis, but not necessary.

- A. Clinically well, exclusive of attacks of major affective disorder ___
- B. Previous episode(s) of major affective disorder ___
- C. Discreteness (and duration) of final attack:
  - 6 months or less ___
  - 12 months or less _X_
- D. "Medical" symptoms:
  - insomnia _X_
  - anorexia _X_
  - weight loss _X_
  - low energy, weakness fatigue ___
  - constipation ___
- E. Psychological symptoms:
  - "blue" feeling, depression, sadness _X_
  - diminished motor activity ___
  - loss of interest ___
  - diminished sexual interest and activity ___
  - undertalkativeness ___
  - low expectancy of recovery; expectation of "black" future _X_
  - feeling of being a burden _X_
  - indecisiveness ___
  - feelings of worthlessness or guilt ___
  - agitation ___
  - personal untidiness ___
  - difficulty in thinking and concentration ___
  - delusions ___
- F. Disturbances in social behavior: decreased social and recreational activity _X_
- G. Miscellaneous items:
  - age of onset 40 and over _X_
  - family history of affective disorder ___

FEIGHNER CRITERIA FOR MAJOR AFFECTIVE DISORDER

Diagnosis required all three of the following categories.

- A. Dysphoric mood (depressed, sad, blue, despondent, hopeless, "down in dumps," irritable, fearful, worried, discouraged) _X_
- B. At least 5 of following for definite; at least 4 of following for probable:
  - poor appetite or weight loss: 2 lb/wk, 10 lb/yr _X_
  - sleep difficulties _X_
  - loss of energy (fatigue, tiredness) ___
  - agitation or retardation ___
  - loss of interest in usual activities or decreased sex drive ___
  - complaints or actual diminished ability to think/concentrate ___
  - feelings of guilt, self-reproach ___
  - recurrent thoughts of death and/or suicide _X_
- C. A psychiatric illness lasting at least one month with no pre-existing psychiatric condition (schizophrenia, anxiety neurosis, phobic neurosis, obsessive-compulsive neurosis, hysteria, alcoholism, drug dependence, antisocial personality, homosexuality, transsexualism, mental retardation, anorexia nervosa, organic brain syndrome) or life-threatening or incapacitating illness _X_

058 Informants: Nephew, physicians, hospital records

This 72-year-old white woman lived all her life on farms in rural Missouri. She married a farmer when she was 22 and spent the 50 years of her marriage on his small farm.

Although she was described by her nephew as having always been a nervous and sensitive person, she had apparently led a relatively peaceful, happy life until about one year prior to her suicide. Very religious, she attended the Christian Church at least twice a week, led several church organizations, and was said to have been religiously opposed to suicide. She had a wide circle of church friends and an active social life. Her husband had clear ownership of 40 acres of farmland and the small house in which they lived.

About a year before her death, her daughter left her husband of 20 years because of his alcoholism and moved in with her parents. The resulting situation was severely upsetting to the subject. Her son-in-law accused her of breaking up his home and, on several occasions, forced his way into his parent-in-law's home and destroyed their belongings. At some point in the last year of the subject's life, he brought suit against her for home breaking. Her nervousness increased and she was said to have felt extreme shame and disgrace over the whole affair and to have feared for her family's personal safety.

Six months before her death, she was ill with flu. Although she recovered physically from flu, she was, according to her doctor, left with a "post flu depression." He described her as having been at that point very nervous, agitated, and restless. Although her nervousness and agitation did not seem to increase over the last six months of her life, she began to complain of insomnia and anorexia two months before she died and, during those last two months, lost a good deal of weight.

Her nephew, who had not seen the subject for about a year before her death, did not believe that she had ever suffered any serious illnesses and he knew of no hospitalizations. He remembered that about six months before her suicide her family had told him that she had become forgetful and that she often had trouble remembering what she had started out to say. He felt that she was very conscious of the effects of old age and she is reported to have made remarks such as "when the body gets bad, the mind gets bad."

Because none of those who lived with her could be interviewed, it is not known whether or not the subject spoke of wanting to die or of suicide in the last months of her life. In any case, when alone one evening she swallowed "Paris Green," a poison containing arsenic. The next morning, her daughter found her vomiting and she admitted having taken the poison. When asked why, she is supposed to have answered that she "just didn't want to live." Her family took her to a nearby clinic. The same day, she was sent to a hospital where she died the following day, having developed pneumonia. Her daughter's explanation for the suicide, according to the hospital records, was that her mother "just couldn't take trouble."

Family history: The nephew was not aware of any family history of psychiatric illness.
Arrest record: None.

Case No *058* M__ F *X* Age *72*

ST. LOUIS SUICIDE STUDY CRITERIA FOR MAJOR AFFECTIVE DISORDER

Diagnosis required four of the six following categories, A-F. Category G was helpful in diagnosis, but not necessary.

- A. Clinically well, exclusive of attacks of major affective disorder *X*
- B. Previous episode(s) of major affective disorder __
- C. Discreteness (and duration) of final attack:
    - 6 months or less *X*
    - 12 months or less __
- D. "Medical" symptoms:
    - insomnia *X*
    - anorexia *X*
    - weight loss *X*
    - low energy, weakness fatigue __
    - constipation __
- E. Psychological symptoms:
    - "blue" feeling, depression, sadness *X*
    - diminished motor activity __
    - loss of interest __
    - diminished sexual interest and activity __
    - undertalkativeness __
    - low expectancy of recovery; expectation of "black" future __
    - feeling of being a burden __
    - indecisiveness __
    - feelings of worthlessness or guilt __
    - agitation *X*
    - personal untidiness __
    - difficulty in thinking and concentration *X*
    - delusions __
- F. Disturbances in social behavior: decreased social and recreational activity __
- G. Miscellaneous items:
    - age of onset 40 and over *X*
    - family history of affective disorder __

FEIGHNER CRITERIA FOR MAJOR AFFECTIVE DISORDER

Diagnosis required all three of the following categories.

A. Dysphoric mood (depressed, sad, blue, despondent, hopeless, "down in dumps," irritable, fearful, worried, discouraged) _X_

B. At least 5 of following for definite; at least 4 of following for probable:
   - poor appetite or weight loss: 2 lb/wk, 10 lb/yr _X_
   - sleep difficulties _X_
   - loss of energy (fatigue, tiredness) ___
   - agitation or retardation _X_
   - loss of interest in usual activities or decreased sex drive _X_
   - complaints or actual diminished ability to think/concentrate _X_
   - feelings of guilt, self-reproach _X_
   - recurrent thoughts of death and/or suicide ___

C. A psychiatric illness lasting <u>at least one month</u> with no pre-existing psychiatric condition (schizophrenia, anxiety neurosis, phobic neurosis, obsessive-compulsive neurosis, hysteria, alcoholism, drug dependence, antisocial personality, homosexuality, transsexualism, mental retardation, anorexia nervosa, organic brain syndrome) or life-threatening or incapacitating illness _X_

5

Alcoholism—Description of the Sample Comprising the Second Largest of the Four Major Diagnostic Groups

There were, among the 134 suicides studied, 33 (about 25%) who were diagnosed as having had alcoholism—28 men and 5 women. The ratio of men to women in alcoholism was 5.6:1. The nine criterion symptoms used initially to diagnose alcoholism in these subjects were, in order of prevalence, 1) drinking alcohol weekly to daily, 2) informant's belief that the subject drank too much, 3) going on benders (at least two incidents of 72 hours or more of drinking in conjunctjon with neglect of duties), 4) families' objection to subjects' drinking, 5) arrests owing to drinking, 6) medical and psychiatric complications of alcoholism, 7) subject's belief that he drank too much, 8) job trouble owing to drinking, and 9) driving trouble associated with drinking.

In regard to criterion symptom 1, 100% of the subjects diagnosed as having alcoholism met that criterion (94% of them drank daily).

Criterion 6, medical and psychiatric complications of alcoholism, involvolved the following specific symptoms in order of prevalence: outbursts of rage (53%), suicidal ideas (48%), anorexia (38%), vomiting (32%), spending binges (32%), loudness and noisiness (29%), abdominal pain (28%), belief would never get well (27%), statement of feeling sad (27%), injuring someone deliberately (27%), sadness (26%), seeming to feel like hurting someone (23%), nausea (21%), fears (21%), threatening to hurt someone (20%), difficulty with simple arithmetic (13%), poor memory (13%), trouble thinking (13%), nightly use of sleeping medicine (10%), belief being spied upon (6%), thoughts about someone being "after" him and trying to annoy him (6%), and reading and understanding less well than usual (3%).

The eight specific criterion symptoms of alcoholism (6 being different in that it is a general symptom) occurred as noted above, in at least 30% of the subjects with alcoholism and half of these symptoms occurred in 66% or more. These criterion symptoms are symptoms proximately related to the excessive use of alcohol, to the subjects' as well as to the informants' views of this misuse, and to its manifestations and consequences, such as periodic benders and a variety of troubles with the police. Since they are so directly concerned with the use of alcohol, it is only logical that they occur with the high prevalence they do in the alcoholic subjects. What is more surprising is that they occur so infrequently in the other three diagnostic groups. For example, the number of alcoholism criterion symptoms that occur in 30% or more in any of the three other major diagnostic groups is only one in each diagnostic group: In the group with affective disorder, depressed phase, only the symptom "drinking alcohol weekly to daily" is present in more than 30% of the subjects (38%). In the third major diagnostic group (which we have called the miscellaneous group), there was, again, only one alcoholism criterion symptom that occurred in more than 30% of cases: "family's objection to subject's drinking" (36%). In the group of subjects which were psychiatrically undiagnosed, once again there was only one symptom—"drinking alcohol weekly to daily"—that was present in more than 30% of subjects (33%).

The 22 symptoms comprising criterion 6 are all included in the list of 100 symptoms shown in Table 3.1. (Alcoholic criteria 1–5 and 7–9 are themselves specific symptoms and each is represented as an entity in Table 3.1.) The selection of those 22 specific symptoms defining criterion 6 was based sometimes on clinical judgment and other times on their prevalences in the alcoholic group as compared with their prevalences in each of the three other major diagnostic groups. There were five symptoms with prevalences in the alcoholic group which were at least twice those of any other diagnostic group: spending binges, loudness and noisiness, injuring someone deliberately, seeming to feel like hurting someone, and threatening someone. One other, outbursts of rage, had a prevalence in the alcoholic group which was somewhat less than twice its prevalence in one of the three non-alcoholic groups, but that prevalence was more than twice those in the other two non-alcoholic groups. Of the 22 symptoms considered to be medical or psychiatric complications of alcoholism, these six indicated that many subjects with alcoholism did behave agressively, or without restraint, in a way not generally characteristic of the illnesses included in the three other diagnostic groups.

The remaining 16 specific symptoms from general criterion 6 fall into three categories. The first category includes symptoms which probably result from at least several years of excessive drinking: nausea, vomiting, anorexia, and abdominal pain. The next category is of symptoms suggestive of organic brain damage presumably related to excessive alcoholic intake and the attendant common brain injury sustained while intoxicated. These include difficulties with simple arithmetic, poor memory, trouble thinking, and not reading or understanding as well as usual. There are two other symptoms which fall into this category but which are typical of a different manifestation of brain syndrome: belief that one is being spied upon and belief that someone is "after" one and trying to annoy one. The last category is of symptoms often seen as indicative of depression: suicidal ideas, subject's belief that he will never get well, statement of feeling sad, sadness, fears, and the taking of drugs every night for sleeping.

Among all of the subjects in this study, the gastrointestinal symptoms turned up second most often in subjects with alcoholism. This finding was assumed to be a direct result of excessive use of alcohol over a period of years. Three of the four symptoms occurred most often in the miscellaneous group and one of them—anorexia—occurred most often in affective disorder, depressed phase. While the high prevalence of these four symptoms in the alcoholic diagnostic group is assumed to be due to excessive use of alcohol, this is not likely to have been the cause of their higher prevalence in the other diagnostic groups which are not characterized by heavy drinking.

The second category of symptoms, those akin to the symptoms of brain damage, are, in subjects with alcoholism, most likely to be the result of years of falling when intoxicated and sustaining blows to the head. These same symptoms occur with a much higher prevalence in the miscellaneous group, in which cases they are apt to be due not to excessive use of alcohol but to organic brain syndrome or schizophrenia.

In the preceding two paragraphs, I have gone to some trouble to describe the way one symptom can—and must—be interpreted differently when the underlying diagnoses are different; i.e., the man with terminal cancer vomits for different reasons than does the man who is drunk. It is useful to keep this rather simplistic example in mind when considering symptom overlap in alcoholism and in affective disorder, depressed phase, in which the differences are more subtle and more easily confused. An example that is particularly illustrative is the symptom "suicidal ideas" (prevalence—38% of subjects with affective disorder; 48% of those with alcoholism). Although the prevalences here are not very different, the interviews with informants showed that, in alcoholism, the suicidal ideas were often directly concerned with disrupted affectional relationships occurring, in most cases, only six weeks prior to suicide. (See replication of this "six-week effect" in the study by Murphy et al.)[1] This did not happen in the lives of those subjects diagnosed as having had affective disorder, depressed phase.

As noted above, some of the 22 symptoms defining criterion 6 were selected by the investigators on the basis of clinical judgment and experience rather than always on the findings of higher prevalence. There are, in addition to the total of 30 criterion symptoms for alcoholism, a further 66 symptoms which occurred in the alcoholic subjects. Twelve were present in 33% or more of the alcoholic subjects. The remaining 54 symptoms occurred in from 32% to 3% of the alcoholic subjects (Table 3.1). There are, in this group of non-criterion symptoms, some that would seem more likely in subjects with affective disorder, depressed phase, while others are more typical of what is expected in alcoholism. As I discussed in regard to the criterion symptoms, alcoholism sometimes manifests itself in ways that, at first look, seem reminiscent of affective disorder, depressed phase, and the observer should remember the likelihood that the same symptom can have, in different illnesses, very different characteristics.

Of the 45 men diagnosed as having had affective disorder, depressed phase, eight (mentioned at the end of the preceding chapter) had symptoms sufficient for a possible second psychiatric diagnosis—alcoholism. All eight had developed serious depressive symptoms from four to ten months prior to suicide. Only two of the eight had ever had significant job troubles, a common symptom of alcoholism. In four of these subjects there were few or no complaints from family members about the alcoholism and, in four cases again, the subjects had stopped drinking or had diminished the amount of their drinking greatly during their last depressions.

I am describing these eight subjects who were diagnosed as having had affective disorder, depressed phase, in spite of the strong evidence of alcoholism to emphasize the occasional difficulty in deciding on the appropriate diagnosis for purposes of classification. Compared with the 33 subjects diagnosed as having had alcoholism, the eight just discussed did not fulfill the alcoholism criteria as completely as they did the affective disorder criteria. It is true that, in these cases in which alcoholism and affective disorder are part of the history, both diseases seem, at first look, to be almost equally prominent. Closer examination of a subject's history tips the scale in the proper direction for classification. An example from the eight cases described above is I.D. number 059, whose wife said that her husband had been a longtime, heavy drinker but that, as a couple, they had a good many close friends and an active social life together, a circumstance not usual in marriages with one alcoholic partner.[2] One of this informant's major complaints was that her husband was subject to spells of moodiness apparently unrelated to excessive drinking. His doctor felt that a brother's death had precipitated a depression that lasted the final year of his life. His wife's description makes it seem likely that a minor automobile accident six weeks before his suicide augmented his depressive symptoms and caused him to stop drinking altogether for the last six weeks of his life. The complete cessation of drinking and the increased number and intensity of depressive symptoms are the reasons that I classified the subject as having had, as his final illness, affective disorder, depressed phase, rather than alcoholism.

Two aspects of seemingly concurrent alcoholism and affective disorder struck me as I was reviewing the data from this study. The first is that alcoholism in combination with affective disorder, depressed phase, is not common. In this study, in only 8 (13%) of 63 cases of affective disorder, depressed phase, had alcoholism been present. In a study designed to investigate this question, 12% of subjects with affective disorder also suffered from alcoholism.[3]

The second aspect is that alcoholism did not, in our study, worsen when affective disorder, depressed phase, supervened. In fact, in half the cases, the alcoholic intake ceased or diminished greatly at that point.

I have included this discussion of overlapping symptoms in order to indicate to the reader how great the range of problems associated with alcoholism can be. While many of these overlapping symptoms are not diagnostically helpful in and of themselves, their presence in whatever combination with criterion symptoms does broaden the understanding of the depth of suffering for which alcoholism is responsible.

It is probable that the most devastating of the effects of alcoholism are not those upon the alcoholic subject's physical being but those upon his and his loved ones' emotions. In this study, the mean and median duration of alcoholism was 20 years. The minimum known duration was 7 years and the maximum duration 46 years. This is in sharp contrast to durations of final episodes of affective disorder, depressed phase, which, in our study, lasted less than one year in 87% of the subjects. Typical of alcoholism, which is a long-term illness, are frequent disruptions of subjects' affectional relationships. An alcoholic of long standing seems able to undergo an almost unlimited number of troubles in his home life and still maintain the urge to renew relationships or form new ones after the most severe emotional upheavals. However, in suicides of alcoholics, it is most often the case that the suicidal act closely follows one last incident in a string of violated and recreated relationships. In the present study, the completed suicide followed such last incidents within six weeks in one-third of the alcoholic subjects and within a year among an additional half of them. Thus, completed suicide occurred within one year of a severe affectional disruption in about 85% of the alcoholic subjects. In comparison, in those subjects with affective disorder, depressed phase, the proportion of suicides that occurred within six weeks of a final disrupted affectional relationship was one-tenth that of the rate among subjects diagnosed as having had alcoholism. Within a one-year period, the affective disorder rate was less than one-third the rate of the alcoholic subjects.[4] So it looks as if it is a matter, in alcoholism and suicide, of there being a straw that breaks the camel's back. What isn't clear is why the individual camel's back breaks under the weight of a given straw at a given time. Because this question is of continuing interest to psychiatrists, an attempt to answer it has been an aspect in studies of attempted suicide. In one such study, the question "What was the chief reason for your attempt?" is included in interviews with such subjects. Persons suffering from affective disorder, depressed phase, most often gave personal reasons such as feelings of guilt or of hopelessness, while, in contrast, subjects suffering from alcoholism gave social reasons such as family trouble, legal trouble, or loss of job.[5]

In the present study, informants provided numerous examples of the particular kinds of suffering experienced by and inflicted on others by alcoholic subjects. These included outbursts of anger causing danger to the safety of those close to the subject, disturbing the privacy and peace of strangers as well as that of acquaintances and neighbors, living in isolation (over half the cases in this study lived alone), violation of marriage to the point of separations and divorce, disregard for the welfare and emotional security of offspring, trouble with police as a result of drunk driving, automobile accidents, peace disturbance, fighting and destruction of property, crass failure to provide financially and emotionally for those for whom the subject was legally responsible.

In addition to the social troubles and indignities inflicted by alcoholics on themselves and on others, there were many cases of their having alcohol-induced physical problems. One-third of the alcoholic subjects in the sample had gastrointestinal illnesses and symptoms—cirrhosis, ascites, alcoholic gastritis, anorexia, nausea, vomiting, and abdominal pain. Besides these frequent gastrointestinal symptoms, there were also many symptoms observed in the histories of the alcoholic subjects which were reminiscent of those seen in affective disorder, depressed phase. These kinds of symptoms were not, of course, sufficiently concentrated for diagnosis of affective disorder, but were scattered symptoms. Therefore, it can be assumed that in alcoholism these scattered symptoms similar to those of affective disorder may be manifestations of brain damage (due to head injuries). These symptoms are mainly those causing psychological pain, but also include a few, like outbursts of rage, which are potentially destructive to others. Some of those causing the alcoholic subjects psychological pain are suicidal ideas, disbelief in the possibility of recovery, sadness, prophecy of black future, and conviction of the loss of mind. Given the apparent difference in the pathogenesis of what sound like the same symptoms, it is likely that they involve and affect differently diagnosed subjects in quite different ways.

The alcoholic is of course aware of society's expectation of "self-control," a possibility beyond the alcoholic's grasp. Thus, he is doubly afflicted and most likely to turn the blame on family, boss, friends—society as it accuses him. Years of alcoholism intensify the uselessness of this reasoning.

Again, as in the previous chapter, the individual case histories of this diagnostic group are arranged by sex and age, along with their "score cards."

REFERENCES

1. Murphy, G.E., Armstrong, J.W., Hermele, S.L., Fischer, J.R. and Clendenin, W.W. Suicide and alcoholism. *Arch. Gen. Psychiat.* 36:65–69, 1979.
2. Amark, C. A study in alcoholism: Clinical, social-psychiatric and genetic investigations. *Acta psychiat. et neurol. Scand.* (suppl. 70) 1951.
3. Pitts, F.N., Jr. and Winokur, G. Affective disorder—VII: Alcoholism and affective disorder. *J. Psychiat. Res.* 4:37–50, 1966.
4. Murphy, G.E. and Robins, E. Social factors in suicide. *JAMA* 199:303–308, 1967.
5. Schmidt, E.H., O'Neal, P. and Robins, E. Evaluation of suicide attempts as guide to therapy: Clinical and follow-up study of 109 patients. *JAMA* 155:549–557, 1954.

ALCOHOLISM, SUBGROUP 1

Men aged 35 and under (N = 4)

022 Informant: Wife

This 34-year-old white unskilled laborer was first married in 1936 and divorced in 1944 because of his wife's infidelity. In spite of the latter, she was awarded alimony for the children. He changed his name and left their hometown in order to avoid paying alimony. After his divorce it was his habit to return periodically to the town where his wife and children lived. There, he would spend hours watching them from a distance, but never approached them or talked to them. In 1954, he married his second wife, the informant. (Since the only informant was his second wife, events prior to the last two years of his life are known sketchily or not at all.) Three characteristics which were most striking to the informant were his excessive alcoholic intake, his ungovernable temper, and his absolute lack of friends. He drank daily and to great excess. About three times a week she would have to go down to the taverns and bring him home. His spells of anger were extremely severe. Frequently he became so angry that everything appeared black to him; the informant believed that on these occasions he may actually have been momentarily blind. On one occasion the light switch in the house trailer did not work. Enraged, he went outside the trailer and threw rocks at the windows until he had broken them all. On another occasion when his car would not start, he kicked off both front fenders. Several times when he did not like his breakfast he had taken the plate and its contents and thrown them out the trailer door. On many occasions when angry he had driven very fast around town. Other times he would drive at high speeds from one city to another. His wife also mentioned that he had frequently left home for periods up to two weeks and returned telling her only that he had been to Indiana. Once he had beaten a drunken man so badly that he had almost killed him. On at least one occasion he and his wife had fought physically. His wife knew that many of these angry episodes had occurred while he was drinking, but she could not be sure whether all of them had. He had absolutely no friends, and, once they married, he did not permit his wife to see her old friends or to make any new ones. He liked no one. He had a special hatred of physicians and would have nothing to do with them.

His wife described him as being disgusted with the world, spiteful, and attention-seeking (from her) during the entire two years she knew him. He was not depressed, and although he had sometimes claimed he was no good, he had always added that he was still better than everyone else. He had great difficulties holding jobs and had at least seven in the year prior to his suicide. He suffered from frequent early morning headaches that usually lasted two days. He had a spell of three or four blackouts once every two weeks. It was not possible to get an adequate description of these from his wife. She believed he lost contact although he never fell. If she attempted to touch him in order to help him during these momentary blackouts he would fight her off violently. He expressed a fear that he might be run over by an automobile and he spoke frequently of being better off dead and of committing suicide, saying "It's hell here on earth; it'll be Heaven after I'm dead." He talked about sex a great deal though he showed no evidence of diminished sex drive, and his wife said that "he was a good man in bed."

On the day of his suicide he had just returned from a ten-day unexplained absence, walked into his wife's place of work and asked her for money. When she gave him some, he complained it was not enough. A few hours later he drove to a bridge, parked his car, and jumped off. His body was recovered from the river some hours later. When his wife was asked why she thought he committed suicide, she responded, "He had no reason to live. No one liked him and he didn't like anyone."

Family history: Alcoholic sister.
Arrest record: None.

Case No. 022 M X F__ Age 34

ST. LOUIS SUICIDE STUDY CRITERIA FOR ALCOHOLISM

At least three of the following selected drinking behaviors were required for diagnosis.

A. Informant thought subject drank too much   X
B. Subject drank daily   X
C. Subject went on benders (at least 48 hours of drinking and neglect of usual routine)   __
D. Family objected to subject's drinking   X
E. Subject's history included arrests related to drinking   __
F. Subject suffered medical and psychiatric complications due to alcoholic intake   X
G. Subject thought he drank too much   __
H. Subject had job difficulties related to drinking   X
I. Subject involved in automobile accident(s) related to drinking   __

FEIGHNER CRITERIA FOR ALCOHOLISM

A definite diagnosis required symptoms in at least three of the following four groups. A probable diagnosis required symptoms in only two of the four groups.

A.
1. Any manifestation of alcohol withdrawal such as tremulousness, convulsions, hallucinations, or delirium _X_
2. History of medical complications, e.g. cirrhosis, gastritis, pancreatitis, myopathy, polyneuropathy, Wernicke-Korsakov's syndrome ___
3. Alcoholic blackouts, i.e., amnesic episodes during heavy drinking not accounted for by head trauma _X_
4. Alcoholic binges or benders (48 hours or more of drinking associated with default of usual obligations): must have occurred more than once ___

B.
1. Subject unable to stop drinking at will ___
2. Subject tried to control drinking by allowing himself to drink only under certain circumstances, such as only after 5:00 p.m., only on weekends, or only with others ___
3. Subject drank before breakfast ___
4. Subject drank nonbeverage forms of alcohol (hair oil, mouthwash, Sterno, etc.) ___

C.
1. Subject arrested for drinking ___
2. Subject involved in traffic difficulties associated with drinking ___
3. Subject had trouble at work because of drinking _X_
4. Subject involved in fights associated with drinking _X_

D.
1. Subject worried about drinking too much ___
2. Family objected to subject's drinking _X_
3. Subject lost friends because of drinking _X_
4. Other people objected to subject's drinking ___
5. Subject felt guilty about his drinking ___

104 Informants: Great-uncle, grandmother

Three months before he committed suicide, this 24-year-old black man had lost his father who had raised him. Informants felt that the subject's behavior after his father's death had become "sullen and withdrawn."

Born in St. Louis, he was his parents' only child. His father had worked as a porter and handyman and the family had always lived in a poor section of St. Louis with a group of older relatives. When the subject was about 10, his parents got divorced. His mother moved to New Mexico and he spent one year there with her. While in New Mexico, he had been thrown from his bicycle by a car and had suffered head injuries resulting for several years in severe headaches accompanied by vomiting. He returned to his father when his mother left New Mexico for Indiana. His great-uncle was not certain how far the subject had gone in school, but remembered that, while still attending, he had often been truant. The uncle said that he had been close to his father who could easily hurt his feelings with criticism, and that though he and his father had often fought, the subject had become furious at his mother when she refused to attend her ex-husband's funeral.

At 18, he joined the military service (his great-uncle did not know which branch), served for three years, and received an honorable discharge. His grandmother and great-uncle both remarked that, once home from the service, he had had "spells," usually after drinking heavily, during which he became angry, loud, abusive, and threw things around. Though he was never known to actually hit anyone, he had often threatened to hit and kill people and had once threatened to kill his mother if she "didn't treat him right." He had apparently told his mother several times that he sometimes wished he were dead. In the last three months of his life, he had seemed to his great-uncle particularly depressed and disgusted with himself and had several times been heard to say that he drank too much, that he was "no good," and that his family would be better off without him. Once, during one of his drunken "spells," he asked his uncle why he didn't "just take [the] shotgun and blow [his] brains out."

He had had about four jobs in the three years following his discharge from the service and was, at the time of his death, a porter at a small St. Louis manufacturing company. His uncle said that he had "money to spend" and "plenty of clothes." Although his relatives knew that he drank heavily on occasion, they were not sure whether or not he took drugs, nor were they sure whether he had ever been arrested even though he bragged that he "had been locked up once or twice." He "ran with a gang" which was said to be a "dope gang" and, two or three weeks before his suicide, he mentioned that the gang "was out to get him" unless he did what they wanted. For the last two months of his life, he never seemed hungry, hardly ate at all, and had obviously begun to lose weight. A month before he died, he was involved in a minor car accident and saw a physician for his "hurt back." During the last month of his life, he was increasingly restless and nervous. The informants said he would suddenly jump up, start packing, say he was leaving and then, just as suddenly, unpack. He borrowed a large sum of money a few weeks before he died. According to his great-uncle, the last two weeks of his life he "looked scared." He had peered out the apartment windows, listened at the front door, and paced nervously. There were nights when he never went to bed at all, but stayed up talking incessantly and unnecessarily.

A few days before his suicide, he left a note with a secretary at his job. The note said: "Gloria, next week, send my last week's pay by money order to (his name) at (his mother's address in Indiana). Don't give anyone my address." On the evening of his death, he lingered after work on the corner of his street with some of his friends. He shook hands with all of them and said to one, "Come on, shake hands with me. This might be the last time you can shake hands with me . . . I'm going to catch up with my daddy." When he left them, he said he had a date that night. Once at home, he told his relatives he was leaving for Milwaukee and got out his packed suitcases. He ate no supper, but stood by the window peering out into the street. When his great-uncle, who was on his way out to church, asked him why he did that, he did not answer. After his uncle had left, he asked his grandmother several times when she was going to bed. When she was in bed, she heard him take something out of a closet and then climb the stairs to his room on the third floor. When his great-uncle returned from church later in the evening, he found the subject's body on the floor of his room, his head wrapped in a pillow. He had shot himself with a .32 caliber automatic pistol which had belonged to his father. He left no note.

Family history: There was no family history of psychiatric illness.
Arrest record: None.

Case No. *104* M X F__ Age *24*

ST. LOUIS SUICIDE STUDY CRITERIA FOR ALCOHOLISM

At least three of the following selected drinking behaviors were required for diagnosis.

A. Informant thought subject drank too much X	F. Subject suffered medical and psychiatric complications due to alcoholic intake	X
B. Subject drank daily __		
C. Subject went on benders (at least 48 hours of drinking and neglect of usual routine) __	G. Subject thought he drank too much	X
D. Family objected to subject's drinking X	H. Subject had job difficulties related to drinking	__
E. Subject's history included arrests related to drinking __	I. Subject involved in automobile accident(s) related to drinking	__

FEIGNER CRITERIA FOR ALCOHOLISM

A definite diagnosis required symptoms in at least three of the following four groups. A probable diagnosis required symptoms in only two of the four groups.

A. 1. Any manifestation of alcohol withdrawal such as tremulousness, convulsions, hallucinations, or delirium ___
   2. History of medical complications, e.g. cirrhosis, gastritis, pancreatitis, myopathy, polyneuropathy, Wernicke-Korsakov's syndrome ___
   3. Alcoholic blackouts, i.e., amnesic episodes during heavy drinking not accounted for by head trauma ___
   4. Alcoholic binges or benders (48 hours or more of drinking associated with default of usual obligations): must have occurred more than once ___

B. 1. Subject unable to stop drinking at will ___
   2. Subject tried to control drinking by allowing himself to drink only under certain circumstances, such as only after 5:00 p.m., only on weekends, or only with others ___
   3. Subject drank before breakfast ___
   4. Subject drank nonbeverage forms of alcohol (hair oil, mouthwash, Sterno, etc.) ___

C. 1. Subject arrested for drinking ___
   2. Subject involved in traffic difficulties associated with drinking ___
   3. Subject had trouble at work because of drinking ___
   4. Subject involved in fights associated with drinking ___

D. 1. Subject worried about drinking too much **X**
   2. Family objected to subject's drinking **X**
   3. Subject lost friends because of drinking ___
   4. Other people objected to subject's drinking ___
   5. Subject felt guilty about his drinking **X**

---

121 Informants: Parents, fellow worker, fellow boarding house roomers

The parents of this 25-year-old, single white man were uncommunicative in the interview concerning their son's death. Beyond simple facts—that he was the 5th of their 10 children, that he had graduated from high school, had never married, had served for two years in the Army, and had been given an honorable discharge—they gave no information about his past, and avoided discussion of his behavior and personality except for a comment that he "might have been more nervous since he got back from the service." As far as events just prior to his suicide were concerned, they reported that he had lived with them for the three years since his discharge from the Army, but had moved six weeks before his death and had been living alone in a rooming house. They had seen him only once in those six weeks, on the day of his suicide. They said he had seemed "fine" then and that he had planned to come back to see them the next day. At 2:00 AM the next morning, they received a telephone call from a hospital and were informed that he had shot himself and had died in the hospital after an unsuccessful emergency operation. He had left a note which said he was sorry for what he was going to do, but that it was "the only way out." His mother reluctantly admitted, at the end of the interview, that her son had been a heavy drinker for a long time.

His record at the chemical company where he worked as a "mill hand" could not be located, but a fellow worker who had known him fairly well said he was a good worker who never caused trouble on the job, that he had been in "good spirits" the day before his suicide, and that there was no question of his being laid off. The fellow worker said that the factory rumor was that he had fought bitterly with his father and had moved away from home at least 8 or 10 months earlier. He felt fairly certain of the truth of that rumor, but another he mentioned—that the subject had "gotten his girlfriend in trouble"—he described as "pure grapevine." He had mentioned having one traffic arrest associated with drinking.

Several of his fellow roomers at the boarding house stated that he drank too much.

Family history: The subject's parents denied any family history of suicide or psychiatric illness.

Arrest record: Hearsay—one traffic arrest for drunken driving.

Case No. 121   M _X_ F __   Age 25

ST. LOUIS SUICIDE STUDY CRITERIA FOR ALCOHOLISM

At least three of the following selected drinking behaviors were required for diagnosis.

A. Informant thought subject drank too much _X_
B. Subject drank daily ___
C. Subject went on benders (at least 48 hours of drinking and neglect of usual routine) ___
D. Family objected to subject's drinking _X_
E. Subject's history included arrests related to drinking ___
F. Subject suffered medical and psychiatric complications due to alcoholic intake ___
G. Subject thought he drank too much ___
H. Subject had job difficulties related to drinking ___
I. Subject involved in automobile accident(s) related to drinking _X_

FEIGHNER CRITERIA FOR ALCOHOLISM

A definite diagnosis required symptoms in at least three of the following four groups. A probable diagnosis required symptoms in only two of the four groups.

A. 1. Any manifestation of alcohol withdrawal such as tremulousness, convulsions, hallucinations, or delirium ___
    2. History of medical complications, e.g. cirrhosis, gastritis, pancreatitis, myopathy, polyneuropathy, Wernicke-Korsakov's syndrome ___
    3. Alcoholic blackouts, i.e., amnesic episodes during heavy drinking not accounted for by head trauma ___
    4. Alcoholic binges or benders (48 hours or more of drinking associated with default of usual obligations): must have occurred more than once ___

B. 1. Subject unable to stop drinking at will ___
    2. Subject tried to control drinking by allowing himself to drink only under certain circumstances, such as only after 5:00 p.m., only on weekends, or only with others ___
    3. Subject drank before breakfast ___
    4. Subject drank nonbeverage forms of alcohol (hair oil, mouthwash, Sterno, etc.) ___

C. 1. Subject arrested for drinking ___
    2. Subject involved in traffic difficulties associated with drinking _X_
    3. Subject had trouble at work because of drinking ___
    4. Subject involved in fights associated with drinking ___

D. 1. Subject worried about drinking too much ___
    2. Family objected to subject's drinking ___
    3. Subject lost friends because of drinking ___
    4. Other people objected to subject's drinking _X_
    5. Subject felt guilty about his drinking ___

129 Informants: Mother, mother-in-law (attempted murder + suicide)

This 31-year-old white attendant and part-owner of a service station was described, by his mother, as being a tolerant man, slow to anger. On the rare occasions he did become angry, however, his anger was extreme. His mother-in-law described him as always having been hot-tempered and easy to anger. Both informants agreed that he was a hard worker and that he had worked steadily at the service station for 14 years. The mother stated that the subject may have had a problem with alcohol, but that it never gave him any trouble. The mother-in-law said that he spent most of his leisure time in taverns, that he drank too much, and that he occasionally went on benders. The mother-in-law, however, did say that he had never been in any serious difficulty because of drinking.

His temper had gotten him into difficulties at the service station and he had had quarrels with his brothers, with whom he managed the station. Some months before his death these quarrels reached such intensity that one of the brothers quit the service station. The subject's irritability had increased over the past two years of his life and become much exacerbated nine months prior to his death when he discovered that his wife was seeing another man. The night he discovered this he had hit his wife, knocking out her front teeth. He then threatened to kill her and himself with a pistol which he pointed at her chest. She locked herself in her room, while he wrote a note in which they jointly bequeathed their property to their two children. He signed it, and told her to sign it. When she refused to do so, he finally went to bed. A few days later his wife asked for a divorce. He refused to give her one because, he said, he loved her too much. He told his mother-in-law, "I can't live without her."

In the ensuing nine months he told his wife on many occasions that he was going to kill himself. He had several times held a knife to his bared chest and whispered to her, "I wonder how it would feel." On other occasions he had put up a rope with a hangman's noose in the basement and taken his wife down to the basement, put his head through and noose, and said, "I wonder how it would feel." The night of his suicide he had been drinking while his wife rested in her room. He entered her room and said, "I'm going to settle this once and for all. I'm going to bring him (his wife's friend) here." She said, "Don't be foolish, it's late." He was adamant. Before he left she got out of bed and began applying cosmetics. He asked, "Getting prettied up for him?" She replied, "I've been asleep and I'm trying to wake up." He left the house, found the man at a tavern, and told him, "We'll settle things peaceably. If my wife tells you she doesn't want to see you any more, will you leave? If she chooses you, I will leave." The two men returned to the subject's home where all three met in the kitchen and a violent argument began. During the argument the subject suddenly pulled a knife and stabbed his wife in the back. He and the other man then ran from the house and grappled in the front yard. He stabbed the other man six times, then stabbed himself and died almost immediately. His wife and the man survived. A note he had written previously and addressed to his parents-in-law stated that he was having trouble with his wife and that he was going to commit suicide. He asked them for forgiveness and said he loved them both.

Family history: There was no family history of psychiatric illness.
Arrest record: None.

Case No. *129* M _X_ F __ Age _31_

ST. LOUIS SUICIDE STUDY CRITERIA FOR ALCOHOLISM

At least three of the following selected drinking behaviors were required for diagnosis.

A. Informant thought subject drank too much _X_

B. Subject drank daily _X_

C. Subject went on benders (at least 48 hours of drinking and neglect of usual routine) _X_

D. Family objected to subject's drinking _X_

E. Subject's history included arrests related to drinking __

F. Subject suffered medical and psychiatric complications due to alcoholic intake __

G. Subject thought he drank too much __

H. Subject had job difficulties related to drinking _X_

I. Subject involved in automobile accident(s) related to drinking __

FEIGHNER CRITERIA FOR ALCOHOLISM

A definite diagnosis required symptoms in at least three of the following four groups. A probable diagnosis required symptoms in only two of the four groups.

A. 1. Any manifestation of alcohol withdrawal such as tremulousness, convulsions, hallucinations, or delirium ___
    2. History of medical complications, e.g. cirrhosis, gastritis, pancreatitis, myopathy, polyneuropathy, Wernicke-Korsakov's syndrome ___
    3. Alcoholic blackouts, i.e., amnesic episodes during heavy drinking not accounted for by head trauma ___
    4. Alcoholic binges or benders (48 hours or more of drinking associated with default of usual obligations): must have occurred more than once _X_

B. 1. Subject unable to stop drinking at will _X_
    2. Subject tried to control drinking by allowing himself to drink only under certain circumstances, such as only after 5:00 p.m., only on weekends, or only with others ___
    3. Subject drank before breakfast ___
    4. Subject drank nonbeverage forms of alcohol (hair oil, mouthwash, Sterno, etc.) ___

C. 1. Subject arrested for drinking ___
    2. Subject involved in traffic difficulties associated with drinking ___
    3. Subject had trouble at work because of drinking _X_
    4. Subject involved in fights associated with drinking ___

D. 1. Subject worried about drinking too much ___
    2. Family objected to subject's drinking _X_
    3. Subject lost friends because of drinking ___
    4. Other people objected to subject's drinking _X_
    5. Subject felt guilty about his drinking ___

ALCOHOLISM, SUBGROUP 2
Men aged 36–56 (N = 9)

007 Informants: Brother, sister-in-law; hospital, social service, and police records

This 43-year-old white, unemployed butcher had a history of excessive alcoholic intake from age 26 or even earlier. When he was 4 years old his parents separated permanently. After a year in an orphan home, he returned to live with his father and step-mother. There seemed to be little parental care—harsh treatment from his step-mother and indifference from his father. He completed nine grades of school and then quit to go to work.

At age 16 he began a lifelong career of trouble with the police (see below). By his early twenties he was drinking excessively. At age 25, he married. Because he changed jobs frequently, and was out of work much of the time, he essentially lived off his wife's salary. At age 28, he enlisted in the Army and received an honorable discharge at the end of World War II. While in the Army he had driven a car for two officers who looted several German homes, but he did not share in the loot. After his discharge he returned home and continued to drink excessively. At his wife's insistence, they moved to Kansas City, where he continued to drink and got into further difficulties with the police. On one occasion, he threatened his wife with a gun and then went to a tavern and threatened a number of people there. One of the informants believes the latter episode involved one of the looting army officers and was an effort to get his share. He was taken to a local hospital and his family was told that he was an alcoholic. During the time in Kansas City, the informants felt that there was a marked worsening in his behavior which never again became even passable.

He was extremely proud of his appearance and strength. In Kansas City, where it was necessary for him to have all his teeth removed, he told the informant, "When a man loses his teeth, he loses his strength." His depression was obvious and he began to wear army clothes around Kansas City until the police stopped him from doing so.

At age 36, he returned again to St. Louis, separated from his wife (their divorce was final three years later), and went to live with his father with whom he remained until his suicide.

Approximately two and a half years prior to his death, his behavior became increasingly disturbed. He complained that the FBI was after him, or, alternatively, that he was an FBI agent. He sometimes thought the house was wired and spoke of being spied on by a man with a telescope. He also spoke of having visions. He realized he was ill and went voluntarily into a mental hospital. There his depression was noted. He complained of severe headaches, said he feared he might commit suicide, and that he wanted help so that he would not. On the day of admission he stated that voices were telling him to kill himself, but no other delusions or hallucinations, including those about the FBI and about being spied on, were elicited at any time during his six-week hospital stay. He was tremulous and fearful on admission but this cleared before discharge. He was oriented and not considered psychotic. Psychological report showed an I.Q. of 114.

After his release he was not depressed for awhile, but "had a peculiar look in his eyes." Later he began to complain of fatigue and some depression. He then developed insomnia and loss of interest and began to neglect his appearance. He was never able to hold a job again. He was known to have hit his elderly and senile father on occasion but only when drinking. During the next 18 months he was readmitted to a general hospital twice with acute intoxication and lacerations. The last time, eight months prior to his death, he stated that a member of a gang was trying to kill him. He believed the gang members were friends of another brother of his who was in prison and was known to be a repetitive criminal. Because of his fear of this gang, he became frightened of going out, and would run and hide when the doorbell rang.

In the month before his suicide his behavior became even worse. He began worrying about losing his mind, feeling he was worthless and no good, and he became preoccupied with religion. He carried a Bible and a picture of Jesus with him everywhere. He lost weight, complained of feeling weak, stopped seeing the informants, and was generally less active. About one week before his suicide he tore the lining out of a suitcase, filled it with water, and said it was an H-bomb. He talked about committing suicide and asked to be buried in the National Cemetery. Once, when visiting his sister-in-law's home, he destroyed all pictures of himself. His drinking continued. The informants were not certain about his orientation and memory, but noted that he could still go from his house to theirs without assistance.

On the day of his suicide he told his father not to bother him, went into his room and remained there all day. The next day his father found that he had hanged himself.

Family history: One brother was a repetitive criminal, currently in prison. Another brother was "nervous" (not further described). His mother had two "nervous breakdowns" and was hospitalized in a mental hospital each time, but seemed to recover both times. A half-sister was hospitalized in a mental hospital (no other details known). His father presumably had a senile psychosis.

Arrest record: 39 arrests between 1930 and 1955, at least one occurring almost every year. These were arrests for drinking, burglary, investigation, peace disturbance, car theft, and carrying a gun.

Case No. 007 M X F __ Age 43

ST. LOUIS SUICIDE STUDY CRITERIA FOR ALCOHOLISM

At least three of the following selected drinking behaviors were required for diagnosis.

- A. Informant thought subject drank too much X
- B. Subject drank daily X
- C. Subject went on benders (at least 48 hours of drinking and neglect of usual routine) ___
- D. Family objected to subject's drinking X
- E. Subject's history included arrests related to drinking X
- F. Subject suffered medical and psychiatric complications due to alcoholic intake X
- G. Subject thought he drank too much X
- H. Subject had job difficulties related to drinking X
- I. Subject involved in automobile accident(s) related to drinking X

FEIGHNER CRITERIA FOR ALCOHOLISM

A definite diagnosis required symptoms in at least three of the following four groups. A probable diagnosis required symptoms in only two of the four groups.

- A.
  1. Any manifestation of alcohol withdrawal such as tremulousness, convulsions, hallucinations, or delirium X
  2. History of medical complications, e.g. cirrhosis, gastritis, pancreatitis, myopathy, polyneuropathy, Wernicke-Korsakov's syndrome ___
  3. Alcoholic blackouts, i.e., amnesic episodes during heavy drinking not accounted for by head trauma ___
  4. Alcoholic binges or benders (48 hours or more of drinking associated with default of usual obligations): must have occurred more than once ___

- B.
  1. Subject unable to stop drinking at will ___
  2. Subject tried to control drinking by allowing himself to drink only under certain circumstances, such as only after 5:00 p.m., only on weekends, or only with others ___
  3. Subject drank before breakfast ___
  4. Subject drank nonbeverage forms of alcohol (hair oil, mouthwash, Sterno, etc.) ___

- C.
  1. Subject arrested for drinking X
  2. Subject involved in traffic difficulties associated with drinking ___
  3. Subject had trouble at work because of drinking X
  4. Subject involved in fights associated with drinking X

- D.
  1. Subject worried about drinking too much X
  2. Family objected to subject's drinking X
  3. Subject lost friends because of drinking ___
  4. Other people objected to subject's drinking ___
  5. Subject felt guilty about his drinking ___

015 Informants: Sister, real estate agent, friend; social service, hospital, and police records

This 49-year-old white unemployed carpenter had been a chronic alcoholic since age 21, if not earlier. He had had job difficulties, arrests, and family troubles related to excessive alcoholic intake. During much of his life he had been able to work as a carpenter although he had at times been fired. His behavior when sober frequently alternated between joviality and moodiness. During alcoholic binges he was usually depressed and mean. Apparently alcohol rarely if ever made him jovial. He was described as cantankerous and depressed following his drinking bouts. He married at age 21, separated from his wife at age 33, and was divorced at age 34. He moved frequently from job to job, remaining out of contact with his family for months and, on at least one occasion, for years. He had three sons who died in infancy and one daughter who survived.

At age 34, two years after a skull fracture, he was admitted to a general hospital with a post-concussion syndrome. At that time he was drinking excessively and complained of vomiting, of marked startle reaction, headache, dizziness, and poor vision with an orange-red color to the environment. Shortly after this admission, social service investigation elicited the information that he had abused his wife prior to their separation and had had several automobile accidents related to his drinking. He had tried to abduct his daughter, who was seven at the time, from her school. The ex-wife applied to the court for custody of the child to prevent him from taking her again.

At age 40, after having been out of St. Louis for some time, he returned. He did not contribute to his child's support. He was described as a "mental case" at the time. At a court hearing concerning his daughter he was noted to be intoxicated, red-eyed, and tremulous. His daughter had been living with him for a few weeks just prior to that time, but she left complaining that he treated her cruelly. He was still very bitter toward his ex-wife, who had remarried, and a year before the court hearing, while still out of St. Louis, he had sent her a (toy) snake in the mail and enclosed a note which read, "This is a mate for you."

Approximately 18 months prior to his death he began living with a woman in a common-law relationship. They were also partners in a venture to convert and rent their house as a rooming house. Having put all his money into the conversion, they found that a zoning law forbade rooming houses in the neighborhood. About four months prior to his suicide his common-law wife left him, taking all of the new furniture and plumbing fixtures. He continued to live alone in the bare house. Approximately four months after his common-law wife left, a neighbor missed seeing him, although his car was still parked in front of the house. On approaching the house, the neighbor noticed an unpleasant smell and a large number of flies, and called the police. The subject's decomposed and almost unrecognizable body was found inside. He had shot himself in the head approximately ten days previously. No empty whiskey bottles were found and only a few of his clothes. Most of his personal possessions, including his watch and photographs of Saudi Arabia and Greenland which he had taken and prized very highly, were gone.

The common-law wife could not be found for interview. His sister, who gave the primary interview, had not seen him for a year. As a result, a detailed description of his symptoms and behavior just before his suicide were not available. A very elderly neighbor (about whose reliability there was some doubt) said that there had been no definite evidence of depression or behavior change.

Family history: A cousin had committed suicide many year previously. His daughter, while still in elementary school, began to behave uncontrollably. Later she became an intractable truant. She was involved in several sexual escapades at a very young age. The later career of the daughter is not known. His ex-wife drank excessively and was said to have "loose morals," including infidelity.

Arrest record: He had five arrests. Three were at age 34 for hitting a pedestrian in a vehicular accident, for peace disturbance, and for driving on the wrong side of the road while intoxicated. A fourth arrest at age 47 was for a minor traffic offense. A fifth arrest at age 48 was for peace disturbance.

Case No. *015* M _X_ F __ Age *49*

ST. LOUIS SUICIDE STUDY CRITERIA FOR ALCOHOLISM

At least three of the following selected drinking behaviors were required for diagnosis.

A. Informant thought subject drank too much __

B. Subject drank daily __

C. Subject went on benders (at least 48 hours of drinking and neglect of usual routine) _X_

D. Family objected to subject's drinking _X_

E. Subject's history included arrests related to drinking _X_

F. Subject suffered medical and psychiatric complications due to alcoholic intake _X_

G. Subject thought he drank too much __

H. Subject had job difficulties related to drinking __

I. Subject involved in automobile accident(s) related to drinking _X_

FEIGHNER CRITERIA FOR ALCOHOLISM

A definite diagnosis required symptoms in at least three of the following four groups. A probable diagnosis required symptoms in only two of the four groups.

A. 1. Any manifestation of alcohol withdrawal such as tremulousness, convulsions, hallucinations, or delirium __X__
    2. History of medical complications, e.g. cirrhosis, gastritis, pancreatitis, myopathy, polyneuropathy, Wernicke-Korsakov's syndrome __X__
    3. Alcoholic blackouts, i.e., amnesic episodes during heavy drinking not accounted for by head trauma ____
    4. Alcoholic binges or benders (48 hours or more of drinking associated with default of usual obligations): must have occurred more than once __X__

B. 1. Subject unable to stop drinking at will ____
    2. Subject tried to control drinking by allowing himself to drink only under certain circumstances, such as only after 5:00 p.m., only on weekends, or only with others ____
    3. Subject drank before breakfast ____
    4. Subject drank nonbeverage forms of alcohol (hair oil, mouthwash, Sterno, etc.) ____

C. 1. Subject arrested for drinking __X__
    2. Subject involved in traffic difficulties associated with drinking __X__
    3. Subject had trouble at work because of drinking __X__
    4. Subject involved in fights associated with drinking __X__

D. 1. Subject worried about drinking too much ____
    2. Family objected to subject's drinking __X__
    3. Subject lost friends because of drinking __X__
    4. Other people objected to subject's drinking ____
    5. Subject felt guilty about his drinking ____

---

017 *Informants: Mother-in-law, friend, employer, fellow worker, attorney, hospital and police records (murder + suicide)*

This 44-year-old white furniture handler was described as having had an explosive temper all of his life. As a young man he was in many fights and was known to strike people without apparent provocation. (There was no history available concerning his behavior prior to age 19.) He frequently spoke of hurting "niggers" and others. He believed he was the "cock of the walk" with women. He was financially irresponsible and had always been so. He was described as erratic in his moods: "He'd smile at you one second and smash your head the next. Five minutes later he'd be all honey and sponge cake again." He always believed and talked about being "extra smart," despite the fact that his accomplishments were few.

His life was punctuated with periods of severe violence. At age 21, he beat a police officer to death and served eight years in prison. While in prison he assaulted a "stool pigeon" and spent 42 days in solitary confinement. At age 36, he was arrested for common assault. Three years later a motorist cut sharply in front of him in traffic. He caught up with the motorist, dragged him from his car, and gave him a severe beating. (His more recent violent behavior is described below.) Subsequent to his discharge from prison at age 29, he had a fear of closed spaces and locked rooms, which he attributed to his time in solitary confinement. He also refused to be around groups of people, whether at parties or at gatherings of persons whom he did not know.

He married for the first time at age 29 and was divorced four or five years later. He accused his first wife of being a drug addict. The informants stated this accusation was false and that their marital difficulties were as much his fault as hers. He married for the second and last time at age 35. About two years after his second marriage his wife went to a physician complaining of scanty menses, flushing, nervousness, and sexual frigidity. She was followed for four months, showing no improvement. She then stopped seeing the physician and there are no further medical records available concerning her.

He began to drink excessively as a young man, and his drinking led him to have troubles at work, with his family, and with the police. He drank daily for years and would go on frequent "benders." During the last few months of his life he was drinking at least 12 bottles of beer daily plus other alcoholic beverages. In spite of this heavy intake, each of the informants agreed that he was drinking less during the last two years of his life than he had for some years previously. Despite the fact that he had trouble on some jobs because of drinking, he was, in general, a good worker. He would often quit a job to get a better one and occasionally would quit because, he alleged, he did not get along with the boss or the fellow workers. In either instance, he was frequently asked back to the old job. His present employer and fellow workers stated that he had been working at one place as a furniture handler for the past two years. He was described as quiet and not aggressive, and was known to have missed work only occasionally and then for a day or at most a few days.

Two years before his death he was admitted to a hospital with a perforated duodenal ulcer which was repaired surgically. He did not return for follow-up attention and, insofar as the informants knew, did not subsequently complain of abdominal symptoms or discomfort.

During the last two years of his life, his relationship with his wife worsened considerably. Informants described among other incidents how he would, while driving his car, pretend to doze, and then permit the car to go off the road at a high speed. His wife's terror only served to make him do this more often. During this period he would undergo rapid changes in his feelings toward his wife, hating her bitterly and then loving her to frenzied excess. In general, however, the bitter feelings began to predominate. He taught his four-year-old son to call his mother names such as "whore" and "bitch." His behavior at home, his fears of closed places, and his avoidance of other people worsened considerably. For the first time his wife felt she could (or should) put him in a mental hospital. Their relationship continued to deteriorate and, finally, six months prior to his death, they separated. His wife filed for divorce. He confided his troubles to a friend at work, who tried to give advice and who found him a place to live. According to two of the informants, he refused to ask his wife to have him back because he was "too proud." During the six months of their separation, he would often come to his wife's home and act in an angry, spiteful, and threatening manner. He threatened to cut his wife's throat if she told the police about his behavior. The informant believed that he was drunk during the vast majority of these episodes. Ten days prior to his death he came to his wife's home and sat across the table from her while fondling the trigger of a shotgun he had brought along. At that time he told her he was going to kill himself. A few days later he also told a friend that he was going to kill himself. Three days later, he came to his wife's home and beat her until she was able to escape and hide in a neighbor's house. He tucked his four-year-old son under his arm and ran over the neighborhood looking for her. He stopped each person he met to ask if they had seen his wife. He called her whore, bitch, etc., and accused her of having had sexual relations with other men.

He had been drinking on the day of his suicide and drove to his wife's house at a high rate of speed. There, he approached her with a gun. When she realized what was happening she screamed to her mother to call the police. Their son begged him not to "shoot [his] mommy." At this, he stopped to give the boy a dime for ice cream. When the child returned some minutes later, the subject shot and killed his wife. The child threw the ice cream at him saying, "Don't hurt Mommy." At that moment, he turned the gun on himself and shot himself in the head.

The informants did not describe any depressive symptoms, affect, or behavior at any time during the last few months of his life.

Family history: There was an equivocal history concerning the possibility of alcoholism in his father.

Arrest record: He had been arrested at least four times—for manslaughter, common asault, careless driving, and peace disturbance.

Case No. 017 M X F__ Age 44

ST. LOUIS SUICIDE STUDY CRITERIA FOR ALCOHOLISM

At least three of the following selected drinking behaviors were required for diagnosis.

- A. Informant thought subject drank too much ___
- B. Subject drank daily X
- C. Subject went on benders (at least 48 hours of drinking and neglect of usual routine) X
- D. Family objected to subject's drinking ___
- E. Subject's history included arrests related to drinking X
- F. Subject suffered medical and psychiatric complications due to alcoholic intake X
- G. Subject thought he drank too much ___
- H. Subject had job difficulties related to drinking X
- I. Subject involved in automobile accident(s) related to drinking X

FEIGHNER CRITERIA FOR ALCOHOLISM

A definite diagnosis required symptoms in at least three of the following four groups. A probable diagnosis required symptoms in only two of the four groups.

- A.
  1. Any manifestation of alcohol withdrawal such as tremulousness, convulsions, hallucinations, or delirium ___
  2. History of medical complications, e.g. cirrhosis, gastritis, pancreatitis, myopathy, polyneuropathy, Wernicke-Korsakov's syndrome X
  3. Alcoholic blackouts, i.e., amnesic episodes during heavy drinking not accounted for by head trauma ___
  4. Alcoholic binges or benders (48 hours or more of drinking associated with default of usual obligations): must have occurred more than once X
- B.
  1. Subject unable to stop drinking at will ___
  2. Subject tried to control drinking by allowing himself to drink only under certain circumstances, such as only after 5:00 p.m., only on weekends, or only with others ___
  3. Subject drank before breakfast ___
  4. Subject drank nonbeverage forms of alcohol (hair oil, mouthwash, Sterno, etc.) ___
- C.
  1. Subject arrested for drinking X
  2. Subject involved in traffic difficulties associated with drinking X
  3. Subject had trouble at work because of drinking X
  4. Subject involved in fights associated with drinking X
- D.
  1. Subject worried about drinking too much ___
  2. Family objected to subject's drinking X
  3. Subject lost friends because of drinking ___
  4. Other people objected to subject's drinking X
  5. Subject felt guilty about his drinking ___

018   Informants: Wife, physician, psychiatrist

This 38-year-old white press-operator and welder was brought up by his father and sisters following his mother's death when he was three months old. He began to drink excessively at age 18 and continued to do so throughout his life. At age 24, he married for the first time, but the marriage ended in annulment—or divorce—for unknown reasons, within a few weeks. He married a second time at age 30. His second wife believed he was a nervous, moody, and sensitive person all of his life. He also was apparently very dependent on her. She would, for instance, go with him to seek new jobs. It was not clear whether these characteristics were the result of excess alcohol or whether they antedated his excessive drinking. His wife felt he had had a "bad" upbringing with too little discipline and too little religion. He ordinarily was affable except when drinking. Then he would become irritable and angry, especially with his wife. He drank daily, went on occasional "benders," fought with his family over his drinking, was arrested repeatedly, and lost many jobs because of drinking. Three years prior to his death he joined Alcoholics Anonymous for six weeks. He then tried counseling with his pastor. Eighteen months prior to his suicide, he was admitted to a mental hospital and was discharged with a diagnosis of chronic alcoholism. In later years, when on drinking sprees, he refused food, suffered from nausea, vomiting, and abdominal pain (diagnosed as alcoholic gastritis), and from insomnia. When he was not on a spree but only consuming his usual amount of alcohol, he did not suffer from these symptoms. He became increasingly concerned with his inability to stop drinking and felt worthless as a result. His bitterness toward his wife increased and there were open and violent arguments between them. About six weeks prior to his death, he made a suicide attempt by hanging. The rope broke. When his wife arrived home she noted the broken rope and he told her, "I wouldn't be here if the rope hadn't broken." The circumstances that precipitated that attempt were not clear. About that time he had said to his wife that she would be better off if he were dead. Four weeks prior to his suicide, he beat his wife around the head, brandished a knife at her, and threatened to kill her. She left him the next day, whereupon he increased his alcohol intake, stopped working, and told his pastor and family he was going to commit suicide. Three weeks prior to his death he again attempted suicide, this time by carbon monoxide poisoning but again failed. He moved in with his brother and sister-in-law, not wishing to remain alone. He appeared sad about his wife's leaving and repeatedly asked her to come back. She refused and four days prior to his suicide he was served with divorce papers. He became much quieter than usual, but continued to drink large quantities. On the morning of the day of his suicide he telephoned his wife, asked for one more chance, and was refused. He said to her, "This is it. You'll have to take care of things." That afternoon, while intoxicated, he called his pastor and asked him to come over for a talk. The pastor was not able to do so. Later that day the subject shot himself in the chest with a shotgun, using a stick to push the trigger.

Family history: A brother was described as a heavy drinker; it is questionable whether or not he was a chronic alcoholic. A sister suffered from "nervous headaches."

Arrest Record: He was arrested five times during the last four years of his life—for careless driving and driving while intoxicated, leaving the scene of an accident, violation of an electric signal, and disturbing the peace.

Case No. 018 M X F__ Age 38

ST. LOUIS SUICIDE STUDY CRITERIA FOR ALCOHOLISM

At least three of the following selected drinking behaviors were required for diagnosis.

A. Informant thought subject drank too much   X
B. Subject drank daily   X
C. Subject went on benders (at least 48 hours of drinking and neglect of usual routine)   X
D. Family objected to subject's drinking   X
E. Subject's history included arrests related to drinking   X
F. Subject suffered medical and psychiatric complications due to alcoholic intake   X
G. Subject thought he drank too much   X
H. Subject had job difficulties related to drinking   X
I. Subject involved in automobile accident(s) related to drinking   X

FEIGHNER CRITERIA FOR ALCOHOLISM

A definite diagnosis required symptoms in at least three of the following four groups. A probable diagnosis required symptoms in only two of the four groups.

A. 1. Any manifestation of alcohol withdrawal such as tremulousness, convulsions, hallucinations, or delirium X
    2. History of medical complications, e.g. cirrhosis, gastritis, pancreatitis, myopathy, polyneuropathy, Wernicke-Korsakov's syndrome X
    3. Alcoholic blackouts, i.e., amnesic episodes during heavy drinking not accounted for by head trauma ___
    4. Alcoholic binges or benders (48 hours or more of drinking associated with default of usual obligations): must have occurred more than once X

B. 1. Subject unable to stop drinking at will X
    2. Subject tried to control drinking by allowing himself to drink only under certain circumstances, such as only after 5:00 p.m., only on weekends, or only with others X
    3. Subject drank before breakfast ___
    4. Subject drank nonbeverage forms of alcohol (hair oil, mouthwash, Sterno, etc.) ___

C. 1. Subject arrested for drinking X
    2. Subject involved in traffic difficulties associated with drinking X
    3. Subject had trouble at work because of drinking X
    4. Subject involved in fights associated with drinking X

D. 1. Subject worried about drinking too much X
    2. Family objected to subject's drinking X
    3. Subject lost friends because of drinking ___
    4. Other people objected to subject's drinking ___
    5. Subject felt guilty about his drinking X

029 Informants: Son, wife, employers

This 53-year-old, 350-pound white man had been a daily drinker for 20 years prior to his suicide. However, until the last few months of his life, his drinking had caused him no trouble on the job nor had it been the cause of any arrests.

He had three siblings, one of whom (a brother) was a chronic alcoholic. One of his five children suffered brief episodes of depression and another drank to excess. His drinking, estimated by his son to be less than a half-pint a day, was evidently a nuisance and worry to his immediate family, all of whom nagged him about it. He himself thought he drank too much for his own good, but his drinking did not interfere with his 35-year-job as a lumberyard foreman until the last months of his life when, according to his employers, he sometimes showed up drunk. Eight years before died, he was "shamed away from church" because of his drinking. Thereafter, he made a habit of listening to Sunday services on the radio.

He appears to have been rather a taciturn man. His social life was restricted to relatives and, to judge from what his son said about him, he led a well-regulated life without much disruption or emotional upheaval. He disliked violence and avoided reading about it. He had headaches for years, he was not comfortable in crowds, and had a tendency toward claustrophobia, but the only strong characteristic mentioned by his son was his life-long fear of physicians and hospitals. Twelve years prior to his suicide, he developed an abdominal tumor which, over the years, grew to the size of a grapefruit. Three or four years before his death, he began to suffer from dyspnea, especially when lying down. One year before he died, the abdominal tumor began to turn dark. At that time, he saw a doctor who advised an operation to remove the tumor. Due to his great fear of medical treatment, he refused to go to the hospital or to return to the doctor. Instead, he made regular visits to a chiropractor. He did not complain of any pain. Six months before his death, he injured his leg in some unspecified way and the injury caused increasing pain in his hips. At the chiropractor's urging, he tried to lose weight and though his appetite continued to be as good as ever, he managed to lose 50 pounds. Despite the weight loss, the pain in his hips got so much worse that it hindered his work. He was forced to use two canes to get around the lumber yard and, according to his employers, the other workers gave him a hard time about this. He began drinking on the job and two weeks before he died, he resigned. His son believed he had been fired, but the owners of the lumber company reported that the decision to resign had been his own.

Disgraced by the loss of his job, he pretended to his family that he was on vacation. The first week he stayed at home, but at the beginning of the second week, he claimed he was going back to work. He had his lunch packed each morning and left the house, returning at the end of what had been his regular working hours. His wife reported that during those two weeks he was "very nervous." Once or twice, when nagged by the family about drinking too much, he said something to the effect that someday he'd be dead and they'd be sorry. He was more irritable and angry toward his family the last four or five days. The chiropractor told his wife after his death that he had not seemed himself during the last two weekly visits to his office. No other depressive symptoms were reported by informants.

On the last morning of his life, he took his lunch and left the house at the usual time. He drove to the bank of a river where a friend saw him and asked why he wasn't at work. He had evidently been drinking heavily and did not give the friend much of an answer. Shortly after the friend left him, he connected a hose to his car's exhaust, ran it inside the car, closed the doors and windows, and turned on the ignition. His body was found by the police when a passer-by reported seeing a car full of smoke. The police record indicates that he was intoxicated "to more than limits that would allow him to drive," which would seem to indicate that once parked by the river, he had continued to drink.

Family history; A brother was a chronic alcoholic. One of his children had had brief episodes of depression and another drank to excess.
Arrest record: None.

Case No. *029* M *X* F ___ Age *53*

ST. LOUIS SUICIDE STUDY CRITERIA FOR ALCOHOLISM

At least three of the following selected drinking behaviors were required for diagnosis.

A. Informant thought subject drank too much	_X_	F. Subject suffered medical and psychiatric complications due to alcoholic intake	___
B. Subject drank daily	_X_		
C. Subject went on benders (at least 48 hours of drinking and neglect of usual routine)	___	G. Subject thought he drank too much	_X_
D. Family objected to subject's drinking	_X_	H. Subject had job difficulties related to drinking	_X_
E. Subject's history included arrests related to drinking	___	I. Subject involved in automobile accident(s) related to drinking	___

FEIGHNER CRITERIA FOR ALCOHOLISM

A definite diagnosis required symptoms in at least three of the following four groups. A probable diagnosis required symptoms in only two of the four groups.

A. 1. Any manifestation of alcohol withdrawal such as tremulousness, convulsions, hallucinations, or delirium ___
    2. History of medical complications, e.g. cirrhosis, gastritis, pancreatitis, myopathy, polyneuropathy, Wernicke-Korsakov's syndrome ___
    3. Alcoholic blackouts, i.e., amnesic episodes during heavy drinking not accounted for by head trauma ___
    4. Alcoholic binges or benders (48 hours or more of drinking associated with default of usual obligations): must have occurred more than once ___

B. 1. Subject unable to stop drinking at will X
    2. Subject tried to control drinking by allowing himself to drink only under certain circumstances, such as only after 5:00 p.m., only on weekends, or only with others ___
    3. Subject drank before breakfast ___
    4. Subject drank nonbeverage forms of alcohol (hair oil, mouthwash, Sterno, etc.) ___

C. 1. Subject arrested for drinking ___
    2. Subject involved in traffic difficulties associated with drinking ___
    3. Subject had trouble at work because of drinking X
    4. Subject involved in fights associated with drinking ___

D. 1. Subject worried about drinking too much X
    2. Family objected to subject's drinking X
    3. Subject lost friends because of drinking ___
    4. Other people objected to subject's drinking ___
    5. Subject felt guilty about his drinking ___

031 Informants: Wife, sister-in-law, physician

This white, 49-year-old man had been an alcoholic for 18 years prior to his suicide. Born and raised in St. Louis, he left school in the ninth grade. He was rejected by the draft for "nerves" and, in his early years, worked at various unspecified jobs. For 18 years prior to his death he suffered from anxiety attacks and had a fear of heights. He is said to have had easily hurt feelings all his life and to have disliked crowds. At 20 he married, but got divorced after only three weeks. The reason given for the divorce was "immaturity."

At age 32, he suffered a "nervous breakdown," after which he was severely phobic for a year. His phobia centered on the fear of being any distance from a hospital in case he "started to die." He was not hospitalized for this first breakdown and, a few weeks after its onset, married for the second time. At the time of his second marriage, he began to drink heavily (averaging a fifth of whiskey a day) "because of his fears." For a full year, he was unable to work due to the phobic symptoms and because "people made him nervous." A year or so after the breakdown, he went to a psychiatrist whom he continued to see for several years and his symptoms gradually diminished.

Ten years before his death, he was self-employed as a used-car salesman and made (and quickly spent) a good deal of money, sometimes, according to informants, as much as $2000–$3000 a month. His drinking was as heavy as ever, his behavior loud, noisy, and clowning. He gave money away impetuously, bought lavish gifts for his friends, and, at bars, frequently bought rounds of drinks for everyone. Always preoccupied by sex, his interest was, at that point, at a peak and he was often away from home for days at a time, returning to brag to his wife of his conquests. At about this time, he began to display outbursts of temper and rage, getting into fights "at the drop of a hat" and beginning a habit of wife-beating that lasted until he and his wife separated. His wife says that during that time he often vomited on arising in the morning and after eating. Seven years prior to his death, he claimed to be "tired of selling cars" and began a career as a heavy equipment mechanic. A year later, he developed liver trouble (cirrhosis).

Four years prior to his suicide, he vomited blood several times and the doctor diagnosed cirrhosis and ascites. Obviously depressed, he complained of fatigue, ennui, and displayed a general loss of interest in life. He saw little of his friends and complained of fatigue, often going to bed immediately after dinner. A year later, he began to suffer from abdominal pain, his sessions of moodiness and sadness increased in frequency, he was less particular about his dress, and he mentioned suicide several times. That year he made one suicide attempt (he took a "lot" of aspirin), and one threat (he cut off some hose for the car exhaust). His wife felt both of these were designed only to frighten her. His relationship with his wife continued to grow worse. Always cheerful and ingratiating with his friends, he was abusive and ugly only toward her. Her explanation of this was, "I think it bothered him that he couldn't leave me alone. All the others he could take or leave." Two years prior to his death, he was beginning to make serious comments about wanting to die. One year before his suicide, his sexual interest declined markedly. He finished with the last of many "girlfriends" and began beating his wife more often and more severely than before. From time to time, he appeared depressed to relatives and friends and, once again, he began to talk about his fears of "dying in the night."

Six months before his death, he hemorrhaged from the mouth and was hospitalized for 19 days. On his doctor's advice, he stopped drinking and did not drink again until a few days before he killed himself. He complained of aches and pains "all over"—in his back, his joints, and his extremities. He ate little, slept poorly, and took many prescribed "pink pills" at night and during the day, even though he said they made him feel groggy. He felt he would never get well, he mentioned suicide many times, and seemed obsessed with the idea of hurting his wife, claiming "it was all [he] could do to keep from choking her" when he could not sleep and she could. The beatings intensified.

One or two months before his death he was laid off a job he'd held for four years. At about the same time, his doctor emphasized to him the seriousness of his condition and indicated that he had only a few months to live. The doctor's warning precipitated an obvious worsening of all his depressive symptoms. He began to cry easily. A week later, he and his stepson fought when the stepson, for the first time in their relationship, defended his mother. At that point, the subject threw his wife out of the house, whereupon she made a firm decision never to return to him. For the last three weeks of his life, he lived alone in ever-increasing desperation. He remained in touch with his wife's sister in an effort to find his wife and bring her back. The sister-in-law remembered that the week before he died, he looked sad, depressed, and somewhat disheveled and that he was irritable to relatives to whom he mentioned suicide four or five times. His physical condition deteriorated—anorexia, bloody stools, loss of bowel control—and he quit the interim job he'd held for two months. Five days prior to his suicide, he threatened to kill his stepson. The following day, he called him to his home to describe to him how he wanted his belongings distributed. In the last days, he paid all his bills, paid a friend's rent, and found the same friend a job.

On the day of his death, he asked his sister-in-law to find his wife so that she could take him to the hospital. When she refused, believing this to be yet another ruse to get his wife home, he said to her, "Tonight's the night." He told her to come by that night and that he'd "be sitting in the Ford." Later that afternoon, he invited the neighbor's children over for ice cream. That night he saw a friend who said the subject was not drunk and had not been drinking. He expressed sadness to this friend, explaining that the doctor had told him he had only months to live and that "time is going fast."

Some time near midnight, he connected a hose to the exhaust of his car, ran the hose through the trunk into the front. He got into the car with his dog, turned on the motor, and put the end of the hose in his mouth. Early the next morning, his body and the dog's were discovered by a neighbor child.

Family history: A sister saw a doctor briefly for "nerves" at menopause. Otherwise, there is no significant family history of psychiatric illness.
Arrest record: None.

Case No. *031* M X F __ Age *49*

ST. LOUIS SUICIDE STUDY CRITERIA FOR ALCOHOLISM

At least three of the following selected drinking behaviors were required for diagnosis.

A. Informant thought subject drank too much   X
B. Subject drank daily   X
C. Subject went on benders (at least 48 hours of drinking and neglect of usual routine)   __
D. Family objected to subject's drinking   X
E. Subject's history included arrests related to drinking   __
F. Subject suffered medical and psychiatric complications due to alcoholic intake   X
G. Subject thought he drank too much   X
H. Subject had job difficulties related to drinking   X
I. Subject involved in automobile accident(s) related to drinking   __

FEIGHNER CRITERIA FOR ALCOHOLISM

A definite diagnosis required symptoms in at least three of the following four groups. A probable diagnosis required symptoms in only two of the four groups.

A. 1. Any manifestation of alcohol withdrawal such as tremulousness, convulsions, hallucinations, or delirium X
    2. History of medical complications, e.g. cirrhosis, gastritis, pancreatitis, myopathy, polyneuropathy, Wernicke-Korsakov's syndrome X
    3. Alcoholic blackouts, i.e., amnesic episodes during heavy drinking not accounted for by head trauma ___
    4. Alcoholic binges or benders (48 hours or more of drinking associated with default of usual obligations): must have occurred more than once ___

B. 1. Subject unable to stop drinking at will X
    2. Subject tried to control drinking by allowing himself to drink only under certain circumstances, such as only after 5:00 p.m., only on weekends, or only with others ___
    3. Subject drank before breakfast ___
    4. Subject drank nonbeverage forms of alcohol (hair oil, mouthwash, Sterno, etc.) ___

C. 1. Subject arrested for drinking ___
    2. Subject involved in traffic difficulties associated with drinking ___
    3. Subject had trouble at work because of drinking ___
    4. Subject involved in fights associated with drinking X

D. 1. Subject worried about drinking too much ___
    2. Family objected to subject's drinking ___
    3. Subject lost friends because of drinking ___
    4. Other people objected to subject's drinking ___
    5. Subject felt guilty about his drinking ___

034 Informants: Neighbor, physician

An only child, this 51-year-old white bachelor had lived with his mother all his life. He committed suicide about a week or so before she died of cancer. Little is known of his family's history or of his life more than five years prior to his death as the only informants available were a neighbor who had known him only five years and a physician who had seen him just once the week before his death.

He appears to have been very dependent on his mother who owned and ran a rooming house and who controlled most of their money. She had been separated from her husband since the subject was a child and she made all the family decisions. Although she did not seem to have been a stingy woman, her son was forced to ask her for whatever he wanted. He drank excessively and, according to the informant, too much for his own good. Because his mother forbade liquor in her house, he often slept in his car or in the garage. She said he always had a bottle of liquor with him, went on benders besides drinking daily, and was rumored to have been drinking heavily for more than 20 years. During the five years the neighbor knew him, he went out with many women, but at the time of his death, had a fairly steady girlfriend. The neighbor, who said he was "always gone," thought he probably stayed with the girlfriend a good deal of the time. At times, his mother was heard screaming at him and, on several occasions, she threw his clothes into the yard and chased him out of the house. He was also known to have outbursts of rage. Despite all this, he and his mother were attached to one another and she had put the bulk of her substantial estate in his name. Nothing is known of his father.

The neighbor described the subject as having been a nervous man—a moody, "high-strung," "neurotic" person who cried easily, was hard of hearing, and was always sniffing at an inhaler. She said he sweated a lot and combed his hair constantly. She knew of only one friend, a man, who visited him at his home, but said there had been many flowers at his funeral.

About eight months before his suicide, his mother was discovered to have cancer. At that point, his nervousness increased noticeably. In the last year of his life, he changed jobs four times, but the neighbor did not know whether he had been fired or had quit these jobs.

One month before his suicide, his mother's condition grew worse and she was taken to the hospital. When she left, he became even more nervous and upset. The neighbor remembers that a few days before the mother's hospitalization, he took $10 from the house and was terribly upset and angry when his mother questioned him about the money. Shortly after his mother went to the hospital, he took 30 days off from work to help care for her and bcause of his nerves. In the weeks that followed, he greatly decreased his drinking and smoking. One week before his death, he saw a doctor about his nerves. The doctor found no serious medical illness, but believed the patient to be depressed and remorseful about having, in the past, left his sick mother alone in order to visit his girlfriend. The doctor referred him to a psychiatrist whom he saw and from whom he received Equanil for his depression and the accompanying anorexia, insomnia, and fatigue which he felt had definitely worsened in parallel with his mother's worsening condition.

Early the next morning he was seen in his garage and appeared to be in pain. Half an hour later, one of the roomers discovered his body in the garage. He had shot himself in the head with a shotgun propped on a shelf.

Later, the neighbor spoke with his girlfriend who, on learning of his suicide, said that they had had a quarrel a week before and that she had been waiting for the note he usually wrote to her after a fight. One day after his death, a large bouquet of flowers bearing his name was delivered to his mother in the hospital.

Family history: There was no information concerning a family history of psychiatric illness.
Arrest record: None.

Case No. *034* M X F __ Age *51*

ST. LOUIS SUICIDE STUDY CRITERIA FOR ALCOHOLISM

At least three of the following selected drinking behaviors were required for diagnosis.

A. Informant thought subject drank too much *X*

B. Subject drank daily *X*

C. Subject went on benders (at least 48 hours of drinking and neglect of usual routine) *X*

D. Family objected to subject's drinking *X*

E. Subject's history included arrests related to drinking ___

F. Subject suffered medical and psychiatric complications due to alcoholic intake *X*

G. Subject thought he drank too much ___

H. Subject had job difficulties related to drinking *X*

I. Subject involved in automobile accident(s) related to drinking ___

FEIGHNER CRITERIA FOR ALCOHOLISM

A definite diagnosis required symptoms in at least three of the following four groups. A probable diagnosis required symptoms in only two of the four groups.

A. 1. Any manifestation of alcohol withdrawal such as tremulousness, convulsions, hallucinations, or delirium ___
    2. History of medical complications, e.g. cirrhosis, gastritis, pancreatitis, myopathy, polyneuropathy, Wernicke-Korsakov's syndrome ___
    3. Alcoholic blackouts, i.e., amnesic episodes during heavy drinking not accounted for by head trauma ___
    4. Alcoholic binges or benders (48 hours or more of drinking associated with default of usual obligations): must have occurred more than once X

B. 1. Subject unable to stop drinking at will ___
    2. Subject tried to control drinking by allowing himself to drink only under certain circumstances, such as only after 5:00 p.m., only on weekends, or only with others ___
    3. Subject drank before breakfast ___
    4. Subject drank nonbeverage forms of alcohol (hair oil, mouthwash, Sterno, etc.) ___

C. 1. Subject arrested for drinking ___
    2. Subject involved in traffic difficulties associated with drinking ___
    3. Subject had trouble at work because of drinking X
    4. Subject involved in fights associated with drinking ___

D. 1. Subject worried about drinking too much ___
    2. Family objected to subject's drinking X
    3. Subject lost friends because of drinking ___
    4. Other people objected to subject's drinking X
    5. Subject felt guilty about his drinking ___

052 Informants: Sisters, bartender

This 53-year-old white man came from a family background of alcoholism and mental illness. His mother, who as a child suffered a severe injury to the head, was "slow" and was sent to an asylum after her husband's death. She died there 16 years later. Thus the subject, educated only through the fifth grade, began his working career at age 13. He apparently also began his career as an alcoholic shortly thereafter as his sisters remembered his having been arrested at least once, at about age 16, for "disturbing the peace."

He married at 23. His wife, who died nine months before his suicide, was also a chronic alcoholic. The subject worked as a handyman and once as a parking lot attendant. His sisters felt that he had lost that one regular job because of his drinking. His wife also worked, to help keep them in alcohol and food. Until her death, he was not in contact with his sisters so they knew him well only in those last months when he sought them out and saw them about three times a week.

According to his sisters, he had been a moody, sensitive person all his life and had been an alcoholic for as long as they could remember. He was also at the time of his wife's death very deaf. Although his sisters denied any sign of change in his behavior or appearance in the months just prior to his suicide, they did feel that he missed his wife badly. They also believed he was worried about not working the last six months of his life and being unable to make the monthly payments on the three mortgages on his small, run-down house or pay any of his bills. His sisters felt certain that any little money he did earn went immediately for drink. They maintained that the subject had made no suicidal comments (although one of them remembered that, after his death, an auto repair shop owner had mentioned his having said to him that he "wouldn't be around much longer") and that he neither looked nor stated feeling depressed or disgusted. He was not under a doctor's care at the time of his death. Born to a Catholic family, he had not attended any church for years. However, one sister reported that, unlike everything else they found in his bedroom after his death, his Bible was not dusty. Also found in his room were a great number of sex magazines.

A bartender who saw the subject daily reported having seen him on the evening of his suicide. He said the subject seemed to be the same as usual—quiet and alone. The bartender said he had come to his tavern every evening for a long time, but that he had no particular friends and, if he grieved over his wife's death, he never showed it. At 7:30 that evening, he parked his car on a street in his neighborhood and fixed a hose to the exhaust pipe of his car. He then sat in the car until 2:00 AM (he was observed from time to time by someone living on the street) at which time he turned on the car's ignition. His dead body was discovered by two young men in the early hours of the morning. He left no note. An autopsy report indicated that he had been drinking just prior to the act.

Family history: Father was an alcoholic. Mother was brain injured and institutionalized. Maternal grandfather had committed suicide. Maternal uncle with advanced cancer had made a serious but unsuccessful suicide attempt. One brother had nervous troubles and two other brothers were chronic alcoholics.

Arrest record: At least one arrest, by age 16, for peace disturbance.

Case No. 052 M X F__ Age 53

ST. LOUIS SUICIDE STUDY CRITERIA FOR ALCOHOLISM

At least three of the following selected drinking behaviors were required for diagnosis.

- A. Informant thought subject drank too much   X
- B. Subject drank daily   X
- C. Subject went on benders (at least 48 hours of drinking and neglect of usual routine)   __
- D. Family objected to subject's drinking   X
- E. Subject's history included arrests related to drinking   X
- F. Subject suffered medical and psychiatric complications due to alcoholic intake   __
- G. Subject thought he drank too much   __
- H. Subject had job difficulties related to drinking   X
- I. Subject involved in automobile accident(s) related to drinking   X

FEIGHNER CRITERIA FOR ALCOHOLISM

A definite diagnosis required symptoms in at least three of the following four groups. A probable diagnosis required symptoms in only two of the four groups.

- A.
  1. Any manifestation of alcohol withdrawal such as tremulousness, convulsions, hallucinations, or delirium   __
  2. History of medical complications, e.g. cirrhosis, gastritis, pancreatitis, myopathy, polyneuropathy, Wernicke-Korsakov's syndrome   __
  3. Alcoholic blackouts, i.e., amnesic episodes during heavy drinking not accounted for by head trauma   __
  4. Alcoholic binges or benders (48 hours or more of drinking associated with default of usual obligations): must have occurred more than once   __
- B.
  1. Subject unable to stop drinking at will   X
  2. Subject tried to control drinking by allowing himself to drink only under certain circumstances, such as only after 5:00 p.m., only on weekends, or only with others   __
  3. Subject drank before breakfast   __
  4. Subject drank nonbeverage forms of alcohol (hair oil, mouthwash, Sterno, etc.)   __
- C.
  1. Subject arrested for drinking   X
  2. Subject involved in traffic difficulties associated with drinking   X
  3. Subject had trouble at work because of drinking   X
  4. Subject involved in fights associated with drinking   __
- D.
  1. Subject worried about drinking too much   __
  2. Family objected to subject's drinking   X
  3. Subject lost friends because of drinking   X
  4. Other people objected to subject's drinking   __
  5. Subject felt guilty about his drinking   __

065 Informants: Wife, social service records

This 52-year-old white man had, at the time of his suicide, been married for 21 years to a woman 13 years his junior. He was the father of seven children. He had quit school in the 11th grade to work on his father's farm. Twenty years before his death, he moved to St. Louis where he found a job working as a "lay-out man" for a real estate and construction company. He was good at this job and held it for 19 years.

According to his wife, the subject was a chronic, long-term (20+ years) alcoholic. She said that his drinking had caused him trouble with the police and with his job (she did not specify what kinds of trouble), that he went on periodic "benders," that his family disapproved of his drinking, and that he himself felt he had a hopeless drinking problem. Though he had not seen a physician for at least the last ten years of his life, he had made several efforts to stop drinking, but "others always forced him back to it." His wife gave as an example her husband's worry over an automobile accident their son had been involved in, a worry which he tried to drink away.

Because of the subject's drinking the family's life was unhappy and chaotic. Social service records showed receipt of an anonymous letter which reported abuse and neglect of the children by the mother. She, in turn, accused her husband of having made the children's lives "a living hell" when he was drunk and she stated, after his death, that the children would be better off without him.

The subject was described as having been an "aloof" man when sober. His wife claimed that he had had no close friends and that though they had been living in the same house for 14 years, he had never spoken to the neighbors. When drunk, he cried easily and was moody. When beginning to sober up, he would become disgusted with himself and blame himself for his troubles and the family's. He had no hobbies, never watched TV or listened to the radio or played cards or read. There were times, throughout his life, when he spoke not at all, not even in answer to questions.

Nine months before his suicide, his wife told him she had decided to sue for a divorce. In response, he threatened to kill himself and went so far as to obtain a gun and leave a note which seemed an attempt at poetry.

> Don't take me to Union Hill
> I have my family
>   But this, is the end.
> Friends on earth, ar
> Very, sweet, shud be.
>   Very, near, But if you had one
> His name is ritten here
>   TVC [his initials] to
> EIC [his wife's initials] Love UHVP

After his first threat, he continued to talk about wanting to die, wanting to kill himself, and about how he and his family would be better off with him dead. He spoke of these things to his wife, his family, and to his relatives for the last nine months of his life.

During the last year of his life, he lost all sexual interest and was essentially impotent, which his wife said worried him. He also began to lose weight and lost a total of 26 pounds by the time he died. Although his wife said that despite his heavy drinking, he had always managed to eat, she mentioned that one week before his suicide he lost his appetite. She also said that that last week he looked depressed, was tired, inert, and indecisive.

On the morning of his suicide, he arose early. He and his wife had quarreled throughout most of the night and had finally agreed on a divorce. He drank beer on arising which she said he had never done (he usually drank whiskey when he drank before breakfast). He drove her to work in his car and explained calmly that if she left him, he would have nothing to live for and that he would kill himself. She replied that they were finished. He took her work phone number, saying she'd get a call before the day was over.

He then returned to his house and kissed each of his children goodbye. His 13-year-old daughter watched as he left the house, went out in the yard, walked in a circle there, and finally drew his gun and shot himself in the head. He died instantly. He had not left a second note.

Family history: One of his three brothers was described as having an unstable personality and an I.Q. of 80. A grandmother had been hospitalized for many years due to "mental breakdown."
Arrest record: Unspecified "trouble with police."

Case No. *065* M _X_ F __ Age *52*

ST. LOUIS SUICIDE STUDY CRITERIA FOR ALCOHOLISM

At least three of the following selected drinking behaviors were required for diagnosis.

A. Informant thought subject drank too much   _X_

B. Subject drank daily   ___

C. Subject went on benders (at least 48 hours of drinking and neglect of usual routine)   _X_

D. Family objected to subject's drinking   ___

E. Subject's history included arrests related to drinking   _X_

F. Subject suffered medical and psychiatric complications due to alcoholic intake   ___

G. Subject thought he drank too much   _X_

H. Subject had job difficulties related to drinking   _X_

I. Subject involved in automobile accident(s) related to drinking   ___

FEIGHNER CRITERIA FOR ALCOHOLISM

A definite diagnosis required symptoms in at least three of the following four groups. A probable diagnosis required symptoms in only two of the four groups.

A. 1. Any manifestation of alcohol withdrawal such as tremulousness, convulsions, hallucinations, or delirium ___
    2. History of medical complications, e.g. cirrhosis, gastritis, pancreatitis, myopathy, polyneuropathy, Wernicke-Korsakov's syndrome ___
    3. Alcoholic blackouts, i.e., amnesic episodes during heavy drinking not accounted for by head trauma ___
    4. Alcoholic binges or benders (48 hours or more of drinking associated with default of usual obligations): must have occurred more than once __X__

B. 1. Subject unable to stop drinking at will __X__
    2. Subject tried to control drinking by allowing himself to drink only under certain circumstances, such as only after 5:00 p.m., only on weekends, or only with others ___
    3. Subject drank before breakfast __X__
    4. Subject drank nonbeverage forms of alcohol (hair oil, mouthwash, Sterno, etc.) ___

C. 1. Subject arrested for drinking __X__
    2. Subject involved in traffic difficulties associated with drinking ___
    3. Subject had trouble at work because of drinking __X__
    4. Subject involved in fights associated with drinking ___

D. 1. Subject worried about drinking too much __X__
    2. Family objected to subject's drinking __X__
    3. Subject lost friends because of drinking ___
    4. Other people objected to subject's drinking ___
    5. Subject felt guilty about his drinking __X__

073 Informants: Mother, physicians, employers

At the time of his suicide, this 36-year-old white married man was considered by his family and friends to be extremely successful. Supervisor of river pilots for a St. Louis river towing company, he had had a promotion and salary raise three months earlier and had recently moved his family into a new, custom designed, nine-room house.

His mother, who had lived with him during most of his 13-year marriage, described him as an enthusiastic, happy "go-getter" who loved his wife and three young children, loved his job, and had everything to live for. She denied any problems in his life though she did admit that "on occasion" he had drunk more than was good for him for about the last seven or eight years and that perhaps his work had been even more demanding since he had been made pilot supervisor three years before. She blamed his "occasional" overdrinking on "big drinking oil men from Texas" he had met in his work and whom she said he was obliged to entertain several times a month. She denied that anybody in his family felt he drank too much, although she remembered that now and then his wife would say to him, "Now, don't drink today." When asked if he himself worried about his drinking, she said that he had often said he was going to quit, but that he never had for any length of time. He did not drink much around his home.

The subject was an only child. His father had been a river steamboat captain and he grew up loving boats. He finished high school and went immediately to work on the river. He married at 23 and, the same year, went overseas with the Army. He was discharged honorably after two years and returned to St. Louis and to his job as a river pilot. When his father died a year later, his mother came to live with him and his wife.

He was healthy all his life. He was a fairly regular church goer, had a great many friends, and enjoyed an active social life with both business and family friends. His mother could think of no reason why he would want to kill himself.

His family physician, who was a close personal friend, reported that the subject's life was not as smooth as his mother had described it. He said that the subject had been drinking heavily with his business associates for the past year or so and that he had often stayed out late at night, coming home drunk. Apparently his wife and his mother did not get along and the wife, whom the doctor described as a "manic-depressive," was sometimes difficult to live with. His doctor also believed that the subject was in debt. The doctor's father, also a physician and family friend, described the subject as a "dipsomaniac" and felt that his extramarital sexual affairs were a "contributing factor." Both doctors denied any recent behavioral change in the subject.

He had never mentioned feelings of depression to the informants, much less made any suicidal comments. As his mother described it, one afternoon, "out of the blue," he called home and told his wife not to start dinner because he was coming home to take the whole family out to eat. On arriving at his house, he drove his car into the garage, closed the garage doors and left the motor of his car running. His wife discovered his body sometime later in the afternoon. No note was found.

Family history: According to the subject's mother, everybody on her side of the family was "a pusher" (by which, it is believed, she meant "go-getter") and "happy." She did recall, however, that two of her brothers were chronic alcoholics.
Arrest record: None.

Case No. 073 M X F__ Age 36

ST. LOUIS SUICIDE STUDY CRITERIA FOR ALCOHOLISM

At least three of the following selected drinking behaviors were required for diagnosis.

A. Informant thought subject drank too much X
B. Subject drank daily X
C. Subject went on benders (at least 48 hours of drinking and neglect of usual routine) __
D. Family objected to subject's drinking X
E. Subject's history included arrests related to drinking __
F. Subject suffered medical and psychiatric complications due to alcoholic intake __
G. Subject thought he drank too much X
H. Subject had job difficulties related to drinking __
I. Subject involved in automobile accident(s) related to drinking __

FEIGHNER CRITERIA FOR ALCOHOLISM

A definite diagnosis required symptoms in at least three of the following four groups. A probable diagnosis required symptoms in only two of the four groups.

A. 1. Any manifestation of alcohol withdrawal such as tremulousness, convulsions, hallucinations, or delirium __
 2. History of medical complications, e.g. cirrhosis, gastritis, pancreatitis, myopathy, polyneuropathy, Wernicke-Korsakov's syndrome __
 3. Alcoholic blackouts, i.e., amnesic episodes during heavy drinking not accounted for by head trauma __
 4. Alcoholic binges or benders (48 hours or more of drinking associated with default of usual obligations): must have occurred more than once __

B. 1. Subject unable to stop drinking at will X
 2. Subject tried to control drinking by allowing himself to drink only under certain circumstances, such as only after 5:00 p.m., only on weekends, or only with others X
 3. Subject drank before breakfast __
 4. Subject drank nonbeverage forms of alcohol (hair oil, mouthwash, Sterno, etc.) __

C. 1. Subject arrested for drinking __
 2. Subject involved in traffic difficulties associated with drinking __
 3. Subject had trouble at work because of drinking __
 4. Subject involved in fights associated with drinking __

D. 1. Subject worried about drinking too much X
 2. Family objected to subject's drinking X
 3. Subject lost friends because of drinking __
 4. Other people objected to subject's drinking X
 5. Subject felt guilty about his drinking __

074 Informants: Wife, friend, hotel manager, physician, bartender

This 47-year-old white man had spent a great deal of time the last five years of his life in a bar drinking. Born on a prosperous farm in Illinois, he finished two years of college before going to work for a chemical company where he was employed for the next 13 years, until the company folded. Afterward he worked as a trailer salesman and was apparently quite successful. About a year before his death, he went to work again for the trailer company, which had moved to Colorado, but for some reason the job lasted only a few months.

He married when he was 30 and he and his wife had one child, a son whom he adored. After 12 years of marriage, his wife divorced him. She said that she had divorced him because of his chronic alcoholism and because, six years before his death, he had quit his job and refused to support her and the boy. Ironically, later the same year, the subject inherited $100,000 from his father's estate. He was then living in Chicago and, shortly after the divorce and the inheritance, his brother had him committed to the psychiatric ward of a Chicago hospital because of his alcoholism. He remained in the hospital for three months.

When he was released from the Chicago hospital, he followed his wife and son to St. Louis and rented a suite of rooms in a hotel near their apartment. It was his plan to retire and live on his inheritance. As mentioned, he spent most of his "retirement" in the hotel bar. There he made several close friends who described him as always having been a charming, soft-spoken, gentlemanly person who was never known to be loud or rowdy. They said he was obviously still very much in love with his wife with whom he was on good terms and that he had occasionally brought her to the bar. His wife's description of him was less flattering. She reported his life-long tendency toward moodiness, nervousness, hypochondria, and, when drunk, outbursts of rage. A daily heavy drinker for many years, he had suffered morning nausea and vomiting for nearly as long as she had known him. He also suffered from frequent anxiety attacks with accompanying apprehension, fears of impending death, palpitation, shortness of breath, weakness, and trembling.

One year before his death, his doctor had admitted him to a St. Louis hospital for his alcoholism and, while there, he suffered an attack of delirium tremens which lasted three days.

Both the subject's wife and his closest barroom friend believed he had begun to get worse about six months before his death. His wife noted that, from that time on, he had looked depressed, that he had said he was depressed, that he had worried about not having money (he had, by then, run through his inheritance), and being in debt. He was extremely disappointed in his son, who was mixed up with a bad gang and in trouble with the police. The subject was sending his son to a private school and felt the son's behavior was poor repayment. He was also worried about his health and thought he might have cirrhosis. His friend said that the subject complained during those six months of abdominal pain, anorexia, weight loss, and insomnia. He also reported that the subject had tried, without much success, to borrow money from friends in the bar, asking each of them what the others were saying about him. He mentioned suicide often to his wife and to his friends and once showed his friend a gun he kept in his room which he said he might use to kill himself. Both informants described the subject during this period as generally less active, less interested in life, joyless, sad, and worried. He was known to be praying, reading the Bible, and talking a great deal about religion, all of which were most unusual for him. His doctor, whom he saw about three months before his death, said that his patient was extremely insecure and that the patient had himself given his "inferiority complex" as one of the reasons for his drinking.

During the week prior to his suicide, the subject spent three days and nights with his wife and son at their apartment. The son was home from school on vacation and his father wanted to try to talk with him and "straighten him out." His wife said that for those three days he seemed greatly improved. He was jovial and obviously happy and even did some of the cooking. At the end of three days, he went back to his hotel. When his family was unable to contact him for a day and a half, they asked the hotel manager to check his apartment and it was discovered that he had shot himself and was dead. He had left a note for the manager asking that he take the rent owed him from his insurance. No other notes were found. The date of his suicide was also the date of his birth.

Family history: One cousin, who was also a good friend of the subject's, had committed suicide some time in the past. There was no other family history of psychiatric illness.
Arrest record: None.

Case No. 074 M X F__ Age 47

ST. LOUIS SUICIDE STUDY CRITERIA FOR ALCOHOLISM

At least three of the following selected drinking behaviors were required for diagnosis.

A. Informant thought subject drank too much X
B. Subject drank daily X
C. Subject went on benders (at least 48 hours of drinking and neglect of usual routine) __
D. Family objected to subject's drinking X
E. Subject's history included arrests related to drinking __
F. Subject suffered medical and psychiatric complications due to alcoholic intake X
G. Subject thought he drank too much __
H. Subject had job difficulties related to drinking __
I. Subject involved in automobile accident(s) related to drinking __

FEIGHNER CRITERIA FOR ALCOHOLISM

A definite diagnosis required symptoms in at least three of the following four groups. A probable diagnosis required symptoms in only two of the four groups.

A. 1. Any manifestation of alcohol withdrawal such as tremulousness, convulsions, hallucinations, or delirium X
   2. History of medical complications, e.g. cirrhosis, gastritis, pancreatitis, myopathy, polyneuropathy, Wernicke-Korsakov's syndrome X
   3. Alcoholic blackouts, i.e., amnesic episodes during heavy drinking not accounted for by head trauma X
   4. Alcoholic binges or benders (48 hours or more of drinking associated with default of usual obligations): must have occurred more than once __

B. 1. Subject unable to stop drinking at will X
   2. Subject tried to control drinking by allowing himself to drink only under certain circumstances, such as only after 5:00 p.m., only on weekends, or only with others __
   3. Subject drank before breakfast __
   4. Subject drank nonbeverage forms of alcohol (hair oil, mouthwash, Sterno, etc.) __

C. 1. Subject arrested for drinking __
   2. Subject involved in traffic difficulties associated with drinking __
   3. Subject had trouble at work because of drinking __
   4. Subject involved in fights associated with drinking __

D. 1. Subject worried about drinking too much X
   2. Family objected to subject's drinking X
   3. Subject lost friends because of drinking __
   4. Other people objected to subject's drinking __
   5. Subject felt guilty about his drinking __

083 Informant: Mother

Born in St. Louis, this 44-year-old white man was the 7th of 16 children. The family was poor and the subject's childhood was spent in at least ten different homes in St. Louis as cheaper and cheaper housing had to be found for the growing family. The subject was in constant trouble throughout his childhood and adolescence because of fights. He finished only five grades of school.

During World War II, he served for three years without being sent overseas and was given an honorable discharge. Having gone to work at age 15, he had had a total of about 15 jobs (excluding the Army) during the 29 years of his working life. The last three jobs he held, each of which lasted an average of two years, were as a bartender, a worker at the St. Louis Zoo, and finally as a bartender again. According to the informant he had been fired from only two jobs.

Described by his mother as always having been a nervous, "highstrung," moody person who cried easily, he began to drink heavily in his mid-twenties and was, by the time he died, consuming a pint of whiskey daily. His drinking caused him frequent trouble with the police and he had a long record of arrests for disorderly conduct, fighting, disturbing the peace, and threatening people. The last arrest recorded before his death was for drunkenness and threatening his mother.

For at least five or six years before he died, he had had drunken attacks of anger, cursing, shouting, ripping off his clothes, tearing out his hair, smashing dishes, and threatening whoever was around. He belonged to a motorcycle club and had often said, "I'm not coming back today, I'm going to ram the cycle into a wall." In the last few years of his life, he became even more specific in his comments about wanting to die, about committing suicide, and about being a burden to his family.

Even so, his mother insisted that there were times when he was a happy, loving person, liked by his friends though despised by the neighbors. He was married four times. Each of his first three wives divorced him, because of his drinking and fighting—the first two after two years of marriage, the third after only three months. He had no children by any of his wives. His fourth, who married him six months prior to his suicide, left him after four months. At that point, all his symptoms grew noticeably worse. He looked depressed and disgusted, he spoke more often of being a burden, of being to blame, of being no good, and talked openly of his depression and sadness. His spells of rage became more frequent and more violent and he drank even more than usual. When he begged his wife to come back, she agreed on the conditions that he quit his job as bartender and that he quit drinking. He promised to try and actually did give up his job. She moved back in with him, but "refused to live as man and wife," which threw him into rages and, about two weeks before his death, he shook her so severely that she left and went to stay with one of the subject's sisters. A week before his suicide, he went after her and pounded wildly on his sister's front door, causing such a commotion that his wife called the police. Because his wife refused to drop the charges of attempted assault, he was notified to appear in court for arraignment a few days later. The day he was due in court, he went to his favorite tavern, shook hands with all his friends there, and told them he had a job to do at home. He told a few of them that they would not see him again. He then went back to his mother's house and ordered his mother to bring his wife and his sisters to him. When she could not carry out this order, he became enraged. He went into his bedroom, sat down on his bed, and put the barrel of a shotgun in his mouth. When his mother tried to stop him, he took the gun away from his mouth, warned her not to come any nearer, replaced the barrel in his mouth, and pulled the trigger. He died instantly with his mother as witness. He did not leave a note.

Family history: The subject's mother had suffered a "nervous breakdown" 20 years previously which lasted two years. She said it was precipitated by the death of one of her children. She had been "nervous" ever since. A sister of the subject's was described as having been "nervous like her brother" since an automobile accident six years earlier.

Arrest record: Prospective arraignment for attempted assault, in addition to a long record of arrests for disorderly conduct, fighting, disturbing the peace, and threatening people.

Case No. *083* M X F __ Age *44*

ST. LOUIS SUICIDE STUDY CRITERIA FOR ALCOHOLISM

At least three of the following selected drinking behaviors were required for diagnosis.

A. Informant thought subject drank too much **X**

B. Subject drank daily **X**

C. Subject went on benders (at least 48 hours of drinking and neglect of usual routine) ___

D. Family objected to subject's drinking **X**

E. Subject's history included arrests related to drinking **X**

F. Subject suffered medical and psychiatric complications due to alcoholic intake **X**

G. Subject thought he drank too much ___

H. Subject had job difficulties related to drinking **X**

I. Subject involved in automobile accident(s) related to drinking ___

FEIGHNER CRITERIA FOR ALCOHOLISM

A definite diagnosis required symptoms in at least three of the following four groups. A probable diagnosis required symptoms in only two of the four groups.

A. 1. Any manifestation of alcohol withdrawal such as tremulousness, convulsions, hallucinations, or delirium ___
    2. History of medical complications, e.g. cirrhosis, gastritis, pancreatitis, myopathy, polyneuropathy, Wernicke-Korsakov's syndrome ___
    3. Alcoholic blackouts, i.e., amnesic episodes during heavy drinking not accounted for by head trauma ___
    4. Alcoholic binges or benders (48 hours or more of drinking associated with default of usual obligations): must have occurred more than once _X_

B. 1. Subject unable to stop drinking at will _X_
    2. Subject tried to control drinking by allowing himself to drink only under certain circumstances, such as only after 5:00 p.m., only on weekends, or only with others ___
    3. Subject drank before breakfast ___
    4. Subject drank nonbeverage forms of alcohol (hair oil, mouthwash, Sterno, etc.) ___

C. 1. Subject arrested for drinking _X_
    2. Subject involved in traffic difficulties associated with drinking ___
    3. Subject had trouble at work because of drinking _X_
    4. Subject involved in fights associated with drinking _X_

D. 1. Subject worried about drinking too much ___
    2. Family objected to subject's drinking _X_
    3. Subject lost friends because of drinking ___
    4. Other people objected to subject's drinking _X_
    5. Subject felt guilty about his drinking _X_

088 Informants: Brother, sister-in-law, friend, hospital records

This 48-year-old white man was, at the time of his suicide, divorced from his third wife and living alone in a rooming house. He completed eight grades in school and worked for 30 years as a foundry "core man" for various St. Louis foundries.

According to his brother, the subject had drunk heavily for 30 years and had been a chronic alcoholic for many years by the time he died. His drinking had caused problems in nearly every aspect of his adult life—he was fired from several jobs because of drunkenness, was arrested numerous times for "peace disturbance," and was involved in a number of automobile accidents. His family nagged him about his drinking and it appeared to have been one of the reasons for his troubled marital life.

His first wife divorced him after ten years of marriage and remarried within 30 days. That incident, which occurred ten years before his death, precipitated his first suicide attempt (by carbon monoxide). The first wife was reported to have been dying at the time of his suicide, a fact he was aware of. His second wife divorced him after only a few months, and his third wife divorced him after one year of marriage, about two years before his suicide.

Five years before his death, he attempted suicide (unknown method) a second time and was hospitalized for an unspecified length of time. Two years before he died, he was hospitalized in a general hospital for two or three weeks for what his brother guessed was a "heart attack." However, a year later, when seen in a hospital emergency room because he had collapsed in a bar, he was diagnosed as an alcoholic and as having "an unstable personality," but was "without heart disease" in spite of his complaint of chest pains for over a year.

Six months before he committed suicide, he was fired from a job. He was able to find work again fairly quickly, but a month before his death he was laid off the new job. Worried, he agreed to work temporarily for a bar owner friend as bartender while the owner had jury duty. When the owner's duty was over, the subject was reluctant to leave the job at the bar and was angry at his friend for not keeping him on.

His sister-in-law felt that he had lost a little weight in the last month. Otherwise, he had shown no signs of sustained depression or behavior change in the weeks just before his suicide. When drunk he cried easily, but this had been true of him for 30 years. He complained of headaches, but these too had been lifelong.

On the day of his suicide, he went to his brother's house to borrow money for his union dues and for something else "in the future." He then went to his "home tavern" where he asked a friend who had once found him a job if he would try to get him another. When the friend refused, saying that he couldn't trust him not to get drunk on the job, the subject, who was drinking, cried and pleaded. When the friend continued to refuse, he left the tavern. A short time later he returned, bought drinks for four of his friends, then walked around behind the bar and shot himself in the head with a pistol. He is said to have written two suicide notes a month earlier and to have shown them to his landlady. One was to the police instructing that his eyes be left to the Eye Bank. The other was addressed to his brother and concerned "personal matters."

Family history: The subject's brother was an alcoholic and had been hospitalized once in a mental hospital because of his alcoholism.

Arrest record: Subject was arrested numerous times for peace disturbance.

Case No. 088 M X F __ Age 48

ST. LOUIS SUICIDE STUDY CRITERIA FOR ALCOHOLISM

At least three of the following selected drinking behaviors were required for diagnosis.

- A. Informant thought subject drank too much X
- B. Subject drank daily __
- C. Subject went on benders (at least 48 hours of drinking and neglect of usual routine) __
- D. Family objected to subject's drinking X
- E. Subject's history included arrests related to drinking X
- F. Subject suffered medical and psychiatric complications due to alcoholic intake X
- G. Subject thought he drank too much __
- H. Subject had job difficulties related to drinking X
- I. Subject involved in automobile accident(s) related to drinking X

FEIGHNER CRITERIA FOR ALCOHOLISM

A definite diagnosis required symptoms in at least three of the following four groups. A probable diagnosis required symptoms in only two of the four groups.

- A.
  1. Any manifestation of alcohol withdrawal such as tremulousness, convulsions, hallucinations, or delirium __
  2. History of medical complications, e.g. cirrhosis, gastritis, pancreatitis, myopathy, polyneuropathy, Wernicke-Korsakov's syndrome X
  3. Alcoholic blackouts, i.e., amnesic episodes during heavy drinking not accounted for by head trauma __
  4. Alcoholic binges or benders (48 hours or more of drinking associated with default of usual obligations): must have occurred more than once __

- B.
  1. Subject unable to stop drinking at will __
  2. Subject tried to control drinking by allowing himself to drink only under certain circumstances, such as only after 5:00 p.m., only on weekends, or only with others __
  3. Subject drank before breakfast __
  4. Subject drank nonbeverage forms of alcohol (hair oil, mouthwash, Sterno, etc.) __

- C.
  1. Subject arrested for drinking X
  2. Subject involved in traffic difficulties associated with drinking X
  3. Subject had trouble at work because of drinking X
  4. Subject involved in fights associated with drinking __

- D.
  1. Subject worried about drinking too much __
  2. Family objected to subject's drinking X
  3. Subject lost friends because of drinking X
  4. Other people objected to subject's drinking X
  5. Subject felt guilty about his drinking __

095   Informants: Mother-in-law, social service records

This 49-year-old white man had been widowed for nine years when he committed suicide. Living alone in a rooming house at the time of his death, he had told an elderly neighbor that he had not wanted to live since his wife's death.

He was the son of a successful undertaker. His father was described as a strong, protective parent who had tried unsuccessfully to keep his son with him in his business. The subject completed two years of college and married at age 27. He and his wife had two daughters. At age 32, he was hospitalized because of frequent "blackouts" and was suspected of being an epileptic. About five years later, he began to drink excessively and, because of his drinking, lost a succession of jobs. Before that, he had been fairly successful as a salesman and had always preferred selling for drug companies. The informant reported that her daughter (the subject's wife) had been content in her marriage until the last three years when the subject's drinking and chronic unemployment had caused problems.

After his wife was killed in an automobile accident, his children went to live with their maternal grandmother. When at the end of a year it was necessary for the grandmother to return to work, they were placed in a children's home. The home records showed that the girls were visited infrequently by their father whose drinking had become increasingly obvious and distressing to his eldest daughter. The records remarked on his good appearance and affectionate approach toward his daughters, but go on to note that he made promises about taking them away with him that he was not able to keep. The older daughter eventually lost all confidence in him and, when she left the home, she went not to her father, but to her grandmother.

For the last eight years of his life, the subject continued to drink, to lose jobs, to move from city to city in search of work, and to suffer from "blackouts." Even though at some earlier time he had been given dilantin and phenobarbital by a doctor and had apparently taken both regularly, the blackouts persisted. Sometime after his wife's death, he ran over and killed a pedestrian while driving and spent eight months in prison for manslaughter.

According to his mother-in-law, the subject had been "nervous," "high-strung," weak-spirited, and moody all his life. After his wife's death, he had gone through a period of depression when he lost weight and cried easily. Since then, though he had not seemed especially depressed, he had complained of headache, dizziness, and back pain, much of which she suspected was "imaginary."

Three months prior to his death, the subject seemed suddenly to worsen. He moved to a rooming house where his fellow roomers found him to be a congenial neighbor, but his mother-in-law said that, from that time until his death, he appeared to be disgusted with himself, greatly upset over his financial difficulties (she said he made only about $500 the last two years of his life), and desperate in his efforts to borrow money from any and every associate and acquaintance. She said he complained of nausea and vomiting and of increasing back pain. She also remembered that, in those three months, he had lost a lot of weight. At Christmas, about a month before his suicide, he tried to persuade his oldest daughter to come out with him alone. She refused, believing that he wanted her to aid in persuading the other daughter to live with him. He also tried to get her to help him in his efforts to borrow money.

A week or so before his death, he visited his mother-in-law and borrowed $18 from her. She said he looked worse than he had when she had seen him at Christmas. None of his relatives saw him again, but his landlady reported that he had joked with her the evening of his suicide and had seemed happy. He took an overdose of digitalis and chloral hydrate (which he had in a salesman's sample case) and died alone in his room. He left a note addressed to his mother-in-law giving as his reason for suicide that he was "at the end of his rope."

Family history: Nothing was known about psychiatric illness in the subject's family.

Arrest record: Eight months in prison for involuntary manslaughter (drunken driving the cause).

Case No *095* M *X* F __ Age *49*

ST. LOUIS SUICIDE STUDY CRITERIA FOR ALCOHOLISM

At least three of the following selected drinking behaviors were required for diagnosis.

A. Informant thought subject drank too much *X*	F. Subject suffered medical and psychiatric complications due to alcoholic intake *X*
B. Subject drank daily __	G. Subject thought he drank too much __
C. Subject went on benders (at least 48 hours of drinking and neglect of usual routine) __	H. Subject had job difficulties related to drinking *X*
D. Family objected to subject's drinking *X*	I. Subject involved in automobile accident(s) related to drinking *X*
E. Subject's history included arrests related to drinking *X*	

FEIGHNER CRITERIA FOR ALCOHOLISM

A definite diagnosis required symptoms in at least three of the following four groups. A probable diagnosis required symptoms in only two of the four groups.

A. 1. Any manifestation of alcohol withdrawal such as tremulousness, convulsions, hallucinations, or delirium ___
2. History of medical complications, e.g. cirrhosis, gastritis, pancreatitis, myopathy, polyneuropathy, Wernicke-Korsakov's syndrome _X_
3. Alcoholic blackouts, i.e., amnesic episodes during heavy drinking not accounted for by head trauma _X_
4. Alcoholic binges or benders (48 hours or more of drinking associated with default of usual obligations): must have occurred more than once ___

B. 1. Subject unable to stop drinking at will _X_
2. Subject tried to control drinking by allowing himself to drink only under certain circumstances, such as only after 5:00 p.m., only on weekends, or only with others ___
3. Subject drank before breakfast ___
4. Subject drank nonbeverage forms of alcohol (hair oil, mouthwash, Sterno, etc.) ___

C. 1. Subject arrested for drinking _X_
2. Subject involved in traffic difficulties associated with drinking ___
3. Subject had trouble at work because of drinking _X_
4. Subject involved in fights associated with drinking ___

D. 1. Subject worried about drinking too much ___
2. Family objected to subject's drinking _X_
3. Subject lost friends because of drinking _X_
4. Other people objected to subject's drinking ___
5. Subject felt guilty about his drinking ___

107 Informants: *Sister-in-law, employer*

This 38-year-old black man was described by his sister-in-law as "just crazy" and as having been so all of the 15 years she had known him.

He had finished eight or nine grades of school and moved to St. Louis with his mother (the father had deserted the family earlier) when he was about 13 years old. He married when he was 26. For the last 15 years of his life, he worked at a steel foundry. His employer described him as a quiet worker who got along well with other employees even though he preferred to work by himself. He had recently been promoted, his salary was good, and he owned a well-maintained, eight-room house.

Despite his success as a provider, he was known to have been a chronic alcoholic for at least 15 years. His drinking had caused him to be arrested three times for drunken driving and his sister-in-law believed it had also caused him some trouble at work though this was not mentioned by his employer. The sister-in-law said he also took drugs for "stomach trouble" which he got from a pharmacist friend without a prescription. He had a hernia surgically repaired 16 years earlier and apparently believed his recent stomach problems were a recurrence of the hernia. He also believed he had high blood pressure, but refused to see a doctor about either of these complaints or for those he suffered in the last year of his life which included dyspnea, palpitation, chest pain, dizziness, headaches, and fatigue.

His sister-in-law said he had been "queer" all his life—"nervous," "high-strung," sensitive, overactive, and overtalkative. She said he had very easily hurt feelings and that he had always cried easily. He was subject to outbursts of rages and during one of these rages he had burned up all his wife's clothes. She emphasized that he was extremely active sexually and expressed this by saying he was "hungry day and night." He had one girlfriend of long standing of whom his family was aware. He also had many good men friends whom he saw regularly, both at bars and in exchanged home visits. Finally, the informant reported that the subject had sometimes acted "silly," that he had a tendency to brag, and that he had a compulsion about brushing his teeth which caused him to get up several times every night to re-brush them.

In the last few days before his suicide, his peculiar behavior worsened. He began to look and act depressed and disgusted. His rages were more frequent and he seemed to be more or less constantly angry. Even so, he was able to serve on jury duty the last week of his life and to continue his duties as Democratic precinct captain, a post he had held for several years.

Three or four days before his suicide, he had a violent fight with his wife and her daughter and "threw them out of the house." Evidently, he was almost immediately overcome by shame, guilt, and self-blame. He called his girlfriend, who is reported to have refused to see him until he returned to his wife. He is said to have answered that the next time she saw him he "would be in a box." He then telephoned his sister-in-law and said he was no good, that he was to blame for all his family's troubles, that he was "too ashamed to live," and was going to "turn on the stove." She persuaded him to wait and to pray. He called again very early the next morning to tell her that praying had done no good and that she must come to his house with the police immediately. When she tried to call him back and got no answer, she called the police. Just as they were approaching his front door, he shot himself. He did not die immediately and was taken to a hospital where he died several hours later. He is said to have left two notes which the coroner's office held.

Family history: According to the sister-in-law, the subject's uncle had committed suicide some years in the past, one of his sisters had committed suicide 19 years prior to his act, and his brother had killed himself one year prior to his act. All of these family members were presumed (by the family) to have had a mental illness and, again according to the informant, "the whole family was alcoholic."
Arrest record: Three arrests for drunken driving.

Case No. *102* M X F __ Age *38*

ST. LOUIS SUICIDE STUDY CRITERIA FOR ALCOHOLISM

At least three of the following selected drinking behaviors were required for diagnosis.

- A. Informant thought subject drank too much   *X*
- B. Subject drank daily   __
- C. Subject went on benders (at least 48 hours of drinking and neglect of usual routine)   __
- D. Family objected to subject's drinking   *X*
- E. Subject's history included arrests related to drinking   *X*
- F. Subject suffered medical and psychiatric complications due to alcoholic intake   *X*
- G. Subject thought he drank too much   __
- H. Subject had job difficulties related to drinking   *X*
- I. Subject involved in automobile accident(s) related to drinking   __

FEIGHNER CRITERIA FOR ALCOHOLISM

A definite diagnosis required symptoms in at least three of the following four groups. A probable diagnosis required symptoms in only two of the four groups.

A. 1. Any manifestation of alcohol withdrawal such as tremulousness, convulsions, hallucinations, or delirium ___
    2. History of medical complications, e.g. cirrhosis, gastritis, pancreatitis, myopathy, polyneuropathy, Wernicke-Korsakov's syndrome ___
    3. Alcoholic blackouts, i.e., amnesic episodes during heavy drinking not accounted for by head trauma ___
    4. Alcoholic binges or benders (48 hours or more of drinking associated with default of usual obligations): must have occurred more than once ___

B. 1. Subject unable to stop drinking at will ___
    2. Subject tried to control drinking by allowing himself to drink only under certain circumstances, such as only after 5:00 p.m., only on weekends, or only with others ___
    3. Subject drank before breakfast ___
    4. Subject drank nonbeverage forms of alcohol (hair oil, mouthwash, Sterno, etc.) ___

C. 1. Subject arrested for drinking   X
    2. Subject involved in traffic difficulties associated with drinking ___
    3. Subject had trouble at work because of drinking   X
    4. Subject involved in fights associated with drinking ___

D. 1. Subject worried about drinking too much ___
    2. Family objected to subject's drinking   X
    3. Subject lost friends because of drinking ___
    4. Other people objected to subject's drinking ___
    5. Subject felt guilty about his drinking ___

109 Informants: Wife, physicians

This 48-year-old white married man was reportedly told by a physician on the morning of his suicide that he had tuberculosis and cancer of the lung.

He was educated through the 8th grade, married at 20, worked as a shoe cutter for most of his adult life, and had worked at his last job for 20 years. He had two children.

His wife described him as a quiet man who had enjoyed life and always been patient and easy-going with his children. Raised a Catholic, he attended church only rarely. Always "nervous," he had been a heavy smoker and had also drunk heavily (ten bottles of beer a night) for most of their marriage. His wife maintained that his drinking, though heavy, had not been a problem until the last few years when he wasn't able "to hold it" as well as he had previously. She said they enjoyed an active social life.

A year and a half before his death, the subject began to show signs of physical weakness and loss of energy. About six months before his death, his loss of energy became much more noticeable and two months later he had begun to lose weight, to tremble, and to display an uncharacteristic joylessness and loss of interest. One month before he died, his children had begun to irritate him. In addition to his ten beers a night, he began to drink whiskey on the sly. His wife and children noticed that he often had a "starry-eyed" expression he had never had before and that he appeared depressed and disgusted a great deal of the time.

By one month before his death, he had begun to cough so much that his wife persuaded him to see a doctor. The doctor ran tests for TB and cancer and, when the x-rays indicated both conditions, referred him to a specialist, but did not tell him of either of his possible diseases. A week before his suicide, he saw the specialist who later reorted that his tests had confirmed the diagnosis of TB and that he also suspected lung cancer. He, too, withheld from the subject his diagnosis and suspicion, but referred him to another lung specialist and, in a long, private talk, tried to prepare him for the possibility of TB. According to his wife, some of the subject's friends at work persuaded him to see another doctor whom they highly recommended and he had indeed seen this man the morning of his suicide. She felt certain that this last doctor had told the subject that "one lung was gone" with cancer and that he had TB as well. The doctor in question denied any knowledge of the subject or ever having seen him.

In any case, following his alleged appointment with the new doctor, the subject spoke on the telephone with his mother-in-law and she reported that he had sounded "OK" and had said he was going to fix himself a sandwich. Instead, he closed himself up in his car inside the garage and started the motor. His wife discovered his body and a note later that afternoon. The note said, "Babe, dear, What I found out this morning—I can't go on."

Family history: There was no family history of psychiatric illness.
Arrest record: None.

Case No. **109** M **X** F___ Age **48**

ST. LOUIS SUICIDE STUDY CRITERIA FOR ALCOHOLISM

At least three of the following selected drinking behaviors were required for diagnosis.

A. Informant thought subject drank too much   **X**
B. Subject drank daily   **X**
C. Subject went on benders (at least 48 hours of drinking and neglect of usual routine)   ___
D. Family objected to subject's drinking   **X**
E. Subject's history included arrests related to drinking   ___
F. Subject suffered medical and psychiatric complications due to alcoholic intake   **X**
G. Subject thought he drank too much   ___
H. Subject had job difficulties related to drinking   ___
I. Subject involved in automobile accident(s) related to drinking   ___

FEIGHNER CRITERIA FOR ALCOHOLISM

A definite diagnosis required symptoms in at least three of the following four groups. A probable diagnosis required symptoms in only two of the four groups.

A.
 1. Any manifestation of alcohol withdrawal such as tremulousness, convulsions, hallucinations, or delirium   ___
 2. History of medical complications, e.g. cirrhosis, gastritis, pancreatitis, myopathy, polyneuropathy, Wernicke-Korsakov's syndrome   ___
 3. Alcoholic blackouts, i.e., amnesic episodes during heavy drinking not accounted for by head trauma   ___
 4. Alcoholic binges or benders (48 hours or more of drinking associated with default of usual obligations): must have occurred more than once   ___

B.
 1. Subject unable to stop drinking at will   ___
 2. Subject tried to control drinking by allowing himself to drink only under certain circumstances, such as only after 5:00 p.m., only on weekends, or only with others   ___
 3. Subject drank before breakfast   ___
 4. Subject drank nonbeverage forms of alcohol (hair oil, mouthwash, Sterno, etc.)   ___

C.
 1. Subject arrested for drinking   ___
 2. Subject involved in traffic difficulties associated with drinking   ___
 3. Subject had trouble at work because of drinking   ___
 4. Subject involved in fights associated with drinking   ___

D.
 1. Subject worried about drinking too much   ___
 2. Family objected to subject's drinking   **X**
 3. Subject lost friends because of drinking   ___
 4. Other people objected to subject's drinking   ___
 5. Subject felt guilty about his drinking   ___

119 Informants: Wife, physicians

This 47-year-old white man committed suicide on the first anniversary of his father's death. He was the oldest of three siblings, all of whom both respected and stood in awe of their successful physician father who specialized in otolaryngology. The subject graduated from college with a degree in civil engineering after switching from a pre-med course. Shortly after his graduation, he married and had one son. This marriage ended in divorce after eight years. He served in the Army as an enlisted man for two years during World War II. Near the end of his service, he allegedly struck an officer, was court martialed, and given a dishonorable discharge. His father wanted to challenge the decision, but, for reasons he would not discuss, the subject refused to let him.

A year after leaving the service, he married his second wife. At that time, he had a job as an engineer for a St. Louis County construction company. After working in St. Louis for one year, he was transferred to a small town where he built and ran a branch plant. According to his wife, his salary had been high and he enjoyed the work. Seven years later, the company closed the plant and he was left without a job. He found another, less interesting job at a great reduction in salary. At the end of one year on the new job, he fractured a vertebra in a drunken fall and, though he returned to work for several weeks after being released from the hospital, he was finally fired for laziness. At that point, he and his wife returned to St. Louis and moved in with his parents. A few weeks after the subject's move to his parents' home, his father died suddenly and, though his wife urged that they find an apartment of their own, he put off leaving his mother. Friction between the recent widow, her unemployed son, and his unhappy wife was such that the wife left twice for long visits to her family in Kentucky. Once during her absence he wrote her that he suspected the maid and his mother of trying to poison his food.

According to his wife, the subject had always been a "nervous," "high-strung," sensitive, "neurotic" person whose feelings were easily hurt and who cried at sad TV programs, movies, and books. She felt that he had a life-long inferiority complex and she said he had mentioned suicide several times when he was drinking and depressed. He had been a heavy drinker for many years and his physician described him as a chronic alcoholic. His wife said he was subject to sudden outbursts of rage, especially when drunk, and that for years he had found Sundays extremely depressing. Once, ten years before his death, he had slashed his wrists in a drunken depression. Generally healthy, he had a long-standing fear of cancer of the nose. Five years before his suicide he began to complain of dyspnea, palpitation, and chest pain, symptoms which were sometimes associated with what appeared to have been anxiety attacks. He did not consult a physician about either his nose worries or his chest pains.

At the time he lost his job with the construction company, his wife noticed a slight change in his behavior, but it wasn't until they had moved to St. Louis that she felt the subject began to display obvious changes. After his father's death, he stopped seeing friends at home and did all his socializing alone at bars. He stopped going to church, and lost all interest in his hobbies. He became less affectionate toward his wife and stopped talking with her when they were alone unless he wanted to pick a fight. His sex drive diminished gradually over the last year of his life to the point of impotence the last month. He began to drink liquor regularly in addition to drinking beer daily. His general attitude was one of joylessness, disinterest, ennui, inertia interspersed with what he called "brain storms." His wife described these as "manic," usually drunken, episodes during which he would talk wildly about schemes for jobs or money-making projects. All this time, he was unable to find a job, a situation he blamed on his dishonorable discharge. He mentioned suicide more and more often and openly stated his feelings of guilt, worthlessness, uselessness, and his belief that his wife and mother would be better off without him. He said occasionally that he feared he was losing his mind and "everything had changed." His worry about cancer of the nose became delusional.

Two weeks before his death, his behavior suddenly worsened. His wife said she hardly spoke to him for fear of starting arguments. He was angry and irritable toward her, his mother, the maid who had helped raise him, and the bartender at his favorite tavern. He complained of a bad headache and was drunk much of the time. The day before his suicide, he took his wife and mother on a tour of cemeteries to look at mausoleums, as he wanted to build one for his father. It was a sad tour and, when they returned home, he was depressed and very quiet. He ate dinner alone in front of the TV. That night, he and his wife went to bed without conversation though he did reach over to touch her hand before going to sleep. The next morning, the first anniversary of his father's death, his mother said at breakfast that the past year had been "the worst of her life." Insulted, he answered her that if she thought that year had been bad, she should remember that she had 20 more ahead of her. Driving his wife to work, he accused her of wanting to "run away" when she commented that it would be nice to own a trailer. When he dropped her off, he said he'd be back to pick her up when she got off or "would see that someone else" came if he couldn't. At about 3:30 that afternoon, he returned to his mother's house. He had been drinking and he went upstairs to his bedroom. About 45 minutes later, the maid heard a "thud" from the bathroom. His mother went up to investigate and found her son's body carefully arranged on his bathroom floor with his head near the shower drain and all the rugs folded and taken up off the floor. He had shot himself in the right temple. He left a note for his wife which said: "My Sweetheart, this cannot go on. We both know that our present existence is not right or circumspect. You have always wanted to run. I have never blamed you. This underlying insult tops everything good that my mother ever did. I can't take any more."

Family history: A maternal uncle had committed suicide. Another uncle and a grandfather had both been alcoholics. The subject's mother and both siblings were described as "nervous" people.
Arrest record: None.

Case No. *119* M *X* F ___ Age *47*

ST. LOUIS SUICIDE STUDY CRITERIA FOR ALCOHOLISM

At least three of the following selected drinking behaviors were required for diagnosis.

A. Informant thought subject drank too much   X

B. Subject drank daily   X

C. Subject went on benders (at least 48 hours of drinking and neglect of usual routine)   ___

D. Family objected to subject's drinking   X

E. Subject's history included arrests related to drinking   ___

F. Subject suffered medical and psychiatric complications due to alcoholic intake   X

G. Subject thought he drank too much   ___

H. Subject had job difficulties related to drinking   X

I. Subject involved in automobile accident(s) related to drinking   ___

FEIGHNER CRITERIA FOR ALCOHOLISM

A definite diagnosis required symptoms in at least three of the following four groups. A probable diagnosis required symptoms in only two of the four groups.

A. 1. Any manifestation of alcohol withdrawal such as tremulousness, convulsions, hallucinations, or delirium ___
   2. History of medical complications, e.g. cirrhosis, gastritis, pancreatitis, myopathy, polyneuropathy, Wernicke-Korsakov's syndrome _X_
   3. Alcoholic blackouts, i.e., amnesic episodes during heavy drinking not accounted for by head trauma ___
   4. Alcoholic binges or benders (48 hours or more of drinking associated with default of usual obligations): must have occurred more than once ___

B. 1. Subject unable to stop drinking at will _X_
   2. Subject tried to control drinking by allowing himself to drink only under certain circumstances, such as only after 5:00 p.m., only on weekends, or only with others ___
   3. Subject drank before breakfast ___
   4. Subject drank nonbeverage forms of alcohol (hair oil, mouthwash, Sterno, etc.) ___

C. 1. Subject arrested for drinking ___
   2. Subject involved in traffic difficulties associated with drinking ___
   3. Subject had trouble at work because of drinking _X_
   4. Subject involved in fights associated with drinking _X_

D. 1. Subject worried about drinking too much _X_
   2. Family objected to subject's drinking _X_
   3. Subject lost friends because of drinking ___
   4. Other people objected to subject's drinking ___
   5. Subject felt guilty about his drinking ___

124 Informants: Sister, former landlady, fellow worker

This 41-year-old white man had married for the first time a year before his suicide and had separated from his wife only a few weeks before his death. He was living with his sister at the time of his suicide.

He had finished the 6th grade of school, served for two years in the Army during World War II, and received an honorable discharge. He had worked at his last job—laborer for an excavation company—for five years and before that he had worked for ten years for a St. Louis department store as an elevator operator.

He had been a heavy drinker since his adolescence and his landlady in the boarding house he lived in before his marriage, whom he called "Mom," said she believed he had, before his marriage, drunk as much as a quart of whiskey a day, but that he had always been a "mannerly" drunk, never loud or bothersome. A fellow worker claimed that his drinking had never affected his work and that he had obviously liked his job and been happy to work right up until the end. The friend and the landlady knew that the subject's marriage had been bad from the beginning even though, once wed, the subject greatly reduced the amount of alcohol he drank and generally settled down. Evidently the couple did not get along at all after the first few weeks and ended up living separate lives in the same house. The subject's fellow worker said that it had been clear that he dreaded going home at night and the landlady said he often cried when he visited her and spoke of his wife's cruelty. When asked why he remained in this intolerable situation, he explained that he was lonely.

A few weeks before his death, his wife left him and arranged for a legal separation. He moved in with his sister who also described the subject's crying over his wife's insults. The sister denied any other problems of her brother's, though she thought he might have been a "little depressed" after his wife left him and perhaps a little more nervous. She said he drank hardly at all while with her and never made suicidal comments, but she did remember that on his birthday two weeks before his death, he had said, "I won't be here for my next birthday."

On the day of his suicide, he got up at the usual time and put on clean work clothes. Although he left his sister's house at the usual time, he did not go to work. Instead he went to his old boarding house to visit his landlady, whom he told that he had been happy the year he spent in her house. She stated that the subject was, that morning, in good spirits, laughing and joking. He had not been drinking and he did not cry, even though he said that he should have stayed single. When he left, before lunch, he said, "I'll be back at 2:00—keep the door open!" Evidently, he then drove around, ending up in a suburban tavern. There he drank two beers and at 5:30 called his sister to say that he would not be home for supper. He ordered and drank one more drink and at 6:45 left the tavern. He was described by the bartender as "happy" as he left. Five minutes later, some boys found him in his car and reported to the bartender that he had been shot. He had managed to shoot himself with his own rifle, but did not die until three weeks later. His family claimed that his death had been accidental. He left no note.

Family history: No family history of psychiatric illness.
Arrest record: None.

Case No. 124 M X F __ Age 41

ST. LOUIS SUICIDE STUDY CRITERIA FOR ALCOHOLISM

At least three of the following selected drinking behaviors were required for diagnosis.

- A. Informant thought subject drank too much __X__
- B. Subject drank daily __X__
- C. Subject went on benders (at least 48 hours of drinking and neglect of usual routine) ___
- D. Family objected to subject's drinking __X__
- E. Subject's history included arrests related to drinking ___
- F. Subject suffered medical and psychiatric complications due to alcoholic intake __X__
- G. Subject thought he drank too much ___
- H. Subject had job difficulties related to drinking ___
- I. Subject involved in automobile accident(s) related to drinking ___

FEIGHNER CRITERIA FOR ALCOHOLISM

A definite diagnosis required symptoms in at least three of the following four groups. A probable diagnosis required symptoms in only two of the four groups.

- A.
  1. Any manifestation of alcohol withdrawal such as tremulousness, convulsions, hallucinations, or delirium ___
  2. History of medical complications, e.g. cirrhosis, gastritis, pancreatitis, myopathy, polyneuropathy, Wernicke-Korsakov's syndrome ___
  3. Alcoholic blackouts, i.e., amnesic episodes during heavy drinking not accounted for by head trauma ___
  4. Alcoholic binges or benders (48 hours or more of drinking associated with default of usual obligations): must have occurred more than once ___
- B.
  1. Subject unable to stop drinking at will ___
  2. Subject tried to control drinking by allowing himself to drink only under certain circumstances, such as only after 5:00 p.m., only on weekends, or only with others __X__
  3. Subject drank before breakfast ___
  4. Subject drank nonbeverage forms of alcohol (hair oil, mouthwash, Sterno, etc.) ___
- C.
  1. Subject arrested for drinking ___
  2. Subject involved in traffic difficulties associated with drinking ___
  3. Subject had trouble at work because of drinking ___
  4. Subject involved in fights associated with drinking ___
- D.
  1. Subject worried about drinking too much ___
  2. Family objected to subject's drinking __X__
  3. Subject lost friends because of drinking __X__
  4. Other people objected to subject's drinking __X__
  5. Subject felt guilty about his drinking ___

128 Informants: Wife, half-brother, social service records

By the time this white man had committed suicide at the age of 37, he had married five women, lived with one other for nine years without marrying her, fathered eight children, none of whom he supported, and at the end of his life, involved himself deeply in seeking custody of a child unrelated to him.

Nothing was known about the extent of his schooling. He served for some time in the Army and claimed he had been given a medical discharge for asthma. He lived in at least five cities and came to St. Louis some time after his release from the service. His half-brother said that he had started drinking at the age of 15. By the time of his death, he was drinking about a quart of wine a day, was nearly always delusional when drunk, suffered frequent amnesic blackouts, and had been hospitalized three times the last year of his life for alcoholism associated with pneumonia, amnesic episode, and attempted suicide. He earned his living as a tree surgeon and was, for the last few years of his life, employed by his half-brother who owned a tree service.

So much went on in the subject's life that, for the sake of brevity, this report will concentrate on the events of the last year which preceded his suicide. Two years before he died, he had married his fourth wife. According to his half-brother, it was during his life with her that his drinking became excessive and the marriage was, as a result, stormy. About a year before his death, he was severely pressed by debts and his fourth wife, so the story went, proposed that she divorce him, marry a man with money, assume the subject's debts, pay them, divorce the monied husband, and remarry the subject. The subject agreed to this plan which she proceeded to carry out. However, when she returned to him, ready for remarriage, he refused the remarriage although he did agree to live with her. His drinking binges grew more frequent, his behavior more inappropriate, and their life more chaotic. He apparently threatened suicide several times and once cut himself on the throat, claiming later that she had cut him. The fourth ex-wife had the subject put in jail on several occasions. The last time, a friend bailed him out and introduced him to an older woman who had a basement room to rent. He took the room and deserted the fourth ex-wife.

Over the next month, the subject became increasingly fond of his landlady and her five-year-old niece. This child, the daughter of the woman's dead sister, had been in her aunt's care since infancy, but her aunt had never been assigned legal custody. Because the subject had become emotionally involved with both the child and her aunt and wished to help ensure custody, he married the aunt. This woman soon discovered the extent and severity of her new husband's alcoholism. She reported that he had many hallucinations (their bed became a "pink coffin," strange men walked about their room, etc.), that he had prolonged periods of confusion and amnesia when drunk, and was always loud when drinking. However, she claimed that when sober, he was coherent, kind, and gentle and that she loved him.

His suicidal preoccupation appeared to have intensified during the last three months of his life and his fifth wife said he called on God nightly to "take him" while he slept. Meanwhile, an extremely jealous and resourceful fourth ex-wife had found out about the subject's fifth marriage and the reasons for it and apparently set out to get revenge. Somehow, in that short period of time, she managed to meet and marry the father of the fifth wife's niece and to persuade him to apply for legal custody of his daughter. She achieved just the effect she intended. The subject became deeply upset at the thought of losing the child and, whenever drunk, wept while cuddling and caressing her. He and the fifth wife appealed to a hospital Social Service Department for help and there is a record of a series of frantic visits during the subject's last month of life.

One month before his suicide, the subject arrived home glassy-eyed and unable to recall where he had been the night before. His fifth wife took him to a psychiatric hospital where he was kept a week for treatment of delirium tremens. On release from the hospital, he immediately got drunk again and made a suicide attempt with pills and some kind of poison. He was hospitalized for one day and released. The last three weeks of his life, he became noticeably worse. He drank, prayed, and cried. On the Friday before his death, he, his wife, and the child moved to a hotel in order to elude the sheriff who wanted to deliver a warrant for the child's custody. When they returned home the day before his death and learned that, despite their efforts, the sheriff would take the child the following day, he devised a last desperate plan which involved divorcing the fifth wife, remarrying the fourth wife, gaining legal custody of the child, divorcing the fourth wife, and returning to the fifth wife with the child. When he telephoned the fourth wife to propose a reconciliation and was refused, he became even more despondent. At bedtime he said to his fifth wife, "Oh Mommy, come and sleep with me this one night more, and hold me tight, I'm so afraid." The next morning, he called his fourth ex-wife's mother and asked her to light a candle for him. He then left for work, taking a religious medal with him. At 9 AM, he returned home and told his fifth wife, "I'm going to have to leave you . . . going to have to go away." He behaved more and more strangely throughout the morning, saying "Remember these words, I love no one but you" and, to a photograph of the fifth wife and her niece, "God, damn you. Why do I have to love her so?" Later, he asked his wife where she would bury him. About 10:30 AM, the child's social worker telephoned and while the fifth wife was talking to her, the child ran in saying "Daddy's got the rifle." His wife screamed at him "not to do it," but he pulled the trigger as she approached him and died immediately. Although he had left suicide notes—to both the fourth and fifth wives—during a previous attempt, he did not leave one at the last.

A month later, the child's custody was legally awarded to her father and stepmother.

Family history: His full brother was an alcoholic and one half-brother was described as "hot tempered" and peculiar.
Arrest record: None.

Case No. 128 M X F __ Age 37

ST. LOUIS SUICIDE STUDY CRITERIA FOR ALCOHOLISM

At least three of the following selected drinking behaviors were required for diagnosis.

A. Informant thought subject drank too much ___
B. Subject drank daily X
C. Subject went on benders (at least 48 hours of drinking and neglect of usual routine) X
D. Family objected to subject's drinking X
E. Subject's history included arrests related to drinking X
F. Subject suffered medical and psychiatric complications due to alcoholic intake X
G. Subject thought he drank too much ___
H. Subject had job difficulties related to drinking ___
I. Subject involved in automobile accident(s) related to drinking ___

FEIGHNER CRITERIA FOR ALCOHOLISM

A definite diagnosis required symptoms in at least three of the following four groups. A probable diagnosis required symptoms in only two of the four groups.

A. 1. Any manifestation of alcohol withdrawal such as tremulousness, convulsions, hallucinations, or delirium __X__
    2. History of medical complications, e.g. cirrhosis, gastritis, pancreatitis, myopathy, polyneuropathy, Wernicke-Korsakov's syndrome __X__
    3. Alcoholic blackouts, i.e., amnesic episodes during heavy drinking not accounted for by head trauma __X__
    4. Alcoholic binges or benders (48 hours or more of drinking associated with default of usual obligations): must have occurred more than once __X__

B. 1. Subject unable to stop drinking at will __X__
    2. Subject tried to control drinking by allowing himself to drink only under certain circumstances, such as only after 5:00 p.m., only on weekends, or only with others ___
    3. Subject drank before breakfast ___
    4. Subject drank nonbeverage forms of alcohol (hair oil, mouthwash, Sterno, etc.) ___

C. 1. Subject arrested for drinking __X__
    2. Subject involved in traffic difficulties associated with drinking ___
    3. Subject had trouble at work because of drinking ___
    4. Subject involved in fights associated with drinking __X__

D. 1. Subject worried about drinking too much ___
    2. Family objected to subject's drinking __X__
    3. Subject lost friends because of drinking ___
    4. Other people objected to subject's drinking __X__
    5. Subject felt guilty about his drinking __X__

ALCOHOLISM, SUBGROUP 3
Men aged 57 and over (N = 5)

003 Informants: Wife, physician, nurse, hospital records

This 58-year-old white man who had been night manager at a motel for 17 years entered a general hospital one month prior to his suicide with an attack of acute pulmonary edema and a coronary thrombosis. At age 40, he was first diagnosed as having hypertension. Seven years later, he developed angina pectoris. By age 48 he was a chronic alcoholic. (He married his current wife at that time and there is no direct confirmed history of excessive drinking prior to this time, but by then he was drinking at least a pint of whiskey daily and both he and his new wife thought he drank too much.) At age 49, his hypertensive cardiovascular disease and coronary insufficiency worsened. From that time he was always sickly. Two years later, he had his first coronary infarction. Three years following the infarction and 18 months prior to his death, he developed diabetes and had a second infarction. From that time he was chronically ill and disabled. During this 18-month period he had the following symptoms: dyspnea, palpitation, chest pain, fatigue, weakness, weight loss, anorexia, impotence, insomnia, constipation, loss of interest, depressed feelings, inertia, and carelessness about his appearance. In the meanwhile, his drinking increased. About four months prior to his death, he developed a hemiparesis of his left arm and leg, which cleared in about a month's time.

During the month in the hospital, his pulmonary edema cleared and his chest pain diminished. There was no note in the record concerning his being depressed or behaving in an unusual fashion until three days before his suicide, when it was noted that he appeared depressed. His sedative medication was increased and on that same day he had a gastric tube passed. He reacted violently to this procedure, saying it was a test for insanity and that they were going to "send me away." Two days before his death, while his wife was visiting, he suddenly removed his clothes and urinated in the corner of his room, giving no explanation for this behavior. That evening he insisted that his wife stay overnight in the hospital with him, although previously he had insisted she abide by the rules of the hospital. The nurse had to persuade him to let his wife go home. The next day he telephoned his wife at home and, when she did not answer, he became very upset, convinced that his wife had "run out" on him. Later that day he suddenly became panicky and yelled to the nurse, "The bugs are going to get me!"

During the afternoon of the day of his suicide he telephoned old friends to whom he had not spoken in ten years "just to say hello." While his wife was visiting he suddenly said to her, "We've got to get out of here! The termites are eating the floor." Later that day he was found with a paring knife in his hand, which he could not explain. During that evening he telephoned his wife three or four times saying, "This is the bluest day of my life," "I won't be in the hospital tomorrow," and "I am going to die tonight." He also told his wife to put his army papers on the dresser at home. Later that evening, an hour after he was supposed to have been asleep for the night, he unlatched the window screen and jumped to his death.

His wife had been unaware of his previous marriages and of his son until three years before his death and she had no knowledge of his early life. She knew that he had been in the army and was honorably discharged at the end of World War I. She believed that prior to his job as night clerk he had been a fairly well-to-do undertaker.

There were no notes in the record demonstrating disorientation for time, place, or person. There was no evidence that his medical disease had worsened in the three days before his death.

His wife regarded her husband as a nervous and sick man who also drank too much. He was in serious debt and there was a question of his having given a diamond ring to another woman some months before his death. Other life stresses that may have played a role included his medical illness and its attendant disability.

Family history: There was no family history of psychiatric illness.
Arrest record: None.

Case No. *003* M *X* F __ Age *58*

ST. LOUIS SUICIDE STUDY CRITERIA FOR ALCOHOLISM

At least three of the following selected drinking behaviors were required for diagnosis.

A. Informant thought subject drank too much   *X*
B. Subject drank daily   *X*
C. Subject went on benders (at least 48 hours of drinking and neglect of usual routine)   __
D. Family objected to subject's drinking   __
E. Subject's history included arrests related to drinking   __
F. Subject suffered medical and psychiatric complications due to alcoholic intake   *X*
G. Subject thought he drank too much   *X*
H. Subject had job difficulties related to drinking   __
I. Subject involved in automobile accident(s) related to drinking   __

FEIGHNER CRITERIA FOR ALCOHOLISM

A definite diagnosis required symptoms in at least three of the following four groups. A probable diagnosis required symptoms in only two of the four groups.

A. 1. Any manifestation of alcohol withdrawal such as tremulousness, convulsions, hallucinations, or delirium _X_
    2. History of medical complications, e.g. cirrhosis, gastritis, pancreatitis, myopathy, polyneuropathy, Wernicke-Korsakov's syndrome _X_
    3. Alcoholic blackouts, i.e., amnesic episodes during heavy drinking not accounted for by head trauma ___
    4. Alcoholic binges or benders (48 hours or more of drinking associated with default of usual obligations): must have occurred more than once ___

B. 1. Subject unable to stop drinking at will ___
    2. Subject tried to control drinking by allowing himself to drink only under certain circumstances, such as only after 5:00 p.m., only on weekends, or only with others ___
    3. Subject drank before breakfast ___
    4. Subject drank nonbeverage forms of alcohol (hair oil, mouthwash, Sterno, etc.) ___

C. 1. Subject arrested for drinking ___
    2. Subject involved in traffic difficulties associated with drinking ___
    3. Subject had trouble at work because of drinking ___
    4. Subject involved in fights associated with drinking ___

D. 1. Subject worried about drinking too much _X_
    2. Family objected to subject's drinking _X_
    3. Subject lost friends because of drinking ___
    4. Other people objected to subject's drinking _X_
    5. Subject felt guilty about his drinking ___

033 Informants: Sister, brother; hospital and social service records

This white 62-year-old man had drunk heavily all of his adult life and was at the time of his death an alcoholic of long standing. He was thought (by "someone," unclear who) to have made one previous attempt on his life. According to his sister, he was an "easygoing," cheerful man for most of his life. He married at age 17 to a decisive and domineering woman who is said to have beaten him in their later years. Informants were vague about his job career, but said he had belonged to the local CIO union and was president of his CIO group for 13 years. Even though his drinking did not, at that point, seem to have interfered with his work, he had a police record of many arrests for drunkenness and disturbing the peace.

Ten years before his death, he joined a Baptist church and became involved in the church's affairs. He left it when his wife, who was apparently jealous of his involvement, insisted. He then opened his own storefront church which he sold some time later.

About six years prior to his suicide, he was hospitalized for a month for stomach pain and vomiting blood. Stomach ulcer was diagnosed and a subtotal gastrectomy performed. A year later, he was hospitalized for nearly a month with homologous serum hepatitis.

Although the informants were uncertain about the exact sequence of events, at some point three or four years before he died his wife began to see another man. It was about this time that he began to show signs of uncharacteristic sadness and nervousness. He cried easily, looked depressed, lost interest in socializing, complained of joint pain, extremity pain, fatigue, and of shortness of breath. He lost weight, and during the last four years of his life, lost 20 pounds. Other complaints mentioned by one informant were dizziness, headaches, palpitation, and chest pains. However, it was not made clear just when these latter symptoms occurred.

Four years before his suicide, the subject's alcoholism began to interfere with his work and, from that time on, he was unable to hold jobs for more than a few weeks at a time. Two years later, his drinking was even heavier and he tended, as he had not previously, to become violent when drunk. Fights with his wife increased and he told relatives that both his wife and his son "beat him up." A year to six months before his death, he claimed that his wife had cut his throat in a quarrel over a man she had slept with some 40 years in the past. Also about that time, he saw a doctor because he was concerned about possible cirrhosis which he maintained had been diagnosed 27 years earlier. There is no record to confirm either his suspicion or his visit to the doctor.

Six months before his suicide, he is said to have weakened in all respects—physical, mental, and moral. His sister reported that, from that point on, he seemed unable to concentrate, to think clearly or talk rationally, that he had memory lapses, and that he often spoke of suicide. Three months later, he tried to give his brother money to pay for his funeral. One month before his death, his wife threw him out, and in the last weeks of his life, he moved from rooming house to rooming house. His appearance was disheveled. He had various short-term jobs and begged money from all his relatives. He tried, on several occasions, to get money from his wife who always refused him. Whatever money he got he spent on alcohol.

Two weeks before his death, he visited his sister and spent 11 days at her home. She said he was extremely depressed, with signs of joylessness and sadness, and that he told her his wife and son had been "mean" to him. He told his brother that he was afraid of his son and spoke to the brother several times about suicide. He was irritable and, when money was refused him, given to outbursts of rage. His weight loss increased and he complained of anorexia and fatigue. During the stay at his sister's, he persuaded her to take him to the country to visit relatives he hadn't seen in years. Just before leaving her home, a week before he committed suicide, he told her that he was "going back . . . but they were going to kill (him)." When she asked who was going to kill him, he answered, "I can't tell you, but they are going to kill me." When he left, he put a letter in her Bible which was not found until after his death. On the outside of the envelope was written, "If anything happens to me, give this to the marshal." The sister was vague about the note itself. It "may have" accused his wife of his death. A similar note, the contents of which are again unknown, was found in his pocket.

No one was certain where he spent the last days and nights of his life, though he did turn up at his brother's once to ask for money. On the last night of his life, he went to a flop house for men, signed the register with his wife's name as well as his own ("Mr. and Mrs. _____"), went to his room, and hanged himself with a sheet thrown over the transom. His shabbily dressed body was found by the owner of the flop house shortly thereafter.

Family history: Although the informants were not entirely clear about his parents' histories, there were indications that both of them were alcoholics. Two sisters had suffered nervous breakdowns in the 1920's and one of them was still in a mental hospital when the subject committed suicide in 1956. A brother was described as having been a "recluse" for 20 years and the family as a whole was described as "nervous."

Arrest record: Many arrests for drunkenness and peace disturbance.

Case No. 033 M X F __ Age 62

ST. LOUIS SUICIDE STUDY CRITERIA FOR ALCOHOLISM

At least three of the following selected drinking behaviors were required for diagnosis.

A. Informant thought subject drank too much X
B. Subject drank daily X
C. Subject went on benders (at least 48 hours of drinking and neglect of usual routine) __
D. Family objected to subject's drinking X
E. Subject's history included arrests related to drinking X
F. Subject suffered medical and psychiatric complications due to alcoholic intake X
G. Subject thought he drank too much __
H. Subject had job difficulties related to drinking X
I. Subject involved in automobile accident(s) related to drinking __

FEIGHNER CRITERIA FOR ALCOHOLISM

A definite diagnosis required symptoms in at least three of the following four groups. A probable diagnosis required symptoms in only two of the four groups.

A. 1. Any manifestation of alcohol withdrawal such as tremulousness, convulsions, hallucinations, or delirium __
   2. History of medical complications, e.g. cirrhosis, gastritis, pancreatitis, myopathy, polyneuropathy, Wernicke-Korsakov's syndrome X
   3. Alcoholic blackouts, i.e., amnesic episodes during heavy drinking not accounted for by head trauma X
   4. Alcoholic binges or benders (48 hours or more of drinking associated with default of usual obligations): must have occurred more than once __

B. 1. Subject unable to stop drinking at will X
   2. Subject tried to control drinking by allowing himself to drink only under certain circumstances, such as only after 5:00 p.m., only on weekends, or only with others __
   3. Subject drank before breakfast __
   4. Subject drank nonbeverage forms of alcohol (hair oil, mouthwash, Sterno, etc.) __

C. 1. Subject arrested for drinking X
   2. Subject involved in traffic difficulties associated with drinking __
   3. Subject had trouble at work because of drinking X
   4. Subject involved in fights associated with drinking X

D. 1. Subject worried about drinking too much X
   2. Family objected to subject's drinking X
   3. Subject lost friends because of drinking __
   4. Other people objected to subject's drinking __
   5. Subject felt guilty about his drinking __

047 Informants: Landlord, bartender, acquaintance (no primary informant)

Three people who knew this 58-year-old unmarried Polish immigrant during his five years in the U.S. were interviewed, but because he lived alone and was able to speak only German, much of his history is unknown and most of the events leading to his suicide are unclear.

It is known that his immigration was sponsored by two elderly friends living in Illinois, that he lived at first, a short while, with a St. Louis druggist and his wife, and that he managed to get a job as a janitor in a grade school. According to the druggist, he complained once too often about the food in their home and they asked him to leave. It was arranged that he take an apartment in the basement of the home of a German-speaking couple. He kept his job until one year before his death. The reasons for its loss varied with the informants. The druggist maintained that the subject, once in the U.S., had begun to drink and that, by the time of his death, he was drinking "at least a half pint of whiskey a day." He believed that the subject had begun to drink on the job and was fired as a result. The landlord reported that he had been laid off to make room for someone else. He said the subject had told him he had been "politically fired." The bartender, on the other hand, said he had never known the subject to drink more than one to three beers a day, never saw him drunk, and that he had had to quit the job because of his poor health. They all agreed that he had liver trouble—probably cirrhosis—and that he had gained a lot of weight in the abdomen and legs. They also agreed that, when he lost his job, he had about $2000 in the bank and that he had said he would hang himself when he ran out of money. He refused to look for other work.

He is remembered as a man who always smiled and said "Hi" to the neighborhood children and he is said to have shown the same amenities on the day of his death. He saw his friend, the bartender, and his landlady early in the afternoon and neither noticed anything unusual in his manner. At 4:30 PM, he was found hanging in the landlord's garage. He was dead when found. He is said to have had no money left in the bank at the time of his death.

Family history: Nothing was known of his family history in regard to psychiatric illness.
Arrest record: None.

Case No. *047* M _X_ F ___ Age *58*

ST. LOUIS SUICIDE STUDY CRITERIA FOR ALCOHOLISM

At least three of the following selected drinking behaviors were required for diagnosis.

- A. Informant thought subject drank too much _X_
- B. Subject drank daily _X_
- C. Subject went on benders (at least 48 hours of drinking and neglect of usual routine) ___
- D. Family objected to subject's drinking ___
- E. Subject's history included arrests related to drinking ___
- F. Subject suffered medical and psychiatric complications due to alcoholic intake _X_
- G. Subject thought he drank too much ___
- H. Subject had job difficulties related to drinking _X_
- I. Subject involved in automobile accident(s) related to drinking ___

FEIGHNER CRITERIA FOR ALCOHOLISM

A definite diagnosis required symptoms in at least three of the following four groups. A probable diagnosis required symptoms in only two of the four groups.

- A.
  1. Any manifestation of alcohol withdrawal such as tremulousness, convulsions, hallucinations, or delirium ___
  2. History of medical complications, e.g. cirrhosis, gastritis, pancreatitis, myopathy, polyneuropathy, Wernicke-Korsakov's syndrome _X_
  3. Alcoholic blackouts, i.e., amnesic episodes during heavy drinking not accounted for by head trauma ___
  4. Alcoholic binges or benders (48 hours or more of drinking associated with default of usual obligations): must have occurred more than once ___

- B.
  1. Subject unable to stop drinking at will ___
  2. Subject tried to control drinking by allowing himself to drink only under certain circumstances, such as only after 5:00 p.m., only on weekends, or only with others ___
  3. Subject drank before breakfast ___
  4. Subject drank nonbeverage forms of alcohol (hair oil, mouthwash, Sterno, etc.) ___

- C.
  1. Subject arrested for drinking ___
  2. Subject involved in traffic difficulties associated with drinking ___
  3. Subject had trouble at work because of drinking _X_
  4. Subject involved in fights associated with drinking ___

- D.
  1. Subject worried about drinking too much ___
  2. Family objected to subject's drinking ___
  3. Subject lost friends because of drinking ___
  4. Other people objected to subject's drinking ___
  5. Subject felt guilty about his drinking ___

097 Informant: Son, hospital records

This 61-year-old white man had been widowed for four years prior to his suicide. Since his wife's death, he had shared his house with his unmarried son.

He left school after the sixth grade, married at age 25, and worked as a stitcher in a shoe factory for 38 years. The subject and his wife were both Catholics and attended church every Sunday throughout their marriage despite the fact that, for at least the last 13 years of it, the subject had spent all his weekends getting drunk. His usual weekend quota was a quart of wine plus a case of beer and almost nothing to eat. According to the son, his mother had kept his father's drinking "in check," though she often joined him in his weekend drunks and at those times the two of them would engage in noisy fighting. Six years before his suicide, the subject spent two weeks in the alcoholic ward of a Catholic hospital where he was diagnosed as having acute alcoholism and depression. The couple was said to have had about five good friends with whom they occasionally went to taverns. The informant described his father as always having been a nervous, moody person whose feelings were easily hurt and who cried easily, especially when he was drunk. He also said that his father was a "frail" man who tended to be sickly.

Almost immediately after his wife's death, the subject extended his drinking habits to week days. At the same time, he lost almost all interest in seeing his relatives and friends and, except to go to his job, rarely left the house. His son said that from then on he was withdrawn, joyless, and often silent. When drunk he made direct statements, to his son and to friends, of his suicidal thoughts, his depression, his sadness, his loneliness, and his disgust at what he considered "a raw deal in life." Always a noisy drunk, he became angry and spiteful when drinking and, when very drunk, suffered spells of dizziness and fainting. When sober, however, he made no suicidal statements and rarely showed obvious signs of self-disgust or self-pity.

Three years before his suicide, he was hospitalized for four days after being brought to the emergency room unconscious, apparently as a result of taking too many sleeping pills along with a large amount of whiskey. His excuse for this was "trouble sleeping," but there was suspicion on his son's part that the episode represented a first attempt at suicide.

A year later, his drinking having increased steadily, he was fired for drunkenness on the job. Unable to find other work, he was unemployed for the last two years of his life. Whatever money he had at the time he was fired he spent on drink and when that was gone, be began to borrow on his life insurance. He let his appearance go and spent most of his time in his house, rarely leaving it for any reason except to buy wine and beer. He had stopped attending church after his wife's death and, by the last year of his life, saw almost no one except his son. During that last year, however, the subject had a "girlfriend," a woman near his age with whom he drank, watched TV, and fought noisily much the way he and his wife had. His son described this relationship as a "rowdy romance."

During the last four years of his life, he was arrested at least twice for drunkenness and twice, when drunk, became uncontrollably frantic because he believed someone had broken into his house and was "robbing" him. Occasionally he complained of weakness and tiredness.

On the evening of his suicide, he was sober when he and his son ate supper. He didn't talk much, but read the newspaper while eating and was still sober when his son went to bed. At 1:00 AM, his son woke to find the hall light still on. He got up and discovered his father's body in the kitchen. He had hanged himself with a rope looped over a cabinet hinge. He left a four-page note which was clearly and legibly written and gave as his reasons for suicide that he had seen his doctor and been told he had cancer and he did not want to become a burden. The family doctor reported that he had not seen the subject for two years and that he had not had cancer when last examined.

Family history: One of the subject's brothers was an alcoholic.
Arrest record: At least two arrests for peace disturbance.

Case No. *097* M *X* F ___ Age *61*

ST. LOUIS SUICIDE STUDY CRITERIA FOR ALCOHOLISM

At least three of the following selected drinking behaviors were required for diagnosis.

A. Informant thought subject drank too much	X	F. Subject suffered medical and psychiatric complications due to alcoholic intake	___
B. Subject drank daily	X		
C. Subject went on benders (at least 48 hours of drinking and neglect of usual routine)	X	G. Subject thought he drank too much	___
D. Family objected to subject's drinking	___	H. Subject had job difficulties related to drinking	X
E. Subject's history included arrests related to drinking	X	I. Subject involved in automobile accident(s) related to drinking	___

FEIGHNER CRITERIA FOR ALCOHOLISM

A definite diagnosis required symptoms in at least three of the following four groups. A probable diagnosis required symptoms in only two of the four groups.

A. 1. Any manifestation of alcohol withdrawal such as tremulousness, convulsions, hallucinations, or delirium ___
    2. History of medical complications, e.g. cirrhosis, gastritis, pancreatitis, myopathy, polyneuropathy, Wernicke-Korsakov's syndrome ___
    3. Alcoholic blackouts, i.e., amnesic episodes during heavy drinking not accounted for by head trauma X
    4. Alcoholic binges or benders (48 hours or more of drinking associated with default of usual obligations): must have occurred more than once X

B. 1. Subject unable to stop drinking at will ___
    2. Subject tried to control drinking by allowing himself to drink only under certain circumstances, such as only after 5:00 p.m., only on weekends, or only with others ___
    3. Subject drank before breakfast ___
    4. Subject drank nonbeverage forms of alcohol (hair oil, mouthwash, Sterno, etc.) ___

C. 1. Subject arrested for drinking X
    2. Subject involved in traffic difficulties associated with drinking ___
    3. Subject had trouble at work because of drinking X
    4. Subject involved in fights associated with drinking X

D. 1. Subject worried about drinking too much ___
    2. Family objected to subject's drinking X
    3. Subject lost friends because of drinking X
    4. Other people objected to subject's drinking ___
    5. Subject felt guilty about his drinking ___

099 Informant: Wife

This 62-year-old white man had remarried only six weeks before he committed suicide. His first wife had died a year earlier and his second wife, the informant, had not known him long before marrying him and thus did not know many details of his background.

She believed that he had been raised in foster homes, but was not certain of this. He finished high school, joined the Army during World War I, and remained in the Army for the next 31 years. He saw combat in both World Wars and was gassed in the first and suffered from shortness of breath and fatigue thereafter. He retired from the Army three years before his death with the rank of Master Sergeant, though he always introduced himself as "Major." Since his retirement from the Army, he had worked as a Civil Servant. He had a GS-9 rating and was a clerk in Army transportation. He had been transferred from Topeka, Kansas, to St. Louis six months before his suicide.

His first marriage lasted 35 years. The second wife did not know anything about the first marriage except that it had produced two daughters—one who died in infancy and a second who was living in Washington state at the time of her father's death. The daughter had received a letter from her father expressing his happiness with his new wife just shortly before the news of his suicide reached her.

His second wife said that they had not been "madly in love" when they married, but had become very congenial companions and, once married, were growing closer and closer. They enjoyed a few drinks together every evening after work, but she began to suspect, shortly after their marriage, that he drank during the day as well. His friends confirmed her suspicions and told her that he drank about a "half bottle" of vodka at work every day. He denied this even though she said she had been careful to assure him it didn't matter to her. She also said that she often heard him swigging from a bottle very late at night.

She described her husband as a "sensitive" man with easily hurt feelings who had been nervous and moody all the time she had known him. She said he had quite a few close friends whom he saw regularly, but that after his second marriage he had seen less of his friends.

The informant had not noticed any change in her new husband's behavior in the weeks and days just prior to his suicide. Two weeks before he died, he went over his Civil Service benefits and papers with his boss to see that they were all in order. And the night before, he had his wife separate her papers from his and tossed three of his, including one stating that she was his beneficiary, at her saying, "Take these, you might need them sometime."

The evening of his suicide, he and his wife had two drinks together before dinner, ate (she said he ate his usual big dinner), read for awhile, then talked. He lay out his clothes for the next day and turned on the radio before getting in bed. She went to sleep before he did, but "something" woke her later. She woke to find him sitting on the edge of the bed facing her. When she asked him what the matter was, he answered, "I think I'll shoot you." She did not realize that he was holding a gun, laughed, and asked, "What did I do now—or didn't do?" He then said, "In that case, I'll shoot myself," and shot himself in the heart. He died immediately. No note was found.

Family history: Nothing was known about the subject's family history.
Arrest record: None.

Case No. *099* M X F __ Age *62*

ST. LOUIS SUICIDE STUDY CRITERIA FOR ALCOHOLISM

At least three of the following selected drinking behaviors were required for diagnosis.

A. Informant thought subject drank too much   X

B. Subject drank daily   X

C. Subject went on benders (at least 48 hours of drinking and neglect of usual routine)   ___

D. Family objected to subject's drinking   X

E. Subject's history included arrests related to drinking   ___

F. Subject suffered medical and psychiatric complications due to alcoholic intake   ___

G. Subject thought he drank too much   X

H. Subject had job difficulties related to drinking   ___

I. Subject involved in automobile accident(s) related to drinking   ___

FEIGHNER CRITERIA FOR ALCOHOLISM

A definite diagnosis required symptoms in at least three of the following four groups. A probable diagnosis required symptoms in only two of the four groups.

- A.
  1. Any manifestation of alcohol withdrawal such as tremulousness, convulsions, hallucinations, or delirium ___
  2. History of medical complications, e.g. cirrhosis, gastritis, pancreatitis, myopathy, polyneuropathy, Wernicke-Korsakov's syndrome ___
  3. Alcoholic blackouts, i.e., amnesic episodes during heavy drinking not accounted for by head trauma ___
  4. Alcoholic binges or benders (48 hours or more of drinking associated with default of usual obligations): must have occurred more than once ___

- B.
  1. Subject unable to stop drinking at will ___
  2. Subject tried to control drinking by allowing himself to drink only under certain circumstances, such as only after 5:00 p.m., only on weekends, or only with others ___
  3. Subject drank before breakfast ___
  4. Subject drank nonbeverage forms of alcohol (hair oil, mouthwash, Sterno, etc.) ___

- C.
  1. Subject arrested for drinking ___
  2. Subject involved in traffic difficulties associated with drinking ___
  3. Subject had trouble at work because of drinking ___
  4. Subject involved in fights associated with drinking ___

- D.
  1. Subject worried about drinking too much ___
  2. Family objected to subject's drinking X
  3. Subject lost friends because of drinking ___
  4. Other people objected to subject's drinking X
  5. Subject felt guilty about his drinking ___

ALCOHOLISM, SUBGROUP 4

Women (N = 5)

060 Informants: Brother of common-law husband, friend, common-law husband, employer

None of the informants had known this 32-year-old black woman, a laundry worker, for longer than six years. During those six years she had been living in a common-law relationship and for the last four years she had worked in a laundry. The laundry manager described her work as good, though he remembers she would occasionally miss work without giving a reason. During this last four-year period she was known to have become a heavy weekend drinker and to drink "pints" over a weekend, but it was not clear whether weekend drinking caused her to miss work.

Without her knowledge, her common-law husband married a close friend of hers, although the man continued to live with her. She learned of his marriage two weeks before her death from the mother of his new wife. She checked, found this was true, and became severely upset. From then on she drank every day, stayed away from work, seldom slept, quit eating, cried continually, screamed and yelled most nights, was indecisive and inert during the daytime hours, and lost interest in everything except drinking. She threatened the man she had been living with.

On the day of her suicide, she went to the laundry to say that she was going to California for good. That evening she ingested some roach powder in water. Shortly thereafter she went next door to her neighbors, handed them a piece of paper with an address on it, and told them her husband could be found there. (The address later proved not to be a valid one.) After a few minutes, the neighbors realized that she had probably done something to herself. Although she denied it, she permitted them to take her to the hospital, where she died within an hour of her arrival. The neighbors believed that she may not have intended to commit suicide, but wanted only to frighten her ex-common-law husband. They could not explain, however, why she had not said anything about having taken poison.

Family history: No family history available.
Arrest record: None.

Case No. *060* M__ F X Age *32*

ST. LOUIS SUICIDE STUDY CRITERIA FOR ALCOHOLISM

At least three of the following selected drinking behaviors were required for diagnosis.

- A. Informant thought subject drank too much X
- B. Subject drank daily X
- C. Subject went on benders (at least 48 hours of drinking and neglect of usual routine) X
- D. Family objected to subject's drinking __
- E. Subject's history included arrests related to drinking __
- F. Subject suffered medical and psychiatric complications due to alcoholic intake X
- G. Subject thought he drank too much __
- H. Subject had job difficulties related to drinking X
- I. Subject involved in automobile accident(s) related to drinking __

FEIGHNER CRITERIA FOR ALCOHOLISM

A definite diagnosis required symptoms in at least three of the following four groups. A probable diagnosis required symptoms in only two of the four groups.

- A.
  1. Any manifestation of alcohol withdrawal such as tremulousness, convulsions, hallucinations, or delirium __
  2. History of medical complications, e.g. cirrhosis, gastritis, pancreatitis, myopathy, polyneuropathy, Wernicke-Korsakov's syndrome __
  3. Alcoholic blackouts, i.e., amnesic episodes during heavy drinking not accounted for by head trauma __
  4. Alcoholic binges or benders (48 hours or more of drinking associated with default of usual obligations): must have occurred more than once X
- B.
  1. Subject unable to stop drinking at will __
  2. Subject tried to control drinking by allowing himself to drink only under certain circumstances, such as only after 5:00 p.m., only on weekends, or only with others __
  3. Subject drank before breakfast __
  4. Subject drank nonbeverage forms of alcohol (hair oil, mouthwash, Sterno, etc.) __
- C.
  1. Subject arrested for drinking __
  2. Subject involved in traffic difficulties associated with drinking __
  3. Subject had trouble at work because of drinking X
  4. Subject involved in fights associated with drinking __
- D.
  1. Subject worried about drinking too much __
  2. Family objected to subject's drinking __
  3. Subject lost friends because of drinking __
  4. Other people objected to subject's drinking X
  5. Subject felt guilty about his drinking __

066 Informants: Younger brother, sister-in-law, close friends, neighbors, internist

Although this 56-year-old white woman had completed only the 10th grade, she seemed to have had a good head for business and financial concerns. At the time of her death she owned a tavern and the apartment building in which it was located. During her last years, the tavern had earned an annual income well above the national median.

She was raised, after her mother's death when she was seven, by her grandmother and led a protected, rather prim life. At 17 she married a local doctor nearly as old as her father and from whom she learned to smoke and to drink whiskey "straight." The marriage appeared happy, but according to her brother, when she was 21 her husband operated on her in some way to sterilize her. The brother said that following the operation she had very painful menstrual periods for many months. In any case, she was never to become pregnant and, after eight or ten years of marriage, the doctor divorced her to marry his office nurse.

She moved then to Florida where she met a man her brother described as a "gigolo" and married him. They were divorced after a year when she accused him of being "after her money." Not long afterward, she met and married a third husband. This marriage seemed a happy one and lasted eight years until the husband was killed in an automobile accident. Her grief was remembered as having been extreme, but she soon fell in love again and was planning to marry for the fourth time when her fiance died suddenly. Again, her grief was extreme.

By this time, she had lived in Miami, New York, Georgia, and San Francisco, had become somewhat coarse and hard, and was drinking heavily. She returned to St. Louis and bought the tavern. About 20 months before her death, she met the man who was to be her fourth husband. Her brother described this man as being like others she had fallen for: "He had a terrific personality, but was otherwise absolutely no good." They lived together for one year, happily, and then were married at her insistence because marriage was, in her words, "a sacred thing." However, after six months, she separated from the fourth husband, accusing him of trying to get money from her and of running around with other women. She stated then her philosophy that "giving money to men ruined them."

When her brother visited her shortly after the separation, he found her to be agitated and upset, so much so that she took issue with everything he said and finally told him to "get the hell out." After her death, he found an unmailed letter addressed to him in which she apologized, explaining that she was distraught and asking him to come back to see her.

About two months before her death the woman's mood became noticeably sadder. She complained of insomnia, loneliness, nervousness, and of greatly missing her fourth husband. She cried whenever he was mentioned and, on several occasions, begged a close friend to come and live with her, saying that she worried about doing herself harm. Two weeks before she died, she told her friend that, if things did not change by November 25th, she would hang herself. A neighbor reported that she claimed she had already tried once to take her life, but had "chickened out."

Sometime after the separation from her last husband, she leased the tavern to a couple, believing she was doing them "a good turn." Later she quarreled with the couple and thereafter feared leaving her apartment above the tavern because, she said, the woman called her "nasty" names whenever she came downstairs. Although she had, in the past, often stated that she did not care what people thought of her, in the last two months of her life she fretted constantly over the woman's having allegedly called her "the meanest woman in the world." Her friends reported that she kept to herself in her apartment, drinking regularly and heavily. They also said she spoke a good deal about sex and she is known to have slept with at least one man she picked up in the tavern. In those last two months, her friends noted that her eyes bulged to an extent they had not previously. Despite her despondency, she kept herself and her apartment clean and tidy and had had her hair freshly tinted the week before she died.

Not long before her death, she saw an internist for menopausal complaints including "nervousness." He gave her estrogen injections and tranquillizers. After the injections were begun, she complained of dizziness, headaches, and painful periods. She told the doctor, who stated that she was an alcoholic (other informants mentioned only that she drank "a lot"), that she was sleeping with many men and that she meant to commit suicide. Her brother did not recall his sister ever suffering from anorexia or weight loss, or having made self-accusatory remarks.

Two days before her death, she called her friend to again beg her to live with her. She said she was afraid she was losing her mind, was drinking too much, and didn't want to be alone. She also said she wanted to get away, but was so mixed up she couldn't even choose clothes to pack.

All day on November 23rd she was heard to be moving furniture and scrubbing floors. At about 11:00 PM, the people downstairs heard something hit the floor. The next day, her friend came to the apartment and found that she had tied a sheet around her neck and then over the transom and had stepped off a box. The apartment was very clean and, stacked neatly on a table near her body, was a pile of sealed, addressed, stamped envelopes and her will. One of the envelopes contained a letter to her brother in which she said she was killing herself because of her loneliness and that the only people she owed money were the newspaper boy and the milkman. She went on to a list of instructions, all of them valid.

She left an estate of about $100,000.

Family history: There was no family history of psychiatric illness.
Arrest record: There was no record of arrest.

Case No. _066_ M ___ F _X_ Age _56_

ST. LOUIS SUICIDE STUDY CRITERIA FOR ALCOHOLISM

At least three of the following selected drinking behaviors were required for diagnosis.

- A. Informant thought subject drank too much _X_
- B. Subject drank daily _X_
- C. Subject went on benders (at least 48 hours of drinking and neglect of usual routine) ___
- D. Family objected to subject's drinking _X_
- E. Subject's history included arrests related to drinking ___
- F. Subject suffered medical and psychiatric complications due to alcoholic intake _X_
- G. Subject thought he drank too much _X_
- H. Subject had job difficulties related to drinking ___
- I. Subject involved in automobile accident(s) related to drinking ___

FEIGHNER CRITERIA FOR ALCOHOLISM

A definite diagnosis required symptoms in at least three of the following four groups. A probable diagnosis required symptoms in only two of the four groups.

- A.
  1. Any manifestation of alcohol withdrawal such as tremulousness, convulsions, hallucinations, or delirium ___
  2. History of medical complications, e.g. cirrhosis, gastritis, pancreatitis, myopathy, polyneuropathy, Wernicke-Korsakov's syndrome ___
  3. Alcoholic blackouts, i.e., amnesic episodes during heavy drinking not accounted for by head trauma ___
  4. Alcoholic binges or benders (48 hours or more of drinking associated with default of usual obligations): must have occurred more than once ___
- B.
  1. Subject unable to stop drinking at will ___
  2. Subject tried to control drinking by allowing himself to drink only under certain circumstances, such as only after 5:00 p.m., only on weekends, or only with others ___
  3. Subject drank before breakfast ___
  4. Subject drank nonbeverage forms of alcohol (hair oil, mouthwash, Sterno, etc.) ___
- C.
  1. Subject arrested for drinking ___
  2. Subject involved in traffic difficulties associated with drinking ___
  3. Subject had trouble at work because of drinking ___
  4. Subject involved in fights associated with drinking ___
- D.
  1. Subject worried about drinking too much _X_
  2. Family objected to subject's drinking _X_
  3. Subject lost friends because of drinking ___
  4. Other people objected to subject's drinking _X_
  5. Subject felt guilty about his drinking ___

070 Informants: Brother, friend

This 46-year-old white woman had moved into a St. Louis hotel about a month before her suicide. Because neither she, her family, nor close friends were from St. Louis, informants had to be interviewed by telephone. There is limited knowledge of the details of the subject's circumstances prior to her death.

She had apparently lived most of her life in the south and, for about six months before her arrival in St. Louis, she had been staying with her brother there. According to him, she was an alcoholic. He said she had been married and divorced twice, the second divorce having been granted two and a half years before. He reported that she had been despondent ever since and that, at the time she had moved in with him, she was drinking excessively. During the time she spent at his home, she had been arrested at least once for disorderly conduct. He said that she was depressed, that she was suffering from insomnia, and that she had no job nor money, which worried her a great deal. He also said that she had seen two psychiatrists in the south.

With her in the hotel near the time of her suicide was a male friend. (It is not clear whether this friend was in St. Louis at the time of her death.) He said that she had told him shortly before her suicide that she might kill herself.

She shot herself and was found in her hotel room where she had left a note saying: "In the event of illness or death, please notify relatives at ———————————(the address of a place where she had once lived)."

Family history: There was no information about a family history of psychiatric illness.
Arrest record: At least one arrest for disorderly conduct.

Case No. 070 M__ F X Age 46

ST. LOUIS SUICIDE STUDY CRITERIA FOR ALCOHOLISM

At least three of the following selected drinking behaviors were required for diagnosis.

- A. Informant thought subject drank too much X
- B. Subject drank daily __
- C. Subject went on benders (at least 48 hours of drinking and neglect of usual routine) __
- D. Family objected to subject's drinking X
- E. Subject's history included arrests related to drinking X
- F. Subject suffered medical and psychiatric complications due to alcoholic intake X
- G. Subject thought he drank too much __
- H. Subject had job difficulties related to drinking __
- I. Subject involved in automobile accident(s) related to drinking __

FEIGHNER CRITERIA FOR ALCOHOLISM

A definite diagnosis required symptoms in at least three of the following four groups. A probable diagnosis required symptoms in only two of the four groups.

- A.
  1. Any manifestation of alcohol withdrawal such as tremulousness, convulsions, hallucinations, or delirium __
  2. History of medical complications, e.g. cirrhosis, gastritis, pancreatitis, myopathy, polyneuropathy, Wernicke-Korsakov's syndrome __
  3. Alcoholic blackouts, i.e., amnesic episodes during heavy drinking not accounted for by head trauma __
  4. Alcoholic binges or benders (48 hours or more of drinking associated with default of usual obligations): must have occurred more than once __
- B.
  1. Subject unable to stop drinking at will __
  2. Subject tried to control drinking by allowing himself to drink only under certain circumstances, such as only after 5:00 p.m., only on weekends, or only with others __
  3. Subject drank before breakfast __
  4. Subject drank nonbeverage forms of alcohol (hair oil, mouthwash, Sterno, etc.) __
- C.
  1. Subject arrested for drinking X
  2. Subject involved in traffic difficulties associated with drinking __
  3. Subject had trouble at work because of drinking __
  4. Subject involved in fights associated with drinking __
- D.
  1. Subject worried about drinking too much __
  2. Family objected to subject's drinking X
  3. Subject lost friends because of drinking __
  4. Other people objected to subject's drinking __
  5. Subject felt guilty about his drinking __

094 Informants: Sister-in-law, hospital and social service records

This 34-year-old white woman finished three years of high school, married at 18, and moved from Illinois with her husband to St. Louis where she lived for the rest of her life. She and her husband, a machinist, had four children.

The subject was described by her sister-in-law as being a pathological liar. She was without any real friends or social life although she had always been a woman with a great deal of nervous energy. Her sister-in-law remarked that she was always "on the go" and "never seemed to eat." While her husband was away in service during World War II, she had begun to drink beer and had been, by the time she died, a chronic alcoholic for at least ten years. Her eldest daughter had left home because of her mother's drinking and her husband, also said to be an alcoholic, had left her many times. He had twice filed for divorce and for custody of their children, accusing her of neglecting and sometimes beating the children, of keeping a dirty house, of constantly cursing at him, of adultery with the man who employed her as a waitress, and of running up bills that he could not afford to pay. She was said to have had at least one abortion during the affair with the restauranteur. She and her husband were separated at the time of her suicide because of a dispute over her purchase of $1200 worth of furniture for which bill collectors had approached her husband.

In the last five years of her life, the subject had twice been arrested for passing forged checks for small amounts. Both times her family paid and she was released from jail after a day or two. A few days prior to her suicide, the bill collectors for the furniture company warned her that if she did not pay something on her bill, they would repossess the furniture. Shortly thereafter, $40 was stolen from the cash register at the restaurant and the day after that, $40 was paid on the furniture bill. The police questioned her at length, but had not, by the time of her suicide, made an arrest.

One year before her death, the subject had made a first suicide attempt with an overdose of sleeping pills. Her children had twarted the attempt with coffee and walking, and she was not seen at a hospital or by a physician. Six days before her second, successful attempt, she attended a picnic given by her husband's employer. There, she got drunk and apparently went "wild," screaming, tearing at her clothes and hair, and weeping. Her brothers-in-law took her to the emergency room at a psychiatric hospital and told the doctors that she had complained of not sleeping or eating for the last week. They also reported that she often beat her children when she was drunk, and that she was a daily drinker. She was kept in the hospital for six days during which time she admitted having often thought of suicide but denied any actual attempts. The hospital records show diagnoses of acute alcoholism and possible brain syndrome. She was released from the hospital and the following evening, went to a tavern, got drunk, returned home, and took nicotine poison. She died in the house during the night. She is reported to have said to her husband earlier that day, "This is the last time I'll see you." She left no note.

Family history: The subject's twin sister, who was born without limbs, attempted suicide with rat poison one year prior to the subject's death. The subject's father, brother, and aunt all suffered from chronic alcoholism.
Arrest record: Two arrests for forgery.

Case No. *094* M___ F _X_ Age _34_

ST. LOUIS SUICIDE STUDY CRITERIA FOR ALCOHOLISM

At least three of the following selected drinking behaviors were required for diagnosis.

- A. Informant thought subject drank too much _X_
- B. Subject drank daily _X_
- C. Subject went on benders (at least 48 hours of drinking and neglect of usual routine) ___
- D. Family objected to subject's drinking _X_
- E. Subject's history included arrests related to drinking ___
- F. Subject suffered medical and psychiatric complications due to alcoholic intake _X_
- G. Subject thought he drank too much ___
- H. Subject had job difficulties related to drinking ___
- I. Subject involved in automobile accident(s) related to drinking ___

FEIGHNER CRITERIA FOR ALCOHOLISM

A definite diagnosis required symptoms in at least three of the following four groups. A probable diagnosis required symptoms in only two of the four groups.

A.
1. Any manifestation of alcohol withdrawal such as tremulousness, convulsions, hallucinations, or delirium ___
2. History of medical complications, e.g. cirrhosis, gastritis, pancreatitis, myopathy, polyneuropathy, Wernicke-Korsakov's syndrome _X_
3. Alcoholic blackouts, i.e., amnesic episodes during heavy drinking not accounted for by head trauma ___
4. Alcoholic binges or benders (48 hours or more of drinking associated with default of usual obligations): must have occurred more than once ___

B.
1. Subject unable to stop drinking at will _X_
2. Subject tried to control drinking by allowing himself to drink only under certain circumstances, such as only after 5:00 p.m., only on weekends, or only with others ___
3. Subject drank before breakfast ___
4. Subject drank nonbeverage forms of alcohol (hair oil, mouthwash, Sterno, etc.) ___

C.
1. Subject arrested for drinking ___
2. Subject involved in traffic difficulties associated with drinking ___
3. Subject had trouble at work because of drinking ___
4. Subject involved in fights associated with drinking _X_

D.
1. Subject worried about drinking too much ___
2. Family objected to subject's drinking _X_
3. Subject lost friends because of drinking _X_
4. Other people objected to subject's drinking _X_
5. Subject felt guilty about his drinking ___

---

111 Informants: Sister, physician

This 54-year-old white woman had been widowed a year before she committed suicide and had, according to her sister, talked often of "joining" her husband after his death.

Born in London, England, the subject and her sister were brought by their parents to St. Louis as adolescents. The subject finished high school and a course in nursing and worked for more than 30 years as a doctor's office nurse and anesthetist. Her sister said she had been employed by a surgeon for 27 years and that he had fired her five years before her death. The subject converted to Catholicism at the time of her marriage at age 40. She was a fervent convert and much more devout than her husband. When she died, she left her money only to those relatives (mostly in-laws) who were Catholics. Her sister described her as always having been "bitchy," self-centered, "nervous," "high-strung," neurotic, and prone to hurt feelings and tantrums. She was known to have been a heavy drinker for many years.

Two years before her death, her mother died. Shortly thereafter, she suffered a "nervous breakdown," took an overdose of sleeping pills, and was hospitalized in a Catholic psychiatric hospital for five weeks. Her psychiatrist there described her condition as "psychotic" with hallucinations and reported that she was treated with barbiturates and bromides and recovered in a few weeks. She was released to her husband who took her to Fort Lauderdale, Florida, for a rest. A year before her suicide, while still in Florida, her husband died. Grief-stricken, she consulted a Fort Lauderdale physician who gave her tranquillizers. She then returned to St. Louis and reentered the Catholic psychiatric hospital where she remained only a few days. She wanted signing out privileges and, when denied them, checked out against advice. By this time, she was taking drugs daily for her "nerves" and nightly for insomnia. She became increasingly preoccupied with the idea of "joining" her husband through suicide.

Despite complaints of "heart trouble" and a long list of associated symptoms, she continued to entertain two or three close friends and to maintain the fairly active social life she had always enjoyed. She saw her psychiatrist once or twice after she left the hospital the second time and, four months before she killed herself, he informed her family that he felt she was suicidal and that they should commit her for her own protection. They failed to take his advice. For the last months, she was more irritable and angry toward her sister than usual and they did not see each other the last five weeks of her life. However, two weeks prior to her death, she arranged a future shopping trip with her sister and consulted her brother-in-law about air conditioning her apartment for the summer. At that time she also telephoned "everyone she had ever known," including friends she had not seen for years. According to her family doctor, she looked very well during that time. She was tanned and had gained weight. He repeatedly told her that he could detect no heart disease that might cause her symptoms of dyspnea, palpitation, chest pain, dizziness, fainting spells, and anxiety attacks, and though he agreed that some of these might have been due to the menopausal syndrome, she refused estrogen treatments because she believed it caused cancer.

Two nights before her suicide, the subject told her sister on the telephone that she "wanted to die." The sister described her voice as "groggy" because of the sleeping medicine she took nightly. The next day, she was told by her family doctor that he was sending her a prescription for barbiturates "for the last time." Apparently, very early the next morning she took an overdose of Amytal. When her sister could not contact her by telephone at 8:30 AM, she went to the apartment building and she and the building manager discovered the subject unconscious on the floor of her bathroom. She was taken to a nearby hospital where she died a few hours later. She left no note. After her death, her family was informed by her psychiatrist that the subject was a chronic alcoholic and that she had been addicted to barbiturates for at least the last five years of her life.

Family history: There was no family history of psychiatric illness.
Arrest record: None.

Case No. *111* M __ F *X* Age *54*

ST. LOUIS SUICIDE STUDY CRITERIA FOR ALCOHOLISM

At least three of the following selected drinking behaviors were required for diagnosis.

A. Informant thought subject drank too much *X*

B. Subject drank daily *X*

C. Subject went on benders (at least 48 hours of drinking and neglect of usual routine) __

D. Family objected to subject's drinking *X*

E. Subject's history included arrests related to drinking __

F. Subject suffered medical and psychiatric complications due to alcoholic intake *X*

G. Subject thought he drank too much __

H. Subject had job difficulties related to drinking __

I. Subject involved in automobile accident(s) related to drinking __

FEIGHNER CRITERIA FOR ALCOHOLISM

A definite diagnosis required symptoms in at least three of the following four groups. A probable diagnosis required symptoms in only two of the four groups.

- A.
  1. Any manifestation of alcohol withdrawal such as tremulousness, convulsions, hallucinations, or delirium ___
  2. History of medical complications, e.g. cirrhosis, gastritis, pancreatitis, myopathy, polyneuropathy, Wernicke-Korsakov's syndrome ___
  3. Alcoholic blackouts, i.e., amnesic episodes during heavy drinking not accounted for by head trauma ___
  4. Alcoholic binges or benders (48 hours or more of drinking associated with default of usual obligations): must have occurred more than once ___

- B.
  1. Subject unable to stop drinking at will ___
  2. Subject tried to control drinking by allowing himself to drink only under certain circumstances, such as only after 5:00 p.m., only on weekends, or only with others ___
  3. Subject drank before breakfast ___
  4. Subject drank nonbeverage forms of alcohol (hair oil, mouthwash, Sterno, etc.) ___

- C.
  1. Subject arrested for drinking ___
  2. Subject involved in traffic difficulties associated with drinking ___
  3. Subject had trouble at work because of drinking ___
  4. Subject involved in fights associated with drinking ___

- D.
  1. Subject worried about drinking too much ___
  2. Family objected to subject's drinking *X*
  3. Subject lost friends because of drinking ___
  4. Other people objected to subject's drinking ___
  5. Subject felt guilty about his drinking *X*

6

The Miscellaneous Group—Description of the Clinical Group Comprising the Smallest Number in the Total Sample

In the 134 subjects, three other psychiatric diagnoses were made as well as two nonpsychiatric diagnoses. Each of these diagnoses occurred in only a few subjects in the total sample—organic brain syndrome in five; schizophrenia in three; drug dependence in two; terminal medical illness with no accompanying psychiatric illness in five; and no psychiatric nor terminal medical illness at time of suicide in three. I gathered these five diagnoses into one miscellaneous group because there are so few subjects in each of them that, even when added together (N = 18), they represent only 13% of the entire sample, or about one in eight. (See Table 6.1)

Only two of the miscellaneous diagnoses—organic brain syndrome and terminal medical illness—applied to as many as five subjects. Although each diagnosis is represented in 5 (4%) of the 134 suicides, it should be noted that, in the general population, there are many more people who are terminally medically ill (from carcinoma or lymphosarcoma—the two illnesses represented in the five terminally ill subjects in this study) than there are people suffering from organic brain syndrome, or, for that matter, from schizophrenia or drug dependence. To give the reader an idea of the difference in numbers, in 1955 there were in the United States about 1,600,000 deaths of which approximately 250,000 were the result of "malignant neoplasms."[1] If one considers that there were at least twice as many cancer patients who did *not* die in 1955 and then compares the resulting estimate of 750,000 sufferers with cancer to the number of resident patients in state and county mental hospitals for the treatment of organic brain syndrome (137,991) or for schizophrenia (267,995),[2] one realizes that, in a given year,

TABLE 6.1 The Miscellaneous Group

Diagnoses	Number	White Men	Black Men	White Women	Black Women	Percent of 134
Psychiatrically ill						
Organic brain syndrome	5	4	0	1	0	4
Schizophrenia	3	3	0	0	0	2
Drug dependence	2	1	0	1	0	1
Not psychiatrically ill						
Terminally medically ill	5	3	0	2	0	4
Neither psychiatrically nor medically ill	3	3	0	0	0	2

the ratio of cancer patients to sufferers of organic brain syndrome would be 5:1, and cancer to schizophrenia, 3:1.

Thus, the prevalence of suicide among the terminally medically ill is far less than it is among people with organic brain syndrome or those with schizophrenia. Based on the same comparisons, the ratio of terminally medically ill patients to those hospitalized in 1955 for drug abuse was about 750:1.[2]

So while suicide in organic brain syndrome, schizophrenia, and drug dependence is rare when compared with suicide in affective disorder, depressed phase, and in alcoholism it is even rarer among people with terminal medical illnesses. Despite the devastation of fatal illnesses, suicide is so rarely associated with them that the physician does not expect it as an outcome and, in fact, its occurrence in 4% of 134 suicides in this study was somewhat of a surprise.

Schizophrenia, on the other hand, has been thought of as being associated with a large proportion of deaths by suicide. That this is not the case has been shown in all 3 studies of 100 or more consecutive suicides and in a recent study of hospitalized psychiatric patients.[3-5] In this study, schizophrenia was present in only three (2%) of the suicide subjects. In the study by Barraclough et al., schizophrenia was present in 3% of the subjects and a related diagnosis, schizo-affective disorder, was shown in 1%. In Dorpat and Ripley's study, schizophrenia was diagnosed in 12% of their 108 suicide subjects. This larger proportion of subjects diagnosed as having had schizophrenia may have been the result of a tendency in U.S. psychiatry to overdiagnose schizophrenia and to underdiagnose affective disorder.[6] This tendency was, by 1974, on the wane. For instance, in the study by Shaffer et al.,[3] 12 of 361 (3%) hospitalized patients diagnosed as having schizophrenia committed suicide within a five-year observation period. This percentage indicates the accuracy of the diagnoses of schizophrenia. The number of resident patients in state and county hospitals for the treatment of schizophrenia dropped from 267,995 in 1955 to 122,587 in 1973, a decrease of almost two-thirds and a further reflection of recent, more stringent diagnostic criteria.

The two other miscellaneous psychiatric diagnoses do not always have counterparts in the two similar studies of suicide. While Barraclough et al. found 1% of their subjects were drug dependent, Dorpat and Ripley found none. And while Dorpat and Ripley's finding that 4% of their suicide subjects had had organic brain syndrome matched our finding, Barraclough et al. made no diagnoses of organic brain syndrome. These matched and mismatched findings in the miscellaneous category suitably reflect the infrequence of suicide among people suffering from organic brain syndrome and drug dependence.

The two nonpsychiatric diagnoses—terminal medical illness and neither terminal medical illness nor psychiatric illness—accounted for 7% (8 subjects) of the St. Louis sample and for 11% of the Barraclough et al. subjects. Dorpat and Ripley reported "no psychiatric information available" in 6 of their 114 cases studied. They therefore based their findings on 108 cases, excluding those 6 about whom they had no psychiatric information. In every one of the 108 cases, there was a diagnosis of a psychiatric illness, even though in 16% the illness was unspecified. (We assume this group was closest, in definition, to our psychiatrically undiagnosed group.)

The reader may wonder—as indeed the author does—about the three subjects who had neither a terminal medical illness nor, as far as could be determined, a psychiatric illness. In all three cases, the informants were candid about the subjects, but both the early criteria developed for the study and later application of the Feighner criteria turned up no evidence of psychiatric illness. Thus the diagnosis "undiagnosed psychiatric illness" did not apply. While there was evidence of physical illness in at least one of the three, the illness was not fatal. Neither of the two other subjects had, at the times of their suicides, any physical illnesses. The reader might ask an obvious question: "Since these three persons did actually take their own lives, were they not by definition depressed?" The answer must necessarily be that the suicidal act was the only overt, reported act interpretable as depressed, psychotic, drug induced, or psychiatrically abnormal. One such act is not enough on which to base a diagnosis. These cases, enigmatic as they are, are not unique to the St. Louis Study. Barraclough and his group of investigators considered seven subjects from their sample "not to be mentally ill." And Dorpat and Ripley's six subjects who were excluded from the sample because of the unavailability of "psychiatric information" probably fall into the same category, although this is not specifically stated in the report.

The following vignettes are presented in groups defined by diagnosis. For three groups there are, as in previous chapters, individual "score cards" tallying the symptoms of the psychiatric diagnoses. Subjects belonging in the two nonpsychiatric diagnostic groups are represented on two group score cards.

REFERENCES

1. U.S. Bureau of the Census, *Statistical Abstract of the United States 1957,* 78th Annual Ed., Edit. Edwin D. Goldfield. U.S. Government Printing Office, Washington, D.C.
2. President's Commission on Mental Health, *Task Panel Report,* Vol. II. Appendix 1978. U.S. Government Printing Office, Washington, D.C.
3. Shaffer, J.W., Perlin, S., Schmidt, C.W., Jr. and Stephens, J.H. The prediction of suicide in schizophrenia. *J. Nerv. Ment. Dis.* 150:349–355, 1974.
4. Barraclough, B., Bunch, J., Nelson, B. and Sainsbury, P. A hundred cases of suicide: Clinical aspects. *Brit. J. Psychiat.* 125:355–373, 1974.
5. Dorpat, T.L. and Ripley, H.S. A study of suicide in the Seattle area. *Comp. Psychiatry* 1(6):349–359, 1960.
6. Cooper, J.E. et al. *Psychiatric Diagnosis in New York and London.* Maudsley Monograph #20. London: Oxford University Press, 1972.

MISCELLANEOUS GROUP, SUBGROUP 1

Men with Organic Brain Syndrome (N = 4)

010 Informants: Wife, two physicians

This 85-year-old white retired stonemason quit work 10 years before his death because of "old age." He had never had any serious illness that his second wife knew of except for a life-long, bothersome skin disease which had been diagnosed neurodermatitis. His first wife had died and he remarried at age 68, seventeen years prior to his suicide. Approximately five years before he died he began to suffer from mild prostatism. One month before his death, a urologist had examined him and found only a mild benign prostatic hypertrophy.

Three to four years before his death he began developing symptoms of senility and of depression. His orientation for time became proor, he had trouble making change, and his memory was said to have started deteriorating, although he could still to some extent get around by himself. He lost sight in one eye and developed a cataract in the other so that he had great difficulty in reading. His depressed mood manifested itself in talk of having lived so long that he might as well die. He also spoke of wanting to die, of being better off dead, and of his family being better off if he were dead. About two years prior to his death he had attempted suicide with a revolver, but the gun had jammed. Later he attempted to jump off a bridge, but was dissuaded by a policeman. He began to worry more about blindness and about being left alone if his wife died before him. On a number of occasions he suggested that his wife and he die together by carbon monoxide poisoning in their automobile. In the six months prior to his death he began to complain bitterly of pain in his groin, allegedly due to his prostatic disease. The urologist who had examined him one month prior to his death felt that the pain was more related to his "senility" than to local urologic disease. He began to suffer from severe insomnia which he laid to his pain. He refused to take "dope" (his word) for the pain or sleeplessness. He also complained of dyspnea, chest pain, and fatigue. He became indecisive and underactive. He began to pray surreptitiously. He felt worthless and was disgusted with himself and with the world.

On the night before his suicide he had been up all night walking around the house and complaining of pain in his groin. On the morning of his suicide he took off his glasses and shot himself in the head while his wife was in the next room with their daughter. He died in two hours without regaining consciousness.

Family history: Seven years previously his daughter had "involutional melancholia" for which she was hospitalized and subsequently recovered.
Arrest record: None

Case No. 010 M X F __ Age 85

ST. LOUIS SUICIDE STUDY CRITERIA FOR ORGANIC BRAIN SYNDROME

Three of the following six symptoms were required for a diagnosis of organic brain syndrome.

A. Memory difficulty	X
B. Disorientation in time	X
C. Inability to find one's way in familiar surroundings	__
D. Inability to be trusted out alone	__
E. Deterioration of reading skills	__
F. Difficulties with simple arithmetic	X

FEIGHNER CRITERIA FOR ORGANIC BRAIN SYNDROME

A definite diagnosis requires one of the two following criteria.

A. Two of the following manifestations must have been present. (In the presence of muteness the diagnosis must be deferred.)

impairment of orientation	X
impairment of memory	X
deterioration of other intellectual functions	__

B. The diagnosis is also made if the subject had at least one (A) manifestation in addition to a known probable cause for organic brain syndrome __

055 Informants: Hospital clinic records, physician, and minister (no primary informant)

This 71-year-old white man shot himself in his garage. Because none of his close relatives would agree to an interview, not a great deal is known about his background or the specific events leading to his suicide.

From hospital clinic records and the statements of his physician and minister, the following facts are known:

He was married and had three grown children. He was a member of the Presbyterian church and a regular church-goer. A friendly man, he was known to have been a good provider for his family. His occupation is not known.

Two or three months before his death, he visited a physician because of difficulty voiding. He complained of pains in his thighs which were temporarily relieved when he was able to void. The doctor, who had been seeing the patient for some years, referred him to a hospital clinic for tests and sent the clinic a letter describing the patient's recent history. For about three years he had been deteriorating mentally due to arteriosclerosis and was at the time of referral frankly senile. He was unable to drive a car and was too forgetful to be left on his own. He had been unable to work for one year and for the last six months had been extremely nervous, forgetful, and unsteady. He had had two falls from his bed, one of which knocked him unconscious for a few minutes. He remembered neither fall the following mornings. He had begun to stutter and have trouble speaking and in the last six months his weight had dropped from 193 to 166 pounds.

The minister remembered that the subject had appeared depressed for the last 12 to 18 months and seemed to have something "preying on his mind." He also remembers the subject having spoken about "how terrible it was for a person to take his own life."

The clinic records indicate that the patient was mainly concerned about the increasingly severe "stabbing" pains in his legs. At the clinic, he underwent a series of tests. Prostatic hypertrophy, mild, and diverticulosis were diagnosed, as well as cerebral arteriosclerosis.

He was seen in the clinic for the last time late in September. His major complaint then was still sharp pains in his thighs. He committed suicide about one week later.

Family history: There was no record of psychiatric illness in the subject's family.
Arrest record: None.

Case No. *055* M X F __ Age *71*

ST. LOUIS SUICIDE STUDY CRITERIA FOR ORGANIC BRAIN SYNDROME

Three of the following six symptoms were required for a diagnosis of organic brain syndrome.

A. Memory difficulty X
B. Disorientation in time __
C. Inability to find one's way in familiar surroundings X
D. Inability to be trusted out alone X
E. Deterioration of reading skills __
F. Difficulties with simple arithmetic __

FEIGHNER CRITERIA FOR ORGANIC BRAIN SYNDROME

A definite diagnosis requires one of the two following criteria.

A. Two of the following manifestations must have been present. (In the presence of muteness the diagnosis must be deferred.)

    impairment of orientation   ___
    impairment of memory   _X_
    deterioration of other intellectual functions   _X_

B. The diagnosis is also made if the subject had at least one (A) manifestation in addition to a known probable cause for organic brain syndrome   ___

100 Informants: Son, daughter-in-law

This 75-year-old white man was separated from his wife and living alone at the time of his suicide. The reasons for and length of his separation from his wife were not given, but he had apparently been living alone for some years and there were hard feelings between him and his wife.

He finished grammar school, but nothing was known about his further education. He was married twice. He and the first wife were divorced after two or three years. He married his second wife 45 years prior to his suicide.

A barber, he owned his own shop and had his living quarters behind it. He had few friends and for many years his only visitors were relatives. He rarely attended church in his later years though he had been a fairly devout Baptist as a child and as a younger man. He had been a heavy drinker for much of his adult life, but had drunk practically not at all in his late years and blamed himself harshly for his earlier drinking. His mental and physical health had evidently been good for most of his life. His son recalled that once, 20 to 25 years earlier, he had threatened suicide. He could not, however, remember the circumstances or whether his father had seemed different at the time. For about the last decade of his life, he was interested in the subject of suicide and often discussed the details of suicides reported in the newspapers.

The subject's son and daughter-in-law felt that his mind had begun "slipping" about five years before he died and that it had gradually worsened. At first, they said, he was just slightly forgetful and seemed to cry easily when he believed he was neglected by his other children or when he thought of his two closest friends, both of whom had recently died. He kept a photograph of the three friends in the room where he slept. In the last year or two, he developed delusional worries about his business, his bank account, and his income tax. He feared that "an organization" would take his business away; he believed that his brother was "tapping" his bank account and giving the money to his estranged wife; and he was certain that he was "in trouble" with the income tax people who were "spying" on him. He was often confused about the date and began to forget his friends' names and his way to familiar places.

For about ten days before he committed suicide, he looked depressed to his son and he complained of back pains which he called "omens." He saw his son the day before his death and seemed all right. From evidence found after his death, on the evening of his suicide he apparently laid out breakfast things for the next day, closed his sleeping quarters off from the shop, went to bed, rose again about midnight, and shot himself behind the right ear. His body was discovered when his son came to the shop a day later on a regular visit his father knew he would be making. No note was found.

Family history: There was no family history of psychiatric illness.
Arrest record: None.

Case No. *100* M _X_ F __ Age _75_

ST. LOUIS SUICIDE STUDY CRITERIA FOR ORGANIC BRAIN SYNDROME

Three of the following six symptoms were required for a diagnosis of organic brain syndrome.

A. Memory difficulty ___
B. Disorientation in time ___
C. Inability to find one's way in familiar surroundings ___
D. Inability to be trusted out alone _X_
E. Deterioration of reading skills _X_
F. Difficulties with simple arithmetic _X_

FEIGHNER CRITERIA FOR ORGANIC BRAIN SYNDROME

A definite diagnosis requires one of the two following criteria.

A. Two of the following manifestations must have been present. (In the presence of muteness the diagnosis must be deferred.)
    impairment of orientation _X_
    impairment of memory _X_
    deterioration of other intellectual functions ___

B. The diagnosis is also made if the subject had at least one (A) manifestation in addition to a known probable cause for organic brain syndrome ___

130 Informant: Wife

This 81-year-old white married man finished the 8th grade of school. At the age of 26, he moved to St. Louis and established himself as a chiropractor. He was married twice. The first marriage, an unhappy one that lasted for 25 years, was ended by his first wife's death. The second marriage lasted 17 years. His second wife described the subject as always having been a "nervous," "high-strung," sensitive person with easily hurt feelings and a tendency toward outbursts of temper. She also said that he had always liked to "run around" with other women and was proud of his success with women.

The subject considered himself to have been the best chiropractor in the area (he "adjusted" himself because no one else was good enough) and he was financially successful in his practice. Although he was a heavy, daily drinker, and probably a chronic alcoholic, his drinking did not seem to interfere with his work. He retired at age 70 because, as no one in his family had ever lived past 74, he expected to die in his early seventies. Ten years before his death, his wife came home late one night to find him with a gun out and declaring that burglars were trying to get him. It was disconcerting to him to find himself living "past his time" and, the last three or four years of his life, he was increasingly depressed and restless. His memory began to slip, he became preoccupied with his waning sexual prowess, his weight dropped, he suffered from fatigue, and he was forced to worry about debts as the money he had saved for retirement dwindled. It angered him that he was ineligible for welfare because he owned a house worth more than $5000. Four years before he died, he sold his car for the money and because his sight was failing. He missed having a car and, more and more, he missed his virility. He felt he would never get well and that he was a burden. He stopped drinking, except at meals, and he developed the delusion that people were trying to annoy him, that the house was being broken into, that his food tasted "funny," and that no one was "honest anymore." He heard voices which he answered and developed phobias about heights, going to public places, and leaving his house. Gradually he lapsed into serious forgetfulness, spoke to people long dead, and, if left to his own devices, ate seven or eight "meals" a day. He had difficulty with everyday arithmetic including making change, lost all interest in seeing friends, was joyless, dressed carelessly, and took no interest in his own cleanliness. He could not be trusted out alone as he would lose his way, nor could he remember the date. He talked more and more about sex until, the last three weeks of life, he simply sat idly and talked to himself about sex.

Two days after his 81st birthday, he ate a big meal at 10:30 PM and made no move toward going to bed. At 4 AM, he took a gun out into the backyard. Fifteen minutes later, a single shot was heard. His wife found his body in the yard, not far from the house. He had made no suicidal comments and left no note.

Family history: There was no history of psychiatric illness in the subject's family.
Arrest record: None.

Case No. *130* M X F __ Age *81*

ST. LOUIS SUICIDE STUDY CRITERIA FOR ORGANIC BRAIN SYNDROME

Three of the following six symptoms were required for a diagnosis of organic brain syndrome.

A. Memory difficulty

B. Disorientation in time   X

C. Inability to find one's way in familiar surroundings

D. Inability to be trusted out alone   X

E. Deterioration of reading skills   X

F. Difficulties with simple arithmetic   X

X (next to A.) X (next to C.)

FEIGHNER CRITERIA FOR ORGANIC BRAIN SYNDROME

A definite diagnosis requires one of the two following criteria.

A. Two of the following manifestations must have been present. (In the presence of muteness the diagnosis must be deferred.)

    impairment of orientation   X
    impairment of memory   X
    deterioration of other intellectual functions   X

B. The diagnosis is also made if the subject had at least one (A) manifestation in addition to a known probable cause for organic brain syndrome   __

MISCELLANEOUS GROUP, SUBGROUP 2

Women with Organic Brain Syndrome (N = 1)

098 Informants: Husband, niece, physician, hospital records

This 58-year-old white woman had suffered a severe stroke two and a half months prior to her suicide. Released from the hospital and at home for six weeks before her death, she was thought by her husband to be rapidly recovering from the effects of the stroke.

The subject finished the 7th grade and was married for the first time at an early age. The first marriage lasted only a year, ending when her husband left her. She was married to her second husband when she was 27 and the marriage lasted, apparently happily, for 31 years until her death. She had only two children, both of whom died at birth. She spent her life as a housewife, and according to her husband they had "innumerable" friends and an active social life. A Lutheran, the subject was a religious woman and though she attended formal church services only twice a year, it was her custom to pray nightly in front of her personal cross at home.

About 20 years before her death, she had a goiter removed and was hospitalized for two weeks following surgery. Five years before she died, she had what was described by her family as a "heart attack" and suffered from "heart trouble" (swollen legs, shortness of breath, chest pain, palpitation, and trouble sleeping) for the rest of her life. She was given sleeping pills and once said to her husband, "If it gets so I can't take the pain, I've got six sleeping pills hidden; I'll end it all." Two years before that statement, she had apologized to her husband for not having been "a really good wife" to him (this remark was in reference to her life-long disinterest in sex) and suggested he needed "a new wife." In retrospect, he considered this a veiled suicidal comment.

Her doctor reported that the subject had seemed an "oddball," that her "hobby was illness," and that she took much pleasure in visiting the sick and sending get-well cards. He believed that before becoming his patient, she had had a first stroke about two years previous to her last and that there was, during the intervening two years, evidence of hypertensive encephalopathy. He had diagnosed her prior to the last stroke as hyperthyroid and hypertensive and noted that she had been, for at least two years, "forgetful, unkempt, and not very clean." The final stroke, which was severe, left her aphasic and paralysed on the right side. After 36 days in the hospital, the paralysis gradually disappeared, but the aphasia remained.

The doctor's description of the patient reinforced the observations of the subject's niece who felt that her aunt had been "odd" for several weeks before the last stroke. Always "safety conscious," she had, a few days before becoming ill, painted green lines from the street to her house as a "safety measure." The niece also noted that for some time before the stroke, she had assumed an awkward, "Knock-kneed" posture. The niece, unlike the husband, felt that after the stroke, the subject had been despondent even in the hospital. Once at home, she believed that people were making fun of her poor speech, was irritable when her husband tried to help her talk, claimed that a dog she had loved before the stroke was "driving her wild." She was impatient and irritable with her sister and often asked her husband to instruct her not to visit.

Both the husband and niece felt that, in the last week of her life, the subject was obviously less interested in what went on around her. Though her husband felt she was "improving daily," she was herself outspokenly discouraged about her speech and her inability to do her housework and complained about both to her sister and niece two days before her death. She answered visitors' reassurances that she looked better with, "I don't think so." She complained bitterly to her husband about what she believed was a recurrence of the goiter. She said it was hurting, keeping her from breathing easily, and that she wanted him to tell the doctor to "cut it out." When he tried to reassure her, she abruptly left the room.

The night before her death, she said the Lord's Prayer aloud all the way through without prompting and slept well that night. The next morning, she kissed her husband goodbye, pinched his cheek affectionately, and told him to come home early. She also reminded him of a chore he had planned for the next day. When he returned from work that evening, he found the house locked. He went to a neighbor's to telephone his wife and, when the phone went unanswered, called the police who helped him break in. He and the police found the house neat, a ladder in the pantry, and his wife's dead body hanging from a hook in the pantry ceiling. She left no note.

Family history: There was no family history of psychiatric illness.
Arrest record: None.

Case No 098 M___ F X Age 58

ST. LOUIS SUICIDE STUDY CRITERIA FOR ORGANIC BRAIN SYNDROME

Three of the following six symptoms were required for a diagnosis of organic brain syndrome.

A. Memory difficulty   X
B. Disorientation in time   ___
C. Inability to find one's way in familiar surroundings ___
D. Inability to be trusted out alone   ___
E. Deterioration of reading skills   X
F. Difficulties with simple arithmetic   X

FEIGHNER CRITERIA FOR ORGANIC BRAIN SYNDROME

A definite diagnosis requires one of the two following criteria.

A. Two of the following manifestations must have been present. (In the presence of muteness the diagnosis must be deferred.)
   impairment of orientation   ___
   impairment of memory   X
   deterioration of other intellectual functions X

B. The diagnosis is also made if the subject had at least one (A) manifestation in addition to a known probable cause for organic brain syndrome ___

MISCELLANEOUS GROUP, SUBGROUP 3

Men with Schizophrenia (N = 3)

039 Informants: Mother-in-law; hospital and Catholic Charities records

This 32-year-old white letter-carrier was a patient home on a weekend pass from a St. Louis veteran's hospital at the time of his suicide. The following history is based on information given by his mother-in-law who had known him well for seven years.

The subject's parents separated when he was about eight and he was raised by his chronically "nervous" mother on whom he was extremely dependent. The mother, who suffered at least one "nervous breakdown," claimed to be a semi-invalid unable to work or to leave her home. The youngest brother was described as behaving "queerly" and the family physician reported that the entire family was of low intelligence. Even so, the subject finished high school and at least two years at the state University. He served overseas as a Navy hospital corpsman for three years during the Second World War and received an honorable discharge.

At age 26, he married the informant's daughter. His mother-in-law opposed the marriage, feeling from the beginning that there was something "odd" about the man. She consulted his parish priest who assured her that he was "a fine young man" and she made no further objections. The priest's assurances to the contrary, her suspicions were confirmed very shortly after the wedding when the couple returned early from their honeymoon and her daughter confided to an aunt that her new husband was sexually "perverted." The only specific example given was his having rubbed semen in her hair, but he was known to have boasted to his fellow postal workers of his homosexual activities. In fact, he could not converse with anyone without getting onto sexual subjects. He had virtually no friends nor social life and refused to allow his wife to have any of her own.

During the six years of their marriage, his wife had three children in quick succession and was seven months pregnant with a fourth at the time of his suicide. He spoiled and overprotected his children, allowing no discipline of any sort, and was constantly rushing one or another of them off to the doctor. He flew into frequent rages without provocation and, during the rages, often struck his wife or smashed china (his mother-in-law said he must have broken up "50 sets of dishes"). Despite a steady income, he was always in debt. He worried a great deal about money, but had no sense of financial management and, though his children were without adequate clothes, he bought a new house with a 35-year mortgage some time in the last year of his life. His excessive dependence on his mother led him to visit her at least once and sometimes several times every evening. It was not unusual for him to leave home to visit her and return only to leave again immediately, return, and repeat the whole thing once again. One of his mother's complaints was heart trouble and he began to worry that he might also have a weak heart because of his intermittent attacks of shortness of breath, chest pain, and a feeling of smothering. At work, he was overindustrious and put much of his energy into outdoing his fellow workers. He wrote many times to the Postmaster, describing his good work and asking for the promotion he felt he deserved. His mother-in-law believed that, among other things including his debts, it was the final realization that these letters were being ignored that led to his first suicide attempt.

One morning four months before his death, he drank a quantity of peroxide, called the police, and claimed that his wife had tried to poison him. He was taken to a hospital, treated, and released, arrangements having been made for him to go to a county mental hospital. His family objected and he was subsequently admitted to a veteran's hospital. There he received psychotherapy but no organic treatment other than Thorazine and, at the end of two months, he signed out against advice. He was at home for one month during which time he made an unsuccessful effort to return to work and three more suicide attempts—the first, by cutting an antecubital vein; the second, by trying to pump air into his veins with his mother's diabetic syringe; and the third, by sticking two knives into an electric outlet in an effort to electrocute himself. When he re-entered the hospital of his own accord, he received only psychotherapy and was given weekend passes to visit home. During both hospitalizations and the month between them, he experienced auditory and visual hallucinations. He believed that the "racket squad," the FBI, and people in red cars were after him. On several occasions, he drove his car around the block to "shake" his pursuers. He believed that his house was wired. He heard voices in the house and sometimes responded to them. He also saw the Blessed Virgin. He believed that his wife was trying to kill him, that she was unfaithful to him, that everybody was trying to do him harm and to put something over on him, and that he had committed too many sins to live. He spoke many times, to anyone who would listen, of his suicidal intentions, explaining that he had nothing to live for, that his future was black, that he was a burden, that his family would be better off without him. His appetite was poor, he lost weight, he slept poorly, he complained of being tired and of not having time to do all that needed doing around his house. Interestingly, he seemed aware of his real trouble for he said at least twice, "You think I'm having a nervous breakdown, but I'm not—I'm insane."

One month after re-entering the hospital, he came home on a weekend pass. Arriving at his house later than expected, he explained that he had stopped off at a tall building intending to jump from its roof, but had lost his nerve. He then accused his wife of being a "kept woman." At this, she lost her temper and shouted at him, enumerating all his faults. Her statements seemed to jolt him and he sat up talking to her until 4 AM, speaking for the first time, according to his mother-in-law, with some "insight" into his illness. A little after 4:00, his wife fell asleep. She was awakened by a loud thud a few minutes later. In the attic she found her husband hanging. She tried to support his body, but could not. She telephoned the police for help, then returned to the attic with a knife to try to cut the rope. She could not do this, and by the time the police arrived, he was dead. The coroner's report indicated that he had probably been dead when she discovered him.

Family history: Two months after the subject's suicide his wife gave birth to a normal son. One month after the birth, suffering from severe depression, she was admitted to a hospital and was given electroshock treatment. A year later, she was still hospitalized and was diagnosed as a schizophrenic. One brother was described as having odd behavior, and the subject's other siblings of having "low intelligence." His mother was chronically "nervous" and had had at least one "nervous breakdown."
Arrest record: None.

Case No. *039* M _X_ F __ Age _32_

ST. LOUIS SUICIDE STUDY CRITERIA FOR SCHIZOPHRENIA

At least seven of the following symptoms were required, in addition to delusions or hallucinations, for a diagnosis of schizophrenia:

A.	Conspicuous delusions or hallucinations	_X_	G.	Silly behavior and mannerisms, unpredictable behavior	_X_
B.	Reduction in attachments and interests, and impoverishment of human relationships	_X_	H.	Dissociative phenomena	__
			I.	Autistic thinking	__
C.	Regressive behavior associated with inappropriate affect	__	J.	Chronic apparent mental deterioration	__
			K.	Rages and fights	_X_
D.	Motor behavior exhibiting either marked generalized inhibition or excessive activity and excitation	__	L.	Hypochondriacal complaints	_X_
			M.	Belief that "people" are spying on one or "after" one	_X_
E.	Expansive delusional system of omnipotence or genius	__	N.	Poor job history	_X_
			O.	Excessive religious preoccupation	__
F.	Ideas of reference	_X_	P.	Muteness	__

FEIGHNER CRITERIA FOR SCHIZOPHRENIA

A definite diagnosis required that the subject met criteria in each of the following categories.

A. Both of the following required:
   A chronic illness with at least six months of symptoms prior to the index evaluation without return to the premorbid level of psychosocial adjustment _X_
   Absence of a period of depressive or manic symptoms sufficient to qualify for affective disorder or probable affective disorder _X_

B. At least one of the following:
   Delusions or hallucinations without significant perplexity or disorientation associated with them. _X_
   Verbal production that makes communication difficult because of a lack of logical or understandable organization. (In the presence of muteness the diagnostic decision must be deferred.) ___

C. At least three of the following symptoms required for "definite" diagnosis of schizophrenia and two for a "probable" diagnosis.
   Single ___
   Poor premorbid social adjustment or work history _X_
   Family history of schizophrenia ___
   Absence of alcoholism or drug abuse within one year of onset of psychosis _X_
   Onset of illness prior to age 40 _X_

087 Informants: Wife, stepfather; Navy, hospital, and police records

This 32-year-old white man had from childhood a troubled and personally violent life. He was an only child, and both his parents were in mental hospitals at the time of his death. The parents separated early in his youth and he spent his school years shuttling back and forth between them. He attended 17 different schools in nearly as many states and finally dropped out of school in the 10th grade to go to work. His school records show that he picked fights and was frequently truant. His father is said to have regularly beaten him, and when his mother remarried, it was to an alcoholic.

His job history is sketchy and an informant commented that he was fired "from about 5 million jobs." He was never known to have had any real friends and was outspokenly prejudiced against Jews, Catholics, and blacks. In fact, he seems to have disliked people in general. He was uncomfortable in crowds and always avoided them. As a very young man, he developed an obsessional love of gambling and was, throughout his adult life, plagued by gambling debts. He is known to have been arrested at least twice—once for fighting and once for attempting to abduct a woman at gun point.

While still in his teens, he joined the Navy and spent six years in the service. For five and a half years his conduct was good, but the last six months he was often in trouble—fighting, going AWOL, talking back to officers. As a result, he was sent to a mental hospital in San Diego but given an honorable discharge.

Shortly after his discharge from the Navy, he went to Chicago and married. His wife had two children from a former marriage whom he promised to support. However, after two years the children had become a source of conflict and his wife was forced to board them. The separation from her children caused further conflict and twice she left him to be with them, but returned to him each time. He often said that he would be better off dead and that she would be, too. The wife said that she became fully aware of his abnormal traits about six months after their marriage. Her realization that he might be mentally ill was gradual though she said he often stated, "I know there is something wrong with me, but I don't know what. I have the feeling of impending disaster as if the sword of Damocles was over me," and that she was his "only outside contact with the world." Though dependent upon her, he often beat her and several times he cut her and once threatened to cut off her breasts. Apparently, his mother had been unfaithful to his father and he irrationally and unjustly accused his wife of being the same way. His own sex life seemed to have been limited. His wife described him as a "not very passionate" man.

At age 25 he attempted suicide (a belt around his neck) for the first time although he had often threatened to kill himself "to get his own way." Because of this attempt, he was hospitalized in a mental hospital for two months. Three years later he shot, but did not kill, his father and was again admitted to a mental hospital. That hospitalization lasted eight months and he seemed better on release, but soon lapsed into his old patterns. At some later time, he threatened to drive his wife and mother off a cliff when his mother refused to give him money.

At that point, he and his wife returned to Chicago where he had a series of jobs. He refused to contribute to the support of his stepchildren and his wife worked to support all of them. She admitted growing cold toward him as his behavior became increasingly bizarre. He made elaborate plans to "deal with" Jews, Catholics, and blacks. He complained of headaches and anxiety attacks, feared brain tumor and other terrible but nameless diseases, believed the police and his wife were spying on him, blamed everyone—especially his parents—for his troubles, was spiteful, angry, felt neglected, felt he was a burden, was at times pathologically overactive, cried easily, paced the floor, and seemed generally enraged and potentially dangerous.

About a year before his death, she left him for the last time and moved to St. Louis. He wrote her that he was turning himself in to a veteran's mental hospital in Illinois. Six months later, he signed himself out of the hospital, came to St. Louis, and asked his wife to return. She refused. A few months later he turned up again. When she again refused to go back to him, he said he would like to meet her to discuss a divorce. He suggested they go to a hotel to talk and have a drink and that they would "part friends." They had some drinks and left. His wife fell asleep in the car and when she woke up, she found he had stopped the car in front of a cheap hotel. At knifepoint he forced her inside and, once in the room, turned on the gas jets. His wife was able to calm him, to turn off the gas, and to open the windows. She told him she thought their "love was dead," but persuaded him to let her go home to think things over. He told her his life was nothing without her, and that he would kill himself if she didn't come back. She was not particularly alarmed by the threat as he had made so many threats in the past.

A week passed during which time his whereabouts were unknown. At the end of that week his wife was walking along her street when he suddenly appeared and said he wanted to talk. When she refused, he told her, "I'm going to kill you. I don't want to kill you, but I have to." He pulled out a handgun and fired it. The gun jammed, she broke loose, and ran across the street. He fired again, wounding her in the neck and chest. He then shot himself in the head and died instantly. His wife recovered.

Family history: At the time of the subject's death, both his parents were in psychiatric hospitals. His father's diagnosis was "paranoia"; his mother's diagnosis was schizophrenia.
Arrest record: None.

Case No. 087 M X F __ Age 32

ST. LOUIS SUICIDE STUDY CRITERIA FOR SCHIZOPHRENIA

At least seven of the following symptoms were required, in addition to delusions or hallucinations, for a diagnosis of schizophrenia:

- A. Conspicuous delusions or hallucinations __X__
- B. Reduction in attachments and interests, and impoverishment of human relationships __—__
- C. Regressive behavior associated with inappropriate affect __X__
- D. Motor behavior exhibiting either marked generalized inhibition or excessive activity and excitation __X__
- E. Expansive delusional system of omnipotence or genius __—__
- F. Ideas of reference __—__
- G. Silly behavior and mannerisms, unpredictable behavior __X__
- H. Dissociative phenomena __X__
- I. Autistic thinking __—__
- J. Chronic apparent mental deterioration __X__
- K. Rages and fights __X__
- L. Hypochondriacal complaints __X__
- M. Belief that "people" are spying on one or "after" one __X__
- N. Poor job history __X__
- O. Excessive religious preoccupation __—__
- P. Muteness __—__

FEIGNER CRITERIA FOR SCHIZOPHRENIA

A definite diagnosis required that the subject met criteria in each of the following categories.

- A. Both of the following required:
  - A chronic illness with at least six months of symptoms prior to the index evaluation without return to the premorbid level of psychosocial adjustment __X__
  - Absence of a period of depressive or manic symptoms sufficient to qualify for affective disorder or probable affective disorder __X__
- B. At least one of the following:
  - Delusions or hallucinations without significant perplexity or disorientation associated with them __X__
  - Verbal production that makes communication difficult because of a lack of logical or understandable organization. (In the presence of muteness the diagnostic decision must be deferred.) __—__
- C. At least three of the following symptoms required for "definite" diagnosis of schizophrenia and two for a "probable" diagnosis.
  - Single __—__
  - Poor premorbid social adjustment or work history __X__
  - Family history of schizophrenia __X__
  - Absence of alcoholism or drug abuse within one year of onset of psychosis __X__
  - Onset of illness prior to age 40 __X__

113 Informants: Hospital records (*no primary informant, refusal*)

Because no one in this 34-year-old white man's family was willing to be interviewed, investigation of his background and the events leading to his suicide was dependent upon records of his several hospitalizations for mental illness.

It was stated by authorities at the psychiatric hospital where he was most often hospitalized that he was the youngest of seven siblings and that there was a possible history of insanity in his family, though his father was said to have denied it. At the age of three, he had suffered a skull fracture (vertex) as the result of an automobile accident and his parents had refused permission for an elevation operation.

At age 16, he was admitted to a general hospital, apparently because he had swallowed several kinds of poison. Although extremely withdrawn at admission, he confessed remembering a quarrel with his brother and feeling great guilt over having recently contracted gonorrhea. He also said he believed "people" were constantly watching him. He was referred to a psychiatric hospital with a preliminary diagnosis of "dementia praecox of a paranoid nature with manifestations of schizophrenia." According to the psychiatric hospital's records, his condition was characterized by "withdrawal, fixed attitude, peculiar facial expression." The hospital notes went on to describe the subject as "frankly delusional and hallucinatory." The final hospital diagnosis was recorded as "dementia praecox, paranoid type." He was treated with 22 Metrazol shock treatments and 50 insulin coma therapy treatments and released after six months.

Three years later, at age 19, he was readmitted to the same hospital. At that time, he reported that in the time that had intervened he had been "okay" until shortly before his admission when he began to have somatic delusions and feelings of persecution. He also said God had been talking to him. He was given insulin and electroshock therapy and released on parole after four months. Six months later, he was fully discharged.

Nine years later, at the age of 28, he was admitted to the psychiatric hospital for the third time. He said he had had the same symptoms as those previously recorded, but added that lately he had begun to drink a lot and to get drunk a lot, as well. He said he had, over a period of six to seven years, until his delusions and hallucinations reappeared, done "okay" on his several jobs, though he admitted he had "walked off" a few of them in anger. He had also developed new olfactory hallucinations and believed he was the cause of a bad odor he smelled. He was, at that time, still single. Once again, he received insulin and electroshock therapy, was paroled at the end of three months, and discharged six months later.

Between his third discharge and his suicide, the hospital had two letters from him. The first, received two years after his last release, was addressed to his doctor there and described a recent "feeling of persecution by my neighbors. . . . As I am more interested in going ahead in a sane manner instead of a crazy one, I would sure appreciate your letting me know if you can prescribe some medicine for me, to help through the rough spots." The doctor replied and sent a prescription (which was not identified in the records). The second letter, received a year later, was addressed to the hospital administrators and enclosed a $5 contribution to the hospital's Assistance League along with a note: "Having been a patient at the hospital and now enjoying good health and prosperity, thanks for the help, I received there, I would like to become a member in your league."

Nothing is known about the subject's life for the four and a half years that elapsed between the letter quoted above and his death. On the day of his suicide, he showed his mother the gun he intended to use to kill himself and, while she was out of the house in search of help, he shot himself.

Family history: No information.
Arrest record: None.

Case No. *113* M *X* F __ Age *34*

ST. LOUIS SUICIDE STUDY CRITERIA FOR SCHIZOPHRENIA

At least seven of the following symptoms were required, in addition to delusions or hallucinations, for a diagnosis of schizophrenia:

A. Conspicuous delusions or hallucinations *X*	G. Silly behavior and mannerisms, unpredictable behavior *X*
B. Reduction in attachments and interests, and impoverishment of human relationships __	H. Dissociative phenomena __
	I. Autistic thinking *X*
C. Regressive behavior associated with inappropriate affect *X*	J. Chronic apparent mental deterioration *X*
	K. Rages and fights __
D. Motor behavior exhibiting either marked generalized inhibition or excessive activity and excitation __	L. Hypochondriacal complaints *X*
	M. Belief that "people" are spying on one or "after" one *X*
E. Expansive delusional system of omnipotence or genius __	N. Poor job history *X*
	O. Excessive religious preoccupation __
F. Ideas of reference __	P. Muteness __

FEIGHNER CRITERIA FOR SCHIZOPHRENIA

A definite diagnosis required that the subject met criteria in each of the following categories.

A. Both of the following required:
   A chronic illness with at least six months of symptoms prior to the index evaluation without return to the premorbid level of psychosocial adjustment _X_
   Absence of a period of depressive or manic symptoms sufficient to qualify for affective disorder or probable affective disorder _X_

B. At least one of the following:
   Delusions or hallucinations without significant perplexity or disorientation associated with them. _X_
   Verbal production that makes communication difficult because of a lack of logical or understandable organization. (In the presence of muteness the diagnostic decision must be deferred.) ___

C. At least three of the following symptoms required for "definite" diagnosis of schizophrenia and two for a "probable" diagnosis.
   Single _X_
   Poor premorbid social adjustment or work history _X_
   Family history of schizophrenia ___
   Absence of alcoholism or drug abuse within one year of onset of psychosis _X_
   Onset of illness prior to age 40 _X_

MISCELLANEOUS GROUP, SUBGROUP 4

Subjects with Drug Dependence (1 man, 1 woman)

020 Informants: Mother, three psychiatrists; hospital and police records

This 29-year-old white unemployed door-to-door salesman began having psychological difficulties as a child. His mother described him as being "nervous," "high-strung," given to outbursts of anger, and as having had occasional convulsions as a child. His mother denied any serious antisocial behavior before age 27, an opinion generally confirmed by his arrest records. His high school record showed truancy, but, according to his mother, he was never expelled or suspended. His first marriage, at age 15, was rapidly annulled. At age 16, he joined the Navy, but was discharged after two months with a (unknown) psychiatric diagnosis. At age 19, he married a second time and remained married until age 27 at which time his wife divorced him because of drug addiction and attendant abnormal behavior. From his discharge from the Navy until age 25 he saw a private psychiatrist sporadically. During the early part of this period, in his late teens and early twenties, he drank heavily, but early in his second marriage he stopped drinking excessively. He was a police chief in a small township for two or three years and simultaneously ran a clinical laboratory. At about age 24, he began to take Seconal excessively, lost both positions, tried many business schemes, and finally became a door-to-door salesman. He and his father "ran through a fortune" of $85,000 during this period.

He was first admitted to a civilian mental hospital at age 26 and a diagnosis of drug addiction was made. He was tremulous and gave a history of difficulty in walking and of a 70-pound weight loss in the preceding year. During that year he became completely derelict and was unable to meet job, financial, and family obligations. Just prior to admission he hallucinated (saw cigarettes and heard his mother call) for a few hours and spoke of suicide. But by the time he was in the hospital he was rational and not hallucinating. It was believed he was having barbiturate withdrawal symptoms. He was discharged within a few days, but was admitted a month later to another mental hospital after having a convulsive seizure, presumably related to barbiturate withdrawal. During the next two years he continued his excessive intake of barbiturates and also complained of palpitation, shortness of breath, and chest pain whenever he was upset. He suffered from chronic fatigue and recurrent fainting spells.

At age 28, he was admitted to a third mental hospital because of Seconal addiction. He remained there only briefly. After his discharge he was unable to work, complained of insomnia, became depressed and disgusted with himself and the world. His mother felt he needed love and wanted attention. Six months prior to his death he married for the third time. He and his wife did not get along. A short time after their marriage his wife found she was pregnant. He stated that he was the father of the unborn child, but his wife contradicted this, saying that another man was the father. About four to six weeks prior to his suicide his wife left him. Because of his drug addiction and generally upset behavior, he was again admitted to a mental hospital for three days about three weeks prior to his death. Two weeks before his suicide he left a suicide note where his mother would see it. She saw it, assumed he was dead inside the house, and called the police. When the police arrived he stuck his head out of a second-story window and asked what all the commotion was about. He continued to feel, according to his mother, neglected, unloved, and depressed and his mother believed that the suicide note had been an attention-getting device.

About a week later he went to Arkansas to attempt to get money from his father, but was unsuccessful. He was worried about his debts and about bogus checks he had passed (see below under arrest history). His worrying continued for the next several days. One morning at 3 AM he wakened his mother and told her how depressed and worried he was. He talked of "needing" someone to love him. His mother warned him about not taking any more drugs and went back to sleep. The next morning she found him dead in bed from an overdose of barbiturates. His mother believed that his debts, his worries about the bad checks, and his wife's leaving him all contributed to his suicide.

Family history: There was no family history of psychiatric illness.
Arrest record: He was arrested five times during the years 1946, 1948, and 1950 for moving traffic offenses, including three speeding tickets. He was arrested in 1947 as a suspect in an affray. He was arrested four times during 1954 and 1955 for passing bad checks. It was recommended that he get extended private psychiatric treatment as an outpatient, but he never did.

Case No. *020* M X F __ Age *29*

ST. LOUIS SUICIDE STUDY CRITERIA FOR DRUG DEPENDENCE

Diagnosis required at least three of the following symptoms:

A. Addiction to drugs as manifested by increased tolerance and withdrawal symptoms when the drugs were unavailable __X__

B. Nightly drugs for sleeping __X__

C. Daily drug abuse __X__

D. Self-concern about taking too many drugs ____

E. Family concern about subject taking too many drugs __X__

F. Inability to stop taking drugs ____

FEIGHNER CRITERIA FOR DRUG DEPENDENCE

A definite diagnosis required any one of the following to be present. The drug type is specified according to DSM-II (with possible change at publication of DSM-III).

A. History of withdrawal symptoms

B. Hospitalization for drug abuse or its complications __X__

C. Indiscriminate prolonged use of central nervous system active drugs __X__

115 Informants: Husband, sister, physicians, hospital records

This 31-year-old white woman had been married to her second husband for just nine months when she committed suicide. Information from her husband was based on what he had observed during their marriage (he had known her only briefly before) and often differed greatly from information given by the subject's sister.

From her sister it was learned that the subject finished the 10th grade, married for the first time at age 17, and had one child. She and her first husband separated after six years of marriage and divorced three years later. The grandparents won custody of their son. The subject moved to St. Louis from Tennessee seven years prior to her suicide. She had several clerical and waitressing jobs, but "always got sick after working a little while on a job." During the seven years she lived in St. Louis, she was hospitalized nine times—twice for surgery (appendectomy and removal of one and a half ovaries and both tubes), five times for medical reasons (twice for laceration, twice for vaginal bleeding, and once for "threatened abortion" which occurred five years after the removal of ovaries and tubes), and twice for psychiatric reasons (once for coma and morphine intoxication and once because of self-inflicted wrist and neck lacerations). She had at least two general practitioners during her years in St. Louis and the medical histories she gave to each of them varied widely. Both record many visits and telephone calls for varying complaints, many of them involving the subject's "need" for sleeping pills, pain killers, and tranquilizers.

About ten months before her death she met her second husband (a man exactly twice her age) and married him a month later. According to him, the subject was "a happy, good girl" who drank too much when she had the chance and got doctors to give her dope. He felt she had been a little tense for several weeks a few months before she died and had lost some weight, but that she'd seemed much "better" the last six weeks and had gained back all her lost weight. He described her as a sensitive ("she was torn up by any little criticism"), moody, and perhaps nervous person, but he did not notice any lasting change in her behavior during the time he knew her. He said he was mainly concerned about the number of drugs she took and had tried to keep them from her. This had always caused her to become very upset, and once or twice she had made suicidal gestures in reaction. About six months before her death, she went as far as slashing her wrists and throat and was hospitalized for several days at a psychiatric hospital. Her husband did not feel that his wife "needed" the drugs, but that she liked the "buzz." He also said that two weeks before her death she had decided she wanted to give them up. He believed she killed herself because "her nerves just ran away with her when she was alone."

The subject's older sister said that she believed her sister had killed herself because her husband was "mean to her" and "she couldn't stand him." She went on to say that the doctors had always mishandled and overtreated her sister, who should never have been trusted to tell doctors the truth. She described the subject as had her husband—sensitive, moody, neurotic, nervous—and went on to list the somatic symptoms she had complained of most of her adult life: headaches, abdominal pain, menstrual pain, menstrual hemorrhages, palpitation, chest pain, dizziness, dyspnea, fainting spells, "fits," amnesia (on one occasion), rapidly fluctuating weight, nausea, and frequent vomiting. The only ones of these that her husband had mentioned were those associated with menstrual problems. Like her husband, the sister had noticed no obvious change in her sister's behavior in the weeks and months prior to her suicide, but she did say she felt she had never "gotten her feet on the ground" after the breakup of her first marriage.

Apparently, the subject had several good friends whom she saw regularly—always in her home, never in theirs. A fairly regular church-goer before her second marriage, she did not go at all after it. There was disagreement about how heavily she drank, but there were no definite indications that she was an alcoholic.

Two weeks before her suicide, she telephoned her doctor to ask for sleeping pills as she had "broken her ankle" and was having trouble sleeping. The doctor referred her to the hospital that had allegedly set the ankle. The autopsy showed no sign of a broken anklebone.

The afternoon of her suicide, a neighbor had visited with her until late afternoon. She reported that the subject was in "good spirits." Sometime in the hour between the neighbor's departure and her husband's return from work, she shot herself. She left the following note: "C., I can't take it, nothing I do is right so you say. I love you, but a person can only take so much, M."

Family history: According to her sister, there was no history of suicide in the subject's family. Her mother was described as "somewhat nervous," but had never been hospitalized for mental illness.
Arrest record: None.

Case No. *115* M __ F X Age *31*

ST. LOUIS SUICIDE STUDY CRITERIA FOR DRUG DEPENDENCE

Diagnosis required at least three of the following symptoms:

A. Addiction to drugs as manifested by increased tolerance and withdrawal symptoms when the drugs were unavailable   X

B. Nightly drugs for sleeping   X

C. Daily drug abuse   X

D. Self-concern about taking too many drugs   X

E. Family concern about subject taking too many drugs   X

F. Inability to stop taking drugs   __

FEIGHNER CRITERIA FOR DRUG DEPENDENCE

A definite diagnosis required any one of the following to be present. The drug type is specified according to DSM-II (with possible change at publication of DSM-III).

A. History of withdrawal symptoms   __

B. Hospitalization for drug abuse or its complications   X

C. Indiscriminate prolonged use of central nervous system active drugs   X

MISCELLANEOUS GROUP, SUBGROUP 5

Subjects with Terminal Medical Illness, no accompanying Psychiatric Disease (3 men, 2 women)

028   Informants: Physician, hospital records (refusal)

At the time of his suicide, this 58-year-old white shoe-salesman was suffering from terminal cancer. His doctor reported that he would probably have lived only two months longer.

Born in Russia, he came to the United States when he was seven. Because neither his children nor his wife was willing to talk to interviewers, no more is known of his background, his family history, or the specific events leading to his death.

Hospital records showed that he had been an in-patient for 17 days one year before his death because of mucinous gastric cancer and that a total gastrectomy had been performed. He had, at that time, no history of psychiatric disorder. After his operation, he was said to have been restless, nervous, apprehensive and, at times, uncooperative.

For the last two months of his life, he was bedridden at home except when he was hospitalized again for about two weeks a month before his death due to the worsening symptoms of the recurrent cancer. The hospital record reported that he was at that time suffering from ascites, peripheral edema, and pleural effusion. Fluid was removed from the chest and the abdomen, after which he was released. According to his doctor, when he returned to his home, the patient was despondent and depressed because he was unable to support his family. However, as far as the doctor knew, he was not in pain, there were no somatic symptoms directly ascribable to psychiatric illness, and he displayed no abnormal behavior. Although he expressed no suicidal intent, his doctor felt that the decision to commit suicide had been a rational one, because he knew he was fatally ill. He had been home from the hospital for two days when he hanged himself.

Family history: There was no information about a family history of psychiatric illness.
Arrest record: None.

081 Informants: Wife, mother-in-law, sister-in-law

This 45-year-old white man was, at the time of his suicide, dying of lung cancer. His wife said that he had not been informed of his cancer. Rather, he had been told that he had a "tumor," but she did not think he had been deceived.

Very little is known about the subject's childhood except that he was raised from infancy by his widowed mother. He saw combat overseas during World War II and received an honorable discharge. On his return to St. Louis he worked for the same shoe company for the next 11 years until shortly before his death when his illness prevented his working.

He and his wife had no children. His wife described him as a "wonderful husband" and a good man in general. She said he had many close friends with whom they enjoyed a full social life.

Seven months before his death, he began to worry about his health because he had lost 15 pounds over several months and because he felt increasingly tired and weak. A month later, he was x-rayed and inoperable cancer of the lung was diagnosed. He was not told the exact nature of his disease. He was given sleeping pills to help counteract his insomnia and he received some x-ray treatments for his "tumor." He continued to keep his life-long good humor and did not seem to worry unduly about himself.

Three months before his death, he was severely burned over the upper part of his body (it was not specified how this happened) and was hospitalized for two weeks. About this time he began to experience symptoms of his progressing cancer—dyspnea and chest pain in particular. He was told that the penicillin he'd been given for his burns had caused him to develop second degree asthma, which was the reason for his breathing discomfort. From that time until his death he referred to his "asthma" and spoke about what he planned when he was "well." His weakness, fatigue, and discomfort increased and he was often unable to sleep because of pain. Although his wife noticed that during the last few months of his life he was less interested in TV and the newspapers, she said his interest in the family grew. He was untempted by most food in the last months and a lot of talking in his presence bothered him. Otherwise, in spite of his progressive weakness and pain, he remained good humored and continued to speak of when he would be "well again."

The last two days and nights of his life, he coughed constantly and could not sleep because the coughing worsened whenever he lay down. On the last night, he finally took several sleeping pills and just before going to sleep, spoke to his wife in symbolic terms about wanting to die. He said he could see her deceased father and could, if she wanted, take her to him. (She declined and wondered later whether, had she said yes, he would have killed her.) Then he told her that there were "two roads—one straight on and one winding" and that she should take the winding one. He then mumbled something like "Wait, George, don't get too far ahead . . . I'll be coming soon." This last was evidently addressed to a friend who had died a few months earlier. In the morning, New Year's Eve, he seemed a little better and was in his usual good spirits. Later in the morning he asked what was for lunch, which was unusual because for weeks he had had no interest in food. When told it would be beef broth, he asked his sister-in-law to get him some. Then he sent his wife to the kitchen after her to see that she didn't make it too hot. The two women talked in the kitchen for about five minutes. He took advantage of that very brief time alone to find a gun he had kept in the next room and to shoot himself. He died immediately. His wife felt that he knew he was dying, that he could no longer bear his pain and the fear of choking, and perhaps because he wanted to spare her the long process a natural death would certainly have been. Not only had he recently lost his friend George, but another of his friends was dying of carcinoma of the stomach. His wife felt he had been upset about both of these friends. He left no note.

Family history: The subject's father had committed suicide when the subject was an infant. There was no other family history of psychiatric illness. *Arrest record:* None.

103 Informants: Wife, physician, hospital records

At the time of his suicide, this 72-year-old white man was dying of cancer and had been bedridden for five months. His wife was not a forthcoming informant and was unable, or unwilling, to distinguish between the subject's medical symptoms and possible depressive symptoms.

Background information was scanty due to the informant's taciturn nature. She did supply basic information that subject was born in a small Illinois town to German immigrant parents; that his father was a cobbler who owned a shoe repair shop; that his mother was a housewife who raised her three children as Catholics; that the subject finished 7th grade; that he did not serve in the military, probably because of poor eyesight. She also reported that he had been married twice. He married the first time when he was 25, was divorced from his first wife after 14 years and married his second wife the same year. The second marriage lasted 34 years, until his death, and produced at least two children whose ages and locations at the time of their father's death were not given. The subject's occupation was described as "self-employed merchant." He had not been able to work for the last two or three years of his life because of his illness and, though his wife worked full-time, finances were tight at the time of his suicide. He had lived in St. Louis for 50 years.

Described by his wife as a "sensitive man" whose feelings had always been easily hurt, the subject was apparently not a particularly social man. He had not attended church regularly since his childhood and had not belonged to the Catholic Church for many years. He had one or two close friends whom he saw, in a social sense, only occasionally. He drank moderately on social occasions. He had enjoyed fishing all his life and, until two or three years before he died, belonged to a local fishing club.

Five years before his suicide, he underwent surgery twice. The first operation, a prostatectomy, was done to relieve hypertrophy of the prostate. A few months later, he was discovered to have cancer of the colon and rectum and a colostomy was performed. Two years before his death, his cancer recurred and his wife felt that from that time on, once he knew he was dying his behavior may have changed slightly. In addition to the worsening symptoms of weakness, fatigue, anorexia, nausea, vomiting, insomnia, and pain associated with his disease, he showed increased irritability and, in the last months, after he had had to be hospitalized several times for complications of his cancer and was finally bedridden, he showed some depression in regard to his condition. In the last five months, he wondered aloud several times "Why this had to happen to me" and displayed a loss of interest and joylessness that was noticeable to his wife. However, his physician did not feel that he was more depressed than might have been expected under the circumstances. A few days before his suicide, he cried briefly "for no reason." He refused all drugs for pain or sleeplessness and was, at the end, in considerable unremitting pain which kept him from sleeping. His eyesight, always poor, was at that point almost gone.

Late on the afternoon of his 72nd birthday, he shot himself while awaiting his wife's return from work. He was still alive when she found him and was taken to St. Louis City Hospital where he died in the early hours of the next morning. No note was found.

Family history: There was no family history of either suicide or mental illness.
Arrest record: None.

035 Informants: Husband, niece, physician, surgeon, hospital records

This 62-year-old white woman, born on a farm in Germany, was brought to the United States by her parents when she was eight. She completed the 8th grade, attended business college, and worked as a secretary until her marriage at 21.

Her husband described a very happy 40-year marriage, although there was some disappointment at not having children. He was fairly successful in his own business, but gave the impression of having made, and then lost, a lot of money. However, he stated that money had never worried him or his wife. After her marriage, she did not work again until the last three years of her life, and then only because she wanted more to keep her busy. At the time of her death, she was employed as a biller at a surgical supply company. She worked until just a few days before she died and seemed to have had no difficulty with her job.

She was described as a sociable woman with wide interests and many close friends. Except for three minor operations she had been well both mentally and physically until four and a half or five years before she died. At that time, she had a sudden onset of hoarseness. The doctor she consulted suggested removal of swollen tonsils, but she procrastinated. Six months later, when her symptoms grew worse, she returned to him and was referred to a surgeon who removed one tonsil. She went back to work a week later, but received regular x-ray therapy. Some time later, she began to develop lymphatic enlargement in the face, neck, and groin. This was treated with x-ray. Despite her obvious and long-standing difficulty, her husband was not told until shortly before her death that she had cancer. She was never told, but he felt certain that she knew. Even so, he insisted that his wife was at no time depressed.

Two or three years before her death, her brother, who had been an invalid for years because of some chronic, wasting muscular disease, died of carcinoma of the lung. She was profoundly affected by this and, at the time, made frequent remarks that she did not intend to die a lingering death as he had done. Though she is said to have remained cheerful throughout her own illness, she continued to make occasional comments about not meaning to prolong her suffering beyond a certain point.

A year before her suicide, she became progressively more fatigued and complained of this. About six months before she died, she began to have severe headaches and dizzy spells accompanied by vomiting. For these, she sometimes took codeine. A few months prior to her death she limited her previously active social life to weekly visits with one friend. During her illness, she lost a good deal of weight (50–75 pounds), but there was no sudden weight loss.

About a month before her suicide, she returned to work from a four-day vacation feeling well and rested. However, after two days of work, she complained of being very tired. The following Monday she went to the doctor. By this time, one leg was badly swollen and she was having great difficulty breathing. On Tuesday, following an x-ray treatment, her doctor, who noted no sign of depression, suggested she enter the hospital for further treatment. She refused, telling her husband she would not "let the doctors needle her to death." She also told him she was "whipped" and that she "just couldn't take it any longer." He handled this by trying to joke with her. Her reply was, "If you only knew how I'm feeling, you'd know I'm not kidding." The next day, when her husband left for work, she seemed cheerful enough, but as she kissed him she said emphatically, "That's your last kiss." Again he kidded her, and she made no reply. She called him at noon to say that she had spoken with her doctor, but did not need to see him that day.

Late that afternoon, a friend telephoned her husband to say that she could not reach his wife by phone. He rushed home and had trouble getting into the house, the doors having been locked from the inside and keys left in each lock. When he got in, he found his wife lying on the kitchen floor with a pistol beside her body. She had shot herself through the heart.

Family history: Mother spent 17 years in a mental hospital where she had been treated for paranoid schizophrenia.
Arrest record: None.

063 Informants: Physician, minister, hospital records (refusal)

Because no one who knew her well was willing to be questioned about this 63-year-old white woman, almost nothing is known of the circumstances of her life except just prior to her suicide.

It is known that she was married and living with her husband to whom she was very close and on whom she was psychologically dependent. He is reported to have described her as having a stable personality and as a person who loved music, poetry, and flowers. She was devoutly religious and a regular church-goer.

Three months before her death, she had undergone exploratory abdominal surgery because she had had complaints of tenderness, physical weakness, and nausea on a full stomach. A large cancerous mass was discovered in her stomach along with pancreatic and pelvic metastases. Her condition was deemed inoperable and she was released to her home a week or so after the operation with a prescription for Thorazine. She was not informed of her cancer.

During the weeks that followed, she suffered increasing abdominal pain and though her minister said that her spirits remained high, she was without vitality. Four days before shooting herself, her minister visited her and found her extremely depressed and complaining of constant pain. She told her husband and minister that she didn't know how much longer she could stand it. Her husband apparently told the minister after her death that although they had sometimes discussed the suicide of others, she had never mentioned thinking of her own.

A little less than eight weeks after her surgery, the subject shot herself in the chest at her home. The minister, her husband, and her doctor were all very much surprised by her act. She was taken to a nearby hospital emergency room where, still conscious and rational, she told doctors that for the last five weeks she had been depressed and despondent, that she had not been able to eat any solids, that she was losing a great deal of weight, and that she was suffering from worsening dyspnea. Although her family doctor claimed she had not been told that she had cancer, she told the doctors caring for her in the emergency room that she had cancer of the "abdomen." The bullet lodged in her chest was removed and for three weeks the subject remained in critical condition in the hospital. At that point, she rallied and improved. Two weeks before her death, her hospital chart read, "Patient continues to improve . . . (beginning) to ambulate." Five days later she relapsed, gradually weakening until, during the last days of her life, she spent most of the days and nights dozing. She died five weeks after shooting herself.

Family history: Nothing is known of the subject's family's medical or psychiatric history. According to her doctor's records, she was supposed to have suffered a "heart attack" nine years prior to her suicide.
Arrest record: None.

Case No. *028* M X F __ Age *58* Medical illness *Mucinous gastric carcinoma*
Case No. *081* M X F __ Age *45* Medical illness *Pulmonary carcinoma*
Case No. *103* M X F __ Age *72* Medical illness *Carcinoma of colon & rectum*
Case No. *035* M __ F X Age *62* Medical illness *Lympho sarcoma*
Case No. *063* M __ F X Age *63* Medical illness *Gastric carcinoma*

The five subjects with terminal medical illnesses who failed to meet the St. Louis suicide study criteria for the following psychiatric illnesses were considered medically ill only and not psychiatrically ill:

Affective disorder, depressed
  phase
Alcoholism
Antisocial personality
Anxiety neurosis
Drug dependence
Homosexuality

Hysteria
Mental retardation
Obsessive-compulsive neurosis
Organic brain syndrome
Phobic neurosis
Schizophrenia
Undiagnosed psychiatric illness

The same five subjects also failed to meet the Feighner criteria for the psychiatric illnesses listed above as well as for:

Anorexia nervosa
Transsexualism

MISCELLANEOUS GROUP, SUBGROUP 6

Subjects without Medical or Psychiatric Illness (3 men)

078 Informants: Daughter-in-law, osteopathic physician, physician

According to his daughter-in-law, this 66-year-old white man was an early-to-work, early-to-bed family man with no hobbies or interests outside his family and work. She described him as a very kind, pleasant man with "no vices."

He was a Catholic, was educated through 8th grade, and had worked for one firm, a bolt and screw company, all of his 50-year-working life. He had begun as an office boy and was at the time of his suicide Secretary-Treasurer of the company. He and his wife of 40 years lived in their own comfortable home and his annual salary was the highest of his career.

For about a year, the subject had been treated by an osteopathic physician for hypertension and probably arteriosclerosis. He had lately complained more and more of chest pain, palpitation, shortness of breath, headache, and a pain in his left arm and had been persuaded by a daughter who worked at a local general hospital to consult a heart specialist there.

Ten days prior to his suicide, he saw the specialist who reported that the subject had seen him for "angina-like pains" and had undergone an examination and some tests. He said that he had seemed happy even though he was planning to retire in two weeks because of his health. The doctor said he appeared content with this decision and pleased about a trip he and his wife were planning. He returned for the test results a week later and was very happy that the doctor did not feel hospitalization was necessary. The doctor said nothing frightening about his heart condition, and felt, on the contrary, that he had been more encouraging than the subject had expected he would be.

No one, including his wife, his children, and his regular osteopathic physician, noticed any symptoms of depression until the day before the subject's suicide, when a son had noticed, while visiting him, that he had sat a long while in a chair looking gloomy and that he had been quieter than usual. His wife did not notice any change and went the next morning, which was Christmas Eve, to her regular hairdressing appointment. When she returned, she found that he had hanged himself in the basement with a clothesline over a rafter. He left no note.

Family history: There was no family history of psychiatric illness.
Arrest record: None.

021 Informants: Wife, osteopathic physician, otolaryngologist, friend and fellow worker

This 47-year-old white manager of a retail store was first married at age 17 and was divorced 14 years later. He did not remarry until age 42. Sometime shortly after his second marriage his wife was injured in an automobile accident. She was unconscious for 14 days. On returning home, she never, according to their family osteopathic physician, regained her previous personality or behavior. She became dull, neglectful of her home, and unresponsive to her husband and friends. It was the belief of the family physician that the change in his wife did not affect the subject too greatly because he was a "well-balanced" man. There was no open fighting between them. The physician also described him as a "ladies' man" who took hormone shots to keep up his sexual vigor. About six months prior to his death he developed hoarseness and had a benign laryngeal tumor removed, which relieved the symptom. Otherwise, except for a slight hypertension, he was medically well.

His wife's story conflicted markedly with the physician's. She described a serious heart attack seven months prior to his death with work incapacity for months. His fellow worker on the job denied this story stating that he had worked every day and was his usual efficient and jovial self until his death. Late in the afternoon of the evening of his suicide he had been playing pool with his friends. He had won the game and come home in good spirits. He put a carton of beer on the kitchen table and went into the bedroom to change his clothes. He called to his wife, asking her when she would be ready to go out to eat. Several minutes later a shot was heard and his wife found him dead. She could offer no explanation for his suicide. It was of interest that his physician, his brothers, his fellow worker, and his mother did not believe he committed suicide. According to his wife, his mother commented to her that "it was better this way," in other words, to have his death called a suicide so that no one would be accused of homicide.

Family history: There was a very questionable history of an uncle who had committed suicide 15 years previously.

Arrest record: In 1936, 1938, and 1941 he was arrested for careless driving twice and speeding once. In 1945, 1953, and 1954 he was arrested for peace disturbance. In 1954 he was arrested for investigation of receiving stolen property.

067 Informants: Older brother, friends

This 64-year-old white owner of a gift shop was described by his older brother as being a kind, sensitive man to whom friends and acquaintances brought their troubles.

During World War I he served in the Army and saw action overseas. He had worked for about 25 years as a retail salesman and as an appraiser for a pawnbroker. According to informants, he had changed jobs only two or three times and was fired once. He kept his last salaried job for ten years until, two years before his death, he opened his own business, the gift shop. Never very successful, the gift shop was beginning to fail badly during the last month of his life.

He married in his mid twenties and had two children. After 30 years of marriage, he and his wife separated by mutual assent and remained so the last ten years of his life. His wife was not interviewed as she was suffering from a terminal illness at the time of the subject's death.

Until shortly before he died, his daughter, son-in-law, and grandson had lived with him. The grandson was, according to his brother, "the pride of his life." He had several close friends whom he saw regularly in their homes and in his own. If he drank at all it was only an occasional social drink.

He was an unusually healthy man. No serious illnesses, physical or emotional, could be recalled by informants and there were no records of surgery or hospitalization of any kind. Various descriptions of his personality include the phrases "soft-hearted," "good-hearted," and "very sensitive." His brother remembered that, as a child, he had always shared whatever he had. The brother also said that it took a great deal of provocation to make him angry, but that once angry, he tended to "blow his stack." Although he had never mentioned any thoughts of suicide to his brother, he is known to have told friends on several occasions that rather than go through "a certain thing" he would prefer to "leave this world."

A few weeks before his death, while he was at work in his shop, a customer—a young solider—rabbit-punched him as he turned his back to reach for an item. He staggered, but did not lose consciousness. He drew a pistol from his cash register, aimed it at the soldier, and ordered him out of the shop. The soldier pulled a knife from a leg sheath and threw it at him before turning to run. He fired at the young man as he ran and later learned that his shot had hit the man's spine, paralysing him from the waist down. He was extremely remorseful about this and spoke of it constantly, emphasizing the "terrible thing" he had done. Despite frequent reassurances from the police about the correctness of his actions, he continued to express the blame he felt.

Sometime after this incident, his daughter and her family moved out of his house and away from St. Louis. At that point, about a month before his death, he moved out of his home himself and into rooms in back of his shop. During that month, his brother and his friends noted that he seemed to be uncharacteristically sad and joyless, though he did not speak directly of his sadness. They felt that he was also increasingly depressed about his shop and by his own failure to keep his stock clean and in order. Although he appeared to be very lonely and depressed, he made no unusual statements to his friends and never remarked on his own troubles except to express the guilt he felt about the soldier's paralysis.

On Thanksgiving Day, he visited friends who noticed nothing strange about his mood or appearance. He was driven home that evening by a friend who noticed no abnormal behavior. The next morning, his brother received a special delivery letter from him which stated, "I can't go on any further . . . When you receive this letter you will find me in the store." The letter went on to describe how he wished to dispose of his property. A second letter was sent to and received by his separated wife (contents unknown). On receiving the letter, his brother contacted his sister-in-law and then the police. An hour later, they met at the shop and found that he had shot himself in the head.

Informants believe that the combination of guilt over injuring the young soldier and loneliness for his daughter and grandson caused his despondency.

Family history: There was no family history of psychiatric illness.
Arrest record: None.

Case No. *021* M *X* F __ Age *42*
Case No. *067* M *X* F __ Age *64*
Case No. *078* M *X* F __ Age *66*

The three subjects failing to meet the St. Louis suicide study criteria for the following psychiatric illnesses were considered not psychiatrically ill:

Affective disorder, depressed phase	Hysteria
	Mental retardation
Alcoholism	Obsessive-compulsive neurosis
Antisocial personality	Organic brain syndrome
Anxiety neurosis	Phobic neurosis
Drug dependence	Schizophrenia
Homosexuality	Undiagnosed psychiatric illness

The same three subjects also failed to meet the Feighner criteria for the illnesses listed above as well as for:

Anorexia nervosa
Transsexualism

7

The Psychiatrically Undiagnosed Group—Description of the 20 Subjects So Categorized

There were, in the total sample of 134 suicide subjects, 20 who were undiagnosed (or undiagnosable) by the criteria described in Chapter 2. In an initial communication, 25 subjects were reported to have been undiagnosed.[1] During the time between the publication of that article and the full consideration of data undertaken for this book, I obtained enough further information on five of the undiagnosed subjects to enable me to diagnose them.

It is important to define the specific meaning of the terms "psychiatrically undiagnosed" and "psychiatrically undiagnosable."[2] In systematic psychiatric research, the terms are used in a fashion analogous to the way the terms "undiagnosed" and "undiagnosable" are used in medicine. The use of the category is not as a residual one for subjects who do not fit into given diagnostic niches. My concept of "undiagnosed" is that it specifies an illness that is suspected but whose symptoms are minimal or one in which the chronology of symptom clusters cannot be determined. It can also indicate the suspected presence of more than one illness in which the symptoms are either insufficient or atypical. It can, finally, indicate the suspected presence of a specific illness in a case without the history necessary to establish a definitive diagnosis.[2-5]

Psychiatric diagnosis relies on a careful and comprehensive description of the clinical picture of a disorder. Such a picture is produced by a certain combination of clinical features—symptoms—or by a single, striking clinical manifestation, along with demographic variables (race, age, and sex), age of onset, and perhaps precipitating factors. Chapter 2 outlines the necessary combination of the above for diagnosis of each psychiatric illness encountered in this study. But what is particularly challenging in a study of completed suicide is the determination of the presence or absence of symptoms in subjects who cannot be interviewed. In an earlier paper,[5] I defined a symptom as being present if it met the following criteria: the symptom led the patient to consult a physician (or osteopath, chiropractor, etc.), the symptom was disabling, the symptom led the subject to take medication, and the symptom is not explicable by known nonpsychiatric disease in the subject. The necessity of using second-hand information to describe the symptoms of subjects who have committed suicide compounds the difficulty of pinpointing the correct psychiatric diagnosis. For example, whether or not a symptom was disabling is sometimes hard to decide even if the informant making such a decision was intimately associated with the subject. For instance, the informant for case #009, the subject's husband, stated that the subject had visited a physician for "nerves" six months prior to her suicide and that she had expressed once the fear of having a "nervous breakdown." He was not, however, able to say that his wife's nervousness was disabling or that it caused her to make even minor changes in her life.

Two further reasons for the absence of definitive diagnoses in 20 subjects in this study were refusals by or unavailability of primary informants in 13 (65%) of these 20 cases, a much higher proportion than occurred in any of the other three major diagnostic groups. "Refusal" signifies that the primary informant—that individual closest to and presumably knowing most about the person who committed suicide—either did not permit an interview or was stopped by protective relatives from granting an interview. Unavailability of a primary informant usually signified that the subject lived alone or that the primary informant lived at a distance from St. Louis more than 500 miles, was himself ill, or in one case had been murdered by the subject just prior to his suicide. In those 13 cases, therefore, information was limited to that given by persons such as brothers, sons, nieces, daughters-in-law, landlords, friends, fellow workers, physicians, and in one case the mother-in-law of a subject's sister.

Of the symptoms asked about by interviewers, there were 38 which did not occur at all in any of the 20 undiagnosed subjects. The 62 symptoms which were present in these subjects occurred with a maximum prevalence of 54% to a minimum prevalence of 6%. In the subjects with affective disorder, 98 symptoms occurred with prevalences from 80% to 2%. In the alcoholic subjects, 98 symptoms occurred with prevalences from 100% to 3%. In the subjects making up the miscellaneous group, 94 symptoms occurred with prevalences from 83% to 7%. A comparison of the low prevalence of relatively few symptoms in the undiagnosed group with those found in the other three groups makes it clear that the undiagnosed group was considered undiagnosed because the information obtained was skimpy.

TABLE 7.1 The "most like" system* as applied to percentages of definite diagnoses

Definite diagnoses	Percents of total sample	Added percents from "most like" category	Resulting distribution if "most like" added
Affective disorder	47	8	55
Alcoholism	25	2	27
Miscellaneous	13	4	17
Psychiatrically undiagnosed	15	0	—

*The third column shows the likely distribution of psychiatric illnesses in the total sample, the result of direct study of case histories instead of applying the percentages determined by the definite diagnoses (e.g.: the extension of 25% for alcoholism would have added 5 of the undiagnosed subjects to the alcoholism group instead of the 3 our system added).

Even so, it was important to try to make as much of this information as useful and as meaningful to the overall study as possible. Therefore, I separated the group of 20 subjects into categories which we call the "most like" groups—i.e. there are 11 subjects who, though undiagnosed, were "most like" sufferers from affective disorder; 3 who were "most like" alcoholics; and 6 whose symptoms seemed to fit most closely with one or another of the criteria for diagnoses in the miscellaneous group (3 "most like" organic brain syndrome, 2 "most like" drug dependence, 1 "most like " schizophrenia). Once one considers the undiagnosed group from this vantage point (albeit an educated hypothesis), it follows that the numbers of subjects from each "most like" category may be added to those in the definite diagnostic groups. The resulting change in percentages (see Table 7.1) probably presents a clearer (if not more provable) picture of the true distribution of diagnoses among the total sample. In other studies, investigators have made similar efforts to deal meaningfully with psychiatrically undiagnosed subjects. An approach that is often used is to apply to the undiagnosed number the distribution of definite diagnoses within the sample. I analyzed the known symptoms to reach the above described "most like" system in an attempt to calculate percentages that would be based more firmly on the actual histories. To at least some extent, I believe this "most like" system succeeded. For example, if I had arbitrarily applied the percentage of definitely diagnosed alcoholics (25% of the total sample) to the number of undiagnosed subjects, there would have been five psychiatrically undiagnosed probable alcoholic subjects. In contrast, when I reviewed the case histories in detail, there were only three subjects in whom any clear alcoholic symptoms were reported by informants.

There follow the case histories of the 20 psychiatrically undiagnosed subjects. They are presented in their "most like" categories.

REFERENCES

1. Robins, E. and Murphy, G.E. Some clinical considerations in the prevention of suicide based on study of 134 successful suicides. *Amer. J. Public Health* 49:888–899, 1959.
2. Welner, A., Liss, J.L. and Robins, E. Undiagnosed psychiatric patients, part III: The undiagnosable patient. *Brit. J. Psychiat.*, 129:91–98, 1973.
3. Welner, A., Liss, J.L. and Robins, E. A systematic approach for making a psychiatric diagnosis. *Arch. Gen. Psychiat.* 31:193–196, 1974.
4. Robins, E. Categories versus dimensions in psychiatric classification. *Psychiatric Annals* 6:368–374, 1976.
5. Robins, E. New concepts in the diagnosis of psychiatric disorders. *Ann. Rev. Med.* 28:67–73, 1977.

PSYCHIATRICALLY UNDIAGNOSED, SUBGROUP 1

"Most Like" Affective Disorder (8 men, 3 women)

005 Informants: Brother, physician

This 37-year-old white handyman suffered from life-long idiopathic epilepsy. He was sheltered by his family because of the epilepsy and was self-conscious because of the illness. His brother joined the army when the subject was 23, which apparently caused him to have marked feelings of worthlessness about which he spoke at length. During the next 13 years he had had more than ten different odd jobs. He had difficulty holding them and on at least two occasions was fired because of his convulsive seizures. About a year prior to death he became depressed and undertalkative, remaining silent for long periods of time even though his family tried to talk with him. At that time he showed interest in a woman for the first time in his life. She, however, refused to go out with him and returned the gifts he sent her, which seemed to make him more moody and depressed than the family had ever seen him. During this period he began to talk about wanting to die and committing suicide. He said he and his mother would be better off if he were dead. He became increasingly irritable and spiteful and stopped doing his usual chores around the house. He wanted a car, but his parents refused him one because of his epilepsy. This refusal made him even more sullen and irritable. He became disgusted with himself and spoke of his worthlessness. His brother felt that at least some of his behavior was an attention-getting device. He had always drunk one or two beers a day, and in the six months prior to his death the amount of his drinking increased. The family did not feel, however, that his drinking was excessive.

Two weeks prior to his suicide he was rebuked by his employer because of his unwanted attentions to the woman in whom he was interested. The rebuke upset him greatly and he quit his job as a gardener and took a job as a handyman. The family believed that his striving for this woman was his first real attempt at adult life and he could not cope with his failure.

On the day of his suicide he invited his immediate family to a barbecue and picnic at his parents' home for which he made all the preparations. That evening, after having five or six beers, he went upstairs to the bathroom. In about 15 minutes he called his brother, who found him vomiting. He told his brother he had taken poison (crabgrass killer) because he had nothing to live for. On the way to the hospital, where he died a short time later, he implied to his brother that he regretted the attempt on his life. The informant believed that his failure with the woman in whom he was interested and his frustration in not being allowed a car were contributing factors to his suicide.

Family history: Maternal uncle committed suicide (by shooting) 15 years previously. The informant stated that the mother had an involutional depression (no details remembered) approximately 20 years previously from which she recovered.
Arrest record: None

UNDIAGNOSED PSYCHIATRIC ILLNESS: Most Like Major Affective Disorder

Case No. *005* M _X_ F __ Age *37*

ST. LOUIS SUICIDE STUDY CRITERIA FOR MAJOR AFFECTIVE DISORDER

Diagnosis required four of the six following categories, A-F. Category G was helpful in diagnosis, but not necessary.

A. Clinically well, exclusive of attacks of major affective disorder ___

B. Previous episode(s) of major affective disorder _X_

C. Discreteness (and duration) of final attack:
   6 months or less ___
   12 months or less _X_

D. "Medical" symptoms:
   insomnia ___
   anorexia ___
   weight loss ___
   low energy, weakness ___
   fatigue ___
   constipation ___

E. Psychological symptoms:
   "blue" feeling, depression, sadness _X_
   diminished motor activity ___
   loss of interest ___
   diminished sexual interest and activity ___
   undertalkativeness _X_
   low expectancy of recovery; expectation of "black" future ___
   feeling of being a burden ___
   indecisiveness ___
   feelings of worthlessness or guilt _X_
   agitation ___
   personal untidiness ___
   difficulty in thinking and concentration ___
   delusions ___

F. Disturbances in social behavior: decreased social and recreational activity ___

G. Miscellaneous items:
   age of onset 40 and over ___
   family history of affective disorder _X_

Failed to meet criteria for diagnosis _X_

FEIGHNER CRITERIA FOR UNDIAGNOSED PSYCHIATRIC ILLNESS

Some patients cannot receive a diagnosis for one or more reasons. Among the more common problems that cause a patient to be considered undiagnosed are the following.

A. Cases in which only one illness is suspected but symptoms are minimal $\underline{X}$

B. Cases in which more than one psychiatric illness is suspected but symptoms are not sufficient to meet the criteria of any of the possibilities ___

C. Cases in which symptoms suggest two or more disorders but in an atypical or confusing manner ___

D. Cases in which the chronology of important symptom clusters cannot be determined ___

E. Cases in which it is impossible to obtain the necessary history to establish a definitive diagnosis ___

032 Informants: Niece, brother, friends, physician, hospital record

This 85-year-old white retired farmer was his usual cheerful and jovial self until approximately three years prior to his death. At that time his sister with whom he lived (he had never married) had suffered a stroke and had become increasingly incapacitated. After his retirement and before his sister's illness, he had tended to most of the outside work while his sister did the inside work. He had also had a relatively active social life outside his home. His sister's illness, which ended in senility, marked motor disability, and deafness, changed the pattern of his life. He took a major responsibility in caring for her, giving up his outside activities.

He and his sister then began having bitter arguments. They argued because she and the remainder of his family wanted him to sell the property and come live with them, because she nagged him, and because she complained about his excessive generosity. It was of interest that after his death very few of his personal possessions were found in the house, and the informants assumed that he had given many of them away.

A little more than one year before his death he became more depressed in marked contrast to his usual good humor. After arguments with his sister, he had frequently threatened to commit suicide, and stated that he would be better off dead. On at least one occasion, he had told his neighbor that he wanted his sister to suffer and to see what it would be like to live without him. At other times he had wondered with foreboding what his future would be like if his sister died before him. His depression and irritability appeared to increase steadily with time. Eleven days before his death he told his neighbors he was going to commit suicide. To dissuade him, they told him they were leaving for a week and that he shouldn't do anything like that while they were away. On the eighth day after this conversation he swallowed a small amount of rat poison which contained phosphorus. It had no effect except to cause epigastric burning. He reiterated his intention to commit suicide, however, and one day later he took a larger amount of the same poison. Within two days he developed jaundice and anuria and died the following day.

Family history: There was no family history of psychiatric illness.
Arrest record: None.

UNDIAGNOSED PSYCHIATRIC ILLNESS: Most Like Major Affective Disorder
Case No. *032* M X F __ Age *85*

ST. LOUIS SUICIDE STUDY CRITERIA FOR MAJOR AFFECTIVE DISORDER

Diagnosis required four of the six following categories, A–F. Category G was helpful in diagnosis, but not necessary.

A. Clinically well, exclusive of attacks of major affective disorder X
B. Previous episode(s) of major affective disorder __
C. Discreteness (and duration) of final attack:
   6 months or less __
   12 months or less __
D. "Medical" symptoms:
   insomnia __
   anorexia __
   weight loss __
   low energy, weakness __
   fatigue __
   constipation __
E. Psychological symptoms:
   "blue" feeling, depression, sadness X
   diminished motor activity __
   loss of interest __
   diminished sexual interest and activity __
   undertalkativeness __
   low expectancy of recovery; expectation of "black" future __
   feeling of being a burden __
   indecisiveness __
   feelings of worthlessness or guilt __
   agitation __
   personal untidiness __
   difficulty in thinking and concentration __
   delusions __
F. Disturbances in social behavior: decreased social and recreational activity X
G. Miscellaneous items:
   age of onset 40 and over X
   family history of affective disorder __

Failed to meet criteria for diagnosis X

FEIGHNER CRITERIA FOR UNDIAGNOSED PSYCHIATRIC ILLNESS

Some patients cannot receive a diagnosis for one or more reasons. Among the more common problems that cause a patient to be considered undiagnosed are the following.

A. Cases in which only one illness is suspected but symptoms are minimal __X__

B. Cases in which more than one psychiatric illness is suspected but symptoms are not sufficient to meet the criteria of any of the possibilities ____

C. Cases in which symptoms suggest two or more disorders but in an atypical or confusing manner ____

D. Cases in which the chronology of important symptom clusters cannot be determined ____

E. Cases in which it is impossible to obtain the necessary history to establish a definitive diagnosis __X__

036 Informants: Hotel manager, physician (no adequate primary interview)

This 82-year-old white retired Western Union mechanic had lived alone in a hotel for several years prior to his retirement at age 79. He had never married. He was described as being extremely "introverted," keeping to himself and rarely speaking to anyone. The hotel manager was struck by the unusualness of his extremely withdrawn behavior, recalling that "he lived for himself and within himself." The only exception to his withdrawn behavior took place during the last few weeks of his life when he had occasionally told the manager that he feared he had cancer.

There was no information concerning symptoms or life stresses except that furnished by a physician whom he visited a few days prior to his death. The physician stated that the patient complained of severe chest pain, had a cancer phobia, and was very depressed, although the physician did not attempt to elicit the usual symptoms of depression. The doctor did attempt to reassure him concerning his fear of cancer. A few days later the hotel manager and clerk noticed that he was agitated and nervous. He spent the whole day running up to his room and down to the lobby and back again. Late that afternoon he returned to his room, spread newspapers over the floor, lay down on them, and shot himself through the head. He left a note saying he could not stand the pain.

Family history: There was no family history of psychiatric illness.
Arrest record: None.

UNDIAGNOSED PSYCHIATRIC ILLNESS: Most Like Major Affective Disorder

Case No. *036* M _X_ F ___ Age *82*

ST. LOUIS SUICIDE STUDY CRITERIA FOR MAJOR AFFECTIVE DISORDER

Diagnosis required four of the six following categories, A–F. Category G was helpful in diagnosis, but not necessary.

- A. Clinically well, exclusive of attacks of major affective disorder _X_
- B. Previous episode(s) of major affective disorder ___
- C. Discreteness (and duration) of final attack:
  - 6 months or less ___
  - 12 months or less ___
- D. "Medical" symptoms:
  - insomnia ___
  - anorexia ___
  - weight loss ___
  - low energy, weakness fatigue ___
  - constipation ___
- E. Psychological symptoms:
  - "blue" feeling, depression, sadness _X_
  - diminished motor activity ___
  - loss of interest ___
  - diminished sexual interest and activity ___
  - undertalkativeness ___
  - low expectancy of recovery; expectation of "black" future _X_
  - feeling of being a burden ___
  - indecisiveness ___
  - feelings of worthlessness or guilt ___
  - agitation _X_
  - personal untidiness ___
  - difficulty in thinking and concentration ___
  - delusions _X_
- F. Disturbances in social behavior: decreased social and recreational activity _X_
- G. Miscellaneous items:
  - age of onset 40 and over _X_
  - family history of affective disorder ___

Failed to meet criteria for diagnosis _X_

FEIGHNER CRITERIA FOR UNDIAGNOSED PSYCHIATRIC ILLNESS

Some patients cannot receive a diagnosis for one or more reasons. Among the more common problems that cause a patient to be considered undiagnosed are the following.

- A. Cases in which only one illness is suspected but symptoms are minimal ___
- B. Cases in which more than one psychiatric illness is suspected but symptoms are not sufficient to meet the criteria of any of the possibilities ___
- C. Cases in which symptoms suggest two or more disorders but in an atypical or confusing manner ___
- D. Cases in which the chronology of important symptom clusters cannot be determined ___
- E. Cases in which it is impossible to obtain the necessary history to establish a definitive diagnosis _X_

053 Informants: Friends, fellow workers; hospital and outpatient records.

A life-long bachelor, this 72-year-old white retired laborer had lived with his mother in a small town in Kentucky until she died 18 years before his death. After his mother's death, he moved to a town in Illinois and went to work for the railroad. He was described as a pleasant, somewhat shy man who never argued with anyone, never became angry, never talked about himself, and almost always wore a smile. Ten months prior to his death he slipped on ice and broke his hip. An open reduction was required after which he used crutches for a few months and later a cane. He had some pain in the affected region, which was lessening with time. However, about six weeks prior to his suicide, he was declared totally and permanently disabled. Shortly before, his physician had noted that he was morbidly despondent and his friends remembered that he had been withdrawn and uncommunicative.

One week prior to his death he came into St. Louis for an overnight check-up at the hospital. His physician's notes recorded improvement of his hip, but also mentioned his despondency and his belief that he would never be all right. Following his discharge from the hospital the next day, he failed to return to his home in Illinois. Six days later he was found dead in a park in St. Louis with his wrist and throat slashed. A razor blade was tucked into his hat band. He had been dead only a few hours before he was found.

Family history: There was no family history of psychiatric illness.
Arrest record: None.

UNDIAGNOSED PSYCHIATRIC ILLNESS: Most Like Major Affective Disorder

Case No. *053* M X F __ Age *22*

ST. LOUIS SUICIDE STUDY CRITERIA FOR MAJOR AFFECTIVE DISORDER

Diagnosis required four of the six following categories, A–F. Category G was helpful in diagnosis, but not necessary.

A. Clinically well, exclusive of attacks of major affective disorder ___
  diminished sexual interest and activity ___
  undertalkativeness X
  low expectancy of recovery; expectation of "black" future X

B. Previous episode(s) of major affective disorder ___
  feeling of being a burden ___
  indecisiveness ___

C. Discreteness (and duration) of final attack:
  6 months or less X
  12 months or less ___
  feelings of worthlessness or guilt ___
  agitation ___
  personal untidiness ___

D. "Medical" symptoms:
  insomnia ___
  anorexia ___
  weight loss ___
  low energy, weakness ___
  fatigue ___
  constipation ___
  difficulty in thinking and concentration ___
  delusions ___

F. Disturbances in social behavior: decreased social and recreational activity ___

E. Psychological symptoms:
  "blue" feeling, depression, sadness X
  diminished motor activity ___
  loss of interest ___

G. Miscellaneous items:
  age of onset 40 and over X
  family history of affective disorder ___

Failed to meet criteria for diagnosis X

FEIGHNER CRITERIA FOR UNDIAGNOSED PSYCHIATRIC ILLNESS

Some patients cannot receive a diagnosis for one or more reasons. Among the more common problems that cause a patient to be considered undiagnosed are the following.

A. Cases in which only one illness is suspected but symptoms are minimal ___

B. Cases in which more than one psychiatric illness is suspected but symptoms are not sufficient to meet the criteria of any of the possibilities ___

C. Cases in which symptoms suggest two or more disorders but in an atypical or confusing manner ___

D. Cases in which the chronology of important symptom clusters cannot be determined ___

E. Cases in which it is impossible to obtain the necessary history to establish a definitive diagnosis X

091   Informant: Brother-in-law (refusal by wife)

This 56-year-old white owner of a truck line was described as always having been hyperactive, "high-strung," and involved in many activities. He was successful in business, having held a high managerial position in a retail chain for some years. Approximately two years prior to his death he lost his job when the firm was sold. He was out of work for nine months and then obtained a job managing a department store in another city. Six months prior to his suicide he returned to St. Louis and, with a relative, opened a trucking firm. The business was unsuccessful and, in the six-month period, he and his relative lost $150,000. In the last few months of his life, after having lost so much money, he began to complain that he had been a failure his whole life, but his wife forbade any talk about his business failure around the house. In the last month of his life he began to suffer from slight fatigue and insomnia.

Two weeks prior to his death one of his best friends committed suicide. The informant believed that this event upset him greatly. For the first time, according to the informant, he became overtly depressed. On the morning of his suicide he called the informant and asked him to meet him at home that afternoon. The informant worried all that day that he might "do something to himself." When the informant came to the house, there was a note directing him to the garage where he found the subject's body, dead from carbon monoxide poisoning.

Family history: There was no family history of psychiatric illness.
Arrest record: None.

UNDIAGNOSED PSYCHIATRIC ILLNESS: Most Like Major Affective Disorder

Case No. _91_ M _X_ F ___ Age _56_

ST. LOUIS SUICIDE STUDY CRITERIA FOR MAJOR AFFECTIVE DISORDER

Diagnosis required four of the six following categories, A-F. Category G was helpful in diagnosis, but not necessary.

A. Clinically well, exclusive of attacks of major affective disorder _X_

B. Previous episode(s) of major affective disorder ___

C. Discreteness (and duration) of final attack:
   6 months or less ___
   12 months or less ___

D. "Medical" symptoms:
   insomnia _X_
   anorexia ___
   weight loss ___
   low energy, weakness fatigue _X_
   constipation ___

E. Psychological symptoms:
   "blue" feeling, depression, sadness _X_
   diminished motor activity ___
   loss of interest ___
   diminished sexual interest and activity ___
   undertalkativeness ___
   low expectancy of recovery; expectation of "black" future ___
   feeling of being a burden ___
   indecisiveness ___
   feelings of worthlessness or guilt _X_
   agitation ___
   personal untidiness ___
   difficulty in thinking and concentration ___
   delusions ___

F. Disturbances in social behavior: decreased social and recreational activity ___

G. Miscellaneous items:
   age of onset 40 and over _X_
   family history of affective disorder ___

Failed to meet criteria for diagnosis _X_

FEIGHNER CRITERIA FOR UNDIAGNOSED PSYCHIATRIC ILLNESS

Some patients cannot receive a diagnosis for one or more reasons. Among the more common problems that cause a patient to be considered undiagnosed are the following.

A. Cases in which only one illness is suspected but symptoms are minimal _X_

B. Cases in which more than one psychiatric illness is suspected but symptoms are not sufficient to meet the criteria of any of the possibilities ___

C. Cases in which symptoms suggest two or more disorders but in an atypical or confusing manner ___

D. Cases in which the chronology of important symptom clusters cannot be determined ___

E. Cases in which it is impossible to obtain the necessary history to establish a definitive diagnosis ___

096 Informants: Daughter, police records (murder + suicide)

This 58-year-old white retired milk-truck driver was first married at age 19 and divorced within a year. At age 20, he married his second wife. Theirs had apparently been a stormy marriage with a great deal of bickering because of his wife's objection to his daily excessive drinking. The informant, however, gave no further definite evidences of alcoholism. At age 35, the subject had hit his wife and broken her nose. She had called the police and he was arrested and fined for disturbing the peace. His job history, until age 46, was a poor one, with frequent job changes and without any advancement. However, from age 46 until his retirement two years before his death he had worked for one company as a milk-truck driver. During this period his relationship with his wife continued to worsen. He apparently was repeatedly unfaithful and three years before his death, he and his wife consulted a priest about their marital problems. These consultations had no effect and 18 months later they were divorced. In the divorce settlement his wife received most of the family money and he planned to live on some personal savings and on income from a small piece of property.

After the divorce, his wife moved to Florida, and a few months later it became evident that he could not live on his income and savings. He made it known then that he wanted to remarry his ex-wife, and his daughter, the informant, was uncertain whether love or money was behind this wish. His wife did not want him back but agreed to see him in Florida. He went there and asked her to marry him. Although she refused his proposal to remarry, they returned together to St. Louis and lived in their daughter's home, but not as man and wife despite the daughter's continual efforts to bring about a reconciliation between them.

During the last nine months of his life he became nervous, moody, irritable, and depressed. He spoke to both his tavern buddies and his ex-wife about committing suicide. He developed insomnia and anxiety attacks. He had reluctantly returned to work, but he was unhappy because going back to work had hurt his pride. His ex-wife became increasingly vexed over living in the same house with him and finally decided to leave. This decision enraged him and he hit his wife. He then got a gun and went to the living room where he shot and killed her. When he returned to the bedroom to hunt for more bullets, his daughter tried to stop him but he shoved her out of the room. In the meantime, his son-in-law had called the police. When they arrived and started toward his bedroom, he shot himself just as they reached his door. He died 45 minutes later at the hospital.

Family history: Father was a chronic alcoholic. One daughter was institutionalized as a child and has remained institutionalized. Her diagnosis is not known.

Arrest history: At age 35, peace disturbance, described above. At ages 40 and 51, moving traffic offenses.

UNDIAGNOSED PSYCHIATRIC ILLNESS: Most Like Major Affective Disorder

Case No. 096 M X F __ Age 58

ST. LOUIS SUICIDE STUDY CRITERIA FOR MAJOR AFFECTIVE DISORDER

Diagnosis required four of the six following categories, A-F. Category G was helpful in diagnosis, but not necessary.

A. Clinically well, exclusive of attacks of major affective disorder ___

B. Previous episode(s) of major affective disorder ___

C. Discreteness (and duration) of final attack:
   6 months or less ___
   12 months or less X

D. "Medical" symptoms:
   insomnia X
   anorexia ___
   weight loss ___
   low energy, weakness fatigue ___
   constipation ___

E. Psychological symptoms:
   "blue" feeling, depression, sadness X
   diminished motor activity ___
   loss of interest ___
   diminished sexual interest and activity ___
   undertalkativeness ___
   low expectancy of recovery; expectation of "black" future ___
   feeling of being a burden ___
   indecisiveness ___
   feelings of worthlessness or guilt ___
   agitation ___
   personal untidiness ___
   difficulty in thinking and concentration ___
   delusions ___

F. Disturbances in social behavior: decreased social and recreational activity ___

G. Miscellaneous items:
   age of onset 40 and over ___
   family history of affective disorder ___

Failed to meet criteria for diagnosis X

FEIGHNER CRITERIA FOR UNDIAGNOSED PSYCHIATRIC ILLNESS

Some patients cannot receive a diagnosis for one or more reasons. Among the more common problems that cause a patient to be considered undiagnosed are the following.

A. Cases in which only one illness is suspected but symptoms are minimal ___

B. Cases in which more than one psychiatric illness is suspected but symptoms are not sufficient to meet the criteria of any of the possibilities X

C. Cases in which symptoms suggest two or more disorders but in an atypical or confusing manner ___

D. Cases in which the chronology of important symptom clusters cannot be determined ___

E. Cases in which it is impossible to obtain the necessary history to establish a definitive diagnosis X

101 Informant: Wife

Although this 58-year-old white printer who owned his own printing company had been having business difficulties for about five years, there was no change in his standard of living and no large debts. When he was in his mid and late forties, he had frequently said that he would not be around at 50. However, once he reached 50, he stopped talking about not being around.

Two years prior to his death, his son found him in his garage with the doors closed and his car's motor running. The son dragged him out of the garage. When the informant was asked about this episode, she said she had never discussed it with her husband because she knew it would have embarrassed him. She answered "I don't know" to most of the questions concerning her husband's recent symptoms, and, while she admitted he had had insomnia for the past few months, she denied knowledge of many other symptoms. Whether this was evasion on the part of the informant could not be determined.

On the morning of his suicide, the subject rose, dressed, went to his car, and found it had three flat tires. He drove to a large municipal park and hooked a hose from the exhaust to the inside of his closed car in which he died of carbon monoxide poisoning.

Family history: There was no family history of psychiatric illness.
Arrest record: None.

UNDIAGNOSED PSYCHIATRIC ILLNESS: Most Like Major Affective Disorder

Case No. 101 M X F __ Age 58

ST. LOUIS SUICIDE STUDY CRITERIA FOR MAJOR AFFECTIVE DISORDER

Diagnosis required four of the six following categories, A–F. Category G was helpful in diagnosis, but not necessary.

A. Clinically well, exclusive of attacks of major affective disorder ___

B. Previous episode(s) of major affective disorder ___

C. Discreteness (and duration) of final attack:
   6 months or less ___
   12 months or less ___

D. "Medical" symptoms:
   insomnia   X
   anorexia ___
   weight loss ___
   low energy, weakness ___
   fatigue ___
   constipation ___

E. Psychological symptoms:
   "blue" feeling, depression, sadness ___
   diminished motor activity ___
   loss of interest ___
   diminished sexual interest and activity ___
   undertalkativeness ___
   low expectancy of recovery; expectation of "black" future ___
   feeling of being a burden ___
   indecisiveness ___
   feelings of worthlessness or guilt ___
   agitation ___
   personal untidiness ___
   difficulty in thinking and concentration ___
   delusions ___

F. Disturbances in social behavior: decreased social and recreational activity ___

G. Miscellaneous items:
   age of onset 40 and over   X
   family history of affective disorder ___

Failed to meet criteria for diagnosis X

FEIGHNER CRITERIA FOR UNDIAGNOSED PSYCHIATRIC ILLNESS

Some patients cannot receive a diagnosis for one or more reasons. Among the more common problems that cause a patient to be considered undiagnosed are the following.

A. Cases in which only one illness is suspected but symptoms are minimal   X

B. Cases in which more than one psychiatric illness is suspected but symptoms are not sufficient to meet the criteria of any of the possibilities ___

C. Cases in which symptoms suggest two or more disorders but in an atypical or confusing manner ___

D. Cases in which the chronology of important symptom clusters cannot be determined ___

E. Cases in which it is impossible to obtain the necessary history to establish a definitive diagnosis   X

116   Informants: Sister, employer

This 45-year-old white butcher completed two years of college and then quit for unknown reasons. He went immediately to work in the butcher shop where he was employed until his death. His employer, who was aware of his college training and of his native intelligence, never understood why he remained as a salaried butcher. In the last eight years of his life, he had missed only one day of work. He refused to take a vacation and had not had one in the 11 years the informant had owned the butcher shop. A teetotaler, his only recreations were a package of cigarettes each Saturday and two movies a week. He never dated and, though he lived with his sister and brother-in-law, he was a solitary person who did not socialize even with his family. His sister believed that he felt neglected. He was described as being a helpful, considerate man who made a habit of going out of his way to help others, but who refused to accept favors of any kind. Always obliging, he had never been known to become angry or to have raised his voice.

Despite his obliging nature, however, he did not get along with his brother-in-law, though neither informant made clear what the difficulty was. He refused all kinds of social invitations. His employer offered, as an example, the fact that he could never get him to go fishing. A man of very few words, he answered most questions with a "yes" or "no" as necessary. His employer was struck by the fact that he never smiled, that he never told or listened to jokes, and that he always looked slightly depressed. Over the years there were on a few occasions periods of days when he appeared more depressed and taciturn than usual. However, in the months that preceded his death, he did not seem to have had one of these spells.

His work was considered satisfactory by his employer except that, in the last few months of his life, he had begun to favor certain of the elderly female customers by selling them meat at reduced prices. When his employer confronted him with this fact, he "broke down" and seemed on the verge of tears. He said he had done it because the women badgered him about the high prices. His employer was surprised by his explanation because he had usually been indecisive and had rarely acted independently. On the day of his suicide, his employer had noticed that he was lax in setting out the meats and in keeping the butcher's table clean. Other than that, his employer noted nothing amiss. That afternoon he went into the bathroom of the shop and shot himself through the roof of the mouth.

Family history: There was no family history of psychiatric illness.
Arrest record: At age 26 for speeding.

UNDIAGNOSED PSYCHIATRIC ILLNESS: Most Like Major Affective Disorder

Case No. *116* M _X_ F __ Age *45*

ST. LOUIS SUICIDE STUDY CRITERIA FOR MAJOR AFFECTIVE DISORDER

Diagnosis required four of the six following categories, A-F. Category G was helpful in diagnosis, but not necessary.

A. Clinically well, exclusive of attacks of major affective disorder ___

B. Previous episode(s) of major affective disorder ___

C. Discreteness (and duration) of final attack:
    6 months or less ___
    12 months or less ___

D. "Medical" symptoms:
    insomnia ___
    anorexia ___
    weight loss ___
    low energy, weakness ___
    fatigue
    constipation ___

E. Psychological symptoms:
    "blue" feeling, depression, sadness ___
    diminished motor activity ___
    loss of interest ___
    diminished sexual interest and activity ___
    undertalkativeness _X_
    low expectancy of recovery; expectation of "black" future ___
    feeling of being a burden ___
    indecisiveness ___
    feelings of worthlessness or guilt ___
    agitation ___
    personal untidiness ___
    difficulty in thinking and concentration ___
    delusions ___

F. Disturbances in social behavior: decreased social and recreational activity ___

G. Miscellaneous items:
    age of onset 40 and over ___
    family history of affective disorder ___

Failed to meet criteria for diagnosis _X_

FEIGHNER CRITERIA FOR UNDIAGNOSED PSYCHIATRIC ILLNESS

Some patients cannot receive a diagnosis for one or more reasons. Among the more common problems that cause a patient to be considered undiagnosed are the following.

A. Cases in which only one illness is suspected but symptoms are minimal _X_

B. Cases in which more than one psychiatric illness is suspected but symptoms are not sufficient to meet the criteria of any of the possibilities ___

C. Cases in which symptoms suggest two or more disorders but in an atypical or confusing manner ___

D. Cases in which the chronology of important symptom clusters cannot be determined ___

E. Cases in which it is impossible to obtain the necessary history to establish a definitive diagnosis _X_

009   Informants: Husband, physician

This 58-year-old white farmer's wife had, according to her husband, given no indication of suicide, either by talking about it or by a change in her behavior. She did, however, go to her physician for "nerves" (not further described by the husband) six months prior to her suicide. At that time the physician noted some weight loss. She also had feelings of inferiority, never looked at the physician, and found it difficult to talk to him. The husband stated that at this time she spoke of wanting to die before or with her husband (who was not ill) so that she would not be left alone. She also had a fear of cancer, which was not completely dispelled by a negative cervical biopsy. The only other abnormality noted by the husband was that her hands shook. Neither the husband nor her physician noted insomnia, depression, or other symptoms. When she went to her physician three months prior to her suicide, she had regained most of her lost weight and he felt that she seemed much better. At about that time her sister had a "nervous breakdown" and was committed to a mental hospital. The husband did not believe this upset her unduly, but he did comment that his wife expressed some fear that some day she might have a "nervous breakdown." During this entire time she continued to perform her usual household duties without any impairment in her efficiency.

Three and one half years previously, she had gone to the same physician complaining of weight loss, constipation, and abdominal cramping. No medical or surgical disease was found to explain these symptoms. About 15 months before her suicide, she again went to her physician complaining of headaches.

On the day of her suicide, she awoke at the usual hour of 5:30 AM, put coffee on for her husband, and woke him. They had breakfast and he went to milk the cows. On returning some minutes later, he found the house tidied, the bed made, and the crock put out for the milk. The basement door was ajar. He called her in the basement and, receiving no answer, went to his son's house for a few minutes. He returned home shortly to tell his wife goodbye before starting to work. Again receiving no answer, he went into the basement and found that his wife had hanged herself.

Family history: Sister had a "nervous breakdown" requiring mental hospitalization three months previously. (A brother-in-law had committed suicide three years previously.)
Arrest history: None.

UNDIAGNOSED PSYCHIATRIC ILLNESS: Most Like Major Affective Disorder

Case No. <u>009</u> M___ F <u>X</u> Age <u>58</u>

ST. LOUIS SUICIDE STUDY CRITERIA FOR MAJOR AFFECTIVE DISORDER

Diagnosis required four of the six following categories, A-F. Category G was helpful in diagnosis, but not necessary.

- A. Clinically well, exclusive of attacks of major affective disorder   X
- B. Previous episode(s) of major affective disorder   ___
- C. Discreteness (and duration) of final attack:
  - 6 months or less   X
  - 12 months or less   ___
- D. "Medical" symptoms:
  - insomnia   ___
  - anorexia   ___
  - weight loss   ___
  - low energy, weakness   ___
  - fatigue   ___
  - constipation   ___
- E. Psychological symptoms:
  - "blue" feeling, depression, sadness   ___
  - diminished motor activity   ___
  - loss of interest   ___
  - diminished sexual interest and activity   ___
  - undertalkativeness   ___
  - low expectancy of recovery; expectation of "black" future   ___
  - feeling of being a burden   ___
  - indecisiveness   ___
  - feelings of worthlessness or guilt   ___
  - agitation   ___
  - personal untidiness   ___
  - difficulty in thinking and concentration   ___
  - delusions   ___
- F. Disturbances in social behavior: decreased social and recreational activity   ___
- G. Miscellaneous items:
  - age of onset 40 and over   X
  - family history of affective disorder   X

Failed to meet criteria for diagnosis X

FEIGHNER CRITERIA FOR UNDIAGNOSED PSYCHIATRIC ILLNESS

Some patients cannot receive a diagnosis for one or more reasons. Among the more common problems that cause a patient to be considered undiagnosed are the following.

- A. Cases in which only one illness is suspected but symptoms are minimal   X
- B. Cases in which more than one psychiatric illness is suspected but symptoms are not sufficient to meet the criteria of any of the possibilities   ___
- C. Cases in which symptoms suggest two or more disorders but in an atypical or confusing manner   ___
- D. Cases in which the chronology of important symptom clusters cannot be determined   ___
- E. Cases in which it is impossible to obtain the necessary history to establish a definitive diagnosis   ___

041 Informants: Mother-in-law of subject's sister, physician (refusal by husband)

This 41-year-old white housewife collapsed in the street two years prior to her death. When taken to a physician's office it became evident she was having a miscarriage. She became pregnant again nine months prior to her suicide. She was observed to behave unusually in that she refused to divulge her expected date of confinement. A few weeks before her suicide her physician recommended that she see a psychiatrist. It was not possible to interview this physician in order to find out exactly why this recommendation was made. Another physician commented that she was despondent about having to live with her mother-in-law. Her husband had said he could not afford to keep up an extra household for his mother.

One week prior to her death she delivered a premature infant who lived only a few minutes. The delivery was at home and a physician was not called until after the baby died. She felt guilty about the baby's death and blamed herself for it. One week after the baby's death, having carefully placed her insurance policy on top of her dresser, she shot herself.

Family history: One sister was in a state mental hospital. She was described as having had a "nervous breakdown" characterized by being "moody, nervous, unstable, and looking as though she was carrying the weight of the world on her shoulders."

Arrest record: None.

UNDIAGNOSED PSYCHIATRIC ILLNESS: Most Like Major Affective Disorder

Case No. 041 M___ F X Age 41

ST. LOUIS SUICIDE STUDY CRITERIA FOR MAJOR AFFECTIVE DISORDER

Diagnosis required four of the six following categories, A-F. Category G was helpful in diagnosis, but not necessary.

- A. Clinically well, exclusive of attacks of major affective disorder ___
- B. Previous episode(s) of major affective disorder ___
- C. Discreteness (and duration) of final attack:
  - 6 months or less ___
  - 12 months or less X
- D. "Medical" symptoms:
  - insomnia ___
  - anorexia ___
  - weight loss ___
  - low energy, weakness ___
  - fatigue ___
  - constipation ___
- E. Psychological symptoms:
  - "blue" feeling, depression, sadness ___
  - diminished motor activity ___
  - loss of interest ___
  - diminished sexual interest and activity ___
  - undertalkativeness ___
  - low expectancy of recovery; expectation of "black" future ___
  - feeling of being a burden ___
  - indecisiveness ___
  - feelings of worthlessness or guilt X
  - agitation ___
  - personal untidiness ___
  - difficulty in thinking and concentration ___
  - delusions ___
- F. Disturbances in social behavior: decreased social and recreational activity ___
- G. Miscellaneous items:
  - age of onset 40 and over X
  - family history of affective disorder X

Failed to meet criteria for diagnosis X

FEIGHNER CRITERIA FOR UNDIAGNOSED PSYCHIATRIC ILLNESS

Some patients cannot receive a diagnosis for one or more reasons. Among the more common problems that cause a patient to be considered undiagnosed are the following.

- A. Cases in which only one illness is suspected but symptoms are minimal X
- B. Cases in which more than one psychiatric illness is suspected but symptoms are not sufficient to meet the criteria of any of the possibilities ___
- C. Cases in which symptoms suggest two or more disorders but in an atypical or confusing manner ___
- D. Cases in which the chronology of important symptom clusters cannot be determined ___
- E. Cases in which it is impossible to obtain the necessary history to establish a definitive diagnosis X

120 Informants: Physician, attorney (refusal by daughter)

This 80-year-old white widowed woman had, several years previously, made a suicide attempt or had stated she was going to commit suicide. The informants knew no details of the earlier circumstances or of her symptoms at the time. Approximately one month before her death, she had injured her head in a revolving door. Although it was a minor injury, it had made her nervous, and she had called the doctor frequently, obviously upset. Following the accident, she had repeatedly told her daughter she wanted to or needed to go to a hospital. She hanged herself while alone at home two weeks after the accident.

Family history: Unknown whether there was a family history of psychiatric illness.
Arrest record: None.

UNDIAGNOSED PSYCHIATRIC ILLNESS: Most Like Major Affective Disorder

Case No. 120 M___ F X Age 80

ST. LOUIS SUICIDE STUDY CRITERIA FOR MAJOR AFFECTIVE DISORDER

Diagnosis required four of the six following categories, A–F. Category G was helpful in diagnosis, but not necessary.

- A. Clinically well, exclusive of attacks of major affective disorder ___
- B. Previous episode(s) of major affective disorder ___
- C. Discreteness (and duration) of final attack:
  - 6 months or less X
  - 12 months or less ___
- D. "Medical" symptoms:
  - insomnia ___
  - anorexia ___
  - weight loss ___
  - low energy, weakness ___
  - fatigue ___
  - constipation ___
- E. Psychological symptoms:
  - "blue" feeling, depression, sadness ___
  - diminished motor activity ___
  - loss of interest ___
  - diminished sexual interest and activity ___
  - undertalkativeness ___
  - low expectancy of recovery; expectation of "black" future ___
  - feeling of being a burden ___
  - indecisiveness X
  - feelings of worthlessness or guilt ___
  - agitation X
  - personal untidiness ___
  - difficulty in thinking and concentration ___
  - delusions ___
- F. Disturbances in social behavior: decreased social and recreational activity ___
- G. Miscellaneous items:
  - age of onset 40 and over ___
  - family history of affective disorder ___

Failed to meet criteria for diagnosis X

FEIGHNER CRITERIA FOR UNDIAGNOSED PSYCHIATRIC ILLNESS

Some patients cannot receive a diagnosis for one or more reasons. Among the more common problems that cause a patient to be considered undiagnosed are the following.

- A. Cases in which only one illness is suspected but symptoms are minimal ___
- B. Cases in which more than one psychiatric illness is suspected but symptoms are not sufficient to meet the criteria of any of the possibilities ___
- C. Cases in which symptoms suggest two or more disorders but in an atypical or confusing manner ___
- D. Cases in which the chronology of important symptom clusters cannot be determined ___
- E. Cases in which it is impossible to obtain the necessary history to establish a definitive diagnosis X

PSYCHIATRICALLY UNDIAGNOSED, SUBGROUP 2

"Most Like" Alcoholism (3 men)

024 Informants: Wife, friend, 2 physicians, employer; hospital, police, and social service records

This 35-year-old white metal-finisher, temporarily unemployed, was raised by his mother who had divorced when the subject was four years old. He married at age 20. His wife, the primary informant, believed that her husband's death was not a suicide and that he may have been murdered. Perhaps as a result of this belief, her interview was full of misleading answers and of omissions (contradictions between her answers and information obtained elsewhere are outlined below).

At age 26, the subject was admitted as a prisoner to a general hospital where diagnoses of alcoholism and contusion of the scalp were made. At age 28, he was admitted to a general hospital with complaints of epigastric burning and of belching. No diagnosis was made; peptic ulcer was not found. At age 32, he was hospitalized because of back pain. At this time, a diagnosis of sacroiliac strain, (?) ruptured intervertebral disc, was made. His wife, who mentioned the two latter hospitalizations, but not the first one, noted that he had suffered from back and joint pain during the last year of his life. She denied that she objected to his drinking, although she stated that he had gone on "benders" recurrently. His employer, however, stated that he had marked unexplained absenteeism during the last five months of his life, missing a total of almost 90 days. On the few occasions when he presented a medical excuse, his physician provided notes stating he was suffering from severe vomiting and gastritis. He was laid off from work because of a slack period during the last seven weeks of his life. His wife stated that during this time he had no symptoms except recurrent headaches. She said that he was more "domestic" than ever and became interested in household affairs. During the same period he was treated for acute gonococcal urethritis by a physician and the police discovered after his death that he had also had a mistress who was pregnant with his child. His wife did not mention any of these events. She stated that she had observed no change in his behavior.

For years, whenever he had felt aggravated he had said, "I feel like jumping off the bridge," but just before his suicide he had not made this statement. The morning of his suicide he told his wife he was going to look for a job. The next morning he was found dead in his car just off a lonely country road. He had shot himself in the lower abdomen with his own gun.

It was the coroner's physician's opinion that it had probably taken him hours to die. The unreliability of the wife's responses during the interview was shown by her insistence that he had never been absent from his job, by her history of his alcoholic intake, and by her failure to mention his arrest at age 26. Whether the omissions on her interview regarding his mistress and his behavior were efforts to "cover up" or whether they were due to unawareness on her part is not known.

Family history: There was no family history of psychiatric illness.
Arrest history: At age 26, drinking and peace disturbance. Ages 32 and 35 for moving traffic violation.

UNDIAGNOSED PSYCHIATRIC ILLNESS: Most Like Alcoholism

Case No. 024 M X F __ Age 35

ST. LOUIS SUICIDE STUDY CRITERIA FOR ALCOHOLISM

At least three of the following selected drinking behaviors were required for diagnosis.

A. Informant thought subject drank too much __
B. Subject drank daily __
C. Subject went on benders (at least 48 hours of drinking and neglect of usual routine) X
D. Family objected to subject's drinking __
E. Subject's history included arrests related to drinking X
F. Subject suffered medical and psychiatric complications due to alcoholic intake __
G. Subject thought he drank too much __
H. Subject had job difficulties related to drinking __
I. Subject involved in automobile accident(s) related to drinking __

Failed to meet criteria for diagnosis X

FEIGHNER CRITERIA FOR UNDIAGNOSED PSYCHIATRIC ILLNESS

Some patients cannot receive a diagnosis for one or more reasons. Among the more common problems that cause a patient to be considered undiagnosed are the following.

A. Cases in which only one illness is suspected but symptoms are minimal ___
B. Cases in which more than one psychiatric illness is suspected but symptoms are not sufficient to meet the criteria of any of the possibilities ___
C. Cases in which symptoms suggest two or more disorders but in an atypical or confusing manner __X__
D. Cases in which the chronology of important symptom clusters cannot be determined ___
E. Cases in which it is impossible to obtain the necessary history to establish a definitive diagnosis ___

084   Informants: Mother, mother-in-law, bartender and friend, physician (murder + suicide)

This 44-year-old white construction laborer had been a farmer until seven years before his death, when he left the farm for his present occupation. A year later he married for the first time and adopted his wife's two small children by a previous marriage. Once he was married, he worked irregularly, about half-time, and it was necessary for his wife to work to support the family. During the first five years of marriage he, his wife, his mother-in-law, and the two children lived in a one-room hovel where he lay around most of the day and complained of being sickly. Even when offered jobs, he usually complained of being too ill to work. His mother and mother-in-law described him as cheerful and not argumentative during this period. They said that he went out to a tavern and drank almost every night, but seldom got "plastered." They also said that he would never go out with his wife or children.

About a year prior to his death the family moved into somewhat better living quarters, but his behavior did not change. About eight months later his wife threw him out because, according to her mother, he would not work. According to *his* mother, she threw him out because she had a lover. At any rate, he went home to live with his mother and her new husband. He pleaded with his wife to take him back, and even promised to return to work, but his wife refused to have him back. One month prior to his death he met his wife outside her house and asked her again to take him back. When she refused and turned to take some groceries out of the car, he hit her over the head twice from behind with a board and, when she fell down, began to kick her. He was arrested and his case, on the charge of common assault, was to come to trial on the day of his suicide. In the meanwhile, his wife had filed for divorce.

On the morning of the day of his suicide, his mother went into his room at 6:30 AM to light a heater. He appeared to be sleeping soundly. Only a few minutes after that, someone knocked on the door of his wife's home. When she asked who was there, a gun was jammed through the screen and window and fired, killing her. The subject was found shot to death in his automobile a few hours later.

His mother-in-law believed he drank too much and she reported that his wife shared this belief. His physician, to whom he had spoken occasionally about his marital difficulties, also said he drank too much. His mother denied that he drank excessively. Neither of the informants who said he drank too much described any prolonged benders or medical or psychiatric complications of alcoholism and police records gave no evidence of arrests associated with drinking.

Family history: The subject had an alcoholic brother.
Arrest history: One arrest one month prior to his suicide for common assault, described above.

UNDIAGNOSED PSYCHIATRIC ILLNESS: Most Like Alcoholism

Case No. 084 M X F __ Age 44

ST. LOUIS SUICIDE STUDY CRITERIA FOR ALCOHOLISM

At least three of the following selected drinking behaviors were required for diagnosis.

A. Informant thought subject drank too much   X
B. Subject drank daily   __
C. Subject went on benders (at least 48 hours of drinking and neglect of usual routine)   __
D. Family objected to subject's drinking   __
E. Subject's history included arrests related to drinking .   __
F. Subject suffered medical and psychiatric complications due to alcoholic intake   __
G. Subject thought he drank too much   __
H. Subject had job difficulties related to drinking   __
I. Subject involved in automobile accident(s) related to drinking   __

Failed to meet criteria for diagnosis X

FEIGHNER CRITERIA FOR UNDIAGNOSED PSYCHIATRIC ILLNESS

Some patients cannot receive a diagnosis for one or more reasons. Among the more common problems that cause a patient to be considered undiagnosed are the following.

A. Cases in which only one illness is suspected but symptoms are minimal __X__

B. Cases in which more than one psychiatric illness is suspected but symptoms are not sufficient to meet the criteria of any of the possibilities ___

C. Cases in which symptoms suggest two or more disorders but in an atypical or confusing manner ___

D. Cases in which the chronology of important symptom clusters cannot be determined ___

E. Cases in which it is impossible to obtain the necessary history to establish a definitive diagnosis ___

106 Informant: Physician, hospital records (refusal by wife)

This 50-year-old white city-engineer first complained of abdominal pain and watery diarrhea nine months prior to his death. The symptoms were fairly severe and he had been frequently wakened during the night by cramping and diarrhea. On one occasion, frank blood was noted in his stool. Four months prior to his death, he was admitted to a general hospital were diagnoses of diverticulum of the second portion of the duodenum and of slight localized diverticulosis of the sigmoid were made. A moderate generalized spasticity of the entire colon was noted on radiological examination. He was treated with antacids and antispasmodics and put on a low calorie diet.

His symptoms, however, continued. During the next four months, he lost 12 pounds on his diet. His physician noted no symptoms of depression or insomnia. Because of continued symptoms, plans were made for him to re-enter the hospital where the possibility of colonic resection with a temporary colostomy was to be considered. His physician observed that he appeared to be stable and not nervous, although he seemed unduly concerned that he might have a carcinoma of the large bowel and worried about needing a permanent colostomy. The negative x-ray findings (for carcinoma) four months previously had failed to reassure him. On the morning of the day he was supposed to re-enter the hospital he was found in his automobile dead from carbon monoxide poisoning. He had 0.10 gm% alcohol in his blood. His wife had made the comment that he "didn't usually drink" and it was not clear whether he drank chronically and excessively.

Family history: There was no information concerning a family history of psychiatric illness.
Arrest history: None.

UNDIAGNOSED PSYCHIATRIC ILLNESS: Most Like Alcoholism

Case No. *106* M *X* F ___ Age *50*

ST. LOUIS SUICIDE STUDY CRITERIA FOR ALCOHOLISM

At least three of the following selected drinking behaviors were required for diagnosis.

A. Informant thought subject drank too much ___

B. Subject drank daily ___

C. Subject went on benders (at least 48 hours of drinking and neglect of usual routine) ___

D. Family objected to subject's drinking ___

E. Subject's history included arrests related to drinking ___

F. Subject suffered medical and psychiatric complications due to alcoholic intake ___

G. Subject thought he drank too much ___

H. Subject had job difficulties related to drinking ___

I. Subject involved in automobile accident(s) related to drinking ___

Failed to meet criteria for diagnosis *X*

FEIGHNER CRITERIA FOR UNDIAGNOSED PSYCHIATRIC ILLNESS

Some patients cannot receive a diagnosis for one or more reasons. Among the more common problems that cause a patient to be considered undiagnosed are the following.

A. Cases in which only one illness is suspected but symptoms are minimal *X*

B. Cases in which more than one psychiatric illness is suspected but symptoms are not sufficient to meet the criteria of any of the possibilities ___

C. Cases in which symptoms suggest two or more disorders but in an atypical or confusing manner ___

D. Cases in which the chronology of important symptom clusters cannot be determined ___

E. Cases in which it is impossible to obtain the necessary history to establish a definitive diagnosis *X*

PSYCHIATRICALLY UNDIAGNOSED, SUBGROUP 3

"Most Like" Organic Brain Syndrome (2 men, 1 woman)

077 Informants: Friend, landlady, cousin; hospital and outpatient record, police records

This 65-year-old white landscape gardener and janitor had deserted his wife and two children 30 years before his suicide and had had no contact with them since. Although he had never been divorced, he told neither his cousin nor the hospital (from the records) about his marriage. About six years prior to his death, he had a gastric resection for peptic ulcer. At that time or shortly before he had attempted suicide by slashing his neck. This information was obtained from police records and the informants knew nothing of the circumstances. Following the resection, he never regained his original weight and was for the rest of his life markedly underweight.

One year before his suicide he began to complain of headaches and dizziness. He also became moody. Six months before his death he visited a physician who found a blood pressure of 170/90, but noted no other positive findings except a history of recent epistaxis and a perforated nasal septum of undetermined etiology. His landlady remembered a definite change in his behavior at about that time. She described him as a "very strange" and "creepy" man whose presence made her nervous. During the last six months of his life, his appearance became sloppy and his room so loaded with "junk" that he could hardly get in and out of it. He had in it, for example, 30 old tattered overcoats, dishes that had never been unpacked, and 20 pairs of eyeglasses. He was described as often staring at the ceiling or floor for hours without saying anything and not answering when spoken to. He appeared depressed. The landlady also believed his memory had been failing, although she had no clear evidence of disorientation or confusion.

Two months prior to his death he again went to an outpatient clinic complaining of headache, cough, urinary frequency, precordial pain, and abdominal bloating. For the last three weeks of his life he did not leave his room except to go once to the emergency room of a hospital where he complained of light-headedness. No diagnosis was made there and he was referred to the clinic. About five days before his death, his landlady took him to two hospitals for admission, which both hospitals refused, referring him again to the outpatient clinic. On that same day a sister sent him an advertisement that his son, whom he had deserted and not seen in 30 years, had placed in a newspaper. The subject contacted his son immediately and received a wire from him setting a date for their reunion. The son came on the given date and spent four or five hours with his father. When the son left in midafternoon, he told the subject's landlady who had taken him to his train, that his father was coming to visit him for Christmas.

An hour later, the landlady went to the subject's room to talk to him and found that he had stabbed himself in the abdomen while leaning over a sink into which he had placed a stopper. The sink had an appreciable amount of blood in it, although he had already fallen to the floor and was dead by the time the landlady found him. The telegram announcing his son's arrival was in his hand. The landlady believed he had leaned over the stoppered sink in an effort to avoid "messing up" the floor of his room. There was no clear history of delusions or hallucinations elicited from any of the informants.

Family history: There was no information concerning a family history of psychiatric illness.
Arrest record: None.

UNDIAGNOSED PSYCHIATRIC ILLNESS: Most Like Organic Brain Syndrome

Case No. *027* M _X_ F __ Age *65*

ST. LOUIS SUICIDE STUDY CRITERIA FOR ORGANIC BRAIN SYNDROME

Three of the following six symptoms were required for a diagnosis of organic brain syndrome.

A. Memory difficulty __X__
B. Disorientation in time ___
C. Inability to find one's way in familiar surroundings ___
D. Inability to be trusted out alone ___
E. Deterioration of reading skills ___
F. Difficulties with simple arithmetic ___

Failed to meet criteria for diagnosis __X__

FEIGHNER CRITERIA FOR UNDIAGNOSED PSYCHIATRIC ILLNESS

Some patients cannot receive a diagnosis for one or more reasons. Among the more common problems that cause a patient to be considered undiagnosed are the following.

A. Cases in which only one illness is suspected but symptoms are minimal __X__
B. Cases in which more than one psychiatric illness is suspected but symptoms are not sufficient to meet the criteria of any of the possibilities ___
C. Cases in which symptoms suggest two or more disorders but in an atypical or confusing manner ___
D. Cases in which the chronology of important symptom clusters cannot be determined __X__
E. Cases in which it is impossible to obtain the necessary history to establish a definitive diagnosis ___

123   Informants: Wife, physician, hospital records

This 72-year-old white owner of a grocery store retired at age 47 because, as he told his wife, he was "nervous" and "jumpy." The informant could not elaborate on the meaning of these terms. Following his retirement, he and his wife had traveled around the United States, living on income from money invested in stocks and bonds. During the 24 years after his retirement he suffered from recurrent nervous spells. Although he had, during the spells, stated that he was "nervous," his wife noted only that he was quieter than usual. The spells lasted days to a week or so. Two years before his death he had a recorded blood pressure of 210/112, but had no symptoms of hypertension. One year later he began to express a fear of cancer and could not be reassured concerning this fear. He also developed an extreme concern about his finances without, according to his wife, having any reason to do so.

Two months before his suicide he noticed rectal bleeding for the first time. Although the cause of the bleeding was ascertained to be hemorrhoids, his cancer phobia increased. For the next two months he refused to leave the house. His wife was not sure of the reasons for his refusal to go out, but she realized that this behavior was unusual for him. Thirteen days before his suicide he entered the hospital and had a hemorrhoidectomy the following day. Sometime after the operation, while still in the hospital, he became confused and overactive and received reserpine as a sedative. On the ninth postoperative day he got out of bed at 1 AM, said that he had to go home, and complained that he had no clothes. The nurse's note described him as "confused." The next day he was discharged from the hospital, although there was an additional nurse's note that he was still confused. During his stay in the hospital there were no relevant medical observations concerning his mental status.

On returning home he was noted by his wife to be underactive, disinterested in things about him, and unusually silent. She did not know whether he was oriented or confused. He ate well and she believed he slept well. He expressed a fear the doctor was trying to dope him and felt that everyone was against him because they would not tell him the truth about having cancer. The fear of doping by the doctor was related to his refusal to take prescribed sleeping medicine and his wife did not believe this was a frank paranoid delusion. Four days after his return from the hospital he drank some weed killer and died within 30 minutes of admission to a hospital. His wife stated that he gave no indication of suicidal intent. After taking the poison in his basement, he came upstairs and told his wife what he had done.

Family history: There was no family history of psychiatric illness.
Arrest record: None.

UNDIAGNOSED PSYCHIATRIC ILLNESS: Most Like Organic Brain Syndrome

Case No. *123* M X F___ Age *72*

ST. LOUIS SUICIDE STUDY CRITERIA FOR ORGANIC BRAIN SYNDROME

Three of the following six symptoms were required for a diagnosis of organic brain syndrome.

A. Memory difficulty ___

B. Disorientation in time   X

C. Inability to find one's way in familiar surroundings ___

D. Inability to be trusted out alone ___

E. Deterioration of reading skills ___

F. Difficulties with simple arithmetic ___

Failed to meet criteria for diagnosis X

FEIGHNER CRITERIA FOR UNDIAGNOSED PSYCHIATRIC ILLNESS

Some patients cannot receive a diagnosis for one or more reasons. Among the more common problems that cause a patient to be considered undiagnosed are the following.

A. Cases in which only one illness is suspected but symptoms are minimal ___

B. Cases in which more than one psychiatric illness is suspected but symptoms are not sufficient to meet the criteria of any of the possibilities ___

C. Cases in which symptoms suggest two or more disorders but in an atypical or confusing manner ___

D. Cases in which the chronology of important symptom clusters cannot be determined   X

E. Cases in which it is impossible to obtain the necessary history to establish a definitive diagnosis ___

---

102 Informants: Internist, hospital records (refusal by daughter)

This 67-year-old white widow lost her husband when she was age 60. Two years later she developed bilateral cataracts and had a cataract extraction. At the time of her operation her blood pressure was 220/125. At age 65 she had a stroke which affected her speech for a few days and from which she apparently completely recovered. Seven months prior to her death she awoke one morning and noted weakness in her legs and difficulty in walking. She fell frequently when attempting to walk. Her hands were also affected in that she had trouble feeding and dressing herself. Her right arm and leg were more severely affected than her left. Two days after the onset of these symptoms she noted speech difficulty characterized by slurring and inability to say what she intended.

On admission to the hospital her blood pressure was 210/100. A physical examination determined that she had suffered narrowing of the retinal vessels, cardiac enlargement, deviation of tongue and uvula to the right, and weakness of the right arm and leg. Mental status examination revealed slurred speech, poor memory, disorientation, and confusion. Spinal puncture was normal. On the second day of her hospitalization she fell out of bed and did not remember the incident the next morning. She was discharged on the fifth day with diagnoses of a cerebral arteriosclerosis with mental deterioration and hypertensive cardiovascular disease.

During the next seven months she became increasingly nervous and restless and complained of dizziness, nausea, aching all over, faint feelings, and spells of nervousness with palpitation, but did not exhibit the disorientation or confusion formerly noted. Six days before her death, she was again hospitalized. There were no notes in the last hospital record concerning the patient's disorientation or confusion. She was described as being extremely nervous and requiring large doses of phenobarbital. Her thyroid was thought to be palpable. Her radioiodine uptake was 42% and her protein-bound iodine was 8.7 μg%. Electrocardiogram was negative. On the sixth day of hospitalization she committed suicide by jumping from an eighth-floor hospital window. The final diagnoses given in the hospital record were "suicide, hypertensive cardiovascular disease, acute anxiety reaction, and (?) thyrotoxicosis."

Family history: There was no available information concerning a family history of psychiatric illness.
Arrest record: None.

UNDIAGNOSED PSYCHIATRIC ILLNESS: Most Like Organic Brain Syndrome
Case No. *102* M __ F X Age *67*

ST. LOUIS SUICIDE STUDY CRITERIA FOR ORGANIC BRAIN SYNDROME

Three of the following six symptoms were required for a diagnosis of organic brain syndrome.

A. Memory difficulty   X
B. Disorientation in time X
C. Inability to find one's way in familiar surroundings   __
D. Inability to be trusted out alone   __
E. Deterioration of reading skills   __
F. Difficulties with simple arithmetic __

Failed to meet criteria for diagnosis X

FEIGHNER CRITERIA FOR UNDIAGNOSED PSYCHIATRIC ILLNESS

Some patients cannot receive a diagnosis for one or more reasons. Among the more common problems that cause a patient to be considered undiagnosed are the following.

A. Cases in which only one illness is suspected but symptoms are minimal ___

B. Cases in which more than one psychiatric illness is suspected but symptoms are not sufficient to meet the criteria of any of the possibilities ___

C. Cases in which symptoms suggest two or more disorders but in an atypical or confusing manner ___

D. Cases in which the chronology of important symptom clusters cannot be determined X

E. Cases in which it is impossible to obtain the necessary history to establish a definitive diagnosis ___

PSYCHIATRICALLY UNDIAGNOSED, SUBGROUP 4

"Most Like" Drug Dependence (2 men)

085 Informants: Friend, another friend (a physician), police records (refusal by wife)

This 61-year-old white retired pharmacist was described by both of his friends, one of whom had known him since his college days, as having been morose, "mad at the world," ready to fight, "ready to explode," tense, irritable, and angry for his entire adult life. He had owned his own drug store in a rather run-down area and had not gotten along well with his customers. During the last 14 years of his life he had made ten complaints to the police about vandalism, bad checks, burglary, and robbery at his drug store. He had shot three or four robbers and had actually killed at least one and probably two. Some years previously he had drunk alcohol to excess, gave up drinking, and, according to the informants, switched to taking barbiturates in excess. However, neither informant could give definite evidence of excess barbiturate ingestion on his part.

For many years he had threatened suicide so often to his wife and his physician that neither paid any attention to these threats, which took the following forms: "I am going to kill myself," "I'd be better off dead," "I'm going to blow my head off," "I'm going to jump off the bridge." There was no increase in the frequency of these suicidal threats in the year preceding his death. One year prior to his suicide he inherited $100,000, retired, and bought a nice home. He became bored and restless and decided to go to Florida for a vacation. The trip did not help and, on the advice of his wife and physician, he decided to go back to work as a pharmacist in someone else's drug store. Once back at work, he complained that the pace was too fast and he quit the job shortly before his suicide.

Neither of his friends had been close enough to him to be aware of any new symptoms he might have had during the last year of his life. His wife refused an interview, saying, "I am under a doctor's care. I'm highly nervous and unstable and I couldn't take an interview." He committed suicide by placing the muzzle of a double-barreled shotgun in his mouth and pulling the trigger.

Family history: There was no available information concerning a family history of psychiatric illness.
Arrest record: One moving traffic offense at age 31.

400   The Final Months

UNDIAGNOSED PSYCHIATRIC ILLNESS: Most Like Drug Dependence

Case No. *085* M X F __ Age *61*

ST. LOUIS SUICIDE STUDY CRITERIA FOR DRUG DEPENDENCE

Diagnosis required at least three of the following symptoms:

A. Addiction to drugs as manifested by increased tolerance and withdrawal symptoms when the drugs were unavailable ___

B. Nightly drugs for sleeping ___

C. Daily drug abuse   X

D. Self-concern about taking too many drugs ___

E. Family concern about subject taking too many drugs ___

F. Inability to stop taking drugs ___

Failed to meet criteria for diagnosis X

FEIGHNER CRITERIA FOR UNDIAGNOSED PSYCHIATRIC ILLNESS

Some patients cannot receive a diagnosis for one or more reasons. Among the more common problems that cause a patient to be considered undiagnosed are the following.

A. Cases in which only one illness is suspected but symptoms are minimal   X

B. Cases in which more than one psychiatric illness is suspected but symptoms are not sufficient to meet the criteria of any of the possibilities ___

C. Cases in which symptoms suggest two or more disorders but in an atypical or confusing manner ___

D. Cases in which the chronology of important symptom clusters cannot be determined   X

E. Cases in which it is impossible to obtain the necessary history to establish a definitive diagnosis ___

108 Informants: Woman friend, physician

This 34-year-old white salaried cabinetmaker had been married and divorced twice. The informant was a 50- to 60-year-old woman who was a friend of his and had known him for four years. During the interview, she began to cry when asked about the effect of his death on her and became so upset that she asked the interviewer to leave. However, it was possible to finish the interview when she was assured the interviewer would not return to the upsetting topic to finish the interview. The subject had told the informant that he had had yellow fever or yellow jaundice or malaria when a soldier in the early 1950's in Korea. During the four years she had known him he repeatedly complained of headaches, weakness, and hot and chilly feelings, saying that it felt as though he had malaria. He continually took pills which he said were for his malaria. Two other friends of his had told the informant that the subject was a "dope" addict, but she had no first-hand knowledge that he was.

Three months before his suicide his twin sister died suddenly. According to the informant, he had been very "upset" by this, but could not elaborate. A few weeks after his sister's death, his father became ill but he did not seem to the informant to have been particularly upset by that event. One month prior to his suicide he had an accident while driving the informant's car. He sustained a scalp laceration and the next day went to a physician complaining of headache and diplopia. The diplopia cleared, but he continued to complain of headache. His physician noted that his liver was six to seven fingerbreadths below the costal margin.

During the last month of his life he felt so ill that his company decided to transfer him to a less taxing job at a branch in another city. On the Saturday two days before his death, he suggested to the informant that he and she go to church the next day. This greatly surprised the informant. On the day of his suicide he moved into her rooming house. Later he called her on the telephone. She noted that he sounded "funny" and nervous and he complained of a headache. After his death, she discovered that he had later called a friend and told him, "We'll go together" (referring to the informant and himself). Still later that day he wrote a letter to the motor vehicle authorities admitting that he had been driving the car at the time of the accident the previous month. The informant had had her driver's license suspended because the police believed that she had been driving and that she had left the scene of the accident. Neither he nor she had previously told the police the truth. On the night of his suicide he entered the rooming house, went to his room, and committed suicide by shooting himself through the roof of his mouth.

Family history: There was no available information concerning a family history of psychiatric illness.
Arrest record: None.

UNDIAGNOSED PSYCHIATRIC ILLNESS: Most Like Drug Dependence

Case No. *108* M X F __ Age *34*

ST. LOUIS SUICIDE STUDY CRITERIA FOR DRUG DEPENDENCE

Diagnosis required at least three of the following symptoms:

A. Addiction to drugs as manifested by increased tolerance and withdrawal symptoms when the drugs were unavailable ___

B. Nightly drugs for sleeping ___

C. Daily drug abuse X

D. Self-concern about taking too many drugs ___

E. Family concern about subject taking too many drugs ___

F. Inability to stop taking drugs ___

Failed to meet criteria for diagnosis X

FEIGHNER CRITERIA FOR UNDIAGNOSED PSYCHIATRIC ILLNESS

Some patients cannot receive a diagnosis for one or more reasons. Among the more common problems that cause a patient to be considered undiagnosed are the following.

A. Cases in which only one illness is suspected but symptoms are minimal ___

B. Cases in which more than one psychiatric illness is suspected but symptoms are not sufficient to meet the criteria of any of the possibilities ___

C. Cases in which symptoms suggest two or more disorders but in an atypical or confusing manner ___

D. Cases in which the chronology of important symptom clusters cannot be determined ___

E. Cases in which it is impossible to obtain the necessary history to establish a definitive diagnosis X

PSYCHIATRICALLY UNDIAGNOSED, SUBGROUP 5

"Most Like" Schizophrenia (1 man)

046 Informant: Brother

This 27-year-old black unmarried, unemployed laborer stopped school in the 10th grade because bronchial asthma had made him miss appreciable amounts of school. He had been suspended once in grammar school because he had refused to participate in manual arts. He was described as moody, serious-minded, and always studying. He owned an encyclopedia, a two-volume dictionary, works of Shakespeare and Kipling, and several mathematics books. He was a jazz fan and had a fair collection of jazz records. His brother said, however, that his studying had not made him a recluse, and that he had gone out frequently with men and women friends. He was sensitive to racial problems and repeatedly spoke out against discrimination. His brother believed that he had been inordinately sensitive and that his feelings about racial discrimination were an extremely important source of dissatisfaction to him.

His work history was poor. He had been fired for unknown reasons from five out of ten jobs. A year prior to his death he had lost a job as a substitute mail handler, was out of work three months, worked for three months as a laborer, and then had been unemployed during the last six months of his life. When working he rented apartments for himself. When not working he moved back with his parents. In the last year he had complained of being a burden on his parents whenever he moved back in to live with them.

During the last year of his life he had looked and acted depressed, stared at the ceiling for long periods of time, and lost 20 pounds in weight. His brother was not aware of other symptoms except that for a few months about a year before his death he had washed his hands excessively, following a soap and water washing with an alcohol rinse. In the last few months of his life he had become more interested in religion, praying more, reading the Bible more, and talking more about religion. He had also spoken occasionally about not minding dying and not being afraid of dying.

In the last few weeks of his life, he had begun writing notes, probably to himself. Some of the notes were in a jazz argot. Although the notes were nonsensical in many places, there was no evidence of delusion or hallucinations in them. Other notes contained many psychiatric and psychologic terms. These notes contained some obscure passages or words in them. An example of one of these notes follows:

Schizophrenic common 22-32
Hallucination
Phinea   New born

So far as the informant was aware there were no further changes in his behavior just prior to his suicide. He shot himself one evening in an automobile, about two blocks from his home.

Family history: There was no family history of psychiatric illness.
Arrest record: None.

UNDIAGNOSED PSYCHIATRIC ILLNESS: Most Like Schizophrenia

Case No. *046* M *X* F ___ Age *27*

ST. LOUIS SUICIDE STUDY CRITERIA FOR SCHIZOPHRENIA

At least seven of the following symptoms were required, in addition to delusions or hallucinations, for a diagnosis of schizophrenia:

A. Conspicuous delusions or hallucinations ___
B. Reduction in attachments and interests, and impoverishment of human relationships ___
C. Regressive behavior associated with inappropriate affect *X*
D. Motor behavior exhibiting either marked generalized inhibition or excessive activity and excitation ___
E. Expansive delusional system of omnipotence or genius ___
F. Ideas of reference ___
G. Silly behavior and mannerisms, unpredictable behavior *X*
H. Dissociative phenomena ___
I. Autistic thinking *X*
J. Chronic apparent mental deterioration ___
K. Rages and fights ___
L. Hypochondriacal complaints ___
M. Belief that "people" are spying on one or "after" one ___
N. Poor job history *X*
O. Excessive religious preoccupation *X*
P. Muteness ___

Failed to meet criteria for diagnosis ___

FEIGHNER CRITERIA FOR UNDIAGNOSED PSYCHIATRIC ILLNESS

Some patients cannot receive a diagnosis for one or more reasons. Among the more common problems that cause a patient to be considered undiagnosed are the following.

A. Cases in which only one illness is suspected but symptoms are minimal ___X___

B. Cases in which more than one psychiatric illness is suspected but symptoms are not sufficient to meet the criteria of any of the possibilities _____

C. Cases in which symptoms suggest two or more disorders but in an atypical or confusing manner _____

D. Cases in which the chronology of important symptom clusters cannot be determined _____

E. Cases in which it is impossible to obtain the necessary history to establish a definitive diagnosis _____

8

How Predictable Are Predictors of Suicide?

Obviously, there is no pathognomic predictor of completed suicide. There are, however, a number of predictors that correlate with completed suicide and are helpful in predicting suicide. The continuing study of suicide shows that some are better than others. For example, recent research has put to rest one of the most popular of the myths about suicide—that "if he talks about it, he won't do it"—as will be shown later in this chapter.

Demographic factors in combination with psychiatric diagnoses

Age, sex, race, and psychiatric diagnosis in certain combinations are probably the most consistently accurate predictors of suicide and, by the same token, are in other combinations equally accurate in predicting a low risk of suicide.

In our study, average age at death was very similar for three of the diagnostic groups—the affective disorder group, the miscellaneous group, and the psychiatrically undiagnosed group. The mean age at death varied only from a minimum age of 53.0 (among women in the miscellaneous group) to a maximum of 59.5 (among women in the undiagnosed group). In contrast, the mean age at death among the alcoholic subjects was a decade younger—the alcoholic men had a mean age of 45.8 years; the women with alcoholism had a mean age of 44.4. In our study, the youngest age at which suicide was committed by a man was 24 (the subject's diagnosis was alcoholism). The youngest woman was a 31-year-old subject suffering from drug dependence (as well as from an associated diagnosis of hysteria which had mani-

TABLE 8.1 Age at Death

	Affective Disorder		Alcoholism		Misc.		Undiagnosed	
	M	F	M	F	M	F	M	F
20–29	2	0	2	0	1	0	1	0
30–39	4	0	6	2	3	1	3	0
40–49	6	5	11	1	2	0	2	1
50–59	5	8	6	2	1	1	4	1
60–69	21	3	3	0	2	2	2	1
70+	7	2	0	0	5	0	4	1
Mean Age	58.5	54.9	45.8	44.4	56.5	53.0	55.1	59.5
Youngest	29	40	24	32	29	31	27	41
Oldest	86	72	62	56	85	63	85	80
Total N	45	18	28	5	14	4	16	4

fested itself earlier in her life). The next youngest woman was a 32-year-old alcoholic. (See Table 8.1.)

There are two diagnostically homogeneous groups of subjects in the St. Louis study: major affective disorder and alcoholism, each of which comprised at least 30 subjects. Of the individual subjects diagnosed as having had affective disorder, the largest number of suicides occurred among those in their sixties (24 of the 63). Of those with alcoholism, the largest number of suicides occurred among subjects in their forties (12 of 33).

This approximately 20-year difference in modal (as opposed to mean) age at death between suicides among diagnosed subjects with affective disorder and those with alcoholism provides additional support to the finding of earlier suicide in alcoholism. The finding that the age at death of women with affective disorder averaged 3.6 years younger than the men's average age at death did not appreciably affect the significant difference between the mean ages at death in alcoholism and affective disorder.

As noted earlier, completed suicide is more than three times as frequent in men as it is in women. Although in affective disorder the ratio was 2.5:1, men to women, the 3:1 ratio still holds for the total sample.

The low numbers of completed suicides among blacks in the study—6:128, blacks to whites (5:98, black men to white men)—reflects the national statistics. The number of suicides by white men in the United States is 20 times the number of suicides by black men. The population ratio is about 10:1, white to black.[1] Therefore the real ratio is about 2:1, white suicides to black suicides. The most complete record of suicide death *rates* for white men and black men, by age and color, is presented in the form of a cohort analysis covering five-year intervals from 1952–1967.[2] During the

20-year interval when death rates for the cohorts were assessed every five years, there was an overall, slight, and insignificant upward trend in the suicide rate for blacks as compared with whites. However, in the cohorts ages 20–24 and ages 60–64, the increases in the white suicide rates were, respectively, 22% and 38% greater than the increases in the black rates. The cohorts in which the black rates increased most significantly as compared with the white rates were ages 40–44 and ages 65–69. In each case, the increase in the black suicide rate was 41% greater than the corresponding rate for whites. Thus of 12 five-year cohorts between ages 20 and 79, there were only two, ages 20–24 and 60–64, in which the white rate increased more than the black rate and two others, 40–44 and 65–69, in which black rates increased the most—41%. In the remaining eight cohorts, the differences in black and white rates averaged only 18% greater in the black rate than in the white. This difference, considering the large numbers involved in a national sample, is an insignificant one.

The rate of suicide among white men over the age of 32 continues then to increase with age and does so beyond age 80. The rate among black men, in contrast, rises more or less parallel with the white male rate to age 32, at which point the rates deviate markedly, the black male rate remaining more or less steady (except for the 2 five-year cohort ages noted above) from 32–80. This deviation between black and white male suicide rates eventuates in an about 5:1 (white to black) ratio of suicidal deaths by age 80.

Thus while there are no specific, individual age, race, sex, or clinical predictors of suicide, certain age, race, and sex factors in combination with particular diagnoses (for example, a white man over age 65 with a diagnosis of major affective disorder) can predict completed suicide with a relatively high degree of accuracy. Conversely, different combinations of the same categories of factors (example: a black woman aged 30 diagnosed as having an uncomplicated neurosis) lead to relatively accurate predictions of low risk of completed suicide.

Communication of intent

Our study found that the kinds of statements most often used to communicate suicidal ideas were: 1. statement of intent to commit suicide; 2. statement of being better off dead and being tired of living; 3. statement of the desire to die; 4. making a suicide attempt; 5. references to methods of suicide; 6. expression of "dire predictions"; and 7. statement that the family would be better off if the subject were dead. The term "dire predictions" was used to gather into one category a number of different kinds of statements that had as their common basis an indirect prediction of death. Examples of these were: "You won't see me again except in a hearse," "If something happens to me, don't be surprised," "This is your last kiss,"

"I won't be around on Thursday," and "I am getting off the face of the earth." The reader will recognize more statements of this nature in the case vignettes. The most common means of communication, occurring in 41% of the sample, was the direct statement of the subject's intention to commit suicide.

Among the 93 subjects who communicated suicidal intent (69%), the mean number of different ways of expression was three per person. Two-thirds of these 93 communicators used more than one way of communication and the maximum number of different kinds of expressions used by any single individual was 12. These expressions were made to a number of people with various relationships to the subjects—60% of the subjects who communicated intentions of suicide did so to their spouses, one-half communicated to relatives including in-laws, one-third communicated to friends, and less than one-fifth communicated intent to physicians, job associates, ministers, police, and landladies.

The expressions were made repeatedly in two-thirds of the 93 cases and only once, or at most, a few times, in the remaining one-third. Almost three-quarters of the first expressions of suicidal ideas occurred within one year of suicide and, strikingly, two-fifths first expressed such ideas within three months of suicide. It was of interest that three-quarters of the informants believed the suicidal communications to have been genuine and only one-quarter did not believe them to have been so—i.e., took as threats not signifying a real intent to commit suicide. We tabulated the informants' responses to communications of suicidal intent as "not believing them to be genuine" when the suicidal idea expressed was not believed serious even if there were, in the same case, other times when statements were taken as genuine. Barraclough et al. reported that, of their 100 subjects, 33 (33%) had made direct threats of suicide within one month of suicide. When less direct communications of intent were considered as threats, the figure rose to 55%.[3] This finding would seem to deflate the old bromide, "If they talk about it, they won't do it."

Because in the St. Louis study the kinds of suicidal communications ranged from specific statements of intent to allusions to the general subject of suicide, it seemed useful to ascertain whether or not some diagnoses reflected specific statements of intent more than others. It turned out that three-fifths of the alchoholics made specific statements of intent to commit suicide as compared with about two-fifths of those diagnosed as having had affective disorder, depressed phase, and less than one-fifth of the remaining subjects in the sample.

The relation of communication of suicidal intent to selected social variables, namely sex, age, marital status, religion, income, education, and occupation, was surprisingly heterogeneous. The only difference that even ap-

TABLE 8.2 Some Features of the Communication of Suicidal Ideas

	Men N = 70	Women N = 23	Total Group N = 93
Kinds of suicidal ideas			
Mean number per person	3.4	2.6	3.2
Proportion of persons with			
>1 way of communication (%)	68	57	65
Maximum number in any 1 person	12	7	12
To whom expressed			
Spouse (%)	65	43	60
Relatives, including in-laws (%)	50	57	51
Friends (%)	34	39	35
Job associates (%)	5	4	5
Physicians (%)	13	35	18
Others: ministers, police, landlady (%)	5	4	5
Mean number per person*	1.8	1.9	1.8
Repeated vs. infrequent expression			
Repeatedly (%)	66	70	67
Once or at most a few times (%)	34	30	33
Time of first expression of suicidal ideas			
Within 1 year of suicide† (%)	74	70	73
More than 1 year, with an			
increase within 1 year (%)	10	22	13
More than 1 year, without			
an increase within 1 year (%)	16	8	14
Considered a genuine warning by respondents			
Genuine (%)	69	87	73
Not genuine‡ (%)	31	13	27

*This number is *not* the mean number of *individuals* to whom the suicidal person communicated his intent, but is the number of different *groups* of individuals to whom a suicidal communication was made. (Only the category spouse necessarily refers to a single individual.)

† It is striking that 39% of the men and 52% of the women (43% of the total group) first expressed suicidal ideas within 3 months of the time of their suicides.

‡ Scored as "not genuine" if there were occasional instances when the person to whom suicidal idea was expressed felt it was a threat and that it did not signify a real intent to commit suicide. It was scored this way even if there were other times when the statement of suicidal intent was considered genuine.

proached significance was that a smaller proportion of the wealthier subjects communicated suicidal ideas than did those in lower income brackets—50% versus 70%.

Because in this study none of the suicide notes were found before death, they cannot here be used in consideration as useful suicide predictors. The contents of those notes which were made available to us are included in the individual vignettes.

Suicide attempts as predictors

Of the 134 cases of suicide, 18% had made suicide attempts sometime prior to the completed suicide. (Barraclough and his group found that 30% of their subjects had made previous attempts;[3] Dorpat and Ripley found 33%.[4]) There were, among the women, a somewhat higher (32%) percent of attempters than among the men (19%). This difference is most clearly seen in the affective disorder group in which there are large enough numbers of each sex to make the results statistically meaningful. Of the ten subjects (in 63) with affective disorder who attempted suicide, six were women (33% of the women with affective disorder) and four were men (9% of the men with

TABLE 8.3 Suicide Attempts (by diagnosis)

Diagnosis	Subjects with previous attempts	% of total subjects	Attempts per subject	Time before completed suicide	Method
Affective Disorder					
Male	4	9			
			1	6 weeks	asphyxia (CO)
			1	3 months	cutting (wrists)
			1	<3 months	starvation
			1	unknown	unknown
Female	6	33			
			1	3 days*	asphyxiation (natural gas)
			4	1 month*	cutting (wrists)
				20 yrs (approx)	drowning
				20 yrs (approx)	drugs
				20 yrs	jumped in front of car
			1	2 months*	drugs
			1	1 year	drugs
			2	2 years	drugs
				6 years	cutting (wrists)
			2	4 years	cutting
				6 years	drugs
Alcoholism					
Male	6	21			
			2	3 weeks*	asphyxiation (CO)
				6 weeks*	hanging
			1	1 year	drugs (aspirin)
			1	unknown	unknown
			1	3 years	drugs (sleeping pills)
			1	10 years	cutting (wrists)
			1	6 months	cutting (throat)
Female	1	†			
			1	1 year	drugs (sleeping pills)

TABLE 8.3 continued

Diagnosis	Subjects with previous attempts	% of total subjects	Attempts per subject	Time before completed suicide	Method
Undiagnosed					
Male	2	13			
			1	3 days*	poison
			1	4 years	asphyxiation (CO)
Female	0	†			
Miscellaneous					
Male	4	29			
			1	1 week*	asphyxiation (natural gas)
			1	12 years	poison
			4	4 months	poison (H_2O_2)
				4 months	cutting (antecubital vein)
				4 months	air into veins
				4 months	electrocution
			2	18 months	jumping
				2 years	shooting
Female	1	†			
			2	6 months	cutting (wrists and neck)
				5 years	cutting (wrists)
Total					
Male	16	16%			
Female	8	26%			
Total	24	18%			

*Indicates suicide attempt(s) 2 months or less prior to completed suicide.
†Percentages of diagnostic-sex groups are not included when the group N was less than 10.

affective disorder). (There are too few women in each of the other three major diagnostic groups to provide statistically interpretable results.)

Multiple attempts, when they occurred, occurred more frequently among the women than among the men; there were 4 women of the entire sample of 31 female subjects who had made more than one previous attempt, whereas there were only 3 men in the male sample of 103 who had made more than one prior attempt. That is, in our sample, 13% of the women versus 3% of the men had made multiple suicide attempts.

As noted in the Introduction, there have been several important studies—by von Andics,[5] Dahlgren,[6] Stengel,[7] and Ettlinger[8]—indicating the overlap in attempted and completed suicide and that the overlap occurs in "two directions"; that is, that a certain percentage of attempters complete suicide (Ettlinger's finding is 1% per year[8]) and that a somewhat higher percentage of completed suicides are preceded by attempts.

Loss of affectional relationships as suicide predictors

During the last year preceding suicide, 33 subjects (25% of the total sample) suffered the loss of an affectional relationship (defined as divorce or separation from a spouse; death of spouse; bereavement not involving spouse but rather the death of another relative or close friend; and a category of loss called "other," which includes separations not described above such as a subject's being left behind by a relative's move from home). Dorpat and Ripley's finding was similar—27% of their subjects suffered the loss of a "love object," identified as loss, by death, of a family member (parent, child, or spouse) or loved one.[4] Eighteen (13%) of these affectional losses took place within six weeks of the suicidal event. The reason so many of the affectional losses occurred in that period is due to the high rate of proximate affectional losses among the alcoholics, an occurrence which seemed to play a relatively important role in precipitating many suicides among the alcoholics. Within the last six-week period, 11 alcoholics suffered such losses, as compared with many fewer losses in the affective disorder group (2), the undiagnosed group (3), and the miscellaneous group (2).

TABLE 8.4 Loss of Affectional Relationships Preceding Suicide

	Affective Disorder	Alcoholism	Miscellaneous	Psychiatrically Undiagnosed
	Within one year			
Separated	3	10	2	1
Divorced	2	1	0	0
Widowed	0	1	0	0
Bereaved	3	1	0	3
Apart (other)	1	3	1	1
Total with Affectional loss	9	16	3	5
% of diagnostic groups	14	48	17	25
	Within six weeks			
Separated	2	8	1	0
Divorced	0	0	0	0
Widowed	0	0	0	0
Bereaved	0	0	0	2
Apart (other)	0	3	1	1
Total with Affectional loss	2	11	2	3
% of diagnostic group	3	33	11	15

It is possible that the higher number of affectional losses among the alcoholics throughout the last year of life is a result of the chronicity of alcoholism and the difficulties involved in living with such chronically ill people. In contrast, affective disorder, as an illness, occurs in infrequent episodes that are not chronic and thus not so apt to lead to separation. (See Table 8.4.)

There was a higher percentage of affectional losses in the last year among the undiagnosed and miscellaneous groups than in the affective disorder group—25% in the undiagnosed, 17% in the miscellaneous, and 15% in the affective disorder group. However, the figures do not lend themselves to valid interpretation because of the small number of patients in these two diagnostic groups which also, by definition, lack cohesive characteristics. The difference between the proportion of patients with affective disorder who had affectional losses and the proportions of patients in the undiagnosed group and the miscellaneous group who had affectional losses was not statistically significant either in comparing the affectional losses within the last year of life or in comparing them within the last six weeks. The difference between the affectional losses in alcoholism compared with those in affective disorder *is* statistically significant both within the last six-week period and the last year.

Antecedent circumstances as predictors

In reviewing the informants' interviews, our study found 19 different antecedent circumstances that were judged "important" in precipitating suicide. Of course, none of the subjects experienced all, or even a majority, of these and thus the number of occurrences of each event is always less than the number of subjects in a given diagnostic/demographic group. These antecedent circumstances were judged by the primary informants as "important," "questionably important," or "not important" in precipitating the suicide. If the informants could not categorize the circumstance definitively as any of the above, there were two other possible interpretations the informants offered: that the antecedent circumstance was not truly antecedent to the psychiatric illness, but rather a symptom of it; or that the role of the circumstance was unknown to the informant.

The 19 antecedent circumstances were: 1. school trouble; 2. job trouble, 3. death of spouse, parent, child, close relative, or 4. death of good friend; 5. friction with spouse or lover; 6. divorce or separation; 7. friction with parents, sibling, or child; 8. financial difficulties; 9. heavy drinking; 10. use of alcohol just prior to suicide; 11. pregnancy (the subject's or that of someone close to the subject); 12. moving to another house; 13. moving to another city; 14. a feeling of disgrace; 15. serious illness of relative; 16. serious illness of close friend; 17. living alone; 18. suffering from a nonpsychiatric illness; and 19. legal trouble. (See Table 8.5.)

TABLE 8.5 "Important" antecedent circumstances in relation to suicide according to informants

	Affective Disorder		Alcoholism		Miscellaneous		Psychiatrically Diagnosed		Total Citations	
	A	B	A	B	A	B	A	B	A	B
School trouble	2	0	0	—	0	—	0	—	2	0
Job trouble	29	8	13	5	9	1	8	2	59	16
Death of close relatives	11	2	7	4	2	0	2	0	23	6
Death of close friend	6	0	1	0	1	1	3	1	11	2
Friction with spouse or lover	13	5	18	8	3	2	4	2	38	17
Divorce or separation	6	3	14	6	2	2	2	1	24	12
Friction with close relative	7	3	12	4	5	0	3	0	27	7
Financial difficulties	13	5	14	3	3	1	4	3	34	12
Heavy drinking	11	4	28	17	1	0	1	0	41	21
Alcohol just prior to suicide	7	2	21	9	1	0	0	—	29	11
Pregnancy	3*	2	0	—	0	—	2	0	5	2
Moved home within city	8	0	11	0	6	0	4	1	29	1
Moved city of residence	2	0	5	0	2	0	0	—	9	0
Feeling of disgrace	13	10	10	1	2	0	0	—	25	11
Sickness of close relatives	13	5	5	0	5	0	0	—	33	5
Sickness of close friend	4	2	0	—	0	—	2	0	6	2
Living alone	10	2	10	1	4	0	3	0	27	3
Medical illness	32	22	10	3	6	1	13	7	61	28
Legal problems	1	0	4	0	1	0	1	1	7	1
No problems described	2	—	0	—	2	0	0	—	4	0

NOTE: Column A is the number of subjects with the event, and Column B is the number of subjects for whom it was rated as "important" by informants.
*Includes male reactions to pregnancy in spouse, lover, or first-degree relative.

The antecedent circumstances that were most often considered by the informants to have been "important" to the suicides of men diagnosed as having affective disorder were nonpsychiatric illness (in 17 of 23 men with affective disorder who had suffered such illnesses); job trouble (in 8 of the 23 men whose histories included job trouble); and feelings of disgrace (in 6 of the 7 men whose histories included statements of such feelings). Despite the investigator's expectation that death of a relative or close friend would be commonly cited as important to suicide by informants on male subjects with affective disorder, in only 1 of the 11 who lost a close relative or friend by death was it so considered.

In women with affective disorder, the antecedent circumstance most frequently believed "important" to suicide by the informants was again nonpsychiatric illness (in 5 of 9). The next most common was the feeling of disgrace (in 4 of 6). The problem least important in the eyes of the informants was job trouble (in 0 of 6). As was true of men with affective disorder, death of relative or friend was infrequently cited (1 of 6). Friction with spouse or lover was mentioned as "important" in only 1 of 5 cases in which such friction was experienced.

As one would expect, the use of alcohol was the circumstance most commonly believed "important" to the suicide of men with alcoholism (17 of 25). Of the 19 alcoholic men who had drunk alcohol just prior to suicide, the informants believed this "unimportant" in 9 cases. Friction with spouse or lover was cited as important in 7 of 15 cases. Those informants who had known the alcoholic men felt job trouble to be "important" in 5 of 12 cases.

Even though there were, in the study, only 5 women diagnosed as alcoholics, it is nonetheless of interest that, unlike the men, heavy drinking was considered "important" to suicide in only 1 of the 5. In the women more importance was placed on the death of a close relative or friend and on divorce or separation (in 3 of 4).

In the undiagnosed group, the informants seemed to have had as much difficulty in judging the importance of specific antecedent circumstances to suicide as the investigators had in making definite diagnoses. This difficulty is illustrated by the finding that only 8 events of 56 cited (or 1 in 7) in the histories of all the undiagnosed subjects, men and women, were considered "important" to suicide, whereas the ratio in the affective disorder and alcoholism groups, men and women, was about 1 in 3. Not only were these "important" events relatively few, they were also scattered among a number of unrelated kinds of circumstances.

In the miscellaneous group, which included 14 men (4 with organic brain syndrome, 3 with schizophrenia, 3 terminally medically ill, 1 with drug dependence, and 3 who had no psychiatric or terminal medical illness at the time of suicide) and 4 women (1 with organic brain syndrome, 2 terminally medically ill, and 1 with drug dependence secondary to hysteria), of 51 antecedent circumstances, 17 were considered by informants to have been "important" to suicide. This one-in-three proportion corresponds to the one-in-three proportion found in both the affective disorder group and the alcoholism group. In the undiagnosed group, the proportion in which important events were reported was, as noted above, only 1 in 7 even though the decision regarding "importance," or lack thereof, was in each case made by an informant close to the subject. This finding presumably underscores the uncertainty in the judgments of the primary informants associated with subjects in the undiagnosed group. Furthermore, difficulty in diagnoses was increased by a higher rate of refusal (5 in 20) among potential primary informants of the undiagnosed subjects in contrast to the rate of refusal in the other three diagnostic groups—2 in 18 in the miscellaneous group, 6 in 63 in the affective disorder group, and 0 in 33 in the alchoholic group.

Physical illness as a predictor of suicide

As discussed above, the most commonly cited antecedent circumstance considered by the informants to be "important" to suicide in the largest of our diagnostic groups—affective disorder (N = 63)—was the occurrence of nonpsychiatric (medical) illness.

Medical illness occurred in 61 (46%) of the 134 subjects and did not occur, at the time of suicide, in 63 (47%) subjects. There were an additional 10 (7%) subjects about whose medical illnesses I had no information. Among the 61 subjects with medical illnesses, the most common illnesses were cardiovascular diseases affecting the heart (and, infrequently, the blood vessels only)—28%. The other organ systems involved were, in order of frequency, the gastrointestinal system (23%), the central nervous system (16%), the musculoskeletal system (13%), the genitourinary system (8%), the respiratory system (7%), the special senses (manifested by deafness or blindness 5%), and the gynecological system (2%). There were, in addition, three kinds of disease not limited to specific organ systems—malignancies (13%), infectious diseases (3%), and diabetes mellitus (2%). (Because some of the subjects had more than one medical illness, the total of these percentages is more than 100%). Table 8.6 shows this division of illnesses among the sample and between the sexes and, finally, among the psychiatric diagnoses.

It is interesting that Dorpat and Ripley's suicide study showed that, of the 80 subjects about whom they had medical information, 56 shared a total of 107 illnesses and 24 were medically well at the time of their suicides. There were 34 subjects about whom the investigators had no medical information. The 107 illnesses were categorized as 47 psychosomatic illnesses (including 17 peptic ulcers, 11 cases of hypertension, 12 cases of rheumatoid arthritis,

TABLE 8.6 Number of Illnesses at Time of Suicide

	Number of subjects without medical illness or about whom no medical information extant (10)	Cardiovascular disease	Gastrointestinal disease	Neurologic disease	Malignancy	Musculoskeletal disease	Genitourinary disease	Respiratory disease	Deafness or blindness	Infectious disease	Diabetes	Gynecological disease
Affective Disorder												
Men	22	8	*4[a]	**4	1	*6	3	*3	1	0	0	0
Women	9	4	2	0	1	*1	1	0	1	0	0	0
Total	31	12	*6	**4	2	**7	**4	*3	2	0	0	0
Alcoholism												
Men	17	1	5	3	*1	0	1	*1	0	1	*1	0
Women	4	1	0	0	0	0	0	0	0	0	0	0
Total	21	2	5	3	*1	0	1	*1	0	1	*1	0
Miscellaneous												
Men	9	1	0	0	0	0	0	0	1	0	0	0
Women	1	0	0	1	0	0	0	0	0	0	0	0
Total	10	1	0	1	0	0	0	0	1	0	0	0
Psychiatrically undiagnosed												
Men	10	1	3	1	3	0	0	0	0	1	0	0
Women	1	1	0	*1	2	1	0	0	0	0	0	1
Total	11	2	3	*2	5	1	0	0	0	1	0	1
Total Sample												
Men	58	11	*12	**8	*5	*6	4	**4	2	2	*1	0
Women	15	6	2	*2	3	2	1	0	1	0	0	1
Total	73	17	*14	***10	*8	**8	**5	**4	3	2	*1	1
Percentages	54[b]	28[c]	23	16	13	13	8	7	5	3	2	2

[a]The number of asterisks by an entry indicates the number of additional illnesses among subjects in that group. Thus, there was a total of 73 illnesses occurring in 61 subjects.

[b]Of 134 subjects, 63 had no physical illness at the time of death. There was no information concerning physical illness in 10 additional subjects. Thus, the percentage of those without physical illness plus those ten of whom there was no knowledge of such is 54% of the total sample. There were 61 subjects who did have at least one physical illness at suicide, i.e. 46% of the total.

[c]The percentages calculated for each disease represent the frequency of occurrence of each of those diseases among the 61 subjects who had definitely suffered from medical illness at the time of suicide.

and 7 unspecified illnesses), 16 cases of cardiovascular and heart disease, 6 malignancies, and 38 unspecified illnesses. Barraclough et al. presumably were not as concerned with medical illnesses as associated with suicide and reported only that 5 of their 100 subjects had suffered from terminal medical illnesses—2 malignancies and 3 nonmalignant illnesses.

In summary, regarding the prediction of suicide, suicide rates for white men increase steadily to age 80 and even beyond. For white women, the rates increase, but less so, until about ages 50–60 and peak during that decade. The overall ratio of white men's to white women's suicide rates is about 3:1 in the United States. White suicide rates in this country are approximately twice those for blacks when correction is made for the population ratio of whites to blacks.

Diagnosis as a predictor gains in importance when one realizes that affective disorder and alcoholism account for the great majority of suicides.

While communication of intent should certainly be considered a red flag, it is not consistently predictive of suicide. Even though 69% of the subjects in this study communicated their intention to commit suicide, in another study, an almost identical percent (68%) of psychiatrically hospitalized patients communicated suicidal intent.[9] Only 2% of the communicators committed suicide during a seven-year follow-up.[10] Suicide attempts are a special form of communication of suicidal intent because subjects who make attempts tend to commit suicide during succeeding years at the rate of about 1% a year. The Hudgens et al. study indicated, but did not make clear, that communication of intent without a suicide attempt may lead to suicide at the same annual rate of about 1% a year (or at a rate slightly less than 1% per year). Viewing attempted suicide in retrospect, from the vantage point of post-completed suicide, it is notable that from one-fifth to one-third of people who completed suicide had made previous attempt(s) at some point.

In this study, affectional losses, defined as separation, divorce, widowhood, bereavement, and being apart ("other"), occurred in only 15% of the subjects with affective disorder in the year preceding their suicides as contrasted with 48% of the subjects with alcoholism. This difference was even more striking if the affectional loss was limited to that occurring within six weeks of the completed suicide: 3% of the subjects with affective disorder as contrasted to 32% with alcoholism.

The most common antecedent circumstances that occurred and were considered by the informants to have been "important to the suicide" were, in order of prevalence, nonpsychiatric illness, heavy drinking, friction with spouse or lover, job troubles, divorce or separation, financial difficulties, drinking just prior to suicide, and feelings of disgrace. Less common were friction with a close relative, death of a close relative, sickness of a relative. Living alone, death of a close friend, sickness of a close friend, pregnancy, moving to another house, and having legal problems were cited as being "important" much less often. Occurring, but never cited as "important," were moving to another city, school problems, and finally, situations in which no problems were known.

Of the 61 subjects who had some medical or surgical illness, in 46% was the illness considered to be "important to the suicide."

The study shows that diagnosis could be more useful as a predictor than the demographic variables and that communication of intent to commit suicide is of less importance as a predictor. I found that even though 69% of the suicide subjects had made such communication, a like percent of psychiatrically hospitalized patients also made such communications and only 2% carried out a completed suicide within the succeeding seven years. Many psychiatrists have written about the possible inherent differences between attempted suicide and completed suicide. I wish only to point out that about a fifth of our sample of 134 completed suicides had made previous suicide attempts and that, while I agree that attempted suicide and completed suicide do occur in different populations, I also believe that some attempts are failures to complete suicide.

REFERENCES

1. *Vital Statistics of the United States, 1975.* Vol II—Mortality (Part B). U.S. Public Health Service, Hyattsville, Md., 1977.
2. Leading Components of Upturn in Mortality for Men, United States—1952–67, *Vital and Health Statistics Series 20,* Number 11, DHEW Publication No. (HSM) 72-1008, Government Printing Office, Washington, D.C., 1971.
3. Barraclough, B., Bunch, J., Nelson, B. and Sainsbury, P. A hundred cases of suicide: Clinical aspects. *Brit. J. Psychiat.* 125:355–373, 1974.
4. Dorpat, T.L. and Ripley, H.S. A study of suicide in the Seattle area. *Comp. Psychiat.* 1:349–359, 1960.
5. von Andics, M., *Über Sinn und Sinnlosigkeit des Lebens.* Vienna: Gerold and Company, 1938.
6. Dahlgren, K.G. *On Suicide and Attempted Suicide.* Lund, Sweden: A.-B. Ph. Lindstedts Univ.-Bokhandel, 1945.
7. Stengel, E. and Cook, N.G. *Attempted Suicide.* Maudsley Monograph #4. London: Chapman and Hall, 1958.
8. Ettlinger, R.W. Suicides in a group of patients who had previously attempted suicide. *Acta. Psychiat. Scand.* 40:363–378, 1964.
9. DeLong, W.B. and Robins, E. The communication of suicidal intent prior to psychiatric hospitalization: A study of 87 patients. *Amer. J. Psychiat.* 117:695–705, 1961.
10. Hudgens, R.W., Robins, E., Lam, J.T. and Meredith, C.H. The communication of suicidal intent in psychiatric illness. In *Life History Research in Psychopathology.* Eds. M. Roff, L.N. Robins, and M. Pollack. Minneapolis: University of Minnesota Press, 1972.

9

Before Suicide

An old question that has been addressed by investigators concerns the difference in the planning of outcome by those who attempt and those who complete suicide.

Ettlinger, in reviewing 11 studies of attempted suicide, reported that the rates of committed suicide among attempters varied narrowly from .5 to 3.5% per year (the periods studied ranged from 1 year to 18 years).[1] In her own ten-year follow-up study of 211 subjects who had made suicide attempts, Ettlinger found that 17 actually committed suicide—8% of the sample in the decade or a rate of .8% per year.[2] Ettlinger's most statistically significant result was a difference in number of attempts between suicide attempters who subsequently committed suicide and those who did not. Among those who did commit suicide, 53% made more than three attempts; whereas, among the attempters who did not commit suicide within the follow-up decade, only 15% had made more than three attempts.[2]

In a more recent follow-up study of attempted suicide, Dahlgren followed 229 suicide attempters hospitalized during the years 1933–42, over a follow-up period of between 21 to 42 years and, to date, the longest of its kind. He showed that, during the first 4 years after hospitalization, 9.7% of the men and 3.7% of the women killed themselves.[3] Further, Dahlgren's study showed that the incidence of completed suicide 15 years or more after the initial attempt was higher—14% of the men and 8.8% of the women.

Our own study looked at the problem from the other side. Of 134 completed suicides, 18%—16% of the men and 26% of the women—had made at least one previous attempt. One subject had made three attempts 20 years

423

prior to suicide and had made one further attempt only one month before killing herself. There were five subjects who had made previous attempts from 5 to 12 years prior to suicide. Four of these did not make attempts within two years of completed suicide. One other of them made an attempt six months prior to suicide.

In Chapter 8, consideration is given to suicide attempts as "predictors" of suicide. In comparison with other predictors, attempted suicide is not a very strong indicator. Communication of intent, for instance, occurred among 69% of the subjects in our study. Even so, the 18% who made suicide attempts must certainly have demonstrated to those around them a high degree of emotional distress. There is, however, a better gauge of the degree to which the subjects in the St. Louis study indicated their distress beyond their immediate families and friends, and that is the extent to which they sought professional help. (See Tables 9.1 and 9.2.)

Almost three-quarters of the subjects diagnosed as having had affective disorder (70% of the total, 100% of the women) had received care for their psychiatric illness within the year preceding their suicides and half (51%) had received such care within one month of suicide. Among the subjects with alcoholism, 39% had had care for alcoholism within one year of suicide and 24% within the last month. Of those subjects in the miscellaneous group, 39% (7 of 18) received care for their various psychiatric illnesses during the final year of their lives, but none had received such care in the last month of that year. Finally, of the psychiatrically undiagnosed subjects, 40% had received care for their psychiatric troubles in the last year preceding suicide and 10% during the last month. In the total sample, 54% had received care for psychiatric problems during the final year prior to suicide and 31% of the total had received such care in the final month.

The care for psychiatric problems referred to above included hospitalization in both psychiatric and general hospitals, consultations with psychiatrists and with nonpsychiatrists, and outpatient care. It is of interest that most of the care for psychiatric illness received by 54% of the suicide subjects was provided by nonpsychiatrists.

In addition to those who did seek and receive care for their psychiatric illnesses within the final year, there were 13 subjects (12 with affective disorder and 1 with alcoholism) who were referred to psychiatric hospitals but did not go.

Within the one-year period prior to suicide, 22% of the total (30 of 134) had been hospitalized for psychiatric treatment. Of these 30 subjects, 8 killed themselves while still hospitalized (3 in psychiatric hospitals and 5 in general hospitals). Of the 30 hospitalized subjects, 17 had affective disorder, depressed phase, 6 had alcoholism, 5 were in the miscellaneous group (1 with organic brain syndrome, 2 with schizophrenia, 2 with drug dependence) and only 2 from the undiagnosed group, both of whom committed suicide shortly after discharge from general hospitals.

TABLE 9.1 Medical and Psychiatric Care in the Year Preceding Suicide

	Psychiatric care only	Psychiatric & medical care	Total Psychiatric care	Medical care only	Total with medical care	No known psychiatric or medical care
Affective disorder						
<1 month	26	6	32	4	36	—
1–3 months	5	4	9	1	10	—
3–12 months	3	0	3	3	6	—
Total	34	10	44	8	52	11
Alcoholism						
<1 month	4	4	8	4	12	—
1–3 months	2	1	3	0	3	—
3–12 months	2	0	2	1	3	—
Total	8	5	13	5	18	15
Miscellaneous						
<1 month	0	0	0	0	0	—
1–3 months	1	0	1	1	2	—
3–12 months	6	0	6	5	11	—
Total	7	0	7	6	13	5
Psychiatrically undiagnosed						
<1 month	1	1	2	2	4	—
1–3 months	2	1	3	0	3	—
3–12 months	1	2	3	5	8	—
Total	4	4	8	7	15	5
Totals						
<1 month	31	11	42	10	52	—
1–3 months	10	6	16	2	18	—
3–12 months	12	2	14	14	28	—
Total	53	19	72	26	98	36

NOTE: Subjects were scored only once each. If a subject received care more than once in the final year, the treatment scored was that which involved the most inclusive care or that of the longest duration.

It is something of a surprise that the percentages of subjects who committed suicide while hospitalized varied so little among diagnostic groups: 8% of subjects with affective disorder, 6% of those with alcoholism, 6% of the miscellaneous group. The numbers of such subjects with affective disorder and alcoholism are large enough to make the percent similarities meaningful. (By the same token, in the miscellaneous group the numbers are too small for percent similarity to have significance.) None of the 20 psychiatrically undiagnosed subjects committed suicide in hospitals. What the significance of this finding might be is unknown.

TABLE 9.2 Hospitalizations in the Year Preceding Suicide

	Affective Disorder	Alcoholism	Miscellaneous	Psychiatrically Undiagnosed
Discharged from psychiatric hospital prior to suicide	7	3	3	0
Suicide while a patient in a psychiatric hospital	2	0	1	0
Discharged from general hospital (for psychiatric treatment) prior to suicide	5	1	1	2
Suicide while a patient in a general hospital	3	2	0	0
Total hospitalizations for psychiatric treatment	17 (27%)	6 (18%)	5 (28%)	2 (10%)
Referred to psychiatric hospital but did not enter	12	1	0	0
Total possible hospitalizations for psychiatric illness	29 (46%)	7 (21%)	5 (28%)	2 (10%)

NOTE: Three additional subjects, not included here, died in general hospitals within one hour of emergency admission following suicide attempt.

Barraclough's group of investigators found that 81% of the suicide subjects they studied in England had received professional treatment for psychiatric problems within the last year of life. Interested in the specific kinds of treatment, Barraclough et al. report further that 80% of the 100 suicide subjects had had psychotrophic drugs prescribed, 53% barbiturates, 21% antidepressants, 21% phenothiazines, 21% minor tranquilizers, 3% electric shock treatments, and 1% haloperidol. In addition, the study reports that 64% of the subjects had had hypnotics prescribed.[4]

Dorpat and Ripley's study of suicide in the Seattle area focused on age in connection with psychiatric treatment. They found that 22% of the subjects had received "some treatment by or consultation with *psychiatrists* [our italics] in the final year." In regard to age and treatment, they found that 60% of the subjects under 40 years of age had had psychiatric care "at some time" in their lives, that 33% of the subjects between 40 and 59 had had psychiatric care at some time, and that only 6% of the subjects over 60 had had psychiatric care at any time during their lives.[5]

In the St. Louis study, the finding that 22 of the 134 subjects killed themselves within a year following discharge from hospitals emphasizes the dangers of premature hospital discharge, since each of these 22 individuals was suffering from the same episode of illness for which he or she had been hospitalized.

A second finding in our study which suggests either or both premature discharge and inadequate outpatient psychiatric care was the occurrence of murder and attempted murder shortly before or immediately prior to suicide. The homicidal acts occurred in the following contexts:

Murders:
Subject with affective disorder (#093) killed wife with ax just prior to suicide.

Subject with alcoholism (#017) shot wife in presence of their four-year-old child just prior to suicide.

Subject with undiagnosed psychiatric illness (alcoholic symptoms) (#084) shot estranged wife from a hiding place outside the window of her house just prior to suicide.

Subject with undiagnosed psychiatric illness (affective disorder symptoms) (#096) shot divorced wife, with whom he was residing in their daughter's home, just prior to suicide.

Attempted Murder:
Subject with affective disorder (#086) shot and wounded estranged wife and both her parents shortly before suicide.

Subject with alcoholism (#129) stabbed and wounded separated wife and her lover just prior to suicide.

Subject with schizophrenia (#087) shot and wounded father three years before suicide; shot and wounded wife on same day as suicide.

Thus, there were seven individuals who committed homicidal acts (5% of the total sample). Four subjects (3%) succeeded in murdering their intended victims; three subjects (2%) did not succeed. These percentages—5%, 3% and 2%—are very similar to those for the United States as a whole, in that 4% of all homicide offenders kill themselves shortly after the offense. This figure contrasts with the figures for England and Wales (where 33% of the homicide offenders commit suicide soon after the offense), Denmark (42%), and Australia (22%).[6] What the reasons for the great discrepancy between the suicide rates among homicidal offenders in the United States and those in other western countries and Australia is unclear.

The 134 subjects in the St. Louis study committed suicide by 11 different methods. (See Table 9.3.) The individual choice of suicide method among the St. Louis suicides of 1956–57 is of interest for several reasons. First, the findings are an indication of the availability of firearms in Missouri in the late 1950's. Twice as many subjects shot themselves (60) than hanged themselves (30). Of the male subjects, more than half (51%) committed suicide by shooting. In 1958, 52% of all suicides in Missouri were by firearms (or explosives). In New York State, where the gun laws are stricter, only 23% of the suicides in 1958 were by firearms or explosives.[7]

TABLE 9.3 Methods of Suicide

	Total N	Affective disorder		Alcoholism		Misc.		Psychiatrically undiagnosed		% of Total	
		M	F	M	F	M	F	M	F	M	F
Shooting	60	20	2	15	1	10	3	8	1	51	23
Hanging	30	12	7	4	1	3	1	—	2	18	35
Drug Ingestion	7	1	3	1	1	1	—	—	—	3	13
Poisoning	8	2	1	—	2	—	—	3	—	5	10
Asphyxiation (carbon monoxide)	13	5	—	5	—	—	—	3	—	13	0
Asphyxiation (natural gas)	1	—	1	—	—	—	—	—	—	—	3
Leaping	6	1	3	1	—	—	—	—	1	2	13
Cutting	5	1	1	1	—	—	—	2	—	4	3
Drowning	2	1	—	1	—	—	—	—	—	2	0
Other*	2	2	—	—	—	—	—	—	—	2	0
Total	134	45	18	28	5	16	4	14	4		

*There were two methods of suicide, performed by two of our subjects, that did not fall into any of the above categories. One subject killed himself by laying his head on a railroad track, in the path of an oncoming train. The other, a patient in a psychiatric hospital, pushed an awl into his chest and through his heart.

Epilogue

Two factors are emphasized in this study of suicide: the circumstances surrounding each of 134 cases of suicide and the psychiatric diagnosis of each of the 134 suicidal individuals. The introduction to this report calls for further such studies for there is clearly more to learn about the general clinical phenomena of suicide. The broader our knowledge of suicide, in terms of numbers, the less likely we are to overlook clues to a biological cause. But ultimately, prevention of suicide cannot be accomplished simply by repeating clinical studies and thereby broadening the fund of clinical information indefinitely. We must be prepared to use the accumulated clinical knowledge in an effort to uncover the biological nature of those psychiatric illnesses most commonly associated with suicide. Suicide is not an isolated event, but rather the last link in a chain of increasingly mortal symptoms.

The first chapter of this book lists seven questions that the St. Louis study was designed to answer. Six of these were answered with numerical results and the sample on which these were based is representative of the U. S. population in terms of race and sex ratios:

1. What proportion of persons who commit suicide are clinically ill psychiatrically? In the St. Louis sample, 94% were diagnosed as having had mental illness.
2. What is the nature and frequency of the illnesses from which these people suffer? Findings of the St. Louis study: affective disorder, depressed phase—47%; alcoholism—25%; organic brain syndrome—4%; schizophrenia—2%; drug dependence—1%; undiagnosed psychiatric illness—15%.

3. Are there mental illnesses which, while common in the population, are rarely or never associated with a completed suicide? In the St. Louis sample, there were no cases of anxiety neurosis, obsessional neurosis, phobic neurosis, or uncomplicated hysteria.
4. What are some of the factors other than diagnosis that may be helpful in assessing the probability of suicide, or indicative of the possibility of suicide (predictors of suicide)? Increasing age, being male, being white. Each of these "predictors" increases in accuracy, positively or negatively, in combination with psychiatric diagnosis.
5. In urban western society, to what degree is suicide a medical problem as measured by the proportion of suicides who have been seen by physicians or psychiatrists or have been hospitalized during or shortly before the last episode of illness? St. Louis study results: 73% of the sample had sought professional clinical help in the last year of life.
6. What proportion of subjects are not psychiatrically ill at the time of suicide? St. Louis study finding: 6%.
7. Does the presence of medical or surgical illness seem to play a role in suicide? This is the single question that the results of the St. Louis study did not answer unequivocally. Some of the informants felt that physical illnesses had played important roles; others felt they had played only minimal roles; still others were uncertain about their significance.

It is my belief that individuals suffering from affective disorder and alcoholism account for 70% to 80% of completed suicides. To answer the larger questions concerning the causes and prevention of suicide will require further investigation of these two illnesses, especially their biological aspects.

Index

abdominal pain, 49, 51, 221, 222
affectional relationships
  alcoholism and, 225
  loss of, as suicide predictor, 414–15, 420
affective disorder (manic depressive disease), 47–56
  age at death and, 408
  alcohol use and, 222
  criteria for diagnosis of, 7–8
  hospitalizations for, 425
  interview design and, 17
  loss of affectional relationships and, 415
  medical illness and, 418
  in men, age 48 and under, 57–84
  in men, age 49 through 67, 85–150
  in men, age 68 and over, 151–72
  number of subjects with, 10–12, 14
  psychiatrically undiagnosed subjects "most like," 363, 365–86
  psychiatric care for, 424
  suicide attempts and, 412–13
  symptoms of, 22–23, 48–55
  symptoms of alcoholism and, 224–26
  underdiagnoses of, 322
  in women, age 45 and under, 173–80
  in women, age 46 through 62, 181–211
  in women, age 63 and over, 212–19
age, at death, 407–8, 420
alcohol, use of
  by alcoholics, 221
  as antecedent circumstance, 417
  gastrointestinal symptoms and, 223
  as symptom, in affective disorder, 53, 222
alcoholism, 221–27
  age at death and, 407, 408
  antecedent circumstances and, 417
  criteria for diagnosis of, 8–9
  hospitalizations for, 425
  loss of affectional relationships and, 414–15
  medical care for, 424
  in men, age 35 and under, 228–38
  in men, age 36 through 56, 239–93
  in men, age 57 and over, 294–307
  number of subjects with, 10, 12, 14
  psychiatrically undiagnosed subjects "most like," 363, 387–92
  symptoms of, 23, 221–26
  weight loss and, 18–21
  in women, 308–20
anorexia, 49, 52, 221–23

433

antecedent circumstances, as suicide predictors, 415–18, 420–21
appetite problems, 52
asphyxiation, 429
attempted murders, 427
attempted suicides, xii–xiii, 412–13, 420, 421, 423–24

Barker, L.F., 47
Barraclough, B. xi, xiv
  on nonpsychiatric subjects, 323
  on psychiatric care for subjects, 426
  on schizophrenia, 322
  on suicide attempts, 412
  on terminal medical illnesses, 420
black future, as symptom, 23, 226
blacks, 13, 14, 408–9, 420
Blashfield, R.K., 11
bodily symptoms, 52, 55
brain damage
  in alcoholism, 223, 226
  see also organic brain syndrome

cancer, 321–22, 418, 420
carcinoma, 321
cardiovascular diseases, 418, 420
case histories
  of affective disorder in men age 48 and under, 57–84
  of affective disorder in men age 49 through 67, 85–150
  of affective disorder in men age 68 and over, 151–72
  of affective disorder in women age 45 and under, 173–80
  of affective disorder in women age 46 through 62, 181–211
  of affective disorder in women age 63 and over, 212–19
  of alcoholism in men age 35 and under, 228–38
  of alcoholism in men age 36 through 56, 239–93
  of alcoholism in men age 57 and over, 294–307
  of alcoholism in women, 308–20
  of drug dependence, 345–49
  of organic brain syndrome in men, 325–31
  of organic brain syndrome in women, 332–34
  of psychiatrically undiagnosed subjects "most like" affective disorder, 365–86
  of psychiatrically undiagnosed subjects "most like" alcoholism, 387–92
  of psychiatrically undiagnosed subjects "most like" drug dependence, 399–402
  of psychiatrically undiagnosed subjects "most like" organic brain syndrome, 393–98
  of psychiatrically undiagnosed subjects "most like" schizophrenia, 403–5
  of schizophrenia, 335–44
  of subjects without medical or psychiatric illness, 357–60
  of terminal medical illness, 350–56
central nervous system diseases, 418
cleanliness, lack of, as symptom, 23
Cohen, M.E., 54
communication of suicide intent, 409–11, 420, 421, 425

Dahlgren, K.G., xii, xiv, 413, 423
death
  of relative or friend, 417
delusions, depressive, 52, 54
demographic factors, as predictors of suicide, 407–9, 420
depressed phase (of affective disorder), 48, 54
  see also affective disorder
depression
  in alcoholism, 223
  consequences of, as symptoms of affective disorder, 52
  suicide as symptom of, 323
  symptoms of, 23
  see also affective disorder
depressive neurosis, 8
diabetes mellitus, 418
diagnoses
  of affective disorder, 7–8
  of chronic alcoholism, 8–9
  of drug dependence, 9
  Feighner criteria for, 11–12
  of medical and surgical illness, 9, 321

of organic brain syndrome, 9, 321
  as predictors, 420, 421
  psychiatrically undiagnosed subjects
    and, 361–63
  of schizophrenia, 9, 322–23
  see also symptoms
"dire predictions," 409–10
disgrace, feelings of, 417
dizziness, 18
Dorpat, T.L., xi, xiv
  on loss of affectional relationships,
    414
  on medical illnesses, 418–20
  on organic brain syndrome, 323
  on psychiatric treatment, 426
  on schizophrenia, 322
  on suicide attempts, 412
drug dependence, 7, 321–23
  case histories of, 345–49
  criteria for diagnosis of, 9
  number of subjects with, 10–11, 13
  psychiatrically undiagnosed subjects
    "most like," 363, 399–402
drugs, use of
  for sleep, in alcoholism, 221, 223
  as symptom, in affective disorder, 53
Durkheim, E., xi
dysphoria, 51–53

Ettlinger, R.W., 413, 423
explosives, 427

family history findings, 51
fears, as symptoms, 20, 52, 221, 223
Feighner criteria, 11–13, 55
firearms, 427, 429
Fremming, K.H., 54

gastrointestinal diseases, 418
  symptoms of, 223, 226
genitourinary system, diseases of, 418
gynecological diseases, 418

hallucinations, 9, 54
hangings, 427, 429
headaches, as symptom, 22, 23
Helgason, T., 14, 54
homicidal acts, 427
homosexuality, 7

hospitalization, for psychiatric treatment, 424–27
Hudgens, R.W., 420
hysteria, 7

illness, medical and surgical, 321–23
  as antecedent circumstance, 417
  case histories of, 350–56
  diagnosis of, 9
  interview design and, 3
  number of subjects with, 10
  as predictor of suicide, 418–20
infectious diseases, 418
insomnia, 53
interviews
  design of, 4–5, 17–18
  form for, 25–46
  refusals of, 362, 418

jobs
  change of, as symptom, 23
  trouble with, as antecedent circumstance, 417

Kantor, J.R., 47
Keller, M., 8
Kraepelin, E., 48

Leighton, D.C., 54
"loss of interest," as symptom, 22
loudness, as symptom of alcoholism,
  221, 222
lymphosarcoma, 321

major affective disorder, see affective
  disorder
malignancies, 321–22, 418, 420
mania, 48
  symptoms of, 52
  see also affective disorder
manic depressive disease, see affective
  disorder
medical illness
  as antecedent circumstance, 417
  as predictor of suicide, 418–20
  terminal, 10, 13, 321–23
  terminal, case histories of, 350–56
medical symptoms
  in affective disorder, 51

medical symptoms (*continued*)
  in alcoholism, 221
memory problems, 221
men
  affective disorder in (age 48 and under), 57–84
  affective disorder in (age 49 through 67), 85–150
  affective disorder in (age 68 and over), 151–72
  alcoholism in (age 35 and under), 228–38
  alcoholism in (age 36 through 56), 239–93
  alcoholism in (age 57 and over), 294–307
  antecedent circumstances in, 417
  drug dependence in, 345–46
  without medical or psychiatric illness, 357–60
  organic brain syndrome in, 325–31
  prediction of suicides in, 420
  in psychiatrically undiagnosed group "most like" affective disorder, 365–80
  in psychiatrically undiagnosed group "most like" alcoholism, 387–92
  in psychiatrically undiagnosed group "most like" drug dependence, 399–402
  in psychiatrically undiagnosed group "most like" organic brain syndrome, 393–96
  in psychiatrically undiagnosed group "most like" schizophrenia, 403–5
  schizophrenia, 335–44
  in subject group, 13
  suicide attempts by, 412–13
  suicide more frequent in, 408
  suicide techniques used by, 429
  terminal medical illness in, 350–53
methodology
  diagnoses, 7–14
  interview forms, 25–46
  refusals of interviews, 5, 362, 418
  symptoms, 18–24
motivation difficulties, 52
murders, 427
Murphy, G.E., 223
musculosketal system, diseases of, 418

natural history findings, 51
nausea, 23, 221, 222
"nervousness"
  in affective disorder, 53–54
  in psychiatrically undiagnosed subjects, 362
neurosis, uncomplicated, 7
noisiness, as symptom of alcoholism, 221, 222
notes, suicide, 411

organic brain syndrome, 321–23
  alcoholism and, 223
  criteria for diagnosis of, 9
  in men, 325–31
  number of subjects with, 10, 13
  psychiatrically undiagnosed subjects "most like," 363, 393–98
  in women, 332–34

paranoid feelings, as symptom, 52
Perris, C., 48
physical illness, *see* medical illness
physicians, in interview sample group, 5
predictors, of suicide, 407–21, 424
psychiatrically undiagnosed subjects, 361–63
  antecedent circumstances in, 417, 418
  loss of affectional relationships by, 415
  "most like" affective disorder. 365–86
  "most like" alcoholism, 387–92
  "most like" drug dependence, 399–402
  "most like" organic brain syndrome, 393–98
  "most like" schizophrenia, 403–5
  psychiatric care for, 424
psychiatric care, 424–27
psychological symptoms
  in affective disorder, 51
  in alcoholism, 221

questions
  in interview form, 25–46

ordering of, 18
in purpose of study, 3, 430–31

race, of subjects, 13, 14, 408–9
rage, as symptom of alcoholism, 221, 222, 226
refusals of interviews, 5, 362, 418
respiratory system, diseases of, 418
retardation, in affective disorder, 52
Ripley, H.S., xi, xiv
   on loss of affectional relationships, 414
   on medical illnesses, 418–20
   on organic brain syndrome, 323
   on psychiatric treatment, 426
   on schizophrenia, 322
   on suicide attempts, 412

sadness, as syndrome, 22, 23
   in alcoholism, 221, 223, 226
schizophrenia, 321–23
   case histories of, 335–44
   criteria for diagnosis of, 9
   number of subjects with, 10, 13
   psychiatrically undiagnosed subject "most like," 363, 403–5
self-blame, in affective disorder, 52
senses, diseases of, 418
sex
   of subjects, 13
   see also affectional relationships; men; women
Schaffer, J.W., 322
shootings, 427, 429
silence, as symptom, 23
sleep problems
   in affective disorder, 52, 53
   in alcoholism, 221, 223
spending binges, 221, 222
Srole, L., 54
Stengel, E., 413
Stenstedt, A., 48
suicidal ideas
   communication of, 409–11, 420, 421, 424
   as symptom, in affective disorder, 52
   as symptom, in alcoholism, 221, 223, 226
suicide
   predictors of, 407–21, 424
   as symptom of depression, 323
   techniques for, 427–29

suicide attempts, 412–13, 420, 421, 423–24
suicide notes, 411
symptoms
   of affective disorder, 48–55
   of alcoholism, 221–26
   in psychiatrically undiagnosed subjects, 361, 362
   in interview design, 18–24
   see also diagnoses

terminal illness, 321–23
   case histories of, 350–56
   number of subjects with, 10, 13

uncomplicated neurosis, 7
undiagnosed subjects, *see* psychiatrically undiagnosed subjects

vomiting, 221, 222
von Andics, M., xii, 413

weight loss, 18–22
   anorexia and, 221–23
whites, 13, 408–9, 420
women
   affective disorder in (age 45 and under), 173–80
   affective disorder in (age 46 through 62), 181–211
   affective disorder in (age 63 and over), 212–19
   age at death of, 407–8
   alcoholism in, 308–20
   antecedent circumstances in, 417
   drug dependence in, 347–49
   organic brain syndrome in, 332–34
   prediction of suicides in, 420
   in psychiatrically undiagnosed group "most like" affective disorder, 381–86
   in psychiatrically undiagnosed group "most like" organic brain syndrome, 396–98
   in subject group, 13
   suicide attempts by, 412–13
   suicide techniques used by, 429
   terminal medical illness in, 353–56

Ziegler, L.H., 47